Citizenship

Citizenship

Dr. Ashok Purohit

RANDOM PUBLICATIONS
NEW DELHI (INDIA)

Citizenship

ISBN 978-93-5111-657-8

Published in 2015 in India by

RANDOM PUBLICATIONS

4376-A/4B, Gali Murari Lal, Ansari Road
New Delhi-110 002
Phone : +9111-43580356, 011-23289044, 011-43142548
e-mail: sales@randompublications.com,
info@randompublications.com, randomexports@gmail.com

Reprinted 2024

Type Setting by : Friends Media, Delhi-110089
Digitally Printed at : Replika Press Pvt. Ltd.

Preface

Citizenship is the status of a person recognized under the custom or law of a state that bestows on that person (called a citizen) the rights and the duties of citizenship. That may include the right to vote, work and live in the country, the right to return to the country, the right to own real estate, legal protections against the country's government, and protection through the military or diplomacy.

A citizen may also be subject to certain duties, such as a duty to follow the country's law, to pay taxes, or to serve in the military. A person may have multiple citizenships and a person who does not have citizenship of any state is said to be stateless. Nationality is often used as a synonym for citizenship in English - notably in international law - although the term is sometimes understood as denoting a person's membership of a nation (a large ethnic group).

Citizenship status, under social contract theory, carries with it both rights and responsibilities. In this sense, citizenship was described as "a bundle of rights -- primarily, political participation in the life of the community, the right to vote, and the right to receive certain protection from the community, as well as obligations." Citizenship is seen by most scholars as culture-specific, in the sense that the meaning of the term varies considerably from culture to culture, and over time.

The expansion of citizenship in the modern state has been both an achievement as well as a limitation. While it declared that all persons as citizens are equal before law, yet the existence of economically unequal classes meant that the practical ability to exercise the rights was not available to all those who possessed them.

In other words, the victims of the class system were unable to participate in the community of citizenship in which they had legal membership. This criticism of modern democratic citizenship has been the hallmark, of Marxist views on citizenship.

This book dealing directly with the historical development of modern citizenship and its social and political consequences.

I would like to thank my team for standing beside me throughout my career and writing this book. My special thanks go to "Random Publications" who have published the book.

– Dr. Ashok Purohit

Contents

1

Introduction to Citizenship

AN OVERVIEW

Since the primary concern of the state is with the people. the first issue of politics is to select the principle that governs this relationship. Some rules must determine who are to be recognized as members of the state and how their membership is acquired.

If membership entails certain rights and responsibilities. these must be allotted according to certain principles. The division of society into government and governed raises a number of questions regarding their mutual relations such as: what kind of persons should compose the government? are all people fit to become the rulers? what are the duties of the rulers? what rights should be extended to everybody? should discrimination be made among the citizens.

All such question involve an enquiry into the nature of citizenship and the relations between those who compose a state. Citizenship has been a persistent social human need. It is as old as settled human community. It defines those who are and those who are not members of a common society. It is more than a label.

According to Heater. he who has no sense of civic bond with his fellows or of some responsibility for civic welfare is not a true citizen. whatever his legal status. The social and political ties which hold an individual in community with his fellows is the essence of citizenship. A citizen needs to understand that his role entails status. a sense of loyality. the discharge certain duties and the enjoyment of rights not at individual leval but in relation to the state as well.

WHAT IS CITIZENSHIP?WHAT IS CITIZENSHIP

During the last 2500 years. the concept of citizenship has been invented and defined. reinvented and redefined in distinct contexts such as Greek city states. Roman Republics and modern nation-state. The nature of citizenship'. wrote Aristotle long back.'...is a question which is often disputed. there is no general agreement on a single definition'. But still the term is very common throughout the world and it is a central concept of everyday political discourse. Formally. it is a relationship between an individual and the state by which the former owes allegiance and the latter owes protection. This relationship is determined by law and recognized by international law.

The citizen is a citizen only through the state. According to Blackwell Encyclopaedia of Political Institutions. citizenship means 'a full and responsible membership of the state'. In social sciences. it has been used to denote the status of individual in the development of the modern state.' According to D.W. Brogan. 'Citizenship has two aspects: i) that every citizen has the right to be consulted in the conduct of political society and the duty to contribute something to the general consultation. and ii) the reverse: the citizen who has a right to be consulted. is bound by the results of that consultation'.

According to Barbalet. 'Citizenship is in the nature of a political bond. Upon it depends how fast the bond is'. According to T.H. Marshal. citizenship is a status attached to full membership of a community. and those who possess this status are equal with respect to the rights and duties associated with it. However. since different societies attach different rights and duties to the status of citizen. there is no universal principle which determines necessary rights and duties of citizenship in general.

Following the line of Marshal. Bryan S. Turner in his book Equality has conceptualized modern citizenship in terms of three major dimensions. They are i) Civil citizenship. *i.e.*. equality before law. personal liberty. the right to own property and freedom of speech. ii) Political citizenship. *i.e.*. political rights and access to popular institutions of political control. and iii) Social citizenship which involves a guarantee of basic level of economic and social welfare. In brief. the crux of citizenship is participation in the political community. However. any theory of political and social participation and rights must acknowledge that the role of the state in the development of citizenship is crucial because the conditions of citizenary are determined within each state depending upon the legal provisions.

Different types of political communities give rise to different forms of citizenship. Making a comparison between the Greek and modern concept of citizenship. Barbalet writes that whereas for Aristotle citizenship was the privileged status of the ruling group of the city state. in the modern democratic states. the basis of citizenship is the capacity to participate in the exercise of political power through the electoral process. Participation by citizens in the modern nation-state entails legal membership of a political community based on universal adult franchise and a civil community based on the rule of law.

Today. it is equated with social. economic and political equality. social welfare and a means to enhance individual liberty. Similarly. according to Heater. though citizenship began as a means of differentiating between inhabitants of the state. yet today it is a means of equalizing their status. The essentials of modern citizenship are political participation. social and welfare rights. communal identity and civic responsibility'.

HISTORY OF CITIZENSHIP

History of citizenship describes the changing relation between an individual and the state. commonly known as citizenship. Citizenship is generally identified not as an aspect of Eastern civilization but of Western civilization. There is a general view that citizenship in ancient times was a simpler relation than modern forms of citizenship. although this view has been challenged.

While there is disagreement about when the relation of citizenship began. many thinkers point to the early city-states of ancient Greece. possibly as a reaction to the fear of slavery. although others see it as primarily a modern phenomenon dating back only a few hundred years. In Roman times. citizenship began to take on more of the character of a relationship based on law. with less political participation than in ancient Greece but a widening sphere of who was considered to be a citizen.In the Middle Ages in Europe. citizenship was primarily identified with commercial and secular life in the growing cities. and it came to be seen as membership in emerging nation-states. In modern democracies. citizenship has contrasting senses. including a *liberal-individualist* view emphasizing needs and entitlements and legal protections for essentially passive political beings. and a *civic-republican* view emphasizing political participation and seeing citizenship as an active relation with specific privileges and obligations.

While citizenship has varied considerably throughout history. there are some common elements of citizenship over time. Citizenship is a bond that extends beyond basic kinship ties to unite people of different genetic backgrounds. that is. it is more than a clan or extended kinship network. It generally describes the relation between a person and an overall political entity such as a city-state or nation and signifies membership in that body. It is often based on. or a function of. some form of military service or expectation of future military service.

It is generally characterized by some form of political participation. although the extent of such participation can vary considerably from minimal duties such as voting to active service in government. And citizenship. throughout history. has often been seen as an ideal state. closely allied with freedom. an important status with legal aspects including rights. and it has sometimes been seen as a*bundle of rights* or a *right to have rights*. Last. citizenship almost always has had an element of exclusion. in the sense that *citizenship*derives meaning. in part. by excluding non-citizens from basic rights and privileges.

OVERVIEW

While a general definition of citizenship is membership in a political society or group. citizenship as a concept is difficult to define. Thinkers as far back as Aristotle realized that there was no agreed-upon definition of citizenship. And modern thinkers. as well. agree that the history of citizenship is complex with no single definition predominating. It is hard to isolate what citizenship means without reference to other terms such as nationalism. civil society. and democracy. According to one view. citizenship as a subject of study is undergoing transformation. with increased interest while the meaning of the term continues to shift.

There is agreement citizenship is culture-specific: it is a function of each political culture. Further. how citizenship is seen and understood depends on the viewpoint of the person making the determination. such that a person from an upper classbackground will have a different notion of citizenship than a person from the lower class. The relation of citizenship has not been a fixed or static relation. but constantly changes within each society. and that according to one view. citizenship might "really have worked" only at select periods during certain times. such as when the Athenian politician Solon made reforms in the early Athenian state.

The history of citizenship has sometimes been presented as a stark contrast between ancient citizenship and post-medieval times. One view is that citizenship should be studied as a long and direct progression throughout Western civilization. beginning from Ancient Greece or perhaps earlier. extending to the present; for example. thinker Feliks Gross examined citizenship as the "history of the continuation of a single institution."

Other views question whether citizenship can be examined as a linear process. growing over time. usually for the better. and see the linear progression approach as an oversimplification possibly leading to incorrect conclusions. According to this view. citizenship should not be considered as a "progressive realisation of the core meanings that are definitionally built into citizenship." Another caveat. offered by some thinkers. is to avoid judging citizenship from one era in terms of the standards of another era; according to this view. citizenship should be understood by examining it within the context of a city-state or nation. and trying to understand it as people from these societies understood it. The rise of citizenship has been studied as an aspect of the development of law.

ANCIENT CONCEPTIONS

Jews in the ancient world

One view is that the beginning of citizenship dates back to the ancient Israelites. These people developed an understanding of themselves as a distinct and unique people—different from the Egyptians or Babylonians. They had a written history. common language and one-deity-only religion sometimes described as ethical monotheism. While most peoples developed a loose identity tied to a specific geographic location. the Jewish people kept their common identity despite being physically moved to different lands. such as when they were held captive as slaves in ancient Egypt or Babylon. The Jewish Covenant has been described as a binding agreement not just with a few people or tribal leaders. but between the whole nation of Israel. including men. women and children. with the Jewish deity Yahweh. Jews. similar to other tribal groups. did not see themselves as citizens per se but they formed a strong attachment to their own group. such that people of different ethnicities were considered as part of an "outgroup". This is in contrast to the modern understanding of citizenship as a way to accept people of different races and ethnicities under the umbrella of being citizens of a nation.

Ancient Greece

Polis citizenship

There is more widespread agreement that the first real instances of citizenship began in ancient Greece. And while there were precursors of the relation in societies before then. it emerged in readily discernible form in the Greek city-states which began to dot the shores of the Aegean Sea. the Black Sea. the Adriatic Sea. and elsewhere around theMediterranean perhaps around the 8th century BCE. The modern day distinction sometimes termed *consent versus descent* distinction—that is. citizenship by choice versusbirthright citizenship. has been traced back to ancient Greece. And thinkers such as J.G.A. Pocock have suggested that the modern-day ideal of citizenship was first articulated by the ancient Athenians and Romans. although he suggested that the "transmission" of the sense of citizenship over two millennia was essentially a myth enshrouding western civilization. One writer suggests that despite the long history of China. there never was a political entity within China similar to the Greek polis.

To the ancients. citizenship was a bond between a person and the city-state. Before Greek times. a person was generally connected to a tribe or kin-group such as an extended family. but citizenship added a layer to these ties—a non-kinship bond between the person and the state. Historian Geoffrey Hosking in his 2005 *Modern Scholar* lecture course suggested that citizenship in ancient Greece arose from an appreciation for the importance of freedom. Hosking explained:

It can be argued that this growth of slavery was what made Greeks particularly conscious of the value of freedom. After all. any Greek farmer might fall into debt and therefore might become a slave. at almost any time... When the Greeks fought together. they fought in order to avoid being enslaved by warfare. to avoid being defeated by those who might take them into slavery.

And they also arranged their political institutions so as to remain free men. —Geoffrey Hosking. 2005The Greek sense of the polis. in which citizenship and the rule of law prevailed. was an important strategic advantage for the Greeks during their wars with Persia.

The polis was grounded in nomos. the rule of law. which meant that no man—no matter who he might be—was master. and all men were subject to the same rules. Any leader who set himself above the law was reckoned to be a tyrannos—a tyrant. It was also grounded in the notion of citizenship—the idea that every man born from the blood of the community has a share in power and responsibility. This notion that... the proper way for us to live is as citizens in communities under the rule of law... is an idea originated by the Greeks and bequeathed by them as their greatest contribution to the rest of mankind and history. It meant that Greeks were willing to live. fight. and die for their poleis... —Robert L. Dise. Jr.. 2009

Greeks could see the benefits of having slaves. since their Labour permitted slaveowners to have substantial free time. enabling participation in public life. While Greeks were spread out in many separate city-states. they had many things in common in addition to shared ideas about citizenship: the Mediterranean trading world. kinship ties. the common Greek language. a shared hostility to the so-called non-Greek-speaking or barbarian peoples. belief in the prescience of the oracle at Delphi. and later on the early Olympic Gameswhich involved generally peaceful athletic competitions between city-states. City-states often feuded with each other; one view was that regular wars were necessary to perpetuate citizenship. since the seized goods and slaves helped make the city-state rich. and that a long peaceful period meant ruin for citizenship.

An important aspect of polis citizenship was exclusivity. *Polis* meant both the political assembly as well as the entire society. Inequality of status was widely accepted. Citizens had a higher status than non-citizens. such as women. slaves or barbarians. For example. women were believed to be irrational and incapable of political participation. although a few writers. most notably Plato. disagreed. Methods used to determine whether someone could be a citizen or not could be based on wealth. identified by the amount of taxes one paid. or political participation. or heritage if both parents had been born in the polis. The first form of citizenship was based on the way people lived in the ancient Greek times. in small-scale organic communities of the polis. Citizenship was not seen as a separate activity from the private life of the individual person. in the sense that there was not a distinction between public and private life. The obligations of citizenship were deeply connected into one's everyday life in the polis.

The Greek sense of citizenship may have arisen from military necessity. since a key military formation demanded cohesion and commitment by each particular soldier. The phalanx formation had hoplite soldiers ranked shoulder-to-shoulder in a "compact mass" with each soldier's shield guarding the soldier to his left. If a single fighter failed to keep his position. then the entire formation could fall apart. Individual soldiers were generally protected provided that the entire mass stayed together. This technique called for large numbers of soldiers. sometimes involving most of the adult male population of a city-state. who supplied weapons at their own expense. The idea of citizenship. then. was that if each man had a say in whether the entire city-state should fight an adversary. and if each man was bound to the will of the group. then battlefield loyalty was much more likely. Political participation was thus linked with military effectiveness. In addition. the Greek city-states were the first instances in which judicial functions were separated from legislativefunctions in the law courts. Selected citizens served as jurors. and they were often paid a modest sum for their service. Greeks often despised tyrannical governments. In a tyrannical arrangement. there was no possibility of citizenship since political life was totally engineered to benefit the ruler.

Spartan citizenship

Several thinkers suggest that ancient Sparta. not Athens. was the originator of the concept of citizenship. Spartan citizenship was based on the principle of equality among a ruling military elite called Spartiates. They were "full Spartan citizens"—men who graduated from a rigorous regimen of military training and at age 30 received a land allotment called a kleros. although they had to keep paying dues to pay for food and drink as was required to maintain citizenship. In the Spartan approach to phalanx warfare. virtues such as courage and loyalty were particularly emphasized relative to other Greek city-states. Each Spartan citizen owned at least a minimum portion of the public land which was sufficient to provide food for a family. although the size of these plots varied. The Spartan citizens relied on the Labour of captured slaves called helots to do the everyday drudgework of farming and maintenance. while the Spartan men underwent a rigorous military regimen. and in a sense it was the Labour of the helots which permitted Spartans to engage in extensive military training and citizenship. Citizenship was viewed as incompatible with manual Labour. Citizens ate meals together in a "communal mess". They were "frugally fed. ferociously disciplined. and kept in constant training through martial games and communal exercises." according to Hosking. As young men. they served in the military. It was seen as virtuous to participate in government when men grew older. Participation was required; failure to appear could entail a loss of citizenship. But thephilosopher Aristotle viewed the Spartan model of citizenship as "artificial and strained". according to one account. While Spartans were expected to learn music andpoetry. serious study was discouraged. Historian Ian Worthington described a "Spartan mirage" in the sense that the mystique about military invincibility tended to obscure weaknesses within the Spartan system. particularly their dependence on helots. In contrast with Athenian women. Spartan women could own property. and owned at one point up to 40per cent of the land according to Aristotle. and they had greater independence and rights. although their main task was not to rule the homes or participate in governance but rather to produce strong and healthy babies.

Athenian citizenship

Aristotle. according to J. G. A. Pocock. suggested that ancient Greeks thought that being a citizen was a natural state. It was an elitist notion. according to Peter Riesenberg. in which small scale communities had generally similar ideas of how people should behave in society and what constituted appropriate conduct. Geoffrey Hosking described a possible Athenian logic leading to participatory democracy:

If you've got a lot of soldiers of rather modest means. and you want them to enthusiastically participate in war. then you've got to have a political and economic system which doesn't allow too many of them to fall into debt. because debt ultimately means slavery. and slaves cannot fight in the army. And it needs a political system which gives them a say on matters that concern their lives. —Geoffrey Hosking. 2005

As a consequence. the original Athenian aristocratic constitution gradually became more inappropriate. and gave way to a more inclusive arrangement. In the early 6th century BCE. the reformer Solon canceled all existing land debts. and enabled free Athenian males to participate in the assembly or ecclesia. In addition. he encouraged foreign craftsmen. particularly skilled in pottery. to move to Athens and offered citizenship by naturalization as an incentive.

Solon expected that aristocratic Athenians would continue running affairs but nevertheless citizens had a "political voice in the Assembly."

Subsequent reformers moved Athens even more towards direct democracy. The Greek reformer Cleisthenes in 508 BC re-engineered Athenian society from organizations based on family-style groupings. or phratries. to larger mixed structures which combined people from different types of geographic areas—coastal areas and cities. hinterlands. and plains—into the same group. Cleisthenes abolished the tribes by "redistributing their identity so radically" so they ceased to exist. The result was that farmers. sailors and sheepherders came together in the same political unit. in effect lessening kinship ties as a basis for citizenship. In this sense. Athenian citizenship extended beyond basic bonds such as ties of family. descent. religion. race. or tribal membership. and reached towards the idea of a civic multiethnic state built on democratic principles.

Cleisthenes took democracy to the masses in a way that Solon didn't.... Cleisthenes gave these same people the opportunity to participate in a political system in which all citizens—noble and non-noble—were in theory equal. and regardless of where they lived in Attica. could take part in some form of state administration. —Ian Worthington. 2009

According to Feliks Gross. such an arrangement can succeed if people from different backgrounds can form constructive associations. The Athenian practice of ostracism. in which citizens could vote anonymously for a fellow citizen to be expelled from Athens for up to ten years. was seen as a way to pre-emptively remove a possible threat to the state. without having to go through legal proceedings. It was intended to promote internal harmony.

Athenian citizenship was based on obligations of citizens towards the community rather than rights given to its members. This was not a problem because people had a strong affinity with the polis; their personal destiny and the destiny of the entire community were strongly linked. Also. citizens of the polis saw obligations to the community as an opportunity to be virtuous. It was a source of honour and respect. According to one view. the citizenry was "its own master". The people were sovereign; there was no sovereignty outside of the people themselves. In Athens. citizens were both ruler and ruled. Further. important political and judicial offices were rotated to widen participation and prevent corruption. and all citizens had the right to speak and vote in the political assembly. Pocock explained:

... what makes the citizen the highest order of being is his capacity to rule. and it follows that rule over one's equal is possible only where one's equal rules over one. Therefore the citizen rules and is ruled; citizens join each other in making decisions where each decider respects the authority of the others. and all join in obeying the decisions (now known as "laws") they have made. —J. G. A. Pocock

The Athenian conception was that "laws that should govern everybody." in the sense of equality under the law or the Greek term *isonomia*. Citizens had certain rights andduties: the rights included the chance to speak and vote in the common assembly. to stand for public office. to serve as jurors. to be protected by the law. to own land. and to participate in public worship; duties included an obligation to obey the law. and to serve in the armed forces which could be "costly" in terms of buying or making expensive war equipment or in risking one's own life. according to Hosking.

This balance of participation. obligations and rights constituted the essence of citizenship. together with the feeling that there was a common interest which imposed its obligations on everyone. —Geoffrey Hosking. 2005

Hosking noticed that citizenship was "relatively narrowly distributed" and excluded all women. all minors. all slaves. all immigrants. and most colonials. that is. citizens who left their city to start another usually lost their rights from their city-state of origin. Many historians felt this exclusiveness was a weakness in Athenian society. according to Hosking. but he noted that there were perhaps

50.000 Athenian citizens overall. and that at most. a tenth of these ever took part in an actual assembly at any one time. Hosking argued that if citizenship had been spread more widely. it would have hurt solidarity.

Pocock expresses a similar sentiment and noted that citizenship requires a certain distance from the day-to-day drudgery of daily living. Greek males solved this problem to some extent with the subjugation of women as well as the institution of slavery which freed their schedules so they could participate in the assembly. Pocock asked: for citizenship to happen. was it necessary to prevent free people from becoming "too much involved in the world of things"? Or. could citizenship be extended to working class persons. and if so. what does this mean for the nature of citizenship itself?

Plato on citizenship

The philosopher Plato envisioned a warrior class similar to the Spartan conception in that these persons did not engage in farming. business. or handicrafts. but their main duty was to prepare for war: to train. to exercise. to train. to exercise. constantly. Like the Spartan practice. Plato's idealized community was one of citizens who kept common meals to build common bonds. Citizenship status. in Plato's ideal view. was inherited. There were four separate classes. There were penalties for failing to vote. A key part of citizenship was obeying the law and being "deferent to the social and political system" and having internal self-control.

Aristotle on citizenship

Writing a generation after Plato. and in contrast with his teacher. Aristotle did not like Sparta's commune-oriented approach. He felt Sparta's land allocation system as well as the communal meals led to a world in which rich and poor were polarized. He recognized differences in citizenship patterns based on age: the young were "underdeveloped" citizens. while the elderly were "superannuated" citizens. And he noted that it was hard to classify the citizenship status of some persons. such as resident aliens who still had access to courts. or citizens who had lost their citizenship franchise.

Still. Aristotle's conception of citizenship was that it was a legally guaranteed role in creating and running government. It reflected the division of Labour which he believed was a good thing; citizenship. in his view. was a commanding role in society with citizens ruling over non-citizens. At the same time. there could not be a permanent barrier between the rulers and the ruled. according to Aristotle's conception. and if there was such a barrier. citizenship could not exist. Aristotle's sense of citizenship depended on a "rigorous separation of public from private. of polis from oikos. of persons and actions from things" which allowed people to interact politically with equals. To be truly human. one had to be an active citizen to the community:

To take no part in the running of the community's affairs is to be either a beast or a god! —Aristotle In Aristotle's view. "man is a political animal". Isolated men were not truly free. in his view. A beast was animal-like without self-control over passions and unable to coordinate with other beasts. and therefore could not be a citizen. And a god was so powerful and immortal that he or she did not need help from others.

In Aristotle's conception. citizenship was possible generally in a small city-state since it required direct participation in public affairs with people knowing "one another's characters". What mattered. according to Pocock's interpretation of Aristotle. was that citizens had the freedom to take part in political discussions if they chose to do so. And citizenship was not merely a means to being free. but was freedom itself. a valued escape from the home-world of the oikos to the political world of the polis. It meant active sharing in civic life. meaning that all men rule. and are ruled. alternatively.

And citizens were those who shared in deliberative and judicial office. and in that sense. attained the status of citizenship. What citizens do should benefit not just a segment of society. but be in the interest of everybody. Unlike Plato. Aristotle believed that women were incapable of citizenship since it did not suit their natures. In Aristotle's conception. humans are destined "by nature" to live in a political association and take short turns at ruling. inclusively. participating in making legislative. judicial and executive decisions. But Aristotle's sense of "inclusiveness" was limited to adult Greek males born in the polity: women. children. slaves. and foreigners (that is. resident aliens). were generally excluded from political participation.

Roman conceptions

Differences from Greece

Roman citizenship was similar to the Greek model but differed in substantive ways. Geoffrey Hosking argued that Greek ideas of citizenship in the city-state. such as the principles of equality under the law. civic participation in government. and notions that "no one citizen should have too much power for too long". were carried forth into the Roman world. But unlike the Greek city-states which enslaved captured peoples following a war. Rome offered relatively generous terms to its captives. including chances for captives to have a "second category of Roman citizenship". Conquered peoples could not vote in the Roman assembly but had full protections of the law. and could make economic contracts and could marry Roman citizens. They blended together with Romans in a culture sometimes described as Romanitas—ceremonies. public baths. games. and a common culture helped unite diverse groups within the empire. One view was that the Greek sense of citizenship was an "emancipation from the world of things" in which citizens essentially acted upon other citizens; material things were left back in the private domestic world of the oikos. But the Roman sensibility took into account to a greater extent that citizens could act upon material things as well as other citizens. in the sense of buying or selling property. possessions. titles. goods. Accordingly. citizens often encountered other citizens on the basis of commerce which often required regulation. It introduced a new level of complexity regarding the concept of citizenship. Pocock explained:

The person was defined and represented through his actions upon things; in the course of time. the term property came to mean. first. the defining characteristic of a human or other being; second. the relation which a person had with a thing; and third. the thing defined as the possession of some person. —J. G. A. Pocock. 1988

Class concerns

A further departure from the Greek model was that the Roman government pitted the upper-class patrician interests against the lower-order working groups known as theplebeian class in a dynamic arrangement. sometimes described as a "tense tug-of-war" between the dignity of the great man and the liberty of the small man. Through worker discontent. the plebs threatened to set up a rival city to Rome. and through negotiation around 494 BCE. won the right to have their interests represented in government by officers known as tribunes. The Roman Republic. according to Hosking. tried to find a balance between the upper and lower classes. And writers such as Burchell have argued that citizenship meant different things depending on what social class one belonged to: for upper-class men. citizenship was an active chance to influence public life; for lower-class men. it was about a respect for "private rights" or ius privatum.

A legal relation

Pocock explained that a citizen came to be understood as a person "free to act by law. free to ask and expect the law's protection. a citizen of such and such a legal community. of such and such a legal standing in that community." An example was Saint Pauldemanding fair treatment after his arrest by claiming to be a Roman citizen. Many thinkers including Pocock suggested that the Roman conception of citizenship had a greater emphasis than the Greek one of it being a legal relationship with the state. described as the "legal and political shield of a free person". And citizenship was believed to have had a "cosmopolitan character". Citizenship meant having rights to have possessions. immunities. expectations. which were "available in many kinds and degrees. available or unavailable to many kinds of person for many kinds of reason." Citizens could "sue and be sued in certain courts". And the law. itself. was a kind of bond uniting people. in the sense of it being the results of past decisions by the assembly. such that citizenship came to mean "membership in a community of shared or common law". According to Pocock. the Roman emphasis on law changed the nature of citizenship: it was more impersonal. universal. multiform. having different degrees and applications. It included many different types of citizenship: sometimes municipal citizenship. sometimes empire-wide citizenship.

Law continued to advance as a subject under the Romans. The Romans developed law into a kind of science known as jurisprudence. Law helped protect citizens:The college of priests agreed to have basic laws inscribed upon twelve stone tablets displayed in the forum for everyone to see... Inscribing these things on stone tablets was very important because it meant. first of all. that law was stable and permanent; the same for everyone. and it could not be altered at the whim of powerful people. And secondly. it was publicly known; it was not secret; it could be consulted by anybody at any time. —Geoffrey Hosking. 2005

Specialists in law found ways to adapt the fixed laws. and to have the common law or jus gentium. work in harmony with natural law or ius naturale. which are rules common to all things. Property was protected by law. and served as a protection of individuals against the power of the state. In addition. unlike the Greek model where laws were mostly made in the assembly. Roman law was often determined in other places than official government bodies. Rules could originate through court rulings. by looking to past court rulings. by sovereign decrees. and the effect was that the assembly's power became increasingly marginalized.

Expansion of citizenship

In the Roman Empire. polis citizenship expanded from small scale communities to the entire empire. In the early years of the Roman Republic. citizenship was a prized relationship which was not widely extended. Romans realised that granting citizenship to people from all over the empire legitimized Roman rule over conquered areas. As the centuries went by. citizenship was no longer a status of political agency. but it had been reduced to a judicial safeguard and the expression of rule and law. The Roman conception of citizenship was relatively more complex and nuanced than the earlier Athenian conception. and it usually did not involve political participation. There was a "multiplicity of roles" for citizens to play. and this sometimes led to "contradictory obligations". Roman citizenship was not a single black-and-white category of *citizen* versus *non-citizen*. but rather there were more gradations and relationships possible. Women were respected to a greater extent with a secure status as what Hosking terms "subsidiary citizens".

But the citizenship rules generally had the effect of building loyalty throughout the empire among highly diverse populations. The Roman statesman Cicero. while encouraging political participation. saw that too much civic activism could have consequences that were possibly dangerous and disruptive. David Burchell argued that in Cicero's time. there were too many citizens pushing to "enhance their dignitas". and the result of a "political stage" with too many actors all wanting to play a leading role. was discord. The problem of extreme inequality of landed wealth led to a decline in the citizen-soldier arrangement. and was one of many causes leading to the dissolution of the Republic and rule by dictators. The Roman Empire gradually expanded the inclusiveness of persons considered as "citizens". while the economic power of persons declined. and fewer men wanted to serve in the military. The granting of citizenship to wide swaths of non-Roman groups diluted its meaning. according to one account.

Decline of Rome

When the Western Roman empire fell in 476 AD. the western part run by Rome was sacked. while the eastern empire headquartered at Constantinople endured. Some thinkers suggest that as a result of historical circumstances. western Europe evolved with two competing sources of authority—religious and secular—and that the ensuingseparation of church and state was a "major step" in bringing forth the modern sense of citizenship. In the eastern half which survived. religious and secular authority were merged in the one emperor. The eastern Roman emperor Justinian. who ruled the eastern empire from 527 to 565. thought that citizenship meant people living with Honour. not causing harm. and to "give each their due" in relation with fellow citizens.

EARLY MODERN IDEAS OF CITIZENSHIP

Feudalism

In the feudal system. there were relationships characterized as reciprocal. with bonds between lords and vassals going both ways: vassals promised loyalty and subsistence. while lords promised protection. The basis of feudal arrangement was control over land.The loyalty of a person was not to a law. or to a constitution. or to an abstract concept such as a nation. but to a person. namely. the next higher-level up. such as a knight. lord. or king. One view is that feudalism's reciprocal obligation system gave rise to the idea of the individual and the citizen.

According to a related view. the Magna Carta. while a sort of "feudal document". marked a transition away from feudalism since the document was not a personal unspoken bond between nobles and the king. but rather was more like acontract between two parties. written in formal language. describing how different parties were supposed to behave towards each other. The Magna Carta posited that the liberty. security and freedom of individuals were "inviolable". Gradually the personal ties linking vassals with lords were replaced with contractual and more impersonal relationships. The early days of medieval communes were marked by intensive citizenship. according to one view. Sometimes there was terrific religious activism. spurred by fanatics and religious zealotry. and as a result of the discord and religious violence. Europeans learned to value the "dutiful passive citizen" as much preferred to the "self-directed religious zealot". according to another.

Early European towns

During the Renaissance and growth of Europe. medieval political scholar Walter Ullmann suggested that the essence of the transition was from people being subjects of a monarch or lord to being citizens of a city and later to a nation. A distinguishing characteristic of a city was having its own law. courts. and independent administration. And being a citizen often meant being subject to the city's law in addition to helping to choose officials. Cities were defensive entities. and its citizens were persons who were "economically competent to bear arms. to equip and train themselves." According to one theorist. the requirement that individual citizen-soldiers provide their own equipment for fighting helped to explain why Western cities evolved the concept of citizenship. while Eastern ones generally did not.

And city dwellers who had fought alongside nobles in battles were no longer content with having a subordinate social status. but demanded a greater role in the form of citizenship. In addition to city administration as a way of participating in political decision-making. membership in guilds was an indirect form of citizenship in that it helped their members succeed financially; guilds exerted considerable political influence in the growing towns.

Emerging nation-states

During European Middle Ages. citizenship was usually associated with cities. Nobility in the aristocracy used to have privileges of a higher nature than commoners. The rise of citizenship was linked to the rise of republicanism. according to one account. since if a republic belongs to its citizens. then kings have less power. In the emerging nation-states. the territory of the nation was its land. and citizenship was an idealized concept. Increasingly. citizenship related not to a person such as a lord or count. but rather citizenship related a person to the state on the basis of more abstract terms such as rights and duties.

Citizenship was increasingly seen as a result of birth. that is. a birthright. But nations often welcomed foreigners with vital skills and capabilities. and came to accept these new people under a process of naturalization. Increasing frequency of cases of naturalization helped people see citizenship as a relationship which was freely chosen by people. Citizens were people who voluntarily chose allegiance to the state. who accepted the legal status of citizenship with its rights and responsibilities. who obeyed its laws. who were loyal to the state.

The American Revolution

British colonists across the Atlantic had grown up in a system in which local government was democratic. marked by participation by affluent men. but after the French and Indian War. colonists came to resent an increase in taxes imposed by Britain to offset expenses. What was particularly irksome to colonists was their lack of representation in the British Parliament. and the phrase no taxation without representation became a common grievance. The struggle between rebelling colonists and British troops was a time when citizenship "worked". according to one view.

American and subsequent French declarations of rights were instrumental in linking the notion of fundamental rights to popular sovereignty in the sense that governments drew their legitimacy and authority from the consent of the governed. The Framers designed the United States Constitution to accommodate a rapidly growing republic by opting for representative democracy as opposed to direct democracy. but this arrangement challenged the idea of citizenship in the sense that citizens were. in effect. choosing other persons to represent them and take their place in government. The revolutionary spirit created a sense of "broadening inclusion". The Constitution specified a three-part structure of government with a federal government and state governments. but it did not specify the relation of citizenship. although the Bill of Rights protected the rights of individuals from intrusion by the federal government. The term *citizen* was not defined by the Constitution until the Fourteenth Amendment was added in 1868. which defined American citizenship as "All persons born or naturalized in the United States." Enlightenment ideas at the heart of the American Revolution were influential worldwide. and helped to precipitate uprisings in France.

The French Revolution

The French Revolution marked major changes and has been widely seen as a watershed event in modern politics. Up until then. the main ties between people under the Ancien Regime were hierarchical. such that each person owed loyalty to the next person further up the chain of command; for example. serfs were loyal to local vassals. who in turn were loyal to nobles. who in turn were loyal to the king. who in turn was presumed to be loyal to God. Clergy and aristocracy had special privileges. including preferential treatment in law courts. and were exempt from taxes; this last privilege had the effect of placing the burden of paying for national expenses on the peasantry.

One scholar who examined pre-Revolutionary France described powerful groups which stifled citizenship and included provincial estates. guilds. military governors. courts with judges who owned their offices. independent church officials. proud nobles. financiers and tax farmers. They blocked citizenship indirectly since they kept a small elite governing group in power. and kept regular people away from participating in political decision-making.These arrangements changed substantially during and after the French Revolution. Louis XVI mismanaged funds. vacillated. was blamed for inaction during a famine. causing the French people to see the interest of the king and the national interest as opposed. During the early stages of the uprising. the abolition of aristocratic privilege happened during a pivotal meeting on August 4. 1789. in which an aristocrat named Vicomte de Noailles proclaimed before the National Assembly that he would renounce all special privileges and would henceforward be known only as the "Citizen of Noailles."

Other aristocrats joined him which helped to dismantle the Ancien Regime's seignorial rights during "one night of heated oratory". according to one historian. Later that month. the Assembly's Declaration of the Rights of Man and Citizen linked the concept of rights with citizenship and asserted that rights of man were "natural. inalienable. and sacred". that all men were "born free and equal. and that the aim of all political association is maintenance of their rights". according to historian Robert Bucholz.

However. the document said nothing about the rights of women. although activist Olympe de Gouge issued a proclamation two years later which argued that women were born with equal rights to men. People began to identify a new loyalty to the nation as a whole. as citizens. and the idea of popular sovereignty earlier espoused by the thinker Rousseau took hold. along with strong feelings of nationalism. Louis XVI and his wife were guillotined.

Citizenship became more inclusive and democratic. aligned with rights and national membership. The king's government was replaced with an administrative hierarchy at all levels. from a national legislature to even power at the local commune. such that power ran both up and down the chain of command. Loyalty became a cornerstone in the concept of citizenship. according to Peter Riesenberg.

One analyst suggested that in the French Revolution. two often polar-opposite versions of citizenship merged: (1) the abstract idea of citizenship as equality before the law caused by the centralizing and rationalizing policies of absolute monarchs and (2) the idea of citizenship as a privileged status reserved for rule-makers. brought forth defensively by an aristocratic elite guarding its exclusiveness.

According to one view by the German philosopher Max Stirner. the Revolution emancipated the citizen but not the individual. since the individuals were not the agents of change. but only the collective force of all individuals; in Stirner's sense. the "agent of change" was effectively the nation. The British thinker T. H. Marshall saw in the 18th century "serious growth" of civil rights. with major growth in the legal aspects of citizenship. often defended through courts of law. These civil rights extended citizenship's legal dimensions: they included the right to free speech. the right to a fair trial. and generally equal access to the legal system. Marshall saw the 18th century as signifying civil rights which was a precursor to political rightssuch as suffrage. and later. in the 20th century. social rights such as welfare.

Early modern: 1700s-1800s

After 1750. states such as Britain and France invested in massive armies and navies which were so expensive to maintain that the option of hiring mercenary soldiers became less attractive. Rulers found troops within the public. and taxed the public to pay for these troops. but one account suggested that the military buildup had a side-effect of undermining the military's autonomous political power. Another view corroborates the idea that military conscription spurred development of a broader role for citizens.

A phenomenon known as the public sphere arose. according to philosopher Jürgen Habermas. as a space between authority and private life in which citizens could meet informally. exchange views on public matters. criticize government choices and suggest reforms. It happened in physical spaces such as public squares as well as in coffeehouses. museums. restaurants. as well as in media such as newspapers. journals. and dramatic performances. It served as a counterweight to government. a check on its power. since a bad ruling could be criticized by the public in places such as editorials. According to Schudson. the public sphere was a "playing field for citizenship".

Eastern conceptions

In the late 19th century. thinking about citizenship began to influence China. Ideas such as legal limits. definitions of monarchy and the state. parliaments and elections. an active press. public opinion. concepts such as civic virtue. national unity. and social progress came to be discussed.

MODERN SENSES

Transitions

John Stuart Mill in his work *On Liberty* (1859) believed that there should be no distinctions between men and women. and that both were capable of citizenship. British sociologist Thomas Humphrey Marshall suggested that the changing patterns of citizenship were as follows: first. a civil relation in the sense of having equality before the law. followed by political citizenship in the sense of having the power to vote. and later a social citizenship in the sense of having the state support individual persons along the lines of a welfare state.Marshall argued in the middle of the 20th century that modern citizenship encompassed all three dimensions: civil. political. and social.He wrote that citizenship required a vital sense of community in the sense of a feeling of loyalty to a common civilization. Thinkers such as Marc Steinberg saw citizenship emerge from a class struggle interrelated with the principle of nationalism. People who were native-born or naturalised members of the state won a greater share of the rights out of "a continuing series of transactions between persons and agents of a given state in which each has enforceable rights and obligations". according to Steinberg. This give-and-take to a common acceptance of the powers of both the citizen and the state. He argued that:

The contingent and uneven development of a bundle of rights understood as citizenship in the early nineteenth century was heavily indebted to class conflict played out in struggles over state policy on trade and Labour. —Marc Steinberg. writing in 1996

Nationalism emerged. Many thinkers suggest that notions of citizenship rights emerged from this spirit of each person identifying strongly with the nation of their birth. A modern type of citizenship is one which lets people participate in a number of different ways.Citizenship is not a "be-all end-all" relation. but only one of many types of relationships which a person might have. It has been seen as an "equalizing principle" in the sense that most other people have the same status. One theory sees different types of citizenship emanating out from concentric circles—from the town. to the state. to the world—and that citizenship can be studied by looking at which types of relations people value at any one time.

The idea that participating in lawmaking is an essential aspect of citizenship continues to be expressed by different thinkers. For example. British journalist and pamphleteerWilliam Cobbett said that the "greatest right". which he called the "right of rights". was having a share in the "making of the laws". and then submitting the laws to the "good of the whole."

The idea of citizenship. and western senses of government. began to emerge in Asia in the 19th and 20th centuries. In Meiji Japan. popular social forces exerted influence against traditional types of authority. and out of a period of negotiations and concessions by the state came a time of "expanding democracy". according to one account. Numerous cause-and-effect relations worked to bring about a Japanese version of citizenship: expanding military activity led to an enlarged state and territory. which furthered direct rule including the power of the military and the Japanese emperor. but this indirectly led to popular resistance. struggle. bargaining. and consequently an expanded role for citizens in early 20th century Japan.

Citizenship today

The concept of citizenship is hard to isolate. since it relates to many other contextual aspects of society such as the family. military service. the individual. freedom. religion. ideas of right and wrong. ethnicity. and patterns for how a person should behave in society.According to British politician Douglas Hurd. citizenship is essentially doing good to others. When there are many different ethnic and religious groups within a nation. citizenship may be the only real bond which unites everybody as equals without discrimination—it is a "broad bond" as one writer described it.Citizenship links "a person with the state" and gives people a universal identity—as a legal member of a nation—besides their identity based on ties of ethnicity or an ethnic self.

But clearly there are wide differences between ancient conceptions of citizenship and modern ones. While the modern one still respects the idea of participation in the political process. it is usually done through "eLabourate systems of political representation at a distance" such as representative democracy. and carried out under the "shadow of a permanent professional administrative apparatus." Unlike the ancient patterns. modern citizenship is much more passive; action is delegated to others; citizenship is often a constraint on acting. not an impetus to act.

Nevertheless. citizens are aware of their obligations to authorities. and they are aware that these bonds "limits their personal political autonomy in a quite profound manner". But there are disagreements that the contrast between ancient and modern versions of citizenship was that sharp; one theorist suggested that the supposedly "modern" aspects of so-called passive citizenship. such as tolerance. respect for others. and simply "minding one's own business". were present in ancient times too.

Citizenship can be seen as both a status and an ideal. Sometimes mentioning the idea of citizenship implies a host of theories as well as the possibility of social reform. according to one view. It invokes a model of what a person should do in relation to the state. and suggests education or punishment for those who stray from the model.

Several thinkers see the modern notion of individualism as being sometimes consistent with citizenship. and other times opposed to it. Accordingly. the *modern individual* and the *modern citizen* seem to be the same. but too much individualism can have the effect of leading to a "crisis of citizenship". Another agreed that individualism can corrupt citizenship. Another sees citizenship as a substantial dilemma between the individual and society. and between the individual and the state. and asked questions such as whether the focus of a person's efforts should be on the collective good or on the individual good? In a Marxist view. the individual and the citizen were both "essentially necessary" to each other in that neither could exist without the other. but both aspects within a person were essentially antagonistic to each other. Habermassuggested in his book *The Structural Transformation of the Public Sphere* that while citizenship widened to include more people. the public sphere shrunk and became commercialized. devoid of serious debate. with media coverage of political campaigns having less focus on issues and more focus on sound bites and political scandals. and in the process. citizenship became more common but meant less. Political participation declined for most people.

Other thinkers echo that citizenship is a vortex for competing ideas and currents. sometimes working against each other. sometimes working in harmony. For example. sociologist T. H. Marshall suggested that citizenship was a contradiction between the "formal political equality of the franchise" and the "persistence of extensive social and economic inequality." In Marshall's sense. citizenship was a way to straddle both issues. A wealthy person and a poor person were both equal in the sense of being citizens. but separated by the economic inequality. Marshall saw citizenship as the basis for awarding social rights. and he made a case that extending such rights would not jeopardize the structure of social classes or end inequality. He saw capitalism as a dynamic system with constant clashes between citizenship and social class. and how these clashes played out determined how a society's political and social life would manifest themselves.Citizenship was not always about including everybody. but was also a powerful force to exclude persons at the margins of society. such as the outcasts. illegal immigrants and others. In this sense. citizenship was not only about getting rights and entitlements but it was a struggle to "reject claims of entitlement by those initially residing outside the core. and subsequently. of migrant and immigrant labour." But one thinker described democratic citizenship as inclusive. generally. and wrote that democratic citizenship:

... (democratic citizenship) extends human. political and civil rights to all inhabitants. regardless of race. religion. ethnicity. or culture. In a civic state. which is based on the concept of such citizenship. even foreigners are protected by the rule of law." —Feliks Gross. 1999

Competing senses

Citizenship in the modern sense is often seen as having two widely divergent strains marked by tension between them.

Liberal-individualist view

The *liberal-individualist* conception of citizenship. or sometimes merely the *liberal* conception. has a concern that the individual's status may be undermined by government. The perspective suggests a language of "needs" and "entitlements" necessary for human dignityand is based on reason for the pursuit of self-interest or more accurately as enlightened self-interest. The conception suggests a focus on the manufacture of material things as well as man's economic vitality. with society seen as a "market-based association of competitive individuals." From this view. citizens are sovereign. morally autonomous beings with duties to pay taxes. obey the law. engage in business transactions. and defend the nation if it comes under attack. but are essentially passive politically. This conception of citizenship has sometimes been termed *conservative* in the sense that passive citizens want to conserve their private interests. and that private people have a right to be left alone. This formulation of citizenship was expressed somewhat in the philosophy of John Rawls. who believed that every person in a society has an "equal right to a fully adequate scheme of equal basic rights and liberties" and that society has an obligation to try to benefit the "least advantaged members of society". But this sense of citizenship has been criticized; according to one view. it can lead to a "culture of subjects" with a "degeneration of public spirit" since *economic man*. or homo economicus. is too focused on material pursuits to engage in civic activity to be true citizens.

Civic-republican view

A competing vision is that democratic citizenship may be founded on a "culture of participation". This orientation has sometimes been termed the *civic-republican* or *classical* conception of citizenship since it focuses on the importance of people practicing citizenship actively and finding places to do this. Unlike the liberal-individualist conception. the civic-republican conception emphasizes man's political nature. and sees citizenship as an active. not passive. activity. A general problem with this conception. according to critics. is that if this model is implemented. it may bring about other issues such as the free rider problem in which some people neglect basic citizenship duties and consequently get a free ride supported by the citizenship efforts of others.

This view emphasizes the democratic participation inherent in citizenship. and can "channel legitimate frustrations and grievances" and bring people together to focus on matters of common concern and lead to a politics of empowerment. according to theorist Dora Kostakopoulou. Like the liberal-individualist conception. it is concerned about government running roughshod over individuals. but unlike the liberal-individualist conception. it is relatively more concerned that government will interfere with popular places to practice citizenship in the public sphere. rather than take away or lessen particular citizenship rights. This sense of citizenship has been described as "active and public citizenship". and has sometimes been called a "revolutionary idea". According to one view. most people today live as citizens according to the liberal-individualist conception but wished they lived more according to the civic-republican ideal.

Other views

The subject of citizenship. including political discussions about what exactly the term describes. can be a battleground for ideologicaldebates. In Canada. *citizenship* and related issues such as civic education are "hotly contested." There continues to be sentiment within the academic community that trying to define one "unitary theory of citizenship" which would describe citizenship in every society. or even in any one society. would be a meaningless exercise.

Citizenship has been described as "multi-layered belongings"—different attachments. different bonds and allegiances. This is the view of Hebert and Wilkinson who suggest there is not one single perspective on citizenship but "multiple citizenship" relations since each person belongs to many different groups which define him or her.

Sociologist Michael Schudson examined changing patterns of citizenship in US history and suggested there were four basic periods:

1. The colonial era was marked by property-owning white males who delegated authority to "gentlemen". and almost all people did not participate as *citizens* according to his research. Early elections didn't generate much interest. were characterized by low voter turnout. and rather reflected an existing social hierarchy. Representative assemblies "barely existed" in the 18th century. according to Schudson.
2. Political parties became prominent in the 19th century to win lucrative patronage jobs. and *citizenship* meant party loyalty.
3. The 20th century citizenship ideal was having an "informed voter". choosing rationally (ie voting) based on information from sources such as newspapers and books.
4. Citizenship came to be seen as a basis for rights and entitlements from government. Schudson predicted the emergence of what he called the *monitorial citizen*: persons engaged in watching for issues such as corruption and government violations of rights.

Schudson chronicled changing patterns in which citizenship expanded to include formerly disenfranchised groups such as women and minorities while parties declined.Interest groups influenced legislators directly via lobbying. Politics retreated to being a peripheral concern for citizens who were often described as "self-absorbed".

In the 21st-century America. citizenship is generally considered to be a legal marker recognizing that a person is an American. *Duty* is generally not part of citizenship. Citizens generally do not see themselves as having a *duty* to provide assistance to one another. although officeholders are seen as having a duty to the public. Rather. citizenship is a bundle of rights which includes being able to get assistance from the federal government. A similar pattern marks the idea of citizenship in many western-style nations. Most Americans do not think much about citizenship except perhaps when applying for a passport and traveling internationally. Feliks Gross sees 20th century America as an "efficient. pluralistic and civic system that extended equal rights to all citizens. irrespective of race. ethnicity and religion." According to Gross. the US can be considered as a "model of a modern civic and democratic state" although discrimination and prejudice still survive. The exception. of course. is that persons living within the borders of America illegally see citizenship as a major issue. Nevertheless. one of the constants is that scholars and thinkers continue to agree that the concept of *citizenship* is hard to define. and lacks a precise meaning.

IDEA DEVELOPMENT OF CITIZENSHIP

The idea of citizenship was developed by Greek city-states. and the classical political thinkers. Because of the internal strifes between rich and poor and wars with neighbours. the problem before these societies was how to bring social peace. *i.e.*. by giving power to a few persons or spread it more widely. While Plato gave the idea of absolute authority to the Guardians. Aristotle developed the idea of citizenship. Political authority was distinctive because it was the authority of the office holder exercised over the members of the political community.

For Aristotle. citizenship was concerned with securing stable government under the law. It consisted in the capacity to govern and to be governed. as a consequence of self-discipline and education. based upon full ownership of property.

He defined citizen as 'one who has a share in the privilege of rule' and excluded certain categories such as slaves. aliens. women from it. In the Republican Rome and in the early imperial Rome. the idea of Roman citizenship also remained as one of privilege. Roman citizens were immune from the more humiliating forms of punishment such as crucification. But the idea of citizenship underwent a slow evolution as the nature of empire changed. The influence of jus gentium on the jus civile in the first two centuries narrowed the gulf between citizens and non-citizens.

The famous decree of Caracalla in 212 extended citizenship to all subjects of the empire. However. as the proportion of citizens increased. its significance declined. The participation in politics became meaningless and the magistracies ceased to have any independent influence and power. What Caracalla did by extending the citizenship to all was primarily to extend the burden of certain taxes and not to expand their political privileges and rights. The breakdown of Greek city states and the Roman empire and intellectual ascendancy of Christianity turned philosophers' gaze inwards or towards the next life.

Man was considered to be the citizen of the whole world. or of the City of God. Earthly citizenship was not an essential.part of good life. The revival of classical argument was done by Machiavelli who asserted that Roman freedom was preserved because of the virtues of its citizens. What citizenship contributed was self-discipline. patriotism. simple piety and a willingness to forgo private gains for the sake of public good.

Reformation. renaissance and industrial revolution in Europe produced a new political and social order. as a result of which the concept of citizenship also underwent a complete transformation. Modern citizenship has a history which parallels the growth of western capitalism. industrialization. creation of propertyless working class. the formation of professional middle class and the development of science and technology. It is associated with the extension of rights to the previously excluded groups such as working class. For example. the idea of citizenship in the French Revolution was associated with the rights.

The declaration of 'Rights of Man and of the Citizens of France' is an important landmark in this direction. It also associated the idea of citizenship with political liberation. At the theoretical level. French Revolution was a major factor for the rise of modern citizenship because it ushered in an era of social change. political liberation and economic equality. Similarly. the fear of social revolutions in Europe led the English capitalist class to legalise the trade unions. extend the suffrage to working class and introduce social reforms. Citizenship was also promoted through warfare.

To wage a war. the state requires the commitment of population and this could be brought through extension of citizenship rights. Also warfare promotes social change through mass mobilization. People come to realize that if the danger to the country is to be shared. then the resources should also be shared. The war promotes full employment and tight labour market and thus labour struggles are likely to put pressure on employers and government for expansion of citizenship rights. Examples of such expansion of democratic citizenship are Austria. Finland. Germany. Italy. Japan. Sweden. etc.

Apart from war. according to Bryan Turner. migration and egalitarian ideologies of twentieth century have also been sufficiently responsible for the growth of modern democratic citizenship. For example. modern citizenship in the American continent has to be understood in terms of the migrant nature of those societies which created a pluralistic culture and supported the struggle for citizenship rights.

Moreover. the ideologies of socialism. communism. welfare state helped in the struggle for political. industrial and social rights. Of late. new social movements such as feminism and sabiteranism have been struggling to extend full citizenship rights to those who are still excluded from them. According to Heater. apart from the political needs of participation and loyalty. three major factors have been responsible for the rise of citizenship. The first was philosophical.

Theories of citizenship contain assumptions and beliefs about the nature of man: that man is a political animal and that the exercise of power is legitimate only if based on the consent and sanctioned by the people. Citizenship evolved as a means of institutionalizing this basic belief. The second factor was the military needs. Every state required for its protection some kind of military service from its members and citizens were those who bore arms in defence of their city. Both the Greek and Roman citizens had this responsibility. Even during the medieval period. conferment of citizenship originated in its recruitment into the defence system. Machiavellian concept of civic virtue also depended upon an armed citizenary. The modern nation-state also universally requires. when necessary. the duty of military service of some kind from its citizens. The third factor was Economic. Theorists from Aristotle onwards were worried whether citizenship should be confined to the propertied class or should be extended to everybody. Initially. only the propertied class was given this status.

Similarly. the modern state which was born in internecine war required money to pursue these conflicts and money was available only with the capitalist class. So 'out of this alliance of the state with capital. dictated by necessity. arose the national citizen class. the bourgeoisie in the modern sense of the word'. It was only when these three factors—philosophical. military. and economic coincided that the idea of modern citizenship evolved.

EXPANSION OF CITIZENSHIP AND MARXISM

The expansion of citizenship in the modern state has been both an achievement as well as a limitation. While it declared that all persons as citizens are equal before law. yet the existence of economically unequal classes meant that the practical ability to exercise the rights was not available to all those who possessed them. In other words. the victims of the class system were unable to participate in the community of citizenship in which they had legal membership. This criticism of modern democratic citizenship has been the hallmark. of Marxist views on citizenship.

Marxism has been suspicious of citizenship and considered it as being contrary to class interest of the proletariat. Since for Marxism. state is an instrument of the dominant class and is likely to wither away in the communist society. it saw citizenship as a subjective and temporary condition. Reacting to the modern democratic citizenship. which Marx called as 'bourgeois citizenship'. he wrote that the state in its own way abolishes distinctions based on birth. rank. education and occupation when it declares birth. rank. education and occupation to be non-political distinctions. when it proclaims that every member of the people is an equal participant in popular sovereignty regardless of these distinctions. Nevertheless. the state allows private property. education and occupation and protects the unequal conditions generated by them.

Far from abolishing these factual distinctions. the state presupposes them in order to exist. Though Marx did not reject the achievements of modern liberal democratic citizenship and believed that the extension of rights has been worthwhile and a 'big step forward' within the 'prevailing scheme of things'. yet his point was that mere political emancipation in citizenship is inadequate. Instead he advocated a general human emancipation in which people were freed from the determining power of private property and its associated institutions.

Thus the limitations of citizenship which arise because of the class division of society could be overcome only through a social revolution in which the class basis of inequalities in social conditions will be overthrown. With. the establishment of a classless and stateless society. there will be no need for the status of citizen since the individual will have no political institutions with which to relate. from which to claim rights. and to which to owe responsibility. However. the theory and practice of citizenship as evolved in the communist states in the twentieth century was quite different. Working on the Marxist line of thinking. Lenin in 1924 constitution banished both 'state' and 'citizen'. and the Soviet people were identified as 'proletariats'. 'peasants' and 'soldiers'.

But the Stalin constitution in 1936 felt the need to restore both the state and the citizen. The constitution provided a number of rights to its citizens including the right to vote. freedom of conscience. speech. assembly and inviolability of person and his home. The list also included a number of duties such as 'observing the law. maintaining the labour discipline. honestly performing public duties. respecting the rules of the socialist community. safeguarding and strengthening. socialist property and defending the socialist fatherland. Above all. the state had the right to 'reform the traitors and counter-reactionaries'.

A novel feature of the communist countries has been that thousands were completely stripped of their right to citizenship such as kulkas in Russia and landlords in China. They were not only disenfranchised but also exterminated. The idea of citizenship in such states placed greater emphasis on the need for a positive commitment by the individual than in the liberal democratic countries.

The citizen was expected to support the state as embodied in the party or the fatherland. In tact. the absorption of Marxist doctrine has often been less in evidence than adherence to collectivist mentality. productive labour. patriotic loyalty and civic duty.

MARSHALL'S THEORY OF CITIZENSHIP

T.H. Marshal in his book Citizenship and Social Class has explained the nature of citizenship in the context of welfare state in Europe. It provides an account of the emergence of citizenship in the modern nation-state in terms of historical development of capitalist society. But contrary to Marxist conclusion. Marshal argues that as capitalism evolved into a social system and as the class structure developed. the concept of citizenship also underwent transformation. From being a system of rights which supported the market system and the propertied class. it changed to a system of rights which were opposed to market and a particular class. *i.e.*. rights of the non-propertied class.

Through their antagonistic relationship. citizenship and class inequality mutually contributed to change each other. The development of citizenship rights helped in the necessary integration of the working class into the capitalist society and the decline of class conflict. Marshal starts from the fact that citizenship is a status attached to full membership of a community and that those who possess this status are equal in respect of rights and duties associated with it. However. since there is no universal principle which determines necessary rights and duties of citizenship in general. different societies attach different rights and duties to the status of citizen.

Talking in the context of England. he wrote that the development of the institutions of modern citizenship coincided with the rise of capitalism. As a doctrine. citizenship was the quest of the bourgeois class for greater representation in society in opposition to aristocratic privileges. Hence it undermined the customary privileges of feudal class and consolidated incipient capitalist class relations. Hence citizenship entailed legal and civil equality. The civil element of citizenship essentially laid in the rights necessary for individual freedom and the institutions most directly associated with it were the rule of law and a system of courts. However. while it undermined one set of class system. it promoted and secured a second because citizenship rights were civil rights and civil rights were those which promoted competitive market economy based upon private property.

During nineteenth century. a number of political rights including the right to franchise were granted to the urban working class through the institution of bourgeois democracy to achieve some regulation of the capitalist economy. However. the full danger to the capitalist class could be avoided because the newly enfranchised working class was too inexperienced to wield political power effectively. But the working class was able to create trade unionism and through collective bargaining was able to wrest a number of concessions from the capitalist class to raise their economic and social status.

Thus the collective exercise of rights by members of the working class in creating and using trade unionism established 'the claim that they. as citizens. were entitled to certain social rights' The addition of social rights in the twentieth century made the situation more complex as well as interesting. It brought 'citizenship and capitalist class' at war. because citizenship is based on the principle of equality. capitalism is based on inequality. Social citizenship attempted to reform capitalism through legislation.

The gradual development of universal provisions for basic education. health and social security changed the nature of cash nexus between capital and labour. Legislation on minimum wages. hours of work. employment of children. working conditions. occupational safety and compensation of occupational accidents made the employees less vulnerable to the capitalist class. Thus the conflict between the two seemed inevitable.

But the problem. according to Marshal. is more complex. Between the rival demands of capitalist class for profit and the working class for welfare.

the state through positive intervention and by reformulating its taxation and expenditure policies has been able to resolve the conflict between the two. Though the creation of social citizenship has not removed the class inequalities. neither has it been able to fundamentally transform the economic basis of capitalism in terms of private appropriation of wealth—rather it has given rise to new forms of inequalities. nevertheless. it has been able to reduce certain social inequalities and especially those associated with the operation of the market.

Thus citizenship has 'imposed modifications on the class'. But on the whole. it has created a 'hyphenated system' because it combines a progressive expansion of egalitarian citizenship rights with the continuity of *de facto*r inequalities in terms of class. status and power.

CONTRIBUTIONS MADE BY ANTHONY GIDDENS

Anthony Giddens gives some other reasons for the development of the idea of citizenship. According to him. citizenship and democracy are both associated with the expansion of state sovereignty. The development of state's sovereignty meant increasing administrative power to supervise the subject population and to collect and store information about them. Since this could not be done through force. cooperation from other sections of the society became necessary.

Hence citizenship was the result of the greater reciprocity between the rulers and the ruled. Giddens calls this as 'two way expansion of power' or 'dialectics of control'. Citizenship was bound up with the new administrative ordering of political power and the politicization of social relations and day-to-day activities which follow in its wake.u The pursuit of equal membership in the new political set up coloured the concept of citizenship. The struggle for citizenship took many forms but the most important has been class conflict. First. it was the conflict of the bourgeoisie against the feudal privileges. followed by the struggle of the working class against the bourgeoisie.

The struggle between the bourgeoisie and feudalism led to the separation of the state from the economy and the establishment of civil and political rights by the state. Also democracy was adopted as a means to protect the freedom and equality of the citizens. Later. the institutional changes led to the success of the working class to gain economic rights. These struggles produced the welfare state—the modern interventionist states.

According to Giddens. the social and economic rights cannot be regarded as a mere extension of civil and political rights. but are a part of an attempt to improve the worse consequences of the worker citizen's lack of control over his working conditions and place. Thus in Gidden's assessment. class conflict has been the medium of extension of citizenship rights and the basis of the creation of an insulated economy. democracy and welfare state. The state sovereignty was a critical factor in the struggle for rights and to remould citizenship.These were major historical changes. But what is important is that there is nothing inherent about them; with the change in political and economic circumstances. they can be eroded. These rights still remain fragile achievements.

CITIZENSHIP EDUCATION CITIZENSHIP EDUCATION

According to Professor Janowitz. effective citizenship rests on a rigourous and viable system of civic rights and obligations. In this context citizenship education becomes very important. The training for citizenship can be traced from Plato and Aristotle onwards. The basic objective of teaching of citizenship in any state is to convey to the learner the body of knowledge. set of values. attitudes and skills which are considered necessary for the sustenance and well-being of the nation. Citizenship education seeks to gain people's support for the nation's civic culture through a variety of educational processes.

The Greeks expected from its citizens to fulfill the functions of politicians. administrators. judges. jurors and soldiers on the one hand and obedience to the laws. submission to the government and a readiness to defend the state by recourse to arms on the other. During the period of Republican Rome. education became largely a family function. and the task of inculcating the characteristic Roman civic qualities into the boys fell on the fathers. The qualities were many: firmness. courage. religious reverence. selfrestraint. dignity. prudence and justice.

The boys were also expected to learn about the exploits of past heroes. singing suitably patriotic songs and learning by recitation the famous Twelve Tables. With the rise of modern-nation state. citizenship education was meant to foster a personal and perpetual relationship of allegiance between king and his subjects. During the eighteenth century Europe and American. it was concerned with the creation of national identity by fostering commitment to slowly evolving democratic values. national loyalty and patriotism. During nineteenth century. which was the century of nationalism. liberal democracy as well as socialism. state intervened to ensure the transmission of political values through the school system.

To this end. the governments made widespread use of flags. patriotic songs and celebration of national anniversaries. The state came increasingly to take interest in the control of schools and a number of theorists argued and justified the 'nationalization of education'. The liberal writers like Bentham and Mill felt the general need for educational provisions. J.S. Mill was convinced that the advance of democracy depended crucially on the general spread of schooling. T.H. Green. who believed in the egalitarian form of citizenship. declared that the task of education should be to undermine the class barriers and create means of bonding its citizens more tightly to the community.During twentieth century. citizenship education is more meaningfully viewed as democratic political education. Primarily political in nature. it addresses public affairs and is not directly concerned with personal or social activities. Its goal is to sustain and refine a democratic political community-a group of people who share both a commitment to certain principles such as freedom. equality. due process of law. justice. diversity. as well as involvement in governing process based on mutual consent.

Here 'we the people' are the ultimate source of legitimate power and authority. The subject matter of citizenship education in these countries consists of a complex inter-relationship between individual and the democratic political community. responsible participation in public affairs. formal and informal political process including critical scrutiny of public officials. institutions and political operations. In short. citizenship knowledge in these countries consists of:

- knowledge of and respect for public law and policy at any level. This does not mean blind and unquestioning obedience to any set of rules; it is individual's duty. however. to abide by laws and policies which are formulated and applied for security and well-being of the society;
- development of the skills and activities which go into making or changing public law and policy. The citizen must accept responsibility for effective participation in shaping or altering the rules which are required by the society at any time;
- acquisition of knowledge necessary for effective participation. Knowledge about public issues and problems is vital for the participatory role of citizens; voting or seeking to influence government officials on the basis of pure emotions in the absence of enlightenment about public policies is not meeting the responsibilities of effective citizenship;
- the knowledge and behaviour which recognize and respect equal rights and opportunities for all in a diverse and pluralistic society. It also includes knowledge and behaviour which advance the individual self-reliance and responsibility in economic and social life.

FEMINIST CRITIQUE OF CITIZENSHIP

The women liberation movements have historically been a struggle against the presumption that sexual distinction made the human female not just different but that in legal. political. social. economic and cultural terms. she is inferior to his male counterpart. Feminists have argued that women are on the whole treated as second class citizen. They are considered as a different social class—defined as a class membership of fathers and husbands. Their opinions on public issues are considered to be borrowed from fathers or husbands. They vote less than men and tend to vote the same way as their men in the family.For much of the historical time. women have been deprived of citizenship rights. As citizens they have been subject to the decisions of male political leaders. Male dominance has been used to exclude women from political and economic decision-making. Women are under-represented in formal political institutions everywhere in the world whether in the legislature. executive. judiciary or bureaucracy. Political activity is primarily considered a masculine activity. Their voting right was achieved in stages even in the liberal democratic countries like England. France. America. Switzerland.

In some countries they still do not have voting rights. Again women have no power over their rights and obligations. Public laws for women are made and enforced by men. whether they are property rights or rights to inheritance. obligations to their children. their education. nourishment. safety. employment selection. conditions of work. etc.

Marriage laws in many countries continue to place women at considerable disadvantage compared to their husbands with regard to property rights and marital status. Another feminist argument is that by making a distinction between public (participation in the political affairs) and private (mainly domestic) spheres. women are deprived of participating and control over their private existence.It is in this context that the slogan of the women liberation movements in 1970s was 'The personal is political'. *i.e.*. the distinction between public and private is a political and manipulative device to perpetuate male dominance and to keep women as second class citizens. How to secure full citizenship for women? On this questions. there is great divergence of opinion within the feminist movement. The primary objective of the liberal feminists has been to bring women into full rights of democratic citizenship. The suffrage rights. more recent reforms such as participation of women on juries. equal pay. anti-discrimination legislation. reform in marriage laws. decriminalization of prostitution are seen as allowing women to become full citizens.

The liberal feminists envisage a future where legal. political. social and economic rights will be achieved and women will be on equal footing with men in all spheres. This will be brought about by reason. persuasion and constitutional reforms. The family will remain but men will have equal role in domestic duties and women's career will not be hampered by rearing of children.This is what they call 'civic feminism'. Socialist feminists want to achieve this objective through expansion of free birth control. abortion. health care for women. child care centres and state recognition of domestic labour. The radical feminists go a step forward and accord less significance to monogamy in order to facilitate the entrance of women into the public world with men.

SUBALTERN CRITIQUE OF CITIZENSHIP

The existence of politically. economically. socially and culturally inferior classes and groups in the underdeveloped countries poses a serious challenge to citizenship. By sublatern groups. we mean people of 'inferior rank'. The word is used for the general attribution of subordination particularly in the underdeveloped countries of South Asian ex-colonial societies irrespective of class. caste. age. gender. office or any other way. This subordination can be understood in contrast to 'domination' by certain privileged groups in each and every sphere of life.

Historically. property has been associated as an essential precondition of citizenship. The poor and the lower classes. because of their inability to meet this criterion. could not be considered as full citizens. Whatever relief to the poor was given was more an act of charity. Although the social citizenship rights in the modern liberal welfare states have changed the position of non-propertied classes and certain rights and services are made available to them irrespective of wealth. yet in the underdeveloped countries. citizenship still means domination of a large portion of population by a few elites.

Though millions are classified as citizens in these states. only a small portion of that number can be truly said to enjoy it as a status of social dignity and source of effective rights. To the peasants and tribals scattered in villages and jungles. or the petty workers and lumpen masses huddled around megalopolitan slums and juggi jhopris. citizenship rights are meaningless. Deprivation experienced by these group is not only physical; it involves breaking down various ties of citizenship— whether it is acquisition of skills. education. access to justice or enjoyment of rights.

Political consciousness. where it exists at all. is resigned acceptance of manipulation by local leaders or of sheer and utter impotence. In many states. social equality is denied as a valid test of citizenship. In short. for such people. the matter of civil. political and social citizenship still remains an act of domination rather than egalitarianism. Effective citizenship in these state in future will depend on how far these groups are integrated into the society.

2

Global Citizenship

INTRODUCTION

Global citizenship applies the whole world to bring world peace and the concept of citizenship to a global level and is strongly connected with the concepts of globalization and cosmopolitanism. World citizenship is a term which can be distinguished from global citizenship. although some may merge the two concepts. Various ideas about what a global citizen is exist. Global citizenship can be defined as a moral and ethical disposition which can guide the understanding of individuals or groups of local and global contexts. and remind them of their relative responsibilities within various communities. The term was used by U.S. President Barack Obama in 2008 in a speech in Berlin.

In this century children and students are meant to become "global citizens" through their education. This is possible through an integration of the "scientific and technical skills" as well as the "traditional academic disciplines". According to some accounts. citizenship is motivated by local interests. global interests. and concern for fellow human beings. human rights and human dignity. The key tenets of global citizenship include respect for any and all fellow global citizens. regardless of race. religion or creed and give rise to a universal sympathy beyond the barriers of nationality.

These sentiments were initially summarized by the British author. pamphleteer and revolutionary Thomas Paine in Rights of Man:

- My country is the world. and my religion is to do good. When translated into participatory action. global citizenship entails a responsibility to reduce international inequality (both social and economic). to refrain from action which compromises an individuals' well-being. and avoids contributing to environmental degradation.

Within the educational system. the concept of global citizenship education (GCE) is at times beginning to supersede movements such as multicultural education. peace education. human rights education and international education. Additionally. GCE rapidly incorporates references to the aforementioned movements. The concept of global citizenship has been linked with awards offered for helping humanity.In international relations. global citizenship can refer to states' responsibility to act with the awareness that the world is a global community. by recognizing and fulfilling its obligations towards the global world. as well as the rights of global citizens. For example. states can choose to recognize the right to freedom of movement. Global citizenship is related to the international relations theory of idealism. which holds that states should include a level of moral goodwill in their foreign policy decisions.

GLOBAL CITIZENSHIP – TOWARDS A DEFINITION

By itself. citizenship has certain legal and democratic overtones. Conceptually. it is wrapped up in rights and obligations. and in owing allegiance to a sovereign state whose power is retained by the citizenry but with rights that are shared by all members of that state. We distinguish "citizen" from "national" or "subject." the latter two implying protection of a state. Citizenship. as it has come down to us via the ancient Greeks and Romans. via the Enlightenment. and the American and French Revolutions. is tied into the emergence of members of a polity with specified privileges and duties. To speak of a "citizen" is thus to speak of individuals with distinct relationships to the state. along with the social status and power these relationships imply.

The lift the citizen concept into the global sphere presents difficulties. not least of which is that global citizens are not legal members in good standing with a sovereign state. More importantly. there are no recognizable privileges and duties associated with the concept that would envelop global citizenship with the status and power (in an ideal world) currently associated with national citizenship.

Since modern nation-states are the repositories and main expression of citizenship. discussion of global citizenship necessarily dictates an existence outside the body politic as we know it. If we follow Preston's (1997) model of citizenship ("who belongs to the polity. how the members of the polity in general are regarded and how they exercise power"). then global citizenship cannot be expressed in any legal sense. It is. however. expressed in other ways that may have a significant and profound impact on the development of civic engagement and citizen-state relations. Three examples are worth mentioning.

Since January 1. 2000. negotiations amongst WTO member states regarding the movement of professionals to and from member countries has taken place. under the General Agreement on Trade in Services. Article XIX. While this does not signal de facto recognition of trans-national citizens. it may indicate halting steps Towards it. This is all the more significant given that around the globe there is greater and easier movement of goods than human beings. The European Community has taken halting steps to change this: it allows the free movement of its peoples to live. work. pay taxes and. significantly. to vote in other member states. Habermas (1994) notes this as a utilitarian model that may have greater implications than merely for Europeans; it is possible the model may be expanded in other regions of the world. or to the entire world itself. The ability of a Spaniard to pick up and move to Germany and be a "citizen" there indicates that notions of ties a country of origin may weaken. The Spaniard may be quite happy living in Germany and not wish to go back to Spain. Is she still a Spaniard. a German. or now a global citizen?

Finally. there is the rising tide of individuals with more than one passport. Where once the U.S. State Department frowned on its citizens carrying more than one passport. the reality is that today that it is turning a blind eye. (In war. this may change). Many immigrants to the U.S. in the 1990s. a decade that saw the largest influx of newcomers to the state. came to work but still retained their old passports. While many immigrants permanently stay in the U.S.. many others either go back to the old country. or travel back and forth. If not global citizens. what label do we give them?

T.H. Marshall (1949). in his classic study on citizenship. noted that citizenship as it arose in Western liberal democracies has both positive and negative connotations. In the positive sense. citizenship is an expression of activism on the part of citizens; in its negative quality. it is the freedom from bureaucratic control and intervention. If his theory is true. where does global citizenship fit into it? Very nicely it would seem.

A visible expression of global citizenship is the many global activists who debuted spectacularly at the Battle in Seattle. These protestors continue to carry on in other venues. such as at meetings for the World Bank and the IMF. and most recently at the Summit of the Americas in Quebec City. Other activists fight for environmental protection. human rights to the impoverished and the unrepresented. and for restrictions on the use of nuclear power and nuclear weapons. Freedom from bureaucratic intervention seems to be a hallmark of global citizenship; the lack of a world body to sanction and protect these citizens also means to a certain degree freedom from bureaucratic control. To return to our Spaniard. how much control does Spain exercise over her when she lives in Germany?

TOWARDS A DEFINITION

Since global citizens are not recognized legally. their existence may be best represented as "associatively."

Global citizenship is less defined by legal sanction than by "associational" status that is different from national citizenship. Since there is no global bureaucracy to give sanction and protect global citizens. and despite intriguing models suggested by the EU. global citizenship remains the purview of individuals to live. work and play within trans-national norms and status that defy national boundaries and sovereignty. Assocational status in this realm does double duty. It serves to explain a unique characteristic of global citizenship while it also expresses that particular lighthouse of post-modernity known as "lifestyle politics." Steenbergen (1994) so far comes closest to explaining this relationship between global citizenry and lifestyle politics as more "sociological" in composition.

Rather than a technical definition of a citizen "on his or her relationship to the state. Steenbergen suggests that the global citizen represents a more wholistic version: you choose where you work. live or play. and therefore are not tied down to your land of birth. The greater number of choices offered by modern life (from consumer products to politics) lies at the root of lifestyle politics. As Falk (1994) put it. in global citizenship there is the rudimentary institutional construction of arenas and allegiance— what many persons are really identifying with— as no longerbounded by or centred upon the formal relationship that anindividual has to his or her own territorial society as embodiedin the form of a state. Traditional citizenship is being challengedand remoulded by the important activism associated with thistrans-national political and social evolution.

Traditional ties between citizen and the state are withering. and are replaced by more fragmented loyalties that explain lifestyle politics. Notions of ties between citizen and state that arose in the aftermath of the American and French Revolution. and the creation of the modern state after the 18 century no longer hold sway. It is not by coincidence. for example. that the first to receive the enfranchisement were adult males who also happened to serve in American and French armies. The citizen army today is replaced by the professional army. and a central cog in the bonds between state and citizen removed. Voting turnout decreases. and the public has low regard for politicians. With such loose ties between citizen and state. does the emergence of global citizenship seem farfetched? Many of newly emerging global citizens are actively engaged in global efforts – whether in business ventures. environmentalism. concern for nuclear weapons. health or immigration problems. Rather than citizenship. being the result of rights and obligations granted by a central authority. the lack of such authority gives primacy to the global citizens themselves: not a top-down but a down-up scenario.

While various types of global citizens exist. a common thread to their emergence is their base in grassroots activism. We may identify different types of global citizens. yet many of these categories are best summarized by their emergence despite a lack of any global governing body. It is as if they have spontaneously erupted of their own volition.

Falk (1994) identified five categories of global citizens which he named as.

- global reformers
- elite global business people
- global environmental managers
- politically conscious regionalists
- trans-national activists

With the exception of global business people. the other categories have grassroots activism at their core. If the Battle in Seattle is an applicable demonstration. these activists are responsible for their own activism rather than "granted" by an institution. This earmarks global citizenship as qualitatively different from the national variety. where rights and obligations came (even when fought and protested for) at the behest and generosity of the state. With global citizenship. individuals exercise communicational and organizational tools such as the Internet to make themselves global citizens. No government sanctioned this development. None. it seems. could.

Jacobson (1996) noted this fracture of the state as dispenser of citizen rights and obligations. although he sees the decline of overall citizenship as a result. Keck and Sikkink (1998) on the other hand. regard such global activism as a possible new engine of civic engagement. These global activists. or "cosmopolitan community of individuals" as they call them. transcend national borders and skillfully use pressure tactics against both government and private corporations that make them viable actors on the emerging global public sphere. A striking example of this pressure is the well-publicized anti-sweatshop campaign against Nike. Literally dozens of websites are devoted to exposing Nike's Labour practices in manufacturing shoes in overseas factories. In 1996. with the aid of Global Exchange. a humanitarian organization that later helped to organize the Battle in Seattle. Nike's Labour practices became the subject of increasing mainstream media attention. In the process. Nike was linked to sweatshop Labour. a label it has tried to shed ever since.

Is the Internet central in the development of these emerging global activists? The Internet and other technologies such as the cell phone play an instrumental role in the development of global activists. as do easy and cheap air travel and the wide use and acceptance of credit cards.

But there are other forces at work: decline in civic engagement. rise of lifestyle politics. homogenization of products. conglomeration in media systems and communicational tools that let us know more about each other than ever before. Add to the mix the rising concern for universal human rights and for trans-global problems such as environmental degradation and global warming. the result is a landscape that tends to be more global than national. This is not the first time in the history of our civilization that society has been "internationalized." but never has it been easier for average citizen to express herself in this globalized fashion – by the clothes she wears. soda she drinks. music she listens to (*e.g.* "world music") and vacation land she visits. It is increasingly obvious that our identities. as Lie and Servaes (2000) and Scammell (2001) suggest. are tied to our roles as citizens. Scammell's "citizen-consumers" vote with their purchases and are engaged in their communities to the extent they have the freedom to shop. Engagement. in this modern sense. is as audience members at a play clapping at the high points of drama. Can we say this is true of global citizenship? The evidence is scanty to make such Judgement; if global activists are replaced by global citizens-consumers the sea change will be complete.

Global citizens may redefine ties between civic engagement and geography. The town hall meetings of New England and other regions of the U.S. seem increasingly supplanted by "electronic spheres" not limited by space and time. This heralds a potentially startling new mechanism in participatory democracy.If we return to the Spaniard living in Germany. what can we say about the geography of community? An output of modernity is greater and greater choice placed upon the individual; the social networks and systems that suited hundreds if not thousands of generations are breaking down in Favour of personal choice and individual responsibility. No longer do we entirely rely on the social bulwarks of the past: the family. the community. the nation. Life is continually being "personalized." Can the Spaniard still be called one while living in Germany? Absentee ballots opened up the way for expatriates to vote while living in another country. The Internet may carry this several steps further. Voting is not limited by time or space: you can be anywhere in the world and still make voting decisions back home.

Most of our nation's history has been bound up in equating geography with sovereignty. It did matter where you lived. worked. played. Since travel was expensive and cumbersome. our lives were tied to geography. No longer can we entirely make this claim.

Thompson (1996). writing in the *Stanford Law Review.* suggests that we can do away with residency and voting in local elections. Frug (1996) even suggests that alienation in the way we regard our geography already creates a disconnect between it and sovereignty. If we are not entirely "home" at home. do boundaries make any difference anymore? This is not just an academic question. but one rife with rich and disheartening social and political possibilities. Global citizens float within. outside and through these boundaries. The implications seem significant.

Many elements seem to spawn global citizenship. but one is noteworthy in this discussion: the continuous tension that globalization has unleashed between various forces local. national and global. An interesting paradox of globalization is while the world is being internationalized at the same time it's also being localized. The world shrinks as the local community (village. town. city) takes on greater and greater importance. Mosco (1999) noted this feature and saw the growing importance of "technopoles." or high-technologized city-states that hark back to classical Greece. If this trend is true. and I believe it is. then it seems global citizens are the glue that may hold these separate entities together. Put another way. global citizens are people that can travel within these various layers or boundaries and somehow still make sense of the world.

Any rights and obligations accorded to the global citizen come from the citizens themselves. growing public Favour for "universal rights." the rise of people migrating around the world. and an increasing tendency to standardize citizenship. Difference may exist on the cultural level. but in bureaucracies. increasing Favour is placed on uniformity. Efficiency and utilitarianism lie at the core of capitalism; naturally a world that lives under its aegis replicates these tendencies. Postal agreements. civil air travel and other inter-governmental agreements are but one small example of standardization that is increasingly moving into the arena of citizenship. The concern is raised that global citizenship may be closer to a "consumer" model than a legal one.

The lack of a world body puts the initiative upon global citizens themselves to create rights and obligations. Rights and obligations as they arose at the formation of nation-states (*e.g.* the right to vote and obligation to serve in time of war) are at the verge of being expanded. So new concepts that accord certain "human rights" which arose in the 20th century are increasingly being universalized across nations and governments. This is the result of many factors. including the Universal Declaration of Human Rights by the United Nations in 1948. the aftermath of World War II and the Holocaust and growing sentiments towards legitimizing marginalized peoples (*e.g.* pre-industrialized peoples found in the jungles of Brazil and Borneo). Couple this with growing awareness of our species' impact on the environment. and there is the rising feeling that citizen rights may extend to include the right to dignity and self-determination. If national citizenship does not foster these new rights. then global citizenship seems more accessible to them.

One cannot overestimate the importance of the rise of human rights discourse within the radar of public opinion. What are the rights and obligations of human beings trapped in conflicts? Or. incarcerated as part of "ethnic cleansing?" Equally striking. are the pre-industrialized tribes newly discovered by scientists living in the depths of dense jungle? Leary (1999). Heater (1999) and Babcock (1994) tend to equate these rights with the rise of global citizenship as normative associations. indicating a national citizenship model that is more closed and a global citizenship one that is more flexible and inclusive. If true. this places a strain in the relationship between national and global citizenship. Boli (1998) tends to see this strain as mutually beneficial. whereas Leary (1999) and McNeely (1998) regard the rupture between the two systems as merely evolutionary rather than combative.

Like much of social change. changing scopes of modern citizenship tend to be played out in both large and minute spheres. Habermas (1994) tends to place global citizenship in a larger. social context. arguing that nation-states can be central engines of citizenship but culture can also be a powerful spurt.

He regards the formation of the "European citizen" as a kind of natural epiphany of governmental conglomeration within the forces of globalization.

only remotely alluding to the corporate conglomeration that has been both the recipient and cause of worldwide economic expansion. Others. including Iyer (2000) see globalization and global citizens as direct descendents of global standardization. which he notes. for instance. in the growing homogeneity of airports.

Standardization and modernity have worked together for the past few centuries. Ellul (1964). Mumford (1963) and other scholars attack this as a form of oppression. in the same vein that Barber (1996) saw the proliferation of carbon-copy fast-food chains around the globe. Why not a set of basic citizen rights followed the world over?

Global citizenship may be the indirect result of Pax Americana. The 20th century. as well as the 21st. may be a time dominated by the United States. America's domination of the WTO. IMF. World Bank and other global institutions creates feelings of imperialism among lesser nations. Cross national cooperation to counter American dominance may result in more global citizens.

If economic. environmental. political and social factors push towards more globalcitizenry. we must also within this camp consider the ramifications of the post cold war world. or *realpolitik*. Modifying Marshall's metaphor. we may ask if global citizenship is not a response *to* the changing factors and response *against* American domination?

In the corporate world. conglomeration leads to larger and larger companies who merge to effectively work against other mega corporations. The evolution of the "United States of Europe" (in theory if not in practice) is in a similar vein; a reaction to the dominating power of the U.S. Other regional alliances may yet emerge. Within such trans-national ties may emerge greater acceptance of one another's citizens. emulating the European model which Habermas. Bellamy (2000). and others so Favour. These alliances may provide the bureaucratic backbone to make global citizenry about more than just lifestyles or personal politics. This development would also change the definition of national citizenry; global citizens may come to Favour their status over those who have no such designation.

Worse. there may emerge two tracks of citizenship: national and global. with the latter being more prestigious. Along with greater separation between rich and poor. educated and not. there would also be those relegated to living out their entire lives in one land. compared to those who freely travel to many.

The darker aspects of this are not hard to miss. Clarke's (1996) contention that citizenship tends to be more exclusive than inclusive would be borne out. Rather than McNeely's (1998) flexible citizenship. or Preston's (1997) multiple loyalty model. we get two separate tracks of citizenship that respond to prestige. wealth and power.

Global citizens may be so favored that nations fight to attract them to their land. similar to today's fight for corporate sites.

ACTIVISM OF GLOBAL CITIZENSHIP

Many citizens could be labeled as emerging global citizens are actively engaged in efforts on a global scale–whether through business ventures. environmentalism. concern for nuclear weapons. health issues or immigration problems. The phenomenon of global citizenship can also be summarized by its lack of any global governing body. In other words. it is as if global citizens spontaneously erupted of their own volition. Some may identify a base in grassroots activism as common thread within the phenomenon of their emergence.

In a document entitled "Global Citizenship - Towards a Definition." scholar Taso G. Lagos writes about the relation between global activism and global citizenship:

Global activity is on the rise. Demonstrations in Seattle in 1999. Genoa in 2001 and at dozens of other sites. brought activists together from a\e and other activities suggest the possibility of an emerging global citizenry. Individuals from a wide variety of nations. both in the North and South. move across boundaries for different activities and reasons. This transnational activity is facilitated by the growing ease of travel and by communication fostered by the Internet and telephony.

Lagos continues later:

- A visible expression of global citizenship is the many global activists who debuted spectacularly at the Battle in Seattle. These protests continue at other venues. such as at meetings for the World Bank and the International Monetary Fund. and most recently at the Summit of the Americas in Quebec City. Other activists fight for environmental protection. human rights to the impoverished and the unrepresented. and for restrictions on the use of nuclear power and nuclear weapons. Freedom from bureaucratic intervention seems to be a hallmark of global citizenship; the lack of a world body to sanction and protect these citizens also means to a certain degree freedom from bureaucratic control.

Further in the article Lagos elaborates:

- Scholars have already noted the emerging power struggle between corporations and global activists who increasingly see the nexus of de facto governance taking place more and more within the corporate world (and as mediated by communication technologies like the Internet) and not in the halls of representative government. Hence. the tendency on the part of activists to promote rallies and events like the protests at WTO. as more effective means of citizen participation and democratic accountability.

In an article entitled "The Making of Global Citizenship." Falk identifies five potential categories of global citizens.

He describes these as "a series of overlapping images of what it might mean to be a global citizen at this stage in history." According to Lagos. the majority of Falk's categories "have grassroots activism at their core" except for the example of elite global business people. Descriptions of the five categories are as follows:

DEFINITION OF GLOBAL CITIZENSHIP

The term "citizenship" refers to an identity between a person and a city. state or nation and their right to work. live and participate politically in a particular geographic area.

When combined with the term "global". it typically defines a person who places their identity with a "global community" above their identity as a citizen of a particular nation or place. The idea is that one's identity transcends geography or political borders and that responsibilities or rights are or can be derived from membership in a broader class: "humanity". This does not mean that such a person denounces or waives their nationality or other. more local identities. but such identities are given "second place" to their membership in a global community. Extended. the idea leads to questions about the state of global society in the age of globalization.In general usage. the term may have much the same meaning as "World Citizen" or Cosmopolitan. but it also has additional. specialized meanings in differing contexts.

USAGE

Education

In education. the term is most often used to describe a worldview or a set of values Towards which education is oriented. The term "global society" is sometimes used to indicate a global studies set of learning objectives for students to prepare them for global citizenship.

Global citizenship education

Within the educational system. the concept of global citizenship education (GCE) is beginning to supersede or overarch movements such as multicultural education. peace education. human rights education. Education for Sustainable Development and international education. Additionally. GCE rapidly incorporates references to the aforementioned movements. The concept of global citizenship has been linked with awards offered for helping humanity. Teachers are being given the responsibility of being social change agents. Audrey Osler. director of the *Centre for Citizenship and Human Rights Education*. the University of Leeds. affirms that "Education for living together in an interdependent world is not an optional extra. but an essential foundation".

Noteworthy. Global Education Magazine is a digital journal supported by UNESCO and UNHCR. inspired in the universal values of the Declaration of Emerging Human Rights that aims to contribute to achieve the Millennium Development Goals by GCE consciousness. An initiative launched by the teaching team that formulated the proposal most voted in the group "Sustainable Development for the Eradication of Poverty in Rio+20".

With GCE gaining attention. scholars are investigating the field and developing perspectives. The following are a few of the more common perspectives:

- *Critical and transformative perspective*. Citizenship is defined by being a member with rights and responsibilities. Therefore. GCE must encourage active involvement. GCE can be taught from a critical and transformative perspective. whereby students are thinking. feeling. and doing. In this approach. GCE requires students to be politically critical and personally transformative. Teachers provide social issues in a neutral and grade-appropriate way for students to understand. grapple with. and do something about.
- *Worldmindedness*. Graham Pike and David Selby view GCE as having two strands. Worldmindedness. the first strand. refers to understanding the world as one unified system and a responsibility to view the interests of individual nations with the overall needs of the planet in mind. The second strand. Child-centeredness. is a pedagogical approach that encourages students to explore and discover on their own and addresses each learner as an individual with inimitable beliefs. experiences. and talents.
- *Holistic Understanding*. The Holistic Understanding perspective was founded by Merry Merryfield. focusing on understanding the self in relation to a global community. This perspective follows a curriculum that attends to human values and beliefs. global systems. issues. history. cross-cultural understandings. and the development of analyticaland evaluative skills.

Philosophy

Global citizenship. in some contexts. may refer to a brand of ethics or political philosophy in which it is proposed that the core social. political. economic and environmentalrealities of the world today should be addressed at all levels—by individuals. civil society organizations. communities and nation states—through a global lens. It refers to a broad. culturally- and environmentally-inclusive worldview that accepts the fundamental interconnectedness of all things. Political. geographic borders become irrelevant and solutions to today's challenges are seen to be beyond the narrow vision of national interests. Proponents of this philosophy often point to Diogenes of

Sinope (c. 412 B.C.) as an example. given his reported declaration that "I am a citizen of the world" in response to a question about his place of origin. A Sanskrit term.*Vasudhaiva Kutumbakam*. has the meaning of 'the world is one family'". The earliest reference to this phrase is found in the Hitopadesha. a collection of parables. In theMahopanishad VI.71-73. œlokas describe how one finds the Brahman (the one supreme. universal Spirit that is the origin and support of the phenomenal universe). The statement is not just about peace and harmony among the societies in the world. but also about a truth that somehow the whole world has to live together like a family.

ASPECTS

Geography. sovereignty. and citizenship

At the same time that globalization is reducing the importance of nation-states. the idea of global citizenship may require a redefinition of ties between civic engagement and geography. Face-to-face town hall meetings seem increasingly supplanted by electronic "town halls" not limited by space and time. Absentee ballots opened the way forexpatriates to vote while living in another country; the Internet may carry this several steps further. Another interpretation given by several scholars of the changing configurations of citizenship due to globalization is the possibility that citizenship becomes a changed institution; even if situated within territorial boundaries that are national. if the meaning of the national itself has changed. then the meaning of being a citizen of that nation changes.

Tension among local. national. and global forces

An interesting feature of globalization is that. while the world is being internationalized. it's also being localized at the same time. The world shrinks as the local community (village. town. city) takes on greater and greater importance. This is reflected in the term glocalization. a portmanteau of the words "global" and "local". Mosco (1999) noted this feature and saw the growing importance of technopoles. If this trend is true. it seems global citizens may be the glue that holds these separate entities together. Put another way. global citizens are people who can travel within these various boundaries and somehow still make sense of the world through a global lens.

Human rights

The lack of a universally recognized world body can put the initiative upon global citizens themselves to create rights and obligations. Rights and obligations as they arose at the formation of nation-states (*e.g.* the right to vote and obligation to serve in time of war) are being expanded. Thus. new concepts that accord certain "human rights" which arose in the 20th century are increasingly being universalized across nations and governments. This is the result of many factors. including the Universal Declaration of Human Rightsby the United Nations in 1948. the aftermath of World War II and the Holocaust and growing sentiments towards legitimizing marginalized peoples (*e.g.*. pre-industrialized peoples found in the jungles of Brazil and Borneo). Couple this with growing awareness of our impact on the environment. and there is the rising feeling that citizen rights may extend to include the right to dignity and self-determination. If national citizenship does not foster these new rights. then global citizenship may seem more accessible.

One cannot overestimate the importance of human rights discourse in shaping public opinion. What are the rights and obligations of human beings trapped in conflicts? Or. incarcerated as part of ethnic cleansing? Equally striking. are the pre-industrialized tribes newly discovered by scientists living in the depths of dense jungle? These rights can be equated with the rise of global citizenship as normative associations. indicating a national citizenship model that is more closed and a global citizenship one that is more flexible and inclusive. If true. this places a strain in the relationship between national and global citizenship.

UN General Assembly

On December 10. 1948. the UN General Assembly Adopted Resolution 217A (III). also known as "The Universal Declaration of Human Rights."

Article 1 states that "All human beings are born free and equal in dignity and rights. They are endowed with reason and conscience and should act towards one another in a spirit of brotherhood."

Article 2 states that "Everyone is entitled to all the rights and freedoms set forth in this Declaration. without distinction of any kind. such as race. colour. sex. language. religion. political or other opinion. national or social origin. property. birth or other status. Furthermore. no distinction shall be made on the basis of the political. jurisdictional or international status of the country or territory to which a person belongs. whether it be independent. trust. non-self-governing or under any other limitation of sovereignty." Article 13(2) states that "Everyone has the right to leave any country. including his own. and to return to his country."

As evidence in today's modern world. events such as the Trial of Saddam Hussein have proven what British jurist A. V. Dicey said in 1885. when he popularized the phrase "rule of law" in 1885. Dicey emphasized three aspects of the rule of law:

1. No one can be punished or made to suffer except for a breach of law proved in an ordinary court.
2. No one is above the law and everyone is equal before the law regardless of social. economic. or political status.
3. The rule of law includes the results of judicial decisions determining the rights of private persons.

US Declaration of Independence

The opening of the United States Declaration of Independence. written by Thomas Jefferson in 1776. states as follows:We hold these truths to be self-evident. that all men are created equal. that they are endowed by their Creator with certain unalienable Rights. that among these areLife. Liberty. and the Pursuit of Happiness. That to secure these rights. Governments are instituted among Men. deriving their just powers from the consent of the governed;

"Global citizenship in the United States" was a term was used by U.S. President Barack Obama in 2008 in a speech in Berlin.

Support for global government

In contrast to questioning definitions. a counter-criticism can be found on the World Alliance of YMCA's Web site. An online article in *YMYCA World* emphasizes the importance of fostering global citizenship and global justice. and states. "Global citizenship might sound like a vague concept for academics but in fact it's a very practical way of looking at the world which anyone. if given the opportunity. can relate to." The author acknowledges the positive and negative outlooks towards globalization. and states. "In the context of globalisation. thinking and acting as global citizens is immensely important and can bring real benefits. as the YMCA experience shows."

SOCIAL MOVEMENTS

World citizen

In general. a World Citizen is a person who places global citizenship above any nationalistic or local identities and relationships. An early expression of this value is found in Diogenes of Sinope (c. 412 B.C.). the founding father of the Cynic movement in Ancient Greece. Of Diogenes it is said: "Asked where he came from. he answered: 'I am a citizen of the world (kosmopolitês)'". This was a ground-breaking concept because the broadest basis of social identity in Greece at that time was either the individual city-state or the Greeks (Hellenes) as a group. The Tamil poet Kaniyan Poongundran wrote in Purananuru. "To us all towns are one. all men our kin." In later years. political philosopher Thomas Paine would declare. "The world is my country. all mankind are my brethren and to do good is my religion." Today. the increase in worldwide globalization has led to the formation of a "world citizen" social movement under a proposed world government. In a non-political definition. it has been suggested that a world citizen may provide value to society by using knowledge acquired across cultural contexts.

Albert Einstein described himself as a world citizen and supported the idea throughout his life. famously saying "Nationalism is an infantile disease. It is the measles of mankind." World citizenship has been promoted by distinguished people including Garry Davis. who lived for 60 years as a citizen of no nation. only the world. Davis founded the World Service Authority in Washington. DC. which issues the World Passport (usually not considered a valid passport) to world citizens. In 1956 Hugh J. Schonfield founded theCommonwealth of World Citizens. later known by its Esperanto name "Mondcivitan Republic". which also issued a world passport; it declined after the 1980s.

The Bahá'í Faith promotes the concept through its founder's proclamation (in the late 19th century) that "The Earth is but one country. and mankind its citizens." As a term defined by the Bahá'í International Community in a concept paper shared at the 1st session of the United Nations Commission on Sustainable Development. New York. U.S.A. on 14–25 June 1993. "World citizenship begins with an acceptance of the oneness of the human family and the interconnectedness of the nations of 'the earth. our home.' While it encourages a sane and legitimate patriotism. it also insists upon a wider loyalty. a love of humanity as a whole. It does not. however. imply abandonment of legitimate loyalties. the suppression of cultural diversity. the abolition of national autonomy. nor the imposition of uniformity. Its hallmark is 'unity in diversity.' World citizenship encompasses the principles of social and economic justice. both within and between nations; non-adversarial decision making at all levels of society; equality of the sexes; racial. ethnic. national and religious harmony; and the willingness to sacrifice for the common good. Other facets of world citizenship—including the promotion of human honour and dignity. understanding. amity. co-operation. trustworthiness. compassion and the desire to serve—can be deduced from those already mentioned."

Mundialization

Philosophically. mundialization (French. *mondialisation*) is seen as a response to globalization's "dehumanisation through [despatialised] planetarisation" (Teilhard de Chardin quoted in Capdepuy 2011). An early use of *mondialisation* was to refer to the act of a city or a local authority declaring itself a "world citizen" city. by voting a charter stating its awareness of global problems and its sense of shared responsibility. The concept was promoted by the self-declared World Citizen Garry Davis in 1949. as a logical extension of the idea of individuals declaring themselves world citizens. and promoted by Robert Sarrazac. a former leader of the French Résistance who created the Human Front of World Citizens in 1945. The first city to be officially mundialised was the small French city of Cahors (only 20.000 in 2006). the capital city of the Département of Lot in central France. on 20 July 1949. Hundreds of cities mundialised themselves over a few years. most of them in France. and then it spread internationally. including to many German cities and to Hiroshima and Nagasaki. In less than a year. 10 General Councils (the elected councils of the French "Départements"). and hundreds of cities in France covering 3.4 million inhabitants voted mundialisation charters. One of the goals was to elect one delegate per million inhabitants to a People's World Constitutional Convention given the already then historical failure of the United Nations in creating a global institution able to negotiate a final world peace. To date. more than 1000 cities and towns have declared themselvesWörld cities. including Beverly Hills. Los Angeles. Minneapolis. St. Louis. Philadelphia. Toronto. Hiroshima. Tokyo. Nivelles. and Königswinter.

As a social movement. mundialization expresses the solidarity of populations of the globe and aims to establish institutions and supranational laws of a federative structure common to them. while respecting the diversity of cultures and peoples. The movement advocates for a new political organization governing all humanity. involving the transfer of certain parts of national sovereignty to a Federal World Authority. Federal World Government and Federal World Court. Basing its authority on the will of the people. and developing new systems to draw the highest and best wisdom of all humanity into the task of governing our world. the collaborative governing system would be capable of solving the problems which call into question the future of man. such as hunger. water. war. peace-keeping. pollution and energy. The mundialization movement includes the declaration of specified territory - a city. town. or state. for example - as world territory. with responsibilities and rights on a world scale. Currently the nation-state system and the United Nations offer no way for the people of the world to vote for world officials or participate in governing our world. International treaties or agreements lack the force of law. Mundialization seeks to address this lack by presenting a way to build. one city at a time. such a system of true World Law based upon the sovereignty of the whole.

Earth Anthem

Author Shashi Tharoor feels that an Earth Anthem sung by people across the world can inspire planetary consciousness and global citizenship among people.

CRITICISMS

Not all interpretations of global citizenship are positive. For example. Parekh advocates what he calls globally oriented citizenship. and states. "If global citizenship means being a citizen of the world. it is neither practicable nor desirable." He argues that global citizenship. defined as an actual membership of a type of worldwide government system. is impractical and dislocated from one's immediate community. He also notes that such a world state would inevitably be "remote. bureaucratic. oppressive. and culturally bland." Parekh presents his alternate option with the statement: "Since the conditions of life of our fellow human beings in distant parts of the world should be a matter of deep moral and political concern to us. our citizenship has an inescapable global dimension. and we should aim to become what I might call a globally oriented citizen." Parekh's concept of globally oriented citizenship consists of identifying with and strengthening ties towards one's political regional community (whether in its current state or an improved. revised form). while recognizing and acting upon obligations towards others in the rest of the world.

Michael Byers. a professor in Political Science at the University of British Columbia. questions the assumption that there is one definition of global citizenship. and unpacks aspects of potential definitions. In the introduction to his public lecture. the UBC Internalization Web site states. "'Global citizenship' remains undefined. What. if anything. does it really mean? Is global citizenship just the latest buzzword?" Byers notes the existence of stateless persons. whom he remarks ought to be the primary candidates for global citizenship. yet continue to live without access to basic freedoms and citizenship rights.

Byers does not oppose the concept of global citizenship. however he criticizes potential implications of the term depending on one's definition of it. such as ones that provide support for the "ruthlessly capitalist economic system that now dominates the planet." Byers states that global citizenship is a "powerful term" because "people that invoke it do so to provoke and justify action." and encourages the attendees of his lecture to re-appropriate it in order for its meaning to have a positive purpose. based on idealistic values.

GLOBAL REFORMERS

Such citizens favour some form of centralized world government or organization in order to avoid global turmoil and maintain some form of unity throughout the world. Falk also points out a tendency for reformers to filter their visions through the cultural and political outlook of their "political community". and thereby impose their framework on the rest of the world.

Falk summarizes the global reformers' "spirit of global citizenship" with the statement. "It is not a matter of being a loyal participant who belongs to a particular political community. whether city or state. but feeling. thinking and acting for the sake of the human species. and all for those most vulnerable and disadvantaged."

A MAN OR WOMAN OF TRANSNATIONAL AFFAIRS

This category of global citizens could also be described as elite global business people. Falk also points out that the vast majority of these people are men.

He writes:

- [T]his second understanding of global citizenship focuses upon the impact on identity of globalization of economic forces. Its guiding image is that the world is becoming unified around a common business elite. an elite that shares interests and experiences. comes to have more in common with each other than it does with the more rooted. ethnically distinct members of its own particular civil society: the result seems to be a denationalized global elite that at the same time lacks any global civic sense of responsibility.

To illustrate the identity. Falk recounts a conversation he had with a Danish business leader on an airplane. The man praised the European Economic Community and its benefits to his business efforts. When Falk asked whether his experiences made him feel less Danish and more European. the man replied. "Oh no. I'm a global citizen."

MANAGERS OF ENVIRONMENTAL AND ECONOMIC GLOBAL ORDER

This perspective focuses more on environmental for that needs but also looks at economic concerns. This view is exemplified by the Bruntland Commission's report. which "stress[es] the shared destiny on the earth as a whole of the human species... [and] argues that unprecedented forms of cooperation among states and a heightened sense of urgency by states will be required to ensure the sustainability of industrial civilization." This perspective is often concerned with "making the planet sustainable at current middle-class lifestyles."

REGIONAL POLITICAL CONSCIOUSNESS

Within Europe. the birthplace of the modern state. "The Euro-federal process is creating a sufficient structure beyond the state so that it becomes necessary. not merely aspirational. to depict a new kind of political community as emergent. although with features that are still far from distinct. and complete."

Falk asks. "Can Europe... forge an ideological and normative identity that becomes more than a strategy to gain a bigger piece of the world economic pie? Can Europe become the bearer of values that are directly related to creating a more peaceful and just world?"

TRANS-NATIONAL ACTIVISTS

Amnesty International and Greenpeace are examples of transnational activism. in part because they transcend national boundaries. Falk writes of the emergence of transnational activism. "the real arena of politics was no longer understood as acting in opposition within a particular state. nor the relation of society and the state. but it consisted more and more of acting to promote a certain kind of political consciousness transnationally that could radiate influence in a variety of directions. including bouncing back to the point of origin." This kind of activism became important to social movements during the 1980s. Falk also emphasizes that "this transnational. grassroots surge. is not. by any means. just a Northern phenomenon."

INTERNATIONAL POLITICAL ISSUES

Global citizenship is qualitatively different from the national variety. where rights and obligations came (even when fought and protested for) at the behest and generosity of the state. With global citizenship. individuals exercise organizational tools such as the Internet to make themselves global citizens. No government sanctioned this development.

Since January 1. 2000. negotiations amongst World Trade Organization member states regarding the movement of professionals to and from member countries has taken place. under the General Agreement on Trade in Services. Article XIX. While this does not signal *de facto* recognition of trans-national citizens. it may indicate halting steps towards it. This is all the more significant given that around the globe there is greater and easier movement of goods than human beings.

The European Community has taken halting steps to change this: it allows the free movement of its people to live. work. pay taxes and. significantly. to vote in other member states. Habermas notes this as a utilitarian model that may have greater implications than merely for Europeans; it is possible the model may be expanded in other regions of the world. or to the entire world itself. The ability of a Spaniard to pick up and move to Germany and be a "citizen" there indicates that notions of ties a country of origin may weaken. The Spaniard may be quite happy living in Germany and not wish to go back to Spain.

There is also the rising tide of individuals with more than one passport. Where once the U.S. State Department frowned on its citizens carrying more than one passport. the reality is that today it is turning a blind eye. (In war. this may change). Many immigrants to the U.S. in the 1990s. a decade that saw the largest influx of newcomers to the state. came to work but still retained their old passports. While many immigrants permanently stay in the U.S.. many others either go back to the old country. or travel back and forth. Such people may be considered global citizens.

Jacobson noted this fracture of the state as dispenser of citizen rights and obligations. although he sees the decline of overall citizenship as a result. Keck and Sikkink on the other hand. regard such global activism as a possible new engine of civic engagement. These global activists. or "cosmopolitan community of individuals" as they call them. transcend national borders and skillfully use pressure tactics against both government and private corporations that make them viable actors on the emerging global public sphere.

A striking example of this pressure is the anti-sweatshop campaign against Nike. Literally dozens of websites are devoted to exposing Nike's labour practices. In 1996. with the aid of Global Exchange. a humanitarian organization that later helped to organize the Battle in Seattle. Nike's labour practices became the subject of increasing mainstream media attention. In the process. Nike was linked to sweatshop labour. a label it has tried to shed ever since.The Internet and other technologies such as the cell phone play an instrumental role in the development of global activists. as does cheaper air travel and the wide acceptance of credit cards.

But there are other forces at work: decline in civic engagement. rise of lifestyle politics. homogenization of products. conglomeration in media systems and communication tools that let us know more about each other than ever before. Add to the mix the rising concern for universal human rights and for trans-global problems such as environmental degradation and global warming. the result is a landscape that tends to be more global than national.

This is not the first time in the history of our civilization that society has been "internationalized". but never has it been easier for average citizens to express themselves in this globalized fashion–by the clothes they wear. the soda they drink. the music they listen to and the vacation land they visit. It is increasingly obvious that our identities. as Lie and Servaes and Scammell suggest. are tied to our roles as citizens.

Scammell's "citizen-consumers" vote with their purchases and are engaged in their communities to the extent they have the freedom to shop.

GEOGRAPHICAL ISSUES

Global citizens may redefine ties between civic engagement and geography. The town hall meetings of New England and other regions of the U.S. seem increasingly supplanted by "electronic spheres" not limited by space and time. This heralds a potentially startling new mechanism in participatory democracy.

Absentee ballots opened up the way for expatriates to vote while living in another country. The Internet may carry this several steps further. Voting is not limited by time or space: you can be anywhere in the world and still make voting decisions back home. Most of U.S. history has been bound up in equating geography with sovereignty. It did matter where you lived. worked. played. Since travel was expensive and cumbersome. our lives were tied to geography. No longer can we entirely make this claim. Thompson. writing in the *Stanford Law Review*. suggests that we can do away with residency and voting in local elections.

Frug even suggests that alienation in the way we regard our geography already creates a disconnect between it and sovereignty. If we are not entirely "home" at home. do boundaries make any difference anymore? This is not just an academic question. but one rife with rich and disheartening social and political possibilities. Global citizens float within. outside and through these boundaries. The implications seem significant.

CAUSES AND INFLUENCES

Many elements seem to spawn global citizenship. but one is noteworthy: the continuous tension that globalization has unleashed between local. national and global forces. An interesting paradox of globalization is while the world is being internationalized at the same time it's also being localized. The world shrinks as the local community (village. town. city) takes on greater and greater importance.

Mosco noted this feature and saw the growing importance of *technopoles*. or highly-technologized city-states that hark back to classical Greece. If this trend is true then it seems global citizens are the glue that may hold these separate entities together. Put another way. global citizens are people that can travel within these various boundaries and somehow still make sense of the world.

Any rights and obligations accorded to the global citizen come from the citizens themselves. growing public favour for "universal rights." the rise of people migrating around the world. and an increasing tendency to standardize citizenship. Difference may exist on the cultural level. but in bureaucracies. increasing favour is placed on uniformity. Efficiency and utilitarianism lie at the core of capitalism; naturally a world that lives under its aegis replicates these tendencies. Postal agreements. civil air travel and other inter-governmental agreements are but one small example of standardization that is increasingly moving into the arena of citizenship. The concern is raised that global citizenship may be closer to a "consumer" model than a legal one.

The lack of a world body puts the initiative upon global citizens themselves to create rights and obligations. Rights and obligations as they arose at the formation of nation-states (*e.g.* the right to vote and obligation to serve in time of war) are at the verge of being expanded. So new concepts that accord certain "human rights" which arose in the 20th century are increasingly being universalized across nations and governments.

This is the result of many factors. including the Universal Declaration of Human Rights by the United Nations in 1948. the aftermath of World War II and the Holocaust and growing sentiments towards legitimizing marginalized peoples (*e.g.*. pre-industrialized peoples found in the jungles of Brazil and Borneo). Couple this with growing awareness of our impact on the environment. and there is the rising feeling that citizen rights may extend to include the right to dignity and self-determination. If national citizenship does not foster these new rights. then global citizenship may seem more accessible.

One cannot overestimate the importance of human rights discourse in shaping public opinion. What are the rights and obligations of human beings trapped in conflicts? Or. incarcerated as part of ethnic cleansing? Equally striking. are the pre-industrialized tribes newly discovered by scientists living in the depths of dense jungle? Leary. Heater and Babcock tend to equate these rights with the rise of global citizenship as normative associations. indicating a national citizenship model that is more closed and a global citizenship one that is more flexible and inclusive. If true. this places a strain in the relationship between national and global citizenship. Boli tends to see this strain as mutually beneficial. whereas Leary and McNeely regard the rupture between the two systems as merely evolutionary rather than combative.

Like much social change. changing scopes of modern citizenship tend to be played out in both large and minute spheres. Habermas tends to place global citizenship in a larger. social context. arguing that nations can be central engines of citizenship but culture can also be powerful. He regards the formation of the "European citizen" as a kind of natural epiphany of governmental conglomeration within the forces of globalization. only remotely alluding to the corporate conglomeration that has been both the recipient and cause of worldwide economic expansion.

Others. including Iyer see globalization and global citizens as direct descendants of global standardization. which he notes. for instance. in the growing homogeneity of airports. Standardization and modernity have worked together for the past few centuries. Ellul. Mumford and other scholars attack this as a form of oppression. in the same vein that Barber saw the proliferation of carbon-copy fast-food chains around the globe. Why not a set of basic citizen rights followed the world over? Global citizenship may be the indirect result of Pax Americana. The 20th century. as well as the 21st. may be a time dominated by the United States. America's domination of the WTO. IMF. World Bank and other global institutions creates feelings of imperialism among smaller nations. Cross national cooperation to counter American dominance may result in more global citizens. If economic. environmental. political and social factors push towards more global citizenry. we must also within this camp consider the ramifications of the post Cold War world. or realpolitik.

Another interpretation given by several scholars of the changing configurations of citizenship due to globalization is the possibility that citizenship is a possibly changed institution. even if situated within territorial boundaries that are national. if the meaning of the national itself has changed.

CRITICISMS

Not all interpretations of global citizenship are positive. For example. Parekh advocates what he calls globally oriented citizenship. and states. "If global citizenship means being a citizen of the world. it is neither practicable nor desirable" He argues that global citizenship. defined as an actual membership of a type of worldwide government system. is impractical and dislocated from one's immediate community. He also notes that such a world state would inevitably be "remote. bureaucratic. oppressive. and culturally bland."Parekh presents his alternate option with the statement: "Since the conditions of life of our fellow human beings in distant parts of the world should be a matter of deep moral and political concern to us. our citizenship has an inescapable global dimension. and we should aim to become what I might call a globally oriented citizen." Parekh's concept of globally oriented citizenship consists of identifying with and strengthening ties towards one's political regional community (whether in its current state or an improved. revised form). while recognizing and acting upon obligations towards others in the rest of the world. In another example. Michael Byers. a professor in Political Science at the University of British Columbia. questions the assumption that there is one definition of global citizenship. and unpacks aspects of potential definitions. In the introduction to his public lecture. the UBC Internalization Web site states. "'Global citizenship' remains undefined. What. if anything. does it really mean? Is global citizenship just the latest buzzword?" Byers notes the existence of stateless persons. whom he remarks ought to be the primary candidates for global citizenship. yet continue to live without access to basic freedoms and citizenship rights.

Byers does not oppose the concept of global citizenship. however he criticizes potential implications of the term depending on one's definition of it. such as ones that provide support for the "ruthlessly capitalist economic system that now dominates the planet." Byers states that global citizenship is a "powerful term" because "people that invoke it do so to provoke and justify action." and encourages the attendees of his lecture to re-appropriate it in order for its meaning to have a positive purpose. based on idealistic values.Many other people believe that global citizenship is a racist concept because it aspires to disengage people from their cultural allegiances and prepare the ground for a world government which. having no cultural connection with its people. would be anti-democratic and oppressive. They also think the concept defies a rational view of human nature in which self-interest is the fundamental guiding principle. albeit with the addition of a humane concern for others.

In contrast to questioning definitions. a counter-criticism can be found on the World Alliance of YMCA's Web site. An online article in *YMYCA World* emphasizes the importance of fostering global citizenship and global social justice. and states.

"Global citizenship might sound like a vague concept for academics but in fact it's a very practical way of looking at the world which anyone. if given the opportunity. can relate to." The author acknowledges the positive and negative outlooks towards globalization. and states. "In the context of globalisation. thinking and acting as global citizens is immensely important and can bring real benefits. as the YMCA experience shows."

INTERNATIONAL CITIZENSHIP

In recent years. some intergovernmental organizations have extended the concept and terminology associated with citizenship to the international level. where it is applied to the totality of the citizens of their constituent countries combined. Citizenship at this level is a secondary concept. with rights deriving from national citizenship.

COMMONWEALTH CITIZENSHIP

The concept of "Commonwealth Citizenship" has been in place ever since the establishment of the Commonwealth of Nations. As with the EU. one holds Commonwealth citizenship only by being a citizen of a Commonwealth member state.

This form of citizenship offers certain privileges within some Commonwealth countries:

- Some such countries do not require tourist visas of citizens of other Commonwealth countries.
- In some Commonwealth countries resident citizens of other Commonwealth countries are entitled to political rights. *e.g.*. the right to vote in local and national elections and in some cases even the right to stand for election.
- In some instances the right to work in any position (including the civil service) is granted. except for certain specific positions (*e.g.* defence. Governor-General or President. Prime Minister).

Although Ireland left the Commonwealth in 1949. it is often treated as if it were a member. with references being made in legal documents to 'the Commonwealth and the Republic of Ireland'. and its citizens are not classified as foreign nationals. particularly in the United Kingdom.

Canada departed from the principle of nationality being defined in terms of allegiance in 1921. In 1935 the Irish Free State was the first to introduce its own citizenship (However. Irish citizens were still treated as subjects of the Crown. and they are still not regarded as foreign. even though Ireland is not a member of the Commonwealth; *Murray v Parkes* All ER 123).

The Canadian Citizenship Act which came into effect on January 1. 1947 provided for a distinct Canadian Citizenship. automatically conferred upon most individuals born in Canada (with certain exceptions) and defined the conditions under which one could become a naturalized citizen. The concept of Commonwealth citizenship was introduced in 1948 in the British Nationality Act 1948. Other Dominions adopted this principle. in New Zealand. in the British Nationality and New Zealand Citizenship Act 1948. Citizenship has replaced allegiance. a more than symbolic change.

CITIZENSHIP OF THE EUROPEAN UNION

Citizenship of the European Union was introduced by theMaastricht Treaty. which was signed in 1992. and has been in force since 1993. European citizenship is supplementary to national citizenship and affords rights such as the right to vote inEuropean elections. the right to free movement. settlement and employment across the EU. and the right to consular protection by other EU states' embassies when a person's country of citizenship does not maintain an embassy or consulate in the country they need protection in.

HISTORY

EU citizenship as a distinct concept was first introduced by the Maastricht Treaty. and was extended by the Treaty of Amsterdam. Prior to the 1992 Maastricht Treaty. theEuropean Communities treaties provided guarantees for the free movement of economically active persons. but not. generally. for others. The 1951 Treaty of Parisestablishing the European Coal and Steel Community established a right to free movement for workers in these industries and the 1957 Treaty of Rome provided for the free movement of workers and services.

However. the Treaty provisions were interpreted by the European Court of Justice not as having a narrow economic purpose. but rather a wider social and economic purpose.

In *Levin*. the Court found that the "freedom to take up employment was important. not just as a means towards the creation of a single market for the benefit of the Member State economies. but as a right for the worker to raise her or his standard of living". Under the ECJ caselaw. the rights of free movement of workers applies regardless of the worker's purpose in taking up employment abroad. to both part-time and full-time work. and whether or not the worker required additional financial assistance from the Member State into which he moves. Since. the ECJ has held that a recipient of service has free movement rights under the treaty and this criterion is easily fulfilled.effectively every national of an EU country within another Member State. whether economically active or not. had a right under Article 12 of the European Community Treaty to non-discrimination even prior to the Maastricht Treaty.In *Martinez Sala*. the European Court of Justice held that the citizenship provisions provided substantive free movement rights in addition to those already granted by Union law.

STATED RIGHTS

Historically. the main benefit of being a citizen of an EU state has been that of free movement. The free movement also applies to the citizens of European Economic Areastates and Switzerland. However with the creation of EU citizenship. certain political rights came into being. The Treaty on the Functioning of the European Unionprovides for citizens to be "*directly represented at Union level in the European Parliament*". and "*to participate in the democratic life of the Union*" (Treaty on the European Union. Title II. Article 10). Specifically. the following rights are afforded;

Political rights

- Voting in European elections: a right to vote and stand in elections to the European Parliament. in any EU member state (Article 22)
- Voting in municipal elections: a right to vote and stand in local elections in an EU state other than their own. under the same conditions as the nationals of that state (Article 22)
- Accessing European government documents: a right to access to European Parliament. Council. and Commission documents (Article 15).
- Petitioning Parliament and the Ombudsman: the right to petition the European Parliament and the right to apply to the European Ombudsman in order to bring to his attention any cases of poor administration by the EU institutions and bodies. with the exception of the legal bodies (Article 24)
- Linguistic rights: the right to apply to the EU institutions in one of the official languages and to receive a reply in that same language (Article 24).

Rights of free movement

- Right to free movement and residence: a right of free movement and residence throughout the Union and the right to work in any position (including national civil services with the exception of those posts in the public sector that involve the exercise of powers conferred by public law and the safeguard of general interests of the State or local authorities (Article 21) for which however there is no one single definition);
- Freedom from discrimination on nationality: a right not to be discriminated against on grounds of nationality within the scope of application of the Treaty (Article 18);

Rights abroad

- Right to consular protection: a right to protection by the diplomatic or consular authorities of other Member States when in a non-EU Member State. if there are no diplomatic or consular authorities from the citizen's own state (Article 23): this is due to the fact that not all member states maintain embassies in every country in the world (16 countries have only one embassy from an EU state).

FREE MOVEMENT RIGHTS

Article 21 Freedom to move and reside

Article 21 (1) of the Treaty on the Functioning of the European Union states thatEvery citizen of the Union shall have the right to move and reside freely within the territory of the Member States. subject to the limitations and conditions laid down in this Treaty and by the measures adopted to give it effect.The European Court of Justice has remarked that.

EU Citizenship is destined to be the fundamental status of nationals of the Member StatesThe ECJ has held that this Article confers a directly effective right upon citizens to reside in another Member State. Before the case of*Baumbast.* it was widely assumed that non-economically active citizens had no rights to residence deriving directly from the EU Treaty. only from directives created under the Treaty. In *Baumbast.* however. the ECJ held that (the then) Article 18 of the EC Treaty granted a generally applicable right to residency. which is limited by secondary legislation. but *only* where that secondary legislation is proportionate. Member States can distinguish between nationals and Union citizens but only if the provisions satisfy the test of proportionality. Migrant EU citizens have a "legitimate expectation of a limited degree of financial solidarity... having regard to their degree of integration into the host society"Length of time is a particularly important factor when considering the degree of integration.

The ECJ's case law on citizenship has been criticised for subjecting an increasing number of national rules to the proportionality assessment.

Article 45 Freedom of movement to work

Article 45 of the Treaty on the Functioning of the European Union states that

1. Freedom of movement for workers shall be secured within the Union.
2. Such freedom of movement shall entail the abolition of any discrimination based on nationality between workers of the Member States as regards employment. remuneration and other conditions of work and employment.

State employment reserved exclusively for nationals varies between member states. For example. training as a barrister in Britain and Ireland is not reserved for nationals. while the corresponding French course qualifies one as a 'juge' and hence can only be taken by French citizens. However. it is broadly limited to those roles that exercise a significant degree of public authority. such as judges. police. the military. diplomats. senior civil servants or politicians. Note that not all Member States choose to restrict all of these posts to nationals.Much of the existing secondary legislation and case law was consolidated in the Citizens' Rights Directive 2004/38/EC on the right to move and reside freely within the EU.

Limitations

New member states may undergo transitional regimes. during which their nationals only enjoy restricted access to labour markets in other member states. EU member states are permitted to keep restrictions on citizens of the newly acceded countries for a maximum of seven years after accession. For the EFTA states (Iceland. Lichtenstein. Norway and Switzerland). the maximum is nine years.

Following the 2004 enlargement. three "old" member states—Ireland. Sweden and the United Kingdom—decided to allow unrestricted access to their labour markets. By December 2009. all but two member states—Austria and Germany—had completely dropped controls. These restrictions too expired on 1 May 2011.Following the 2007 enlargement. all pre-2004 member states except Finland and Sweden imposed restrictions on Bulgarian and Romanian citizens. as did two member states that joined in 2004: Malta and Hungary. As of November 2012. all but 8 EU countries have dropped restrictions entirely. These restrictions too expired on 1 January 2014. Norway opened its labour market in June 2012. while Switzerland and Lichtenstein may keep restrictions in place until 2016.Following the 2013 enlargement. it is expected that some countries will implement restrictions on Croatian nationals following the country's EU accession on 1 July 2013. As of July 2013. all but 13 EU countries have dropped restrictions entirely. The UK Home Office has announced a bill to this effect.

ACQUISITION

There is no common EU policy on the acquisition of European citizenship as it is supplementary to national citizenship (one cannot be an EU citizen without being a national of a member state). Article 20 (1) of the Treaty on the Functioning of the European Union states that:

"Citizenship of the Union is hereby established. Every person holding the nationality of a Member State shall be a citizen of the Union. Citizenship of the Union shall be additional to and not replace national citizenship."

While nationals of Member States are citizens of the union. "It is for each Member State. having due regard to Union law. to lay down the conditions for the acquisition and loss of nationality." As a result. there is a great variety in rules and practices with regard to the acquisition and loss of citizenship in EU member states. Thus in practice. a member state may withhold EU citizenship from certain groups of citizens — namely some in overseas territories of member states outside the EU. One example would be the Faroe Islands of Denmark which. though a part of Denmark. are outside the EU and do not have EU citizenship.

EUROPEAN UNION (EU) CITIZENSHIP

The Maastricht Treaty introduced the concept of citizenship of the European Union.

Article 17 (1) of the Treaty on European Union (consolidated version) states that:

- Citizenship of the Union is hereby established. Every person holding the nationality of a Member State shall be a citizen of the Union. Citizenship of the Union shall be additional to and not replace national citizenship.

The amended EC Treaty establishes certain minimal rights for EU citizens. Article 12 of the amended EC Treaty guarantees a general right of non-discrimination within the scope of the Treaty. Article 18 provides a limited right to free movement and residence in Member States other than that of which the EU citizen is a national. Articles 18-21 and 225 provide certain political rights.

Union citizens have also extensive rights to move in order to exercise economic activity in any of the Member States (Articles 39. 43. 49 EC). which predate the introduction of Union citizenship.

SUBNATIONAL CITIZENSHIP

Citizenship most usually relates to membership of the nation state. but the term can also apply at subnational level. Subnational entities may impose requirements. of residency or otherwise. which permit citizens to participate in the political life of that entity. or to enjoy benefits provided by the government of that entity. But in such cases. those eligible are also sometimes seen as "citizens" of the relevant state. province. or region.

An example of this is how the fundamental basis of Swiss citizenship is citizenship of an individual commune. from which follows citizenship of a canton and of the Confederation. Another example is Åland where the residents enjoy a special provincial citizenship within Finland. *hembygdsrätt*.

The United States has a system of dual citizenship where one is a citizen of the state of residence as well as a citizen of the United States. State constitutions may grant certain rights above and beyond what are granted under the US Constitution and may impose their own obligations including the sovereign right of taxation and military service (each state maintains at least one military force subject to national militia transfer service. the state's national guard. while some maintain a second military force not subject to nationalization).

HISTORY

The concept of citizenship arose with the first laws.

POLIS CITIZENSHIP

The first form of citizenship was based on the way people lived in the ancient Greek times. in small-scale organic communities of the polis. In those days citizenship was not seen as a public matter. separated from the private life of the individual person. The obligations of citizenship were deeply connected into one's everyday life in the polis. To be truly human. one had to be an active citizen to the community. which Aristotle famously expressed: "To take no part in the running of the community's affairs is to be either a beast or a god!"

This form of citizenship was based on obligations of citizens towards the community. rather than rights given to the citizens of the community. This was not a problem because they all had a strong affinity with the polis; their own destiny and the destiny of the community were strongly linked. Also. citizens of the polis saw obligations to the community as an opportunity to be virtuous. it was a source of honour and respect. In Athens. citizens were both ruler and ruled. important political and judicial offices were rotated and all citizens had the right to speak and vote in the political assembly.

However. an important aspect of polis citizenship was exclusivity. Citizenship in ancient Greece and Rome. as well as Medieval cities that practiced polis citizenship. was exclusive and inequality of status was widely accepted. Citizens had a much higher status than non-citizens: Women. slaves or 'barbarians'. For example. women were seen to be irrational and incapable of political participation (although some. most notably Plato. disagreed). Methods used to determine whether someone could be a citizen or not could be based on wealth (the amount of taxes one paid). political participation. or heritage (both parents had to be born in the polis).

In the Roman Empire. polis citizenship changed form: Citizenship was expanded from small scale communities to the entire empire. Romans realised that granting citizenship to people from all over the empire legitimized Roman rule over conquered areas. Citizenship in the Roman era was no longer a status of political agency; it had been reduced to a judicial safeguard and the expression of rule and law.

MEDIEVAL AND EARLY MODERN CITIZENSHIP

During European Middle Ages. citizenship was usually associated with cities Great Burgher and Bourgeoisie. Nobility used to have privileges above commoners but the French Revolution and other revolutions revoked these privileges and made citizens.

HONORARY CITIZENSHIP

Some countries extend "honorary citizenship" to those whom they consider to be especially admirable or worthy of the distinction.

By act of United States Congress and presidential assent. honorary United States citizenship has been awarded to only seven individuals. Honorary Canadian citizenship requires the unanimous approval of Parliament. The only people to ever receive honorary Canadian citizenship are Raoul Wallenberg posthumously in 1985. Nelson Mandela in 2001. the 14th Dalai Lama. Tenzin Gyatso in 2006. Aung San Suu Kyi in 2007 and Prince Karim Aga Khan in 2009.

In 2002 South Korea awarded honorary citizenship to Dutch football (soccer) coach Guus Hiddink who successfully and unexpectedly took the national team to the semi-finals of the 2002 FIFA World Cup. Honorary citizenship was also awarded to Hines Ward. a black Korean American football player. in 2006 for his efforts to minimize discrimination in Korea against half-Koreans.

American actress Angelina Jolie received an honorary Cambodian citizenship in 2005 due to her humanitarian efforts. Cricketers Matthew Hayden and Herschelle Gibbs were awarded honorary citizenship of St. Kitts and Nevis in March 2007 due to their record-breaking innings in the 2007 Cricket World Cup.

In Germany the honorary citizenship is awarded by cities. towns and sometimes federal states. The honorary citizenship ends with the death of the honoured. or. in exceptional cases. when it is taken away by the council or parliament of the city. town. or state. In the case of war criminals. all such honours were taken away by "Article VIII. section II. letter i of the directive 38 of the Allied Control Council for Germany" on October 12. 1946. In some cases. honorary citizenship was taken away from members of the former GDR regime. *e.g.*

Erich Honecker. after the collapse of the GDR in 1989/90. In Ireland. "honorary citizenship" bestowed on a foreigner is in fact full legal citizenship including the right to reside in Ireland. to vote etc.. Cuban citizens by birth are those foreigners who. by virtue of their exceptional merits won in the struggles for Cuba's liberation. were considered Cuban citizens by birth. Che Guevara was made an honorary citizen of Cuba by Fidel Castro for his part in the Cuban Revolution. of which Guevara later renounced in his well known farewell letter.

Historically. many states limited citizenship to only a proportion of their population. thereby creating a citizen class with political rights superior to other sections of the population. but equal with each other. The classical example of a limited citizenry was Athens where slaves. women. and resident foreigners (called metics) were excluded from political rights. The Roman Republic forms another example and. more recently. the nobility of the Polish-Lithuanian Commonwealth had some of the same characteristics.

RESPONSIBILITIES OR DUTIES OF CITIZENSHIP

The legally enforceable duties of citizenship vary depending on one's country. and may include such items as:

- Conscription (or volunteer in fighting in the armed forces. in countries without a conscription)

- Paying taxes
- Serving on a jury
- Voting
- Obeying the criminal laws enacted by one's government. even while abroad
- For children and teens. attending school; per law by compulsory education

CITIZENSHIP IN THE UNITED STATES

Citizenship in the United States. being a citizen. is a status that entails specific rights. privileges. and duties. Citizenship is understood as a "right to have rights" since it serves as a foundation for a bundle of subsequent rights. such as the right to live and work in the United States and to receive federal assistance.There are two primary sources of citizenship: birthright citizenship. in which a person is presumed to be a citizen provided that he is born within the territorial limits of the United States. and naturalization. a process in which an immigrant applies for citizenship and is accepted. These two pathways to citizenship are specified in the Citizenship Clause of the Constitution's 1868 Fourteenth Amendmentwhich reads:

All persons born or naturalized in the United States. and subject to the jurisdiction thereof. are citizens of the United States and of the State wherein they reside. —from the Fourteenth Amendment.

National citizenship signifies membership in the country as a whole; *state citizenship*. in contrast. signifies a relation between a person and a particular state and has application generally limited to domestic matters. State citizenship may affect (1) tax decisions and (2) eligibility for some state-provided benefits such as higher education and (3) eligibility for state political posts such as U.S. Senator.

In Article One of the Constitution. the power to establish a "uniform rule of naturalization" is granted explicitly to Congress.

U.S. law permits multiple citizenship. A citizen of another country naturalized as a U.S. citizen may retain their previous *citizenship*. though they must renounce allegiance to the other country. A U.S. citizen retains U.S. citizenship when becoming the citizen of another country. should that country's laws allow it. Citizenship can be renounced by American citizens who also hold another citizenship via a formal procedure at a U.S. Embassy. and it can also be restored.

NATURE OF CITIZENSHIP

Citizenship is the legal status of membership in the United States. Citizens have the right to live and work without fear of deportation. The activities associated with citizenship typically include duties and privileges.

Duties

- Jury duty is only imposed upon citizens. Jury duty may be considered the "sole differential obligation" between non-citizens and citizens; the federal and state courts "uniformly exclude non-citizens from jury pools today. and with the exception of a few states in the past. this has always been the case.
- Military participation is not currently required in the United States. but a policy of conscription of men has been in place at various times (both in war and in peace) in American history. most recently during the Vietnam War. Currently. the United States armed forces are a professional all-volunteer force. although both male U.S. citizens and male non-citizen permanent residents are required to register with the Selective Service System and may be called up in the event of a future draft. Johns Hopkins University political scientist Benjamin Ginsberg writes. "The professional military has limited the need for citizen soldiers."
- Taxes. In the United States today. everyone except those whose income is derived from tax exempt revenue (Subchapter N. Section 861 of the U.S. Tax Code) is required to pay taxes. and this has been the case for many years. The U.S. requires that aliens who are present in the United States. including non-immigrants and illegal immigrants. for more than 180 days must file tax returns.American citizens are subject to federal income tax on worldwide income regardless of their country of residence.

Rights

- Freedom to reside and work. United States citizens have the right to reside and work in the United States. Certain non-citizens. such as permanent residents. have similar rights. However. non-citizens. unlike citizens. may have the right taken away: for example. they may be deported if convicted of a serious crime.
- Freedom to enter and leave the United States. United States citizens have the right to enter and leave the United States freely. Certain non-citizens. such as permanent residents. have similar rights. Unlike permanent residents. U.S. citizens do not have an obligation to maintain residence in the U.S. – they can leave for any length of time and return freely at any time.
- Voting for federal office in all fifty states and the District of Columbia is restricted to citizens only. States are not required to extend the franchise to all citizens: for example. several states bar citizen felons from voting. even after they have completed any custodial sentence. The United States Constitution bars states from restricting citizens

from voting on grounds of race. Colour. previous condition of servitude. sex. failure to pay any tax. or age (for citizens who are at least eighteen years old). Historically. many states and local jurisdictions have allowed non-citizens to vote; however. today this is limited to local elections in very few places. Citizens are notcompelled to vote.

- Freedom to stand for public office. The United States Constitution requires that all members of the United States House of Representatives have been citizens for seven years. and that all senators have been citizens for nine years. before taking office. Most states have similar requirements: for example California requires that legislators have been citizens for three years. and the Governor have been a citizen for five years. upon taking office. The U.S. Constitution requires that one be "a natural born Citizen" and a U.S. resident for fourteen years in order to be President of the United States. The Constitution also stipulates that otherwise eligible citizens must meet certain age requirements for these offices.

Benefits

- Consular protection outside the United States. While traveling abroad. if a person is arrested or detained by foreign authorities. the person can request to speak to somebody from the U.S. Embassy or Consulate. Consular officials can provide resources for Americans incarcerated abroad. such as a list of local attorneys who speak English. The U.S. government may even intervene on the person's behalf. Non-citizen U.S. nationals also have this benefit.
- Increased ability to sponsor relatives living abroad. Several types of immigrant visas require that the person requesting the visa be directly related to a U.S. citizen. Having U.S. citizenship facilitates the granting of IR and F visas to family members.
- Ability to invest in U.S. real property without triggering FIRPTA. Perhaps the only quantifiable economic benefit of U.S. citizenship. citizens are not subject to additional withholding tax on income and capital gains derived from U.S. real estate under theForeign Investment in Real Property Tax Act (FIRPTA).
- Transmission of U.S. citizenship to children born abroad. Generally. children born to two U.S. citizen parents abroad are automatically U.S. citizens at birth. When the parents are one U.S. citizen and one non-U.S. citizen. certain conditions about the U.S. citizen's parent's length of time spent in the U.S. need to be met. See United States nationality law for more details. Non-citizen U.S. nationals also have a similar benefit (transmission of non-citizen U.S. nationality to children born abroad).

- Protection from deportation. Naturalized U.S. citizens are no longer considered aliens and cannot be placed into deportation proceedings.
- Other benefits. The USCIS sometimes honors the achievements of naturalized U.S. citizens. The 'Outstanding American by Choice Award' was created by the USCIS to recognize the outstanding achievements of naturalized U.S. citizens. and past recipients include author Elie Wiesel who won the Nobel Peace Prize; Indra K. Nooyi who is CEO of PepsiCo; John Shalikashvili who was Chairman of the Joint Chiefs of Staff; and others. Further. citizenship status can affect which country an athlete can compete as a member of in competitions such as the Olympics.

Civic participation

Civic participation is not required in the United States. There is no requirement to attend town meetings. belong to a political party. or vote in elections. However. a benefit of naturalization is the ability to "participate fully in the civic life of the country". There is disagreement about whether popular lack of involvement in politics is helpful or harmful. Vanderbilt professor Dana D. Nelson suggests that most Americans merely vote for president every four years. and that's all they do. and she sees this pattern as undemocratic. In her book *Bad for Democracy*. Nelson argues that declining citizen participation in politics is unhealthy for long term prospects for democracy.

However. writers such as Robert D. Kaplan in *The Atlantic* see benefits to non-involvement; he wrote "the very indifference of most people allows for a calm and healthy political climate". Kaplan elaborated: "Apathy. after all. often means that the political situation is healthy enough to be ignored. The last thing America needs is more voters—particularly badly educated and alienated ones—with a passion for politics." He argued that civic participation. in itself. is not always a sufficient condition to bring good outcomes. and pointed to authoritarian societies such as Singapore which prospered because it had "relative safety from corruption. from breach of contract. from property expropriation. and from bureaucratic inefficiency".

DUAL CITIZENSHIP

A person who is considered a citizen by more than one nation has *dual citizenship*. It is possible for a United States citizen to have dual citizenship; this can be achieved in various ways. such as by birth in the United States to a parent. or in certain circumstances even grandparent. who is a citizen of a foreign country. by birth in another country to a parent(s) who is/are a United States citizen/s. or by having parents who are citizens of different countries. Anyone who becomes a naturalized U.S. citizen is required to renounce any prior "allegiance" to other countries during the naturalization ceremony; however.

this renunciation of allegiance is generally not considered renunciation of citizenship to those countries. Under certain circumstances there are relevant distinctions between dual citizens who hold a "substantial contact" with a country. for example by holding a passport or by residing in the country for a certain period of time. and those who do not. For example. under the Heroes Earnings Assistance and Relief Tax (HEART) Act of 2008. U.S. citizens in general are subject to an expatriation tax if they give up U.S. citizenship. but there are exceptions (specifically 26 U.S.C. § 877A(g)(1)(b)) for those who are either under age 18½ upon giving up U.S. citizenship and have lived in the U.S. for less than ten years in their lives. or who are dual citizens by birth residing in their other country of citizenship at the time of giving up U.S. citizenship and have lived in the U.S. for less than ten out of the past fifteen years. Similarly. the United States consider holders of a foreign passport to have a substantial contact with the country that issued the passport. which may preclude security clearance.

United States citizens are required by federal law to identify themselves with a U.S. passport. not with any other foreign passport. when entering or leaving the US. The Supreme Court case of *Afroyim v. Rusk* declared that a U.S. citizen did not lose his citizenship by voting in an election in a foreign country. or by acquiring foreign citizenship. if they did not intend to lose U.S. citizenship. U.S. citizens who have dual citizenship do not lose their United States citizenship unless they renounce it officially.

HISTORY OF CITIZENSHIP IN THE UNITED STATES

Citizenship began in colonial times as an active relation between people working cooperatively to solve municipal problems and participating actively in democratic decision-making. such as in New England town hall meetings. People met regularly to discuss local affairs and make decisions. These town meetings were described as the "earliest form of American democracy" which was vital since citizen participation in public affairs helped keep democracy "sturdy". according to Alexis de Tocqueville in 1835. A variety of forces changed this relation during the nation's history. Citizenship became less defined by participation in politics and more defined as a legal relation with accompanying rightsand privileges.

While the realm of civic participation in the public sphere has shrunk. the citizenship franchise has been expanded to include not just propertied white adult men but black men and adult women.

Earlier on. US citizenship was not given to people of Indian or East Asian descent. A. K. Mozumdar was the first person born in the Indian sub-continent to attain US citizenship. Few years earlier. as a result of the 1898 United States v. Wong Kim Ark Supreme Court decision. ethnic Chinese born in the United States became citizens. During World War II. due to Japan's heavy involvement as an aggressor. it was decided to restrict many Japanese citizens from applying for US citizenship. while Chinese citizens encountered no trouble. because of China's alliance with the US.

BIRTHRIGHT CITIZENSHIP

U.S. citizenship is usually acquired by birth when a child is born in the territory of the United States. In addition to the U.S. States. this includes the District of Columbia. Guam.Puerto Rico. the Northern Mariana Islands and the U.S. Virgin Islands. Citizenship. however. was not specified in the original Constitution. In 1868 the Fourteenth Amendment specifically defined persons who were either born or naturalized in the United States and subject to its jurisdiction as citizens. All babies born in the United States—except those born to enemy aliens in wartime or the children of foreign diplomats—enjoy U.S. citizenship under the Supreme Court's long-standing interpretation of the Fourteenth Amendment. The amendment states: "All persons born or naturalized in the United States. and subject to the jurisdiction thereof. are citizens of the United States and of the State wherein they reside." There remains dispute as to who is "subject to the jurisdiction" of the United States at birth.By acts of Congress. every person born in Puerto Rico. the U.S. Virgin Islands. Guam. and the Northern Mariana Islands is a United States citizen by birth. Also. every person born in the former Panama Canal Zone whose father or mother (or both) are or were a citizen is a United States citizen by birth. Regardless of where they are born. children of U.S. citizens are U.S. citizens in most cases. Children born outside the United States with at least one U.S. citizen parent usually have birthright citizenship by parentage.

While persons born in the United States are considered to be citizens and can have passports. children under age eighteen are legally considered to be minors and cannot vote or hold office. Upon the event of their eighteenth birthday. they are considered full citizens but there is no ceremony acknowledging this relation or any correspondence between the new citizen and the government to this effect. Citizenship is assumed to exist. and the relation is assumed to remain viable until death or until it is renounced or dissolved by some other legal process. Secondary schools teach the basics of citizenship and create "informed and responsible citizens" who are "skilled in the arts of effective deliberation and action".

Americans who live in foreign countries and become members of other governments have. in some instances. been stripped of citizenship. although there have been court cases where decisions regarding citizenship have been reversed.

NATURALIZED CITIZENSHIP

Acts of Congress provide for acquisition of citizenship by persons born abroad.

Agency in charge

The agency in charge of admitting new citizens is the United States Citizenship and Immigration Services. commonly abbreviated as USCIS. It is a bureau of the Department of Homeland Security. It offers web-based services. The agency depends on application fees for revenue; in 2009. with a struggling economy. applications were down sharply. and consequently there was much less revenue to upgrade and streamline services. There was speculation that if the administration of president Barack Obama passes immigration reform. then the agency could face a "welcome but overwhelming surge of Americans-in-waiting" and longer processing times for citizenship applications. The USCIS has made efforts to digitize records.

A USCIS Web site says the "U.S. Citizenship and Immigration Services (USCIS) is committed to offering the best possible service to you. our customer" and which says "With our focus on customer service. we offer you a variety of services both before and after you file your case." The Web site allowed applicants to estimate the length of time required to process specific types of cases. to check application status. and to access a customer guide.The USCIS processes cases in the order they're received.

Pathways to citizenship

People applying to become citizens must satisfy certain requirements. For example. there have been requirements for applicants to have lived in the nation for five years (three if married to a U.S. citizen.) be of "good moral character" meaning no felony convictions. be of "sound mind" in the Judgement of immigration officials. have knowledge of the Constitution. and be able to speak and understand English unless they are elderly or disabled. Applicants must also pass a simple citizenship test.

Up until recently. a test published by theImmigration and Naturalization Service asked questions such as "How many stars are there in our flag?" and "What is the Constitution?" and "Who is the president of the United States today?" At one point. the Government Printing Office sold flashcards for $8.50 to help test takers prepare for the test. In 2006. the government replaced the former trivia test with a ten-question oral test designed to "shun simple historical facts about

America that can be recounted in a few words for more explanation about the principles of American democracy. such as freedom". One reviewer described the new citizenship test as "thoughtful". While some have criticized the new version of the test. officials counter that the new test is a "teachable moment" without making it conceptually more difficult. since the list of possible questions and answers. as before. will be publicly available. Six correct answers constitutes a passing grade. The new test probes for signs that immigrants "understand and share American values".

- Military participation is often a way for immigrant residents to become citizens. Since many people seek citizenship for its financial and social benefits. the promise of citizenship can be seen as a means of motivating persons to do dangerous activities such as fight in wars. For example. a 2009 article in the *New York Times* said that the United States Military was recruiting "skilled immigrants who are living in this country with temporary visas" by promising an opportunity to become citizens "in as little as six months" in exchange for service in Afghanistan and Iraq where US forces are "stretched thin". The option was not open to illegal immigrants. One estimate was that in 2009 the US military had 29.000 foreign-born people currently serving who were not American citizens. Spouses of citizens or non-citizens who served in the military also have less difficulty becoming citizens. One analyst noted that "many immigrants. not yet citizens. have volunteered to serve in the United States military forces... Some have been killed and others wounded... Perhaps this can be seen as a cynical attempt to qualify more easily for U.S. citizenship... But I think that service in the U.S. military has to be taken as a pretty serious commitment to the United States."Immigrant soldiers who fight for the US often have an easier and faster path to citizenship. In 2002. President Bush signed an executive order to eliminate the three-year waiting period and made service personnel immediately eligible for citizenship. In 2003. Congress voted to "cut the waiting period to become a citizen from three years down to one year" for immigrants who had served in the armed forces. In 2003. of 1.4 million service members. 37.000 active-duty members were not citizens. and of these. 20 percent had applied for citizenship. By June 2003. 12 non-citizens had died fighting for the United States in the Iraqi war. The military has had a tradition of "filling out its ranks" with aliens living in the U.S. Non-citizens fought in World War II. The military has struggled to "fill its depleted ranks" by recruiting more non-US citizens. But there is considerable anxiety about using foreigners to serve in the U.S. armed forces. General Dwight D. Eisenhower was quoted as saying: "When Rome went out and hired mercenary soldiers. Rome fell."
- Grandparent rule. Section 322 of the INA. added in 1994. enabled children of a U.S. citizen who did not get citizenship at birth. to use the physical presence period in the U.S. of a grandparent who was a citizen to qualify for U.S. citizenship. In 2006. there were 4.000 applications of citizenship using the physical presence of grandparents.Israelis comprise 90per cent of those taking advantage of the clause.

Strong demand

According to a senior fellow at the Migration Policy Institute. "citizenship is a very. very valuable commodity". However. one study suggested legal residents eligible for citizenship. but who don't apply. tend to have low incomes (41 percent). do not speak English well (60 percent). or have low levels of education (25 percent). There is strong demand for citizenship based on the numbers of applications filed. From 1920 to 1940. the number of immigrants to the United States who became citizens numbered about 200.000 each year; there was a spike after World War II. and then the level reduced to about 150.000 per year until resuming to the 200.000 level beginning about 1980. In the mid-1990s to 2009. the levels rose to about 500.000 per year with considerable variation.

In 1996. more than one million people became citizens through naturalization. In 1997. there were 1.41 million applications filed; in 2006. 1.38 million. The number of naturalized citizens in the United States rose from 6.5 million in the mid-1990s to 11 million in 2002. By 2003. the pool of immigrants eligible to become naturalized citizens was 8 million. and of these. 2.7 million lived in California. In 2003. the number of new citizens from naturalization was 463.204. In 2007. the number was 702.589. In 2007. 1.38 million people applied for citizenship creating a backlog. In 2008. applications decreased to 525.786.

Naturalization fees were $60 in 1989; $90 in 1991; $95 in 1994; $225 in 1999; $260 in 2002; $320 in 2003; $330 in 2005. Application fees were increased from $330 to $595 and an additional $80 computerized fingerprinting fee was added. The high fees have been criticized as putting up one more wall to citizenship. Increases in fees for citizenship have drawn criticism. Doris Meissner. a senior fellow at the Migration Policy Institute and former Immigration and Naturalization Service Commissioner. doubted that fee increases deter citizenship-seekers. In 2009. the number of immigrants applying for citizenship plunged 62 percent; reasons cited were the slowing economy and the cost of naturalization.

Citizenship ceremonies

The citizenship process has been described as a ritual that is meaningful for many immigrants. Many new citizens are sworn in during Fourth of July ceremonies. Most citizenship ceremonies take place at offices of the U.S. Citizenship and Immigration Services. However. one swearing-in ceremony was held at Arlington National Cemetery inVirginia in 2008. The judge who chose this venue explained: "I did it to Honour our country's warriors and to give the new citizens a sense for what makes this country great."According to federal law. citizenship applicants who are also changing their names must appear before a federal judge.

HONORARY CITIZENSHIP

The title of "Honorary Citizen of the United States" has been granted seven times by an act of Congress or by a proclamation issued by the President pursuant to authorization granted by Congress. The seven individuals are Sir Winston Churchill. Raoul Wallenberg. William Penn. Hannah Callowhill Penn. Mother Teresa. the Marquis de Lafayette. and Casimir Pulaski.

Sometimes. the government awarded non-citizen immigrants who died fighting for American forces with the posthumous title of U.S. citizen. but this is not considered honorary citizenship. In June 2003. Congress approved legislation to help families of fallen non-citizen soldiers.

CORPORATE CITIZENSHIP

There is a sense in which corporations can be considered "citizens". Since *corporations* are considered persons in the eyes of the law. it is possible to think of corporations as being like citizens. For example. the airline Virgin America asked the United States Department of Transportation to be treated as an American air carrier. The advantage of "citizenship" is having the protection and support of the United States government when jockeying with foreign governments for access to air routes and overseas airports. A competitor of Virgin America called Alaska Airlines asked for a review of the situation; according to "U.S. law. foreign ownership in a U.S. air carrier is limited to 25per cent of the voting interest in the carrier". but executives at Virgin America insisted the airline met this requirement.

For the purposes of diversity jurisdiction in the United States civil procedure. corporate citizenship is determined by the principal place of business of the corporation. There is some degree of disagreement among legal authorities as to how exactly this may be determined. Another sense of "corporate citizenship" is a way to show support for causes such as social issues and the environment and. indirectly. gain a kind of "reputational advantage".

CONTROVERSIES

The issue of citizenship naturalization is a highly contentious matter in American politics. particularly regarding illegal immigrants. Candidates in the 2008 presidential election such as Rudolph Giuliani tried to "carve out a middle ground" on the issue of illegal immigration. but rivals such as John McCain advocated legislation requiring illegal immigrants to first leave the country before being eligible to apply as citizens. Some measures to require proof of citizenship upon registering to vote have met with controversy.

Issues such as whether to include questions about current citizenship status in census questions have been debated in the Senate. Generally. there tends to be controversy when citizenship impacts political issues. For example. issues such as asking questions about citizenship on the United States Census tend to cause controversy. Census data affects state electoral clout; it also affects budgetary allocations. Including non-citizens in Census counts also shifts political power to states that have large numbers of non-citizens due to the fact that reapportionment of congressional seats is based on Census data.

There have been controversies based on speculation about which way newly naturalized citizens are likely to vote. Since immigrants from many countries have been presumed to vote Democratic if naturalized. there have been efforts by Democratic administrations to streamline citizenship applications before elections to increase turnout; Republicans. in contrast. have exerted pressure to slow down the process. In 1997. there were efforts to strip the citizenship of 5.000 newly approved immigrants who. it was thought. had been "wrongly naturalized"; a legal effort to do this presented enormous challenges. An examination by the Immigration and Naturalization Service of 1.1 million people who were granted citizenship from September 1995 to September 1996 found 4.946 cases in which a criminal arrest should have disqualified an applicant or in which an applicant lied about his or her criminal history. Before the 2008 election. there was controversy about the speed of the USCIS in processing applications; one report suggested that the agency would complete 930.000 applications in time for the newly processed citizens to vote in the November 2008 election. Foreign-born naturalized citizens tend to vote at the same rates as natives. For example. in the state of New Jersey in the 2008 election. the foreign born represented 20.1 percent of the state's population of 8.754.560; of these. 636.000 were eighteen or older and hence eligible to vote; of eligible voters. 396.000 actually voted. which was about 62per cent. So foreign-born citizens vote in roughly the same proportion (62per cent) as native citizens (67per cent).

There has been controversy about the agency in charge of citizenship. The USCIS has been criticized as being a "notoriously surly. inattentive bureaucracy" with long backlogs in which "would-be citizens spent years waiting for paperwork". Rules made by United States Congress and the federal government regarding citizenship are highly technical and often confusing. and the agency is forced to cope with enforcement within a complex regulatory milieu.

There have been instances in which applicants for citizenship have been deported on technicalities. One Pennsylvania doctor and his wife. both from the Philippines who applied for citizenship. and one Mr. Darnell from Canada who was married to an American with two children from this marriage. ran afoul of legal technicalities and faced deportation. The New York Times reported that "Mr. Darnell discovered that a 10-year-old conviction for domestic violence involving a former girlfriend. even though it had been reduced to a misdemeanor and erased from his public record. made him ineligible to become a citizen—or even to continue living in the United States."

Overworked federal examiners under pressure to make "quick decisions" as well as "weed out security risks" have been described as preferring "to err on the side of rejection". In 2000. 399.670 applications were denied (about 1/3 of all applications); in 2007. 89.683 applications for naturalization were denied. about 12 percent of those presented.

Generally. eligibility for citizenship is denied for the millions of people living in the United States illegally. although from time to time. there have been amnesties. In 2006. there were mass protests numbering hundreds of thousands of people throughout the US demanding U.S. citizenship for illegal immigrants. Many carried banners which read "We Have A Dream Too". One estimate is that there are 12 million illegal immigrants in the USA in 2006. There are many American high school students with citizenship issues. One estimate is that there are 65.000 illegal immigrant students in 2008. A 1982 Supreme Court decision entitled illegal immigrants to free education fromkindergarten through high school. But it is less clear about post-secondary education.

Illegal aliens who get arrested face difficulties in the courtroom as they have no constitutional right to challenge the outcome of their deportation hearings. Writer Tom Barry of the *Boston Review* criticizes the crackdown against illegal immigrants since it has "flooded the federal courts with Non-violent offenders. besieged poor communities. and dramatically increased the U.S. prison population. while doing little to solve the problem itself". Barry criticizes the United States' high incarceration rate as being "fives times greater than the average rate in the rest of the world". Virginia Senator Jim Webb agreed that "we are doing something dramatically wrong in our criminal justice system".

CANADIAN NATIONALITY LAW

Canadian nationality law determines who is and who is not a Canadian citizen. Canadian nationality is typically obtained by birth in Canada. birth abroad when at least one parent is a Canadian citizen and was born or naturalized in Canada. or by adoption abroad by at least one Canadian citizen. It can also be granted to a permanent resident who has lived in Canada for a period of time.

HISTORY OF BRITISH SUBJECT INTO CANADIAN CITIZENSHIP

After Canadian Confederation was achieved in 1867. the new Dominion's "nationality law" initially closely mirrored that of the United Kingdom and all Canadians were classified as "British subject"s. Section 91(25) of the "British North America Act". 1867. passed by the British Parliament in London. (now referred to as the "Constitution Act". 1867). however. gave the Parliament of Canada authority over "Naturalization and Aliens." The "Immigration Act". 1910. for example. created the status of "Canadian citizen." This distinguished those "British subjects" who were born. naturalized. or domiciled in Canada from those who were not. but was only applied for the purpose of determining whether someone was free of immigration controls. The Naturalization Act. 1914. increased the period of residence required to qualify for naturalization in Canada as a "British subject" from three years to five years. A separate additional status of "Canadian national" was created under the Canadian Nationals Act. 1921. in order that Canada could participate in international forces or military expeditions separately from Britain.

Canadian independence from Britain was obtained incrementally between 1867 (confederation and Dominion status within the Empire) and 1982 (patriation of the Canadian constitution). In 1931. the Statute of Westminster provided that the United Kingdom would have no legislative authority over Dominions without the request and consent of that Dominion's government to have a British law become part of the law of the Dominion. The law also left the British North America Acts within the purvue of the British parliament. because the federal government and the provinces could not agree on an amending formula for the Canadian constitution. (Similarly. the neighbouring Dominion of Newfoundland did not become independent because it never ratified the Statute.) When. in 1982. the British and Canadian parliaments produced the mutual Canada Act 1982 (UK) and Constitution Act 1982 (Canada). which included a constitutional amendment process. the UK ceased to have any legislative authority whatsoever over Canada.

By the 1930s and the outbreak of World War II. Canada's naturalization laws consisted of a hodgepodge of confusing acts. which still retained the term "British subject" as the designation for "Canadian nationals." This eventually conflicted with the nationalism that eventually rose amongst North America's Canadians following the sacrifices and heroism shown by Canadian troops on their own in various war fronts in the First World War and later increasing following the publicity of the larger Canadian Army in theSecond World War. the spreading use of newspapers with the installation of radios in most homes by the 1920s and 1930s beaming news and entertainment into all homes. followed by television's impact after World War II. and with the increasing population with the domestic. cultural and artistic accomplishments of native Canadians and increased participation of assimilated immigrant groups brought an accompanying desire to have the Dominion of Canada's sovereign status reflected in distinct nationalistic symbols (such as flags. anthem seal. etc.). This. plus the muddled nature of existing nationality law. prompted the enactment of the "Canadian Citizenship Act. 1946". which took effect on 1 January 1947. On that date. "Canadian citizenship" was conferred on most Canadians previously classified as "British subjects." Subsequently. on 1 April 1949. Canadian nationality law was extended to the Newfoundland. upon the former British colony (but long-time Canadian neighbour and cooperative government) joining the Canadian confederation as the Province of Newfoundland. Canadian nationality law was substantially revised again on 15 February 1977. when the new "Citizenship Act" came into force. From that date. multiple citizenship became legal. However. those who had lost Canadian citizenship before that date did not automatically have it restored until 17 April 2009. when Bill C-37 became law. The 2009 act. the most recent major change to laws governing Canadian citizenship. limited the issuance of citizenship to children born outside Canada to Canadian ancestors (jus sanguinis) to one generation abroad.

BIRTH IN CANADA

In general. everyone born in Canada from 1947 or later acquires Canadian citizenship at birth. In one 2008 case. a girl born to a Ugandan mother aboard a Northwest Airlinesflight from Amsterdam to Boston was deemed a Canadian citizen for customs' purposes because she was born over Canada's airspace.The only exceptions concern children born to diplomats. where additional requirements apply.

Section 3(2) of the current act states that Canadian citizenship is not granted to a child born in Canada if either parent was a diplomatic or consular officer or other representative at the time of birth and neither parent was a Canadian citizen or Canadian permanent resident. However. should the immigration status of the parents of such persons change to permanent resident. a child may be granted citizenship immediately. or when the parents acquire citizenship through naturalization. at the discretion of Citizenship and Immigration Canada.In 2012. Citizenship and Immigration Minister Jason Kenney proposed to modify the jus soli birthright citizenship recognised in Canadian law as a means of discouraging birth tourism. most likely by requiring at least one of the parents be resident in Canada.

CANADIAN CITIZENSHIP BY DESCENT

Every person born outside of Canada in the first generation abroad is a Canadian citizen by descent. Prior to Bill C-37 becoming law on 17 April 2009. this only applied to those people born after 15 February 1977 (those born prior to this date but who did not have citizenship reacquired it or gained it retroactive to their date of birth or date citizenship was lost). Every such person whose Canadian parent or parents were also not born in Canada and obtained their citizenship at birth by descent (second generation born abroad) must have successfully applied to maintain their Canadian citizenship before their 28th birthday. that is. if their 28th birthday took place before 17 April 2009. People falling into that category who did not take steps to maintain their citizenship lost their citizenship on that birthday.

With Bill C-37 coming into effect on 17 April 2009. there is no longer a requirement or any allowance to apply to maintain citizenship. Additionally.

the first generation rule requires at least one parent to be born in Canada or be a naturalized Canadian citizen in order to pass citizenship to their children born outside of Canada (government and Canadian Forces employees are exempt from this rule).

2009 AMENDMENTS TO THE CITIZENSHIP ACT

An Act to amend the Citizenship Act (S.C. 2008. c. 14) came into effect on 17 April 2009 and changed the rules for Canadian citizenship. Individuals born outside of Canada can now become Canadian citizens by descent if one of their parents is a citizen of Canada either by having been born in Canada or by naturalization. The new law limits citizenship by descent to one generation born outside Canada. One of the changes instituted by the Government of Canada. is the "first generation limitation." considered a punitive measure by some against naturalized citizens who reside abroad for lengthy periods of time. Jason Kenney Minister for Citizenship. Immigration and Multiculturalism said the following in the House of Commons of Canada on 10 June 2010: "That's why we must protect the values of Canadian citizenship and must take steps against those who would cheapen it.... We will strengthen the new limitation on the ability to acquire citizenship for the second generation born abroad." The new rules would not confer a Canadian citizenship on children born outside of Canada to parents who were themselves Canadian citizens by birth but not born in Canada. Thus the new rule makes a distinction between Canadian citizens born in Canada and immigrants granted citizenship on the one hand and citizens by birth who were born outside Canada on the other who have attenuated rights to pass on citizenship to their children.

In a scenario. the new rules would apply like this: A child is born in Brazil in 2005 (*before* the new rules came in effect) to a Canadian citizen father. who himself is a born abroad citizen by descent. and a Brazilian mother who is only a Permanent Resident of Canada. Child automatically becomes a Canadian citizen at birth. Another child born *after* 17 April 2009 in the same scenario would not be considered a Canadian citizen. The child is considered born past "first generation limitation" and the parents (the father) would have to sponsor the child to Canada to become a Permanent Resident. (a lengthy process which may take from one to four years) Once the Permanent Residency is granted. a Canadian parent can apply for Canadian citizenship on behalf of the child. without the required three-year-residency rule. however.

Every person born outside Canada but within one generation of the native-born or naturalized citizen parent is automatically a Canadian citizen by descent (retroactive to date of birth or date citizenship was lost). The second generation born abroad. however. is not a citizen of Canada at birth. Such an individual might even be stateless if without claim to any other citizenship. (This situation actually occurred to a child born in China to a father who is a Canadian citizen born outside Canada.) The second generation born abroad can gain Canadian citizenship only by immigrating to Canada; this can be done by the Canadian citizen's parents sponsoring as a dependent children. a category with fewer requirements. which would also take less time than most other immigration application categories.

Under new rules. introduced in 2009. foreign nationals being adopted by Canadian citizens can now acquire Canadian citizenship immediately upon completion of the adoption. without entering Canada as a permanent resident as under the previous rules.

NATURALIZATION AS A CANADIAN CITIZEN

A person who is a permanent resident may apply for Canadian citizenship by naturalization (grant) subject to the following conditions.

The person:

- is aged 18 years or over
- is a permanent resident
- has lived in Canada for a total of 1095 days during the four years preceding the application for citizenship. including a minimum of two years as a permanent resident
- has knowledge of Canada (as demonstrated by taking the Canadian Citizenship Test. which is required as part of the application process. but only if the applicant is between 18 and 54 years of age)
- is not a subject to any criminal prohibitions
- is not a war criminal
- is able to speak English or French well enough to communicate with people

Bill C-24. the *Strengthening Canadian Citizenship Act*. was introduced in February 2014. The bill would raise citizenship requirements from 1095 days (3 years total) during the four years preceding the application to 1460 days (4 years total) during the six years preceding the application. with the minimum time as a permanent resident also raised to 4 years as no credit would be given for time spent in Canada as a temporary resident. Applicants must also have been in Canada for 183 days in four of the six years relevant to their application date. The language and knowledge requirement is extended to those 14 to 64 years of age.

Children aged under 18

The naturalization requirements for children under 18 are different from those for adults.

- the child should be a permanent resident
- a parent of the child should be a Canadian citizen or in the process of applying for Canadian citizenship The residence and other requirements do not normally apply to those aged under 18.

Citizenship ceremonies

All applicants for Canadian citizenship aged 14 or over must attend a citizenship ceremony as the final stage of their application.

CANADIAN CITIZENSHIP BY ADOPTION

In May 2006 the Canadian government introduced draft legislation. Bill C-14: An Act to Amend the Citizenship Act (Adoption) which is designed to allow adopted children the right to apply for immediate citizenship. This bill received Royal Assent on 22 June 2007.

Bill C-14 consists of only four clauses. Clause 1 amends section 3 of the Citizenship Act so that adopted children who attain citizenship without first obtaining permanent resident status are Canadian citizens. Clause 2 applies to adopted children who are minors and also to those who are at least 18 years of age; it amends section 5 of the Citizenship Act and provides that. subject to certain conditions. the Minister shall grant citizenship to children who are adopted abroad after 14 February 1977. Clause 2 also has a special provision for adoptions that are under the jurisdiction of Quebec.

LOSS OF CANADIAN CITIZENSHIP

Under Canadian law there was no provision for involuntary loss of Canadian citizenship except:

- naturalized Canadians can have their citizenship revoked if convicted of fraud in relation to their citizenship application. or their original admission to Canada as an immigrant

Similar provisions also exist under the nationality laws of the UK. US. Israel. Australia. New Zealand and Spain.

However Bill C-24 has added other conditions under which a Canadian can lose their citizenship. Thereby returning the punishment of "exile" to Canada for certain crimes including but not limited to:

- Committing an act of terrorism
- Being convicted of an act of terrorism by a foreign court

Many Canadians lost their citizenship prior to 15 February 1977 through:

- naturalization in another country
- long residence overseas (prior to 1967)
- if a child. based on a parent's loss of Canadian citizenship

A Canadian citizen who holds another nationality may in some cases renounce their Canadian status.

Lost Canadians

In February 2007. the House of Commons Standing Committee on Citizenship and Immigration held hearings on so-called Lost Canadians. who found out recently. on applying for passports. that for various reasons they may not be Canadian citizens as they thought. Don Chapman. a witness before the committee. estimated that 700.000 Canadians have either lost their citizenship or are at risk of having it stripped. However. Citizenship and Immigration Minister Diane Finley said her office has had just 881 calls on the subject. On 19 February 2007. she signed documents granting citizenship to 33 such individuals. Some of the reasons citizenship may have been lost is if the individual was born out of wedlock before 1977. or to a father who took a second citizenship.

Another reason is if the child was born outside Canada. and failed to confirm their citizenship before turning 24 or 28. Some of the people affected reside in towns near the southern border. and hence were born in American hospitals. Others. particularly Mennonites. were born to Canadian parents in Mexico or Paraguay. An investigation by the CBC. based on Canadian census data. concluded that the problem could affect an estimated 10.000 to 20.000 individuals currently residing in Canada.

On 29 May 2007. Canadian Minister of Citizenship and Immigration Diane Finley announced her proposal to amend the *Citizenship Act*. Under the proposal. anyone naturalized in Canada since 1947 would have citizenship even if they lost it under the 1947 Act. Also. anyone born since 1947 outside the country to a Canadian mother or father. in or out of wedlock. would have citizenship if they are the first generation born abroad. Appearing before the Standing Committee on Citizenship and Immigration.

Finley asserted that as of 24 May 2007. there were only 285 cases of individuals in Canada whose citizenship status needs to be resolved. Under the proposed legislation. anyone born before 1947 to a Canadian citizen abroad would be dealt with on a case-by-case basis; such individuals would have to apply for a ministerial permit.

Bill C-37. which received Royal Assent on 17 April 2009. amended the *Citizenship Act* to give Canadian citizenship to those who lost or never had it. due to outdated provisions in existing and former legislation. The law came into effect on 17 April 2009.

RESUMPTION OF CANADIAN CITIZENSHIP

Former Canadian citizens who lost their citizenship as adults are generally required to obtain landed immigrant (permanent resident) status under normal rules and live in Canada for one year in order to resume Canadian citizenship. Former Canadians who lost British subject status before 1947 have no specific rights to Canadian citizenship. except in the case of women who lost British subject status on marriage to a foreign man.

On 22 September 1988. Prime Minister Brian Mulroney agreed to a redress package for Japanese-Canadians deported from Canada between 1941 and 1946 (about 4.000 in total) and their descendants. The package authorized a special grant of Canadian citizenship for any such person. All descendants of deported persons were also eligible for the grant of citizenship provided that they were living on 22 September 1988. regardless of whether the person actually deported from Canada was still alive.

THE ROYAL FAMILY

Though she resides predominantly in the United Kingdom and it is uncertain whether a monarch is subject to his or her own citizenship laws. the Queen of Canada is considered Canadian. She and those others in the Royal Family who do not meet the requirements of Canadian citizenship (there are four Canadian citizens within the Royal Family) are not classified by either the government or some constitutional experts as foreigners to Canada; in the Canadian context. members of the Royal Family are subjects specifically of the monarch of Canada. Members of the Royal Family have also. on occasion. declared themselves to be Canadian and called Canada "home".

JUDICIAL REVIEW OF PROVISIONS OF CURRENT AND PREVIOUS CITIZENSHIP ACTS

There has been a number of court decisions dealing with the subject of Canadian citizenship. In particular. the interpretation of the 3-year (1.095-day) residence requirement enacted by the 1977 *Citizenship Act*. which does not define the term "residence" and. further. prohibits an appeal of a Federal Court decision in a citizenship matter to the Federal Court of Appeal or the Supreme Court. has "led to a great deal of mischief and agony" and generated considerable judicial controversy.Over the years 2 principal schools of thought with respect to residence have emerged from the Federal Court.

Early on. in 1978. Associate Chief Justice Arthur L. Thurlow in *Papadogiorgakis (Re)*. [1978] 2 F.C. 208. opined that residency entails more than a mere counting of days. He held that residency is a matter of the degree to which a person. in mind or fact. settles into or maintains or centralizes his or her ordinary mode of living. including social relations. interests and conveniences. The question becomes whether an applicant's linkages suggest that Canada is his or her home. regardless of any absences from the country.

In *Re Koo*. Justice Barbara Reed further elaborated that in residency cases the question before the Court is whether Canada is the country in which an applicant has centralized his or her mode of existence. Resolving such a question involves consideration of several factors:

1. Was the individual physically present in Canada for a long period prior to recent absences which occurred immediately before the application for citizenship?
2. Where are the applicant's immediate family and dependents (and extended family) resident?

3. Does the pattern of physical presence in Canada indicate a returning home or merely visiting the country?
4. What is the extent of the physical absences – if an applicant is only a few days short of the 1095 day total it is easier to find deemed residence than if those absences are extensive?
5. Is the physical absence caused by a clearly temporary situation such as employment as a missionary abroad. following a course of study abroad as a student. accepting temporary employment abroad. accompanying a spouse who has accepted temporary employment abroad?
6. What is the quality of the connection with Canada: is it more substantial than that which exists with any other country?

The general principle is that the quality of residence in Canada must be more substantial than elsewhere.

In contrast. a line of jurisprudence flowing from the decision in *Re Pourghasemi (1993)*. 62 F.T.R. 122. 19 Imm. L.R. (2d) 259. emphasized how important it is for a potential new citizen to be immersed in Canadian society and that a person cannot reside in a place where the person is not physically present. Thus. it is necessary for a potential citizen to establish that he or she has been physically present in Canada for the requisite period of time.

In the words of Justice Francis Muldoon:

It is clear that the purpose of paragraph 5(1)(c) is to ensure that everyone who is granted precious Canadian citizenship has become. or at least has been compulsorily presented with the everyday opportunity to become "Canadianized." This happens by "rubbing elbows" with Canadians in shopping malls. corner stores. libraries. concert halls. auto repair shops. pubs. cabarets. elevators. churches. synagogues. mosques and temples – in a word wherever one can meet and converse with Canadians – during the prescribed three years. One can observe Canadian society for all its virtues. decadence. values. dangers and freedoms. just as it is. That is little enough time in which to become Canadianized. If a citizenship candidate misses that qualifying experience. then Canadian citizenship can be conferred. in effect. on a person who is still a foreigner in experience. social adaptation. and often in thought and outlook... So those who would throw in their lot with Canadians by becoming citizens must first throw in their lot with Canadians by residing among Canadians. in Canada. during three of the preceding four years. in order to Canadianize themselves. It is not something one can do while abroad. for Canadian life and society exist only in Canada and nowhere else.

The co-existence of such disparate. yet equally valid approaches has led some judges to comment that the citizenship "law is in a sorry state." that "there cannot be two correct interpretations of a statute." that "it does not engender confidence in the system for conferring citizenship if an applicant is.

in the course of a single application. subjected to different legal tests because of the differing legal views of the Citizenship Court." that there's a "scandalous incertitude in the law." and that "there is no doubt that a review of the citizenship decisions of this Court. on that issue. demonstrates that the process of gaining citizenship in such circumstances is akin to a lottery."

In 2010 it seemed that a relative judicial consensus with respect to decision-making in residence cases might emerge. In several Federal Court decisions it was held that the Citizenship Judge must apply a hybrid two-test approach by firstly ascertaining whether. on the balance of probabilities. the applicant has accumulated 1.095 days of physical presence. If so. the residency requirement is considered to have been met. If not. then the judge must additionally assess the application under the "centralized mode of existence" approach. guided by the non-exhaustive factors set out in *Koo (Re)*.

However. most recently. this compromise formula was rejected by the Federal Court judges. who continued to plead for legislative intervention as the means to settle the residency requirement debacle.

GLOBAL CITIZENS MOVEMENT

In most discussions. the global citizens movement is a socio-political process rather than a political organization or party structure. The term is often used synonymously with the anti-globalization movement or the global justice movement. Colloquially the term is also used in this imprecise manner. Global citizens movement has been used by activists to refer to a number of organized and overlapping citizens groups who seek to influence public policy often with the hope of establishing global solidarity on an issue. Such efforts include advocacy on ecological sustainability. corporate responsibility. social justice and similar progressive issues.

In theoretical discussions of social movements. global citizens movement refers to a complex and unprecedented phenomena made possible by the unique subjective and objective conditions of the planetary phase of civilization. The term is used to distinguish the latent potential for a profound shift in values among an aware and engaged citizenry from existing transnational citizens movements which tend to focus on specific issues (such as the anti-war movement or the labour movement).

BACKGROUND

The concept of *global citizenship* first emerged among the Greek Cynics in the 4th Century BCE (9.6 ky). who coined the term "cosmopolitan" – meaning *citizen of the world*. TheRoman Stoics later elaborated on the concept. The contemporary concept of cosmopolitanism. which proposes that all individuals belong to a single moral community. has gained a new salience as scholars examine the ethical requirements of the planetary phase of civilization.

The idea that today's objective and subjective conditions have increased the latency for an emergent global civic identity has been argued by the authors of the Global Scenario Group's final report Great Transition: the Promise and Lure of the Times Ahead. Similar arguments for the existence of a latent pool of tens of millions of people ready to identify around new values of earth consciousness have been put forth by such authors as Paul Raskin. Paul H. Ray. and David Korten. Organizations. such as Oxfam International believe that a global citizens movement rooted in social and economic justice is emerging and is necessary for ending global poverty.

VISIONS OF A GLOBAL CITIZENS MOVEMENT

Orion Kriegman. author of Dawn of the Cosmopolitan: The Hope of a Global Citizens Movement. states. "Transnational corporations. governments. and non-governmental organizations (NGOs) remain powerful global actors. but all of these would be deeply influenced by a coherent. worldwide association of millions of people who call for priority to be placed on new values of quality of life. human solidarity. and environmental sustainability."

Kriegman distinguishes this "coherent. worldwide association of millions" from the existing fragmented social movements active in the World Social Forum. These movements tend to be issue-specific – focused on Labour. environment. human rights. feminist issues. indigenous struggles. poverty. AIDS. and numerous other interrelated but "siloed" efforts. Coherence among these movements would require a reframing of their work under the rubric of the struggle for a socially just and ecologically sustainable global society and the establishment of an institutional structure to defend the rights of humanity. future generations. and the biosphere. Kriegman asserts. "The upsurge of civil society activity. in the form of NGOs and social movements. over the past few decades can be understood as an early manifestation of the latency in the global system. and at the same time this transnational activity helps deepen the latency. However. existing social movements have not found a way to effectively balance the creative tension between pluralism and coherence to provide a collective framework for theory and action. Without a shared framework. it is hard to imagine how the latent potential would coalesce into a global systemic movement. The development of a shared framework will depend on new forms of leadership to facilitate engaged dialogue inclusive of diverse voices."

CRITIQUES OF A GLOBAL CITIZENS MOVEMENT

The major critique of the notion of a global citizens movement centers on the potential for the emergence of solidarity on issues at the global level. Nationalism. racism. and the dominance of the Westphalian state system are considered antithetical to the adoption of a global civic identity. However. some scholars point out that the historical emergence of nationalism must have felt just as improbable in a time of warring city-states. and yet in retrospect it appears inevitable. A more radical critique stems from the arguments put forth by Michael Hardt and Antonio Negri in their book Multitude and enshrines Foucault's notion of a "plurality of resistance" as the only legitimate path forward. This argument asserts that an organized movement among the vast multitude is both undesirable and impossible. Instead of leadership and organizational structures. Hardt and Negri put faith in the emergence of spontaneous coherence due to increasing self-organized networks among various autonomous resistance movements. They critique the notion that there could be legitimate leaders. democratically chosen through a formal network of grassroots structures. acting on behalf of a big-tent pluralistic association of global citizens to directly confront the entrenched power of transnational corporations and state governments. However. it remains unclear how a network of autonomous movements would differ in practice from the vision of an authentic global citizens movement.

3

National Citizenship

INTRODUCTION

Generally citizenship is seen as the relationship between an individual and a particular nation. In ancient Greece. the main political entity was the city-state. and citizens were members of particular city-states. In the past five hundred years. with the rise of the nation-state. citizenship is most closely identified with being a member of a particular nation. To some extent. certain entities cross national boundaries such as trade organizations. non-governmental organizations as well as multi-national corporations. and sometimes the term "citizen of the world" applies in the sense of people having less ties to a particular nation and more of a sense of belonging to the world in general.

In modern times. citizenship policy is divided between *jus sanguinis* ("right of blood") and *jus soli* ("right of soil") nations. A *jus sanguinis* policy grants citizenship based on ancestry or ethnicity. and is related to the concept of a nation state common in Europe. A *jus soli* policy grants citizenship to anyone born on the territory of the state. a policy practiced by many countries in the Americas. Many countries have a hybrid birthright requirement of local nativity and citizenship of at least one parent.

Citizenship can also commonly be obtained through marriage to a person holding the citizenship (*jure matrimonii*). or through naturalization.

FULL AND EQUAL MEMBERSHIP FULL AND EQUAL MEMBERSHIP

If you have ever travelled in a crowded railway compartment or bus you will be familiar with the way in which those who may have earlier fought each other to enter. once inside discover a shared interest in keeping others out! A division soon develops between 'insiders' and 'outsiders' with 'outsiders' being seen as a threat. Similar processes take place from time to time in cities. regions. or even the nation as a while. If jobs. facilities like medical care or education. and natural resources like land or water. are limited. demands may be made to restrict entry to 'outsiders' even though they may be fellow citizens. You may remember the slogan 'Mumbai for Mumbaikars' which expressed such feelings.

Many similar struggles have taken place in different parts of India and the world. This raises questions about what 'full and equal membership' really means? Does it mean that citizens should enjoy equal rights and opportunities wherever in the country they may decide to live. study. or work? Does it mean that all citizens. rich or poor. should enjoy certain basic rights and facilities? In this section as suggested. explore the meaning of citizenship by focusing on the first of these questions. One of the rights granted to citizens in our country. and in many others. is freedom of movement. This right is of particular importance for workers.

Labour tends to migrate in search of jobs when opportunities are not available near their homes. Some people may even travel outside the country in search of jobs. Markets for skilled and unskilled workers have developed in different parts of our country. For instance. I.T. workers may flock to towns like Bangalore. Nurses from Kerala may be found all over the country. The booming building industry in town attracts workers from different parts of the country. So do infrastructure projects like road making. You may have come across workers from different regions near your home or school.

However. often resistance builds up among the local people against so many jobs going to people from outside the area. sometimes at lower wages. A demand may develop to restrict certain jobs to those who belong to the state. or those who know the local language. Political parties may take up the issue. Resistance could even take the form of organised violence against 'outsiders'. Almost every region of India has experienced such movements. Are such movements ever justified?

We all become indignant. if Indian workers in other countries are ill-treated by the local population. Some of us may also feel that skilled and educated workers have the right to migrate for work. States may even be proud of their ability to attract such workers. But if jobs are scarce in a region. local residents may resent competition from 'outsiders'. Does the right to freedom of movement include the right to live or work in any part of the country?

Another factor that we need to consider is that there may sometimes be a difference between our response to poor migrants and to skilled migrants. We may not always be as welcoming to poor migrants who move into our areas as we may be to skilled and affluent workers. This raises the question of whether poor and unskilled workers should have the same right to live and work anywhere in the country as do skilled workers? These are some of the issues which being debated in our country today regarding 'full and equal membership' for all citizens of the country.

However. disputes may sometimes arise even in democratic societies. How can such disputes be resolved? The right to protest is an aspect of the freedom of expression guaranteed to citizens in our Constitution. provided protest does not harm the life or property of other people or the State. Citizens are free to try and influence public opinion and government policy by forming groups. holding demonstrations. using the media. appealing to political parties. or by approaching the courts. The courts may give a decision on the matter. or they may urge the government to address the issue. It may be a slow process but varying degrees of success are sometimes possible. If the guiding principle of providing full and equal membership to all citizens is kept in mind. it should be possible to arrive at an acceptable solution to the problems that may arise from time to time in a society. A basic principle of democracy is that such disputes should be settled by negotiation and discussion rather than force. This is one of the obligations of citizenship.

CITIZEN AND NATION

The concept of nation state evolved in the modern period. One of the earliest assertions regarding the sovereignty of the nation state and democratic rights of citizens was made by the revolutionaries in France in 1789. Nation states claim that their boundaries define not just a territory but also a unique culture and shared history. The national identity may be expressed through symbols like a flag. national anthem. national language. or certain ceremonial practices. among other things.

Most modern states include people of different religions. languages. and cultural traditions. But the national identity of a democratic state is supposed to provide citizens with a political identity that can be shared by all the members of the state. Democratic states usually try to define their identity so that it is as inclusive as possible — that is. which allows all citizens to identify themselves as part of the nation. But in practice. most countries tend to define their identity in a way which makes it easier for some citizens to identify with the state than others. It may also make it easier for the state to extend citizenship to some people and not others. This would be as true of the United States. which prides itself on being a country of immigrants. as any other country.

France. for instance. is a country which claims to be both secular and inclusive. It includes not only people of European origin but also citizens who originally came from other areas such as North Africa. Culture and language are important features of its national identity and all citizens are expected to assimilate into it in the public aspects of their lives. They may. however. retain their personal beliefs and practices in their private lives. This may seem like a reasonable policy but it is not always simple to define what is public and what is private and this has given rise to some controversies.Religious belief is supposed to belong to the private sphere of citizens but sometimes religious symbols and practices may enter into their public lives. You may have heard about the demand of Sikh school boys in France to wear the turban to school. and of Muslim girls to wear the head scarf with their school uniforms.

This was disallowed by some schools on the ground that it involved bringing religious symbols into the public sphere of state education. Those whose religions did not demand such practices naturally did not face the same problem. Clearly. assimilation into the national culture would be easier for some groups than for others.

The criteria for granting citizenship to new applicants varies from country to country. In countries such as Israel. or Germany. factors like religion. or ethnic origin. may be given priority when granting citizenship. In Germany there has been a persistent demand from Turkish workers. who were at one time encouraged to come and work in Germany. that their children who have been born and brought up in Germany should automatically be granted citizenship. This is still being debated. These are only a few examples of the kinds of restrictions which may be placed on citizenship even in democratic countries which pride themselves on being inclusive.

India defines itself as a secular. democratic. nation state. The movement for independence was a broad based one and deliberate attempts were made to bind together people of different religions. regions and cultures. True. Partition of the country did take place in 1947 when differences with the Muslim League could not be resolved. but this only strengthened the resolve of Indian national leaders to maintain the secular and inclusive character of the Indian nation state they were committed to build. This resolve was embodied in the Constitution.

The Indian Constitution attempted to accommodate a very diverse society. To mention just a few of these diversities. it attempted to provide full and equal citizenship to groups as different as the Scheduled Castes and Scheduled Tribes. many women who had not previously enjoyed equal rights. some remote communities in the Andaman and Nicobar islands who had had little contact with modern civilization. and many others. It also attempted to find a place for the different languages. religions and practices found in different parts of the country.

It had to provide equal rights to all without at the same time forcing people to give up their personal beliefs. languages or cultural practices. It was therefore a unique experiment which was undertaken through the Constitution. The Republic Day parade in Delhi symbolises the attempt of the state to include people of different regions. cultures and religions.

The provisions about citizenship in the Constitution can be found in Part Three and in subsequent laws passed by Parliament. The Constitution adopted an essentially democratic and inclusive notion of citizenship. In India. citizenship can be acquired by birth. descent. registration. naturalisation. or inclusion of territory. The rights and obligations of citizens are listed in the Constitution. There is also a provision that the state should not discriminate against citizens on the grounds of race/caste/sex/place of birth. or any of them. The rights of religious and linguistic minorities are also protected.

However. even such inclusive provisions have given rise to struggles and controversies. The women's movement. the dalit movement. or struggles of people displaced by development projects. represent only a few of the struggles being waged by people who feel that they are being denied full rights of citizenship. The experience of India indicates that democratic citizenship in any country is a project. an ideal to work towards. New issues are constantly being raised as societies change and new demands are made by groups who feel they are being marginalised. In a democratic state these demands have to be negotiated.

CIVIL AND POLITICAL RIGHTS

Civil and political rights are a class of rights that protect individuals' freedom from unwarranted infringement by governments and private organizations. and ensure one's ability to participate in the civil and political life of the state without discrimination or repression.

Civil rights include the ensuring of peoples' physical integrity and safety; protection from discrimination on grounds such as physical or mental disability. gender. religion. race. national origin. age. sexual orientation. or gender identity; and individual rights such as the freedoms of thought and conscience. speech and expression. religion. the press. and movement.

Political rights include natural justice (procedural fairness) in law. such as the rights of the accused. including the right to a fair trial; due process; the right to seek redress or a legal remedy; and rights of participation in civil society and politics such as freedom of association. the right to assemble. the right to petition. the right of self-defence as supported by the Bill of Rights. and the right to vote.

Civil and political rights form the original and main part of international human rights. They comprise the first portion of the 1948 Universal Declaration of Human Rights (with economic. social and cultural rights comprising the second portion).

The theory of three generations of human rights considers this group of rights to be "first-generation rights". and the theory of negative and positive rights considers them to be generally negative rights. The phrase "civil rights" is a translation of Latin *ius civis* (rights of citizens). Roman citizens could be either free (*libertas*) or servile (*servitus*). but they all had rights in law. After the Edict of the Milan in 313. these rights included the freedom of religion. Roman legal doctrine was lost during the Middle Ages. but claims of universal rights could still be made based on religious doctrine. According to the leaders of Kett's Rebellion (1549). "all bond men may be made free. for God made all free with his precious blood-shedding."

In the 17th century. English common law judge Sir Edward Coke revived the idea of rights based on citizenship by arguing that Englishman had historically enjoyed such rights The English Bill of Rights was adopted in 1689. The Virginia Declaration of Rights. by George Mason and James Madison. was adopted in 1776. The Virginia declaration is the direct ancestor and model for the U.S. Bill of Rights.

In early 19th century Britain. the phrase "civil rights" most commonly referred to the problem of legal discrimination against Catholics. In the House of Commons support for the British civil rights movement was divided. many more largely known politicians supported the discrimination towards Catholics. Independent MPs applied pressure on the larger parties to pàss the civil rights act of the 1920s.In the 1860s. Americans adapted this usage to newly freed blacks. Congress enacted civil rights acts in 1866. 1871. 1875. 1957. 1960. 1964. 1968. and 1991.

GUARANTEES OF RIGHTS

T.H. Marshall Notes that civil rights were among the first to be recognized and codified. followed later by political rights and still later by social rights. In many countries. they are constitutional rights and are included in a bill of rights or similar document. They are also defined in international human rights instruments. such as the 1948 Universal Declaration of Human Rights and the 1966 International Covenant on Civil and Political Rights.

Civil and political rights need not be codified to be protected. although most democracies worldwide do have formal written guarantees of civil and political rights. Civil rights are often considered to be natural rights. Thomas Jefferson wrote in his 1774 *A Summary View of the Rights of British America* that "a free people their rights as derived from the laws of nature. and not as the gift of their chief magistrate." Custom also plays a role. Implied or unenumerated rights are rights that courts may find to exist even though not expressly guaranteed by written law or custom; one example is the right to privacy in the United States.

The question of to whom civil and political rights apply is a subject of controversy. In many countries. citizens have greater protections against infringement of rights than non-citizens; at the same time. civil and political rights are considered to be universal rights that apply to all persons.

Civil Rights Movement

When civil and political rights are not guaranteed to all as part of equal protection of laws. or when such guarantees exist on paper but are not respected in practice. opposition and even social unrest may ensue.

Civil Rights movements began as early as 1848 in the USA with such documents as the Declaration of Sentiment. Consciously modeled after the Declaration of Independence. the Declaration of Rights and Sentiments became the founding document of the American women's movement. and it was adopted at the Seneca Falls Convention. July 19 and 20. 1848 The civil rights movement was a worldwide political movement for equality before the law occurring between approximately 1950 and 1980. The movement had a legal and constitutional aspect. and resulting in much law-making at both national and international levels. It also had an activist side. particularly in situations where violations of rights were widespread.

Movements with the proclaimed aim of securing observance of civil and political rights included:

- The US civil rights struggle in the 1960s in the southern United States. where rights of black citizens had been violated;
- The Northern Ireland Civil Rights Association. formed in 1967 following failures in this province of the United Kingdom to respect the Catholic minority's rights; and
- Movements in many Communist countries. such as Charter 77 in Czechoslovakia.

Most civil rights movements relied on the technique of civil resistance. using Non-violent methods of struggle. to achieve their aims. In some countries. struggles for civil rights were accompanied. or followed. by civil unrest and even armed rebellion. While civil rights movements over the last 60 years have resulted in an extension of civil and political rights. the process was long and tenuous in many countries. and many of these movements did not achieve or fully achieve their objectives.

PROBLEMS AND ANALYSIS

Questions about civil and political rights have frequently emerged. For example. to what extent should the government intervene to protect individuals from infringement on their rights by other individuals. or from corporations — *e.g.*. in what way should employment discrimination in the private sector be dealt with?

Political theory deals with civil and political rights. Robert Nozick and John Rawls expressed competing visions in Nozick's *Anarchy. State. and Utopia* and Rawls' *A Theory of Justice*. Other influential authors in the area include Wesley Newcomb Hohfeld and Jean Edward Smith.

CITIZENS. RESIDENT ALIENS AND RIGHTS

Should one infer from the preceding discussion that citizenship is "hard on the outside and soft on the inside" with the border representing a firm line between those who are part of the community of equal citizens and those who remain outside? The short answer is no. International migration produces what Bauböck calls a "mismatch between citizenship and the territorial scope of legitimate authority" with "citizens living outside the country whose government is supposed to be accountable to them and inside a country whose government is not accountable to them". To resident aliens who live within a specific community of citizens. the border is not something they have left behind. it effectively follows them inside the state. denying them many of the rights enjoyed by full citizens or making their enjoyment less secure.

One way to address this mismatch is to reconsider how entitlement to citizenship is determined. In a world characterized by significant levels of migration across states. birthright citizenship — acquired either through descent (*jus sanguinis*) or birth in the territory (*jus soli*) — may lead to counterintuitive results: while a regime of pure *jus sanguinis* systematically excludes immigrants and their children. though the latter may be born and bred in their parents' new home. it includes descendents of expatriates who may never have set foot in their forebears' homeland. On the other hand. a regime of *jus soli* may attribute citizenship to children whose birth in the territory is accidental while denying it to those children who have arrived in the country at a very young age.

The stakeholder principle (or *jus nexi*) is proposed as an alternative (or a supplement) to birthright citizenship: individuals who have a "real and effective link" to the political community. or a "permanent interest in membership" should be entitled to claim citizenship. This new criterion aims at securing citizenship for those who are truly members of the political community. in the sense that their life prospects depend on the country's laws and policy choices.

If the stakeholder principle alleviates the mismatch. it does not question the tight association between rights. citizenship. territory and authority. For some. it is precisely this association that should be questioned since it contradicts the increasing fluidity of the relations between individuals and polities in a globalized world. This new context is thought to necessitate more than a friendly amendment to current principles of citizenship allocation: it requires the disaggregation of rights. commonly associated with citizenship. from the legal status of citizen. This process is thought to have already begun in contemporary democracies since. as noted above. many of the civil and social rights associated with citizenship are now extended to all individuals residing in the state. notwithstanding their legal status. Political rights to participation should likewise be extended to resident Non-citizens. and perhaps even to those "Non-citizen Non-residents" who have fundamental interests that are affected by a particular state.

The emergence of human rights instruments at the international and transnational levels has lent some credibility to the perspective of a deterritorialization of rights regimes and the possibility of securing a person's basic rights irrespective of her formal membership status in a given polity. In this context. it is not in virtue of our (particular) citizenship that we are recognized rights. but in virtue of our (universal) personhood. Over and above diverging assessments of the empirical plausibility of such unbundling. some authors highlight the risks involved and contest its desirability. Stable citizenship regimes "promote internal redistribution and support co-governance". "By encouraging the dissolution of the bundle of benefits and protections that currently attach to citizenship. proponents of the unbundling vision will also begin to fuel an alternative discourse as well – one that urges the privatization and fragmentation of citizenship. and that implies less collective responsibility for the well being of members".

THE PROMISE OF TRANSNATIONAL CITIZENSHIP

The nation-state's sovereignty is often understood as an impediment to global justice. Its capacity to deal with economic. social and environmental problems that increasingly cut across borders is also questioned. Under such circumstances. should the sovereign. territorial state still be seen as the necessary institutional context for justice and democracy? Should we not explore possibilities beyond its boundaries?

Such questioning has sparked two responses from theorists of citizenship. 'Voluntarists' insist on the need to rethink democracy and citizenship beyond the nation-state. proposing schemes to extend democratic politics to the regional and global levels. 'Sceptics'. on the other hand. argue that democratic citizenship requires a bounded territorial space. in which citizens see themselves as part of a common *demos*. At the heart of this debate is the contested meaning of democratic political agency and its conditions. which must be clarified if the debate is to get anywhere.

Citizenship as legal status is what makes global citizenship conceivable. since there is no limit to the potential extension of rights. while the political dimension of citizenship presupposes a concept of political community that is richer but more limited. The sceptics consider that citizenship at the global level entails a weakening of its political dimension. a waning of its democratic character. The voluntarists respond that transnational political citizenship is not an oxymoron if we rid ourselves of the blinkers inherited from the past. Both sceptics and voluntarists acknowledge that meaningful citizenship cannot simply be legal in nature. It's their assumptions about the political dimension of democratic citizenship and its background conditions that set them apart.

We will examine two versions of this disagreement. In the first. disagreement centres upon the basic conditions of democratic political agency rather than on its meaning. This is a crucial issue since how we define these conditions can limit the potential extension of the political community. In the second. the disagreement is over the meaning of democratic agency itself. To what extent should political agency be understood as a form of collective agency? Should we characterize political action as a common practice. which requires that citizens be in a relation of interaction and mutual awareness. or can we define it as primarily individual?

Supporters of global democracy reject the conventional identification between *demos*. territory and citizenship. In their view. citizenship is not a set of practices and rights that need to be anchored in a particular *demos* defined by specific territorial boundaries. On the contrary. citizenship is ideally exercised in a multiplicity of 'sites'. situated at different levels of governance: local. national. regional and global. Global democrats sketch a multilayered. global democratic order in which no single layer or site is dominant. This scheme implies a 'vertical' dispersal of power above and below existing sovereign states. which are stripped of their centrality. This would give less of an incentive for conflicts over power and wealth within and between states. "'thereby reducing the incidence of war. poverty. and oppression' and environmental degradation".

Voluntarists would balance this dilution of state power by strengthening certain global regulatory regimes in areas like peace and security. human rights. the environment. trade and finances. etc. These regimes would set down general rules "regarding that small but vital set of issues around which peace and justice call for global co-operation". A set of global institutions would be needed to ensure the application of these rules; though voluntarists are quick to point out the importance of democratic principles — consent. self-determination and autonomy — and their institutional implications.

The formal political institutions and procedures envisaged are largely familiar: representative assemblies based on elections and referenda. Such institutions would exist at each level of the multilayered scheme: local. national. regional and global. Following the European Union model. continent-wide parliaments are envisaged. as well as a reformed general assembly of the United Nations. At the informal level. voluntarists insist on the need for globally active organizations of civil society. welcome the emergence of a transnational public opinion and call on global agencies such as the World Trade Organization and the International Monetary Fund to commit themselves to basic principles of publicity. Global democrats assume that the extension of democracy beyond the limits of the nation-state is neither conceptually nor practically impossible. Their response to claims that scale constitutes a major obstacle is twofold: first. they put the principle of subsidiarity at the front and centre of their institutional scheme; second. they insist that robust democratic politics is truly possible only at the local level. In existing. large nation-states. representative institutions are already far removed from ordinary citizens. who feel largely disempowered and disaffected. Since the multilayered scheme they propose involves significant decentralization from the national to the sub-national level. the argument runs that global democracy would. in fact. translate into more. rather than less. 'real' democracy. It would serve to increase the ability of citizens to participate effectively in shaping the policies that concern them directly (. But no matter how forcefully the principle of subsidiarity is applied. the global democratic project would still entail the implementation of global principles and standards (*e.g.* (re)distributive principles. human rights standards) that would rely on coercive enforcement agencies. Given this reality. the democratic legitimacy of political institutions above the level of the state is an issue that cannot be avoided.

Sceptics of global democracy have worked to identify basic background conditions to democratic institutions and procedures while showing that they cannot be satisfied beyond a certain threshold. Their argument is empirical. rather than conceptual. A common language is one plausible candidate put forward by Will Kymlicka. He insists that linguistic/territorial political associations are the primary forum for democratic participation. rather than higher-level political associations that cut across linguistic lines. because democratic politics is essentially "politics in the vernacular". Even in cases where average citizens are conversant in one or more foreign language. they rarely have the level of fluency necessary to participate in political debate in a language other than their own: only a select few have the ability and opportunity to acquire and sustain the necessary language skills. Political debate in multilingual settings is essentially an elitist pursuit.

In fact. political discussions require a higher degree of fluency than what is needed for business transactions or tourism: "political communication has a large ritualistic component. and these ritualized forms of communication are typically language-specific. Even if one understands a foreign language in the technical sense. without knowledge of these ritualistic elements one may be unable to understand political debates". If he is right. the hope that English's emergence as a new *lingua franca* in Europe and globally could overcome the linguistic obstacles that impede the development of transnational democratic politics are overstated. English's growing use may be enough to increase mutual understanding between individuals. but it is unlikely that it could become a transnational vernacular allowing democratic politics to transcend national boundaries.

Most voluntarists and sceptics rely on the same implicit view of democratic political agency: citizens are political agents through their participation in institutions and procedures that require significant interaction and mutual awareness. In this sense. democratic political agency appears collective rather than individual. Yet this leaves the door open to the sceptics' objections. If we believe that formal and informal democratic institutions like Parliaments and the public sphere require relatively high levels of horizontal communication between citizens. the existence of a common language appears a necessary condition to democratic agency. This. in turn. sets limits to the potential extension of the political community. Schemes that call for the "institutionalization of national and transnational forms of public debate. democratic participation. and accountability" for democracy's global extension appear misguided.

It might be argued. however. that the development of transnational advocacy networks shows that the sceptics' criticisms are overstated. These networks are proof that it is possible for individuals to exercise political agency in forums other than those provided by democratic states and that the absence of a common vernacular does not impede participation. Global democracy becomes thinkable once we focus on the development of transnational civil society rather than on the transposing of representative institutions at the global level. In response. it should be noted that such networks coalesce around a common ideology or conception of the good (*e.g.* the environment; rights of indigenous peoples. critique of neo-liberal forms of globalisation. etc.). which serves as a functional equivalent to a common vernacular. More important. these networks are composed of voluntary associations organized around shared interests and cannot stand as a surrogate for the political community *per se*. which acts as the addressee of claims made by the organisations and groups of civil society.

Which political community or communities can act as the addressee of claims made by organisations of transnational civil society? If one answers national political communities and their formal institutions. one agrees with Kymlicka that: "the weak transnationalism of advocacy networks is predicated on. even parasitic on. the ongoing existence of bounded political communities". Surely. we cannot point to a constituted cosmopolitan political community. which as yet does not exist and. if the sceptics are to be believed. has very little chances of ever coming into existence. If this is right. then the organisations of an emerging transnational civil society can offer possibilities of political agency for certain committed individuals and groups. but they do not offer a solution to the problem posed by the extension of democratic citizenship to the global level.

There is another version of the global democratic project. however. that involves an individualist conception of democratic political agency. Here citizens can engage in significant political activities that do not require high levels of interaction and cooperation between them. This is a position developed recently by Andrew Kuper (2004). It involves. first. that we abandon the conception of democratic legitimacy implicit in deliberative. participatory and republican conceptions of democracy. which all attempt to maintain a broadly Rousseauian understanding of legitimacy: laws are legitimate only if citizens can see themselves. somehow. as their coauthors. Kuper suggests that we discard this vision of democratic legitimacy in favour of one focusing on the responsiveness of the political system as a whole. The central issue becomes whether this system is made to act "in the best interests of the public. in a manner responsive to them". On this view. the vertical. rather than horizontal. dimension of communication is of overarching importance: individual citizens must have access to relevant information about what various authorities are doing. there must exist institutional channels through which they can pressure authorities and let them know their views on proposed policies. Doing so does not require that they "act together with high levels of mutual awareness"; they can exercise these capacities individually. via specific agencies. Responsiveness is also a dimension of democratic legitimacy favored by some empirical social scientists. Responsiveness itself means that representatives respond to the opinions. preferences and concerns of citizens communicated via various agencies. it is measured. however through statistical correlation. in which public opinion is the dependent variable and policy output is the independent variable. For an overview see. for example Page (1994).

In contrast to the vertical and sometimes causal picture citizenship depicted in responsiveness. one could insist. as does Bernard Manin. that meaningful political agency in a representative democracy requires that citizens be capable of learning what their co-citizens think about important policy issues or events independent of the authorities. Horizontal communication between citizens appears as a necessary condition to their being capable of political action. The thing that makes citizens political agents is their capacity to act independently of authorities and this ability. in turn. depends on whether they regularly act and communicate together. even if this interaction is often mediated through institutions like the electronic media.

DIMENSIONS OF CITIZENSHIP

DEFINITIONS

The concept of citizenship is composed of three main elements or dimensions. The first is citizenship as legal status. defined by civil. political and social rights. Here. the citizen is the legal person free to act according to the law and having the right to claim the law's protection. It need not mean that the citizen takes part in the law's formulation. nor does it require that rights be uniform between citizens. The second considers citizens specifically as political agents. actively participating in a society's political institutions. The third refers to citizenship as membership in a political community that furnishes a distinct source of identity.

In many ways. the identity dimension is the least straightforward of the three. Authors tend to include under this heading many different things related to identity. both individual and collective. and social integration. Arguably. this is inescapable since citizens' subjective sense of belonging. sometimes called the "psychological" dimension of citizenship. necessarily affects the strength of the political community's collective identity. If enough citizens display a robust sense of belonging to the same political community. social cohesion is obviously strengthened. However. since many other factors can impede or encourage it. social integration should be seen as an important goal (or problem) that citizenship aims to achieve (or resolve). rather than as one of its elements. As we will see. one crucial test for any conception of citizenship is whether or not it can be said to contribute to social integration.

Relations between the three dimensions are complex: the rights a citizen enjoys will partly define the range of available political activities while explaining how citizenship can be a source of identity by strengthening her sense of self-respect. A strong civic identity can itself motivate citizens to participate actively in their society's political life. That distinct groups within a state do not share the same sense of identity towards 'their' political community (or communities) can be a reason to argue in favour of a differentiated allocation of rights.

The differences between conceptions of citizenship centre around four disagreements: over the precise definition of each element (legal. political and identity); over their relative importance; over the causal and/or conceptual relations between them; over appropriate normative standards.

TWO MODELS OF CITIZENSHIP: REPUBLICAN AND LIBERAL

Discussions about citizenship usually have. as their point of reference. one of two models: the republican or the liberal. The republican model's sources can be found in the writings of authors like Aristotle. Tacitus. Cicero. Machiavelli. Harrington and Rousseau. and in distinct historical experiences: from Athenian democracy and Republican Rome to the Italian city-states and workers' councils.

The key principle of the republican model is civic self-rule. embodied in classical institutions and practices like the rotation of offices. underpinning Aristotle's characterization of the citizen as one capable of ruling and being ruled in turn. Citizens are. first and foremost. "those who share in the holding of office" (Aristotle *Politics*. 1275a8). Civic self-rule is also at the heart of Rousseau's project in the *Contrat Social*: it is their co-authoring of the laws via the general will that makes citizens free and laws legitimate. Active participation in processes of deliberation and decision-making ensures that individuals are citizens. not subjects. In essence. the republican model emphasizes the second dimension of citizenship. that of political agency.

The liberal model's origins are traceable to the Roman Empire and early-modern reflections on Roman law. The Empire's expansion resulted in citizenship rights being extended to conquered peoples. profoundly transforming the concept's meaning. Citizenship meant being protected by the law rather than participating in its formulation or execution. It became an "important but occasional identity. a legal status rather than a fact of everyday life". The focus here is obviously the first dimension: citizenship is primarily understood as a legal status rather than as a political office. It now "denotes membership in a community of shared or common law. which may or may not be identical with a territorial community". The Roman experience shows that the legal dimension of citizenship is potentially inclusive and indefinitely extensible. The liberal tradition. which developed from the 17 century onwards. understands citizenship primarily as a legal status: political liberty is important as a means to protecting individual freedoms from interference by other individuals or the authorities themselves. But citizens exercise these freedoms primarily in the world of private associations and attachments. rather than in the political domain.

At first glance. the two models present us with a clear set of alternatives: citizenship as a political office or a legal status; central to an individual's sense of self or as an "occasional identity". The citizen appears either as the primary political agent or as an individual whose private activities leave little time or inclination to engage actively in politics. entrusting the business of law-making to representatives. If the liberal model of citizenship dominates contemporary constitutional democracies. the republican critique of the *private* citizen's passivity and insignificance is still alive and well.

Republicans have problems of their own. First and foremost is a concern. often repeated since Benjamin Constant. that their ideal has become largely obsolete in the changed circumstances of the "*grands États modernes*". Aiming to realize the original republican ideal in the present context would be a disaster. as was the Jacobins' attempt during the French revolution. Today's citizens will not be Romans: first. the scale and complexity of modern states seem to preclude the kind of civic engagement required by the republican model. If an individual's chances of having an impact as an active citizen are close to nil. then it makes more sense for him to commit himself to non-political activities. be they economic. social or familial. His identity as citizen is not central to his sense of self and politics is only one of his many interests. Second. the heterogeneity of modern states does not allow the kind of "moral unity" and mutual trust that has been projected onto the ancient *polis*. qualities deemed necessary to the functioning of republican institutions. But if ancient virtue is irrecoverable. the republican model may still act today as "a benchmark that we appeal to when assessing how well our institutions and practices are functioning". In essence. this involves a reformulation of the model. questioning some of its original premises while holding onto the ideal of the citizen as an active political agent.

Instead of opposing the two models. we could reasonably see them as complementary. Political liberty. as Constant pointed out. is the necessary guarantee of individual liberty. Echoing Constant. Michael Walzer considers that the two conceptions "go hand in hand" since "the security provided by the authorities cannot just be enjoyed; it must itself be secured. and sometimes against the authorities themselves.

The passive enjoyment of citizenship requires. at least intermittently. the activist politics of citizens". There are times when individuals need only be "*private* citizens" and others when they must become "private *citizens*". But can we expect passive spectators of political life to become active citizens should the need arise? This is no easy question and may explain why Constant ended his famous essay by insisting that the regular exercise of political liberty is the surest means of moral improvement. opening citizens' minds and spirits to the public interest. and to the importance of defending their freedoms. Such habituation underpins their capacity and willingness to protect their liberties and the institutions that support them.

THE FEMINIST CRITIQUE

Since the 1970s. feminist theorists have sharply criticized the republican and liberal models' shared assumption of a rigid separation between the private and the public spheres. Their critique has provided the impetus to the development of alternative conceptions of politics and citizenship.

In its classical formulation. the republican conception sees the public/political sphere as the realm of liberty and equality: it is there that free. male citizens engage with their peers and deliberate over the common good. deciding what is just or unjust. advantageous or harmful. The political space must be protected from the private sphere. defined as the domain of necessity and inequality. where the material reproduction of the *polis* is secured. Women. associated with the 'natural world' of reproduction. are denied citizenship and relegated to the household.

Feminists have criticized this rigid division as mythical since both the separation itself and the radically unequal conception of the household that it presupposed "were clearly the outcome of political decisions made in the public sphere". If the division ostensibly made it possible for citizens to engage with each other as equa

ls. feminists doubt whether it ever was the ideal way of achieving this goal. Hence Susan Okin's question to republicans: "Which is likely to produce better citizens. capable of acting as each other's equals? Having to deal with things part of the time — even the 'mundane' things of daily life? Or *treating most people as things?*". An egalitarian family is a much more fertile ground for equal citizens than one organized like a school for despotism (J.S. Mill); if this means that the political space cannot remain insulated from the world of things. there's no great loss.

The liberal model. for its part. gives primacy to the private sphere. Political liberty is seen in instrumental terms: the formal rights of individuals secure the private sphere from outside interference. allowing the free pursuit of their particular interests. But the neutral language of Lockean egalitarian individualism hides the reality of women's subjection: "woman's sphere" can be read as "male property" since wives are described as naturally subordinated to their husbands. Here as well. the division between private and public has prevented women from gaining access to the public.

Since the public and private "are. and always have been. inextricably connected". the upshot of the feminist critique is not simply to make models of citizenship inclusive by recognizing that women are individuals or to acknowledge that they too can be citizens. Rather. we must see how laws and policies structure personal circumstances (*e.g.* laws about rape and abortion. child-care policies. allocation of welfare benefits. etc.) and how some 'personal problems' have wider significance and can only be solved collectively through political action.

This does not make the distinction irrelevant and the categories collapsible. But it does mean that the boundaries between public and private should be seen as a social construction subject to change and contestation and that their hierarchical characterization should be resisted.

If we discard the abstractions that characterize both the classical and the liberal conceptions. the citizen sheds his "political lion skin" and appears as "situated" in a social world characterized by differences of gender. class. language. race. ethnicity. culture. etc. To accept that politics cannot and should not be insulated from private/social/economic life is not to dissolve the political. but. rather. to revive it since anything is as political as citizens choose to make it. This contextualized conception of the political has informed much of the criticism aimed at the universalist model of citizenship and has inspired the formulation of a differentialist alternative.

THE CHALLENGE OF INTERNAL DIVERSITY

UNIVERSALIST VS DIFFERENTIALIST CONCEPTIONS OF CITIZENSHIP

The universalist or unitary model defines citizenship primarily as a legal status through which an identical set of civil. political and social rights are accorded to all members of the polity. T.H. Marshall's seminal essay "Citizenship and Social Class" is the main reference for this model. which became progressively dominant in post-World War II liberal democracies. Marshall's central thesis was that the 20th century's expansion of social rights was crucial to the working class's progressive integration in British society. Similar stories were told in other Western democracies: the development of welfare policies aimed at softening the impact of unemployment. sickness and distress was fundamental to political and social stability. The apparent success of the post-war welfare state in securing social cohesion was a strong argument in favour of a conception of citizenship focused on the securing of equal civil. political and social rights.

The universalist model was aggressively targeted at the end of the 1980s as the moral and cultural pluralism of contemporary liberal societies elicited increasing theoretical attention. Scepticism towards the universalist model was spurred by concerns that the extension of citizenship rights to groups previously excluded had not translated into equality and full integration. notably in the case of Afro-Americans and women. A questioning of the causal relation assumed between citizenship as a uniform legal status and civic integration followed.

Critics argued that the model proves exclusionary if one interprets universal citizenship as requiring (a) the transcendence of particular. situated perspectives to achieve a common. general point of view and (b) the formulation of laws and policies that are difference-blind. The first requirement seems particularly odious once generality is exposed as a myth covering the majority's culture and conventions. The call to transcend particularity too often translates into the imposition of the majority perspective on minorities. The second requirement may produce more inequality rather than less since the purported neutrality of difference-blind institutions often belies an implicit bias towards the needs. interests and identities of the majority group. This bias often creates specific burdens for members of minorities. *i.e.* more inequality.

Critics of this (failed) universalism have proposed an alternative conception of citizenship based on the acknowledgment of the political relevance of difference (cultural. gender. class. race. etc.). This means. first. the recognition of the pluralist character of the democratic public. composed of many perspectives. none of which should be considered *a priori* more legitimate. Second. it entails that. in certain cases at least. equal respect may justify differential treatment and the recognition of special minority rights.

Once these two points are conceded. the question becomes when. and for what reason. the recognition of particular rights is either justified or illegitimate. This discussion is necessarily context specific. focusing on concrete demands made by groups in particular circumstances. and shies away from easy generalizations. It has led to an array of publications covering issues ranging from the fate of 'minorities within minorities' to how tolerant liberal societies should be of illiberal groups. etc.

But the model of differentiated citizenship has generated its own share of criticisms and queries. particularly with regards to the overall effects of its implementation. Critics focus on its impact on the possibility of a common political practice. Consider Iris Young's vision of a heterogeneous public where participants start from their "situated positions" and attempt to construct a dialogue across differences. This dialogue requires participants to be 'public-spirited' — open to the claims of others and not single-mindedly self-interested. Unlike interest group pluralism. which does not require justifying one's interest as right or as compatible with social justice. participants are supposed to use deliberation to come to a decision that they determine to be best or more just. While welcoming Young's conception of the democratic public. one may doubt that the policies and institutions associated with a differentiated model of citizenship would either motivate or enable citizens to engage in such dialogue. This analysis is tied to a wider literature on the virtues required of citizens in pluralist liberal democracies and on ways to favour their development. Stephen Macedo (1990). William Galston (1991). and Eamonn Callan (1997). among others. have all emphasized the importance of public reasonableness. This virtue is defined as the ability to listen to others and formulate one's own position in a way that is sensitive to. and respectful of. the different experiences and identities of fellow citizens. acknowledging that these differences may affect political views. But how and where does one develop this and related virtue(s)? If a differentiated model of citizenship simply allows individuals and groups to retreat into their particular enclaves. how are they to develop either the motivation or the capacity to participate in a common forum?

One immediately understands political philosophers' renewed interest in education over the last twenty years. If we want citizens of diverse societies to develop the 'right' attitudes and dispositions. should we not encourage a common education. school them in a curriculum that teaches respect for difference. while providing the necessary skills for democratic discussion across these differences? If so. should we not resist demands for separate schools or dispensations for minorities? How flexible should public schools be towards minorities if the goal is to make them feel welcome and ensure that they do not retreat into parochial institutions?

Critics of differentiated citizenship have also argued that policies that break with difference-blind universalism can only weaken the integrative function of citizenship. If embracing multicultural and minority rights means that citizens lose their sense of collective belonging. it may also affect their willingness to compromise and make sacrifices for each other. Citizens may then develop a purely strategic attitude towards those of different backgrounds. As Joseph Carens puts it: "From this perspective. the danger of [...] differentiated citizenship is that the emphasis [it] place[s] on the recognition and institutionalization of difference could undermine the conditions that make a sense of common identification and thus mutuality possible". Critics of Aboriginal demands for self-government rights have pressed this concern with force.

In addressing these and similar queries. Will Kymlicka and Wayne Norman have broadly distinguished between three types of demands: special representation rights (for disadvantaged groups). multicultural rights (for immigrant and religious groups) and self-government rights (for national minorities) (Kymlicka and Norman 1994; Kymlicka. 1995. 176–187). The first two are really demands for inclusion into mainstream society: special representation rights are best understood as (temporary) measures to alleviate the obstacles that minorities and/or historically disadvantaged groups face in having their voices heard in majoritarian democratic institutions. Reforming the electoral system to ensure the better representation of minorities may raise all sorts of difficult issues. but the aim is clearly integration into the larger political society. not isolation.

Similarly. the demands for multicultural rights made by immigrant groups are usually aimed either at exemption from laws and policies that disadvantage them because of their religious practices or at ensuring public support for particular education and/or cultural initiatives to maintain and transmit elements of their cultural and religious heritage. These should be seen as measures designed to facilitate their inclusion in the larger society rather than as a way to avoid integration. It is only claims to self-government rights. grounded in a principle of self-determination. that potentially endanger civic integration since their aim is not to achieve a greater presence in the institutions of the central government. but to gain a greater share of power and legislative jurisdiction for institutions controlled by national minorities.

Addressing such demands through a simple reaffirmation of the ideal of common citizenship is not a serious option. It may only aggravate the alienation felt by members of these groups and feed into more radical political projects. including secession. Further. to say that recognition of self-government rights may weaken the bonds of the larger community is to suppose that these bonds exist in the first place and that a significant proportion of national minorities identify with the larger society. Yet such assumptions are often overly optimistic. If these bonds do not exist. or remain quite weak. what is needed is the construction of a genuine dialogue between the majority society and minorities over what constitutes just relations. through which difference can be recognized. The hope is that such dialogue would strengthen. rather than weaken. their relationship by putting it on firmer moral and political grounds.

This broadly positive assessment of the effects of differentiated citizenship on civic integration is increasingly being questioned. On the one hand. left-leaning authors have complained that multicultural politics make egalitarian policies more difficult to achieve by diverting "political effort away from universalistic goals" and by undermining efforts to build a broadly based coalition supporting ambitious policies of redistribution. On the other hand. events like September 11. the killing of Dutch film director Theo Van Gogh (2004) and the Mohammed cartoons affair have chilled the enthusiasm for and led to something of a backlash against the recognition of multicultural rights. The belief that such demands are really demands for inclusion in the larger society has been thrown into doubt. notably in the case of Muslim immigrants. The debate has increasingly focused on the place of women in traditional religious conceptions. again more specifically in Islam. Does the accommodation of religious sensitivities come at the price of a weakening of women's rights? What is the right balance between the principle of sexual equality affirmed in constitutional democracies and the respect of religious liberty?

Increasingly wary. some European countries have introduced legislation aimed at better securing the integration of immigrants: by requiring minimal linguistic proficiency in the majority language as a condition of citizenship or by banning religious symbols from public schools. More recently. France has gone so far as to legally ban the wearing of full veils in public places in the name of the liberty and equality of women in a secular country. Such initiatives can only rekindle debate about what constitutes legitimate conditions of integration as opposed to the illegitimate imposition of the majority culture.

To allay fears about the supposed trade-off between cultural recognition and redistribution. supporters of multiculturalism cite the lack of empirical studies establishing a negative correlation between the adoption of multicultural policies and a robust welfare state. Further. claims that the push for multicultural policies diverts energies. time and resources from the struggle for redistributive policies assume that the pursuit of justice is zero-sum. seemingly a false generalization. On the contrary. it can be argued that: "the pursuit of justice in one dimension helps build a broader political culture that supports struggles for justice in other dimensions". In the same vein. to claim that paying attention to issues of cultural recognition tends to warp our sensitivity to economic injustice is to assume that we can only be sensitive to one dimension of injustice at a time. But it is equally plausible that sensitivity to a particular type of injustice may favour. rather than hinder. sensitivity to other injustices. Still. it is difficult not to agree with Anne Phillips' assessment that. in debates on democracy. there has been a tendency in the 1990s to focus either on political and cultural issues or on social and economic concerns. As she points out. there is a real need to reconnect reflections on socio-economic and political/cultural equality.

Supporters of multicultural rights are also responding to the changed climate surrounding multicultural demands of immigrant groups. Since the main worry relates to the ability and willingness of Muslim immigrants to integrate into Western liberal democracies. there has been a steady upsurge of interest in these groups. On an empirical level. there is a growing interest in research focusing on the particular challenges Europe faces in integrating Muslim minorities. At a more theoretical level. there is a call to re-examine the complex relations between the secular liberal political cultures dominant in the West and religion. more particularly with regards to the difficult question of religion's place in the public sphere.

LIBERAL NATIONALISTS VS POSTNATIONALISTS

The debate between supporters and critics of differentiated citizenship centres on the model's supposed effect on civic integration. It is assumed that democratic citizenship. properly construed. can indeed function as a significant lever of integration. The idea is that citizenship as a set of civil. political and social rights and as a political practice can help generate desirable feelings of identity and belonging. This statement hides significant disagreement over how to characterize the relation between citizenship and nationality. Some consider that citizenship's capacity to fulfil its integrative function depends on. and feeds upon. the prior existence of a common nationality while others counter that. under conditions of pluralism. nationality cannot function as a suitable focus of allegiance and identity. The collective identity of modern democratic states should rather be based upon more abstract and universalistic political and legal principles that transcend cultural difference. This debate brings to the fore differing assessments of the role that citizenship can play in contemporary societies characterized by a high degree of complexity and internal diversity.

Liberal nationalists like David Miller have argued that only specific forms of political practice can produce high levels of trust and loyalty between citizens. The political activities of the citizens of Athens or of Rousseau's ideal Republic presumed face-to-face relations of cooperation that favour the growth of such sentiments. The scale and complexity of modern states have made the kind of political practice envisaged by Rousseau and described by Aristotle at best marginal. Citizens do not meet under an oak tree to formulate the laws; they are basically strangers and citizens' involvement in the politics of representative democracies is episodic and diluted. Politics in this context cannot be expected to play a central role in most individuals' lives; something else must generate the trust and loyalty necessary to the functioning of a political community. Historically. it is the nation that has allowed large numbers of individuals to feel a sense of commonality. setting them apart from others and making solidarity among strangers possible.

Postnationalists do not dispute the key role played by the nation in making republican politics possible in large modern states. They agree that reference to a common nationality allowed the political mobilization of their inhabitants. calling on their shared descent. history or language. But democracy's association with the nation-state is contingent rather than necessary. And this. it is argued. means that democratic politics can. in principle. free itself from its historical moorings. Postnationalists claim that this dissociation is not only possible. but necessary for moral and pragmatic reasons.

On the one hand. the historical balance sheet of the nation-state reveals a legacy of oppression of minority cultures within and cultural. political and economic imperialism outside its borders. On the other hand. the acknowledgment of the nation-state's (growing) internal diversity and sensitivity to the injustice of forced assimilation undermine its ability to continue playing the role it fulfilled in the 19th and early 20th centuries. Imposing the majority culture upon minorities may simply make it more difficult for them to identify with the nation-state and weaken its legitimacy.

In conditions of pluralism. therefore. the majority culture cannot serve as the grounding of a shared identity. It must be replaced by universalistic principles of human rights and the rule of law. which do not. it is argued. imply the imposition of a particular majority culture on minorities. Each political community develops distinctive interpretations of the meaning of these principles over time. which become embodied in its political and legal institutions and practices. These in turn form a political culture that crystallizes around the country's constitution and makes those principles into a 'concrete universal'. This embedding of democratic and liberal principles in a distinctive political culture can. in turn. give rise to what Jürgen Habermas has called a "constitutional patriotism". which should replace nationalism as the focus of a common identity. In countries that have achieved a strong national consciousness. the political culture has long been entangled with the majority culture. This "fusion". argues Habermas. "must be dissolved if it is to be possible for different cultural. ethnic. and religious forms of life to coexist and interact on equal terms within *the same*political community".

The thrust of the argument is that democratic political practice can provide a sufficient stimulus to integration in complex democratic societies. and is indeed the only one properly available to them. There is no need for a background consensus based on cultural homogeneity to act as a 'catalyzing condition' for democracy to the extent that the democratic political process. involving public deliberation and decision-making. makes "a reasonable political understanding possible. even among strangers." Democracy. as a set of procedures. can secure legitimacy in the absence of more substantive commonalities between citizens and achieve social integration. Since it is not wedded to particular cultural premises. it can be responsive to changes in the cultural composition of the citizenry and generate a common political culture (Habermas 2001a. 73–74). Habermas's position. then. gives pride of place to the democratic process and to the political participation of citizens. which play a key role in securing social integration: "In complex societies. it is the deliberative opinion- and will-formation of citizens. grounded in the principles of popular sovereignty. that forms the ultimate medium for a form of abstract. legally constructed solidarity that reproduces itself through political participation".

But the democratic process can fulfil its role only if it achieves a certain level of output legitimacy: appropriate levels of solidarity are sustainable only if basic standards of social justice are satisfied. If it is to remain a source of solidarity. citizenship has to be seen as a valuable status. associated not only with civil and political rights. but also with the fulfilment of fundamental social and cultural rights.

For most liberal nationalists. this seems like putting the cart before the horse since a successful welfare state. they argue. is possible only if citizens already enjoy high levels of mutual trust and loyalty. Welfare policies suppose that we make sacrifices for anonymous others who differ from us in terms of their ethnic origin. religion and way of life. But in democracies. redistributive policies can be sustained only if they enjoy strong levels of public support. This support is dependent on a sense of common identity that transcends difference and motivates citizens to share their revenues with people whom they do not know. but to whom they feel related by common bonds. This sentiment implies reciprocity: the expectation that. in times of need. one could also benefit from the solidarity of fellow citizens.

Liberal nationalists and other critics of the postnationalist position go on to argue that freeing the liberal democratic state from its historical moorings is neither possible. nor necessary. They recognize that the link between liberal democracy and the nation is historically contingent rather than necessary or conceptual while adding that this does not mean that they can or should be dissociated Calling for the separation of a country's political culture from the majority group's culture is easier said than done. While it may be comparably easy to discard the most egregious forms of fusion. if there is the political will to do so (for instance. by de-establishing the Anglican church in the case of England). any political culture will be ethically patterned in ways that are difficult for members of the majority to appreciate. Expressions such as "cutting the umbilical cord" or "dissolving" the fusion overstate the extent to which a political culture may be disengaged from the background culture. This is not necessarily cause for alarm. it is argued. since the nation need not be construed in ways that exclude minorities. Nationhood can be understood in sufficiently 'thin' terms to accommodate minorities while being 'thick' enough to generate appropriate sentiments of solidarity. loyalty. and trust.

There are different versions of this thin understanding of nationhood. What they all share is the downplaying of substantive commonalities of descent. culture and religion to the benefit of political and legal principles and institutions. Still there are variations: David Miller defends a conception of public culture that goes beyond the political to cover social norms (such as honesty in filling tax returns) and may include certain cultural ideals (for instance. "religious beliefs or a commitment to preserve the purity of the national language") while Kymlicka argues that an appropriately thin conception of nationhood also discards assumptions that "members of the nation should share the same [...] life-style".

These differences notwithstanding. both conceptions are affirmed as inclusive since they describe national identity as flexible and open to change. Once immigrants are citizens. they can participate in the collective conversation by which citizens debate and constantly reinterpret the nation's identity. What immigrants are required to display is a "willingness to accept current political structures and to engage with the host community so that a new common identity can be forged". They are expected "to speak a common national language". "feel loyalty to national institutions" and "share a commitment to maintaining the nation as a single. self-governing community into the indefinite future".Given the thin version of national identity they propose. one might conclude that liberal nationalists are not that far from the constitutional patriotism of Jürgen Habermas. After all. both positions seem to give the central role to a common political culture.

The distance separating them becomes clear when we look at the political implications of their respective views. like when evaluating the prospects of the European Union. Liberal nationalists are often sceptical towards the European experiment while postnationalists are firm supporters. This difference flows from their respective conceptions of what makes and sustains a political culture as a source of integration. For liberal nationalists. continuity is essential: a political culture derives much of its strength from an anchoring in the history and narrative of a distinct political community extending backwards and forwards in time. They are sceptical of political voluntarism and. more specifically. towards what can be achieved through formal political institutions. Democratic procedures alone. divorced from a richer background. can neither generate nor sustain a robust political culture or a sense of common identity.

In contrast. postnationalists like Habermas consider that the democratic process is crucial. The postnationalist conception gives greater weight to political practice and to the legal and political institutions that sustain it rather than their cultural and historical moorings. This explains Habermas's militant support of the European project and. more specifically. his belief that adopting a constitution could have a "catalytic effect" on the process of constructing a 'more perfect Union'.

THE CHALLENGE OF GLOBALISATION

For the better part of the last century. conceptions of citizenship. despite many differences. have had one thing in common: the idea that the necessary framework for citizenship is the sovereign. territorial state. The legal status of citizen is essentially the formal expression of membership in a polity that has definite territorial boundaries within which citizens enjoy equal rights and exercise their political agency. In other words. citizenship. both as a legal status and as an activity. is thought to presuppose the existence of a territorially bounded political community. which extends over time and is the focus of a common identity. In the last twenty years. this premise has come under close scrutiny.

A host of phenomena. loosely associated under the heading 'globalisation'. have encouraged this critical awakening: exploding transnational economic exchange. competition and communication as well as high levels of migration. of cultural and social interactions have shown how porous those borders have become and led people to contest the relevance and legitimacy of state sovereignty. Three questions are particularly salient. First. the intensification of migratory movements from poorer to richer countries in the context of growing inequalities between North and South has led some authors to contest the state's moral right to choose its members by selectively closing its borders. Second. what R. Bauböck calls the "mismatch between citizenship and the territorial scope of legitimate authority" has prompted a growing questioning of the acceptability of the different rights accorded to citizens and non-citizens living within the same state. But if we question the tight association between the territorial state. citizenship and rights. are we not weakening the very institutional framework that makes citizenship a meaningful practice? This question raises a third set of issues as it assumes that the democratic nation-state is the only institutional context in which citizenship can thrive. This is contested by those who claim that citizenship can be exercised in a multiplicity of 'sites' both below and above the nation-state.

CITIZENSHIP AND BORDERS

Does the political community have the moral right to decide who can/cannot become a citizen or mustn't we recognize the right to free movement? Much of the philosophical debate has turned around two issues: firstly. on the nature of our obligations towards people from impoverished countries who seek better lives for themselves and their families; secondly. on the moral status of political communities and their supposed right to protect their integrity by excluding Non- members.

One way of characterizing our obligation to strangers insists that. absent any relations of cooperation. common humanity is our only bond. It is argued that only a rather weak. imperfect or conditional duty of assistance can be inferred from such a premise. This duty limits the basic right of the political community to distribute membership as it wishes without. in any way. displacing it. Individuals have a duty to assist strangers in urgent need if they can provide assistance without exposing themselves to significant risk or cost. At a collective level. the implications are more considerable as political communities have greater resources and can consider a broader range of benevolent actions at comparably negligible cost. The principle of mutual aid may justify redistribution of membership. territory. wealth and resources to the extent that certain states have more than they can reasonably be said to need. In this framework. redistributive policies remain. however. entirely dependent on wealthier countries' understanding of their needs and of the urgency of a stranger's situation. There is no obligation to give equal weight to the interests of non-members.

Institutionally. this position supports what the Geneva Convention on the Status of Refugees (United Nations 1951) calls the principle of "*non refoulement*": signatory states are not to deport refugees and asylum seekers to their countries of origin if this threatens their lives and freedom. It can also support claims in favour of increasing the number of immigrants admitted into richer countries. depending on how the latter evaluate the potential effects on their own interests.

Critics contend that our obligations towards migrants and asylum-seekers go well beyond this and call for a policy of open borders and/or deny the state's right to decide alone who exactly. and how many people. may enter its territory. Three basic strategies are employed: the first consists of arguing that freedom of movement is a fundamental human right. For example. some have argued that any theory recognizing the equal moral value of individuals and giving them moral primacy over communities cannot justify rejecting aliens' claims to admission and citizenship. As Joseph Carens demonstrated in an early article. this argument applies to the three main strands of contemporary liberal theory: libertarianism (*a la* Nozick). Rawlsianism and utilitarianism. If we give the principle of moral equality its full extension. the distinction between citizen and alien is morally arbitrary. justified neither by nature nor achievement. When evaluating border and immigration policies. the equal consideration of the interests of all affected (be they aliens or citizens) is required. Political communities cannot decide whether they can afford to accept refugee claimants or prospective immigrants simply according to their understanding of their own situation. needs and interests. Consideration of consequences (*e.g.* in terms of public order. the sustainability of welfare policies. the potential effects of a brain drain in developing countries. etc.) is not prohibited; what changes radically is how we are to evaluate them. Institutionally. this would doubtless lead to substantial changes in the immigration and refugee policies of most Western democracies.

A second strategy recently advocated by Arash Abizadeh (2008) relies on the principle of democratic legitimacy. holding that the exercise of coercive power is legitimate "only insofar as it is actually *justified by and to* the very people over whom it is exercised" (41). Since a regime of border control subjects both citizens and non-citizens to the state's coercive use of power. "the justification for a particular regime of border control is owed not just to those whom the boundary marks as members. but to Non-members as well" (45). The upshot to this argument is that. contrary to a long-held assumption. no democratic state has the right to unilaterally control its own borders. but must either allow freedom of movement or. at the very least. give voice to prospective immigrants when formulating border policy. The latter condition would itself lead to significant changes in immigration policies in the Western world. since jointly controlled borders would presumably be more porous as well.

The third strategy is less direct. To the extent that states do not satisfy their moral obligations to guarantee the universal human right to security and subsistence through international redistributive policies. they have a moral obligation to admit those wishing to enter. Here the idea of open borders is an instrumental. rather than intrinsic. moral principle: it is a means towards achieving global distributive justice. The advantage of this line of argument is that it faithfully reflects a central motivation for open borders: the outrage provoked by the huge inequalities between North and South and rich countries' role in perpetuating this situation. This strategy. if successful. would establish specific rights for people from poorer countries towards the North. and not simply a broadly framed right to free movement. to be 'equally' enjoyed by individuals of rich and poor countries alike.

To be convincing the argument must show: firstly. that severe global poverty requires immediate action; secondly. that it is a matter of justice. not charity. To that effect. it is crucial to show that the extreme poverty of some countries is not simply the result of endogenous factors (*e.g.* bad governance; corrupt political culture. etc.). but is linked to a global political and economic order that systematically produces an unjust distribution of resources and political power. which rich northern countries. as its main beneficiaries. are in no hurry to reform. The third step in this schema purportedly shows that justifications of restrictive immigration policies premised on ethico-political claims lose much of their force in the context of profound international inequalities and injustice. Proponents claim that regulating immigration in order to preserve the integrity of the political community is a legitimate goal only if duties of international distributive justice are satisfied. The argument's upshot is that "[r]ich Northern states have a double moral obligation to seriously fight global poverty and to let more people in".

Both supporters and critics of (more) open borders agree that liberal democratic political communities have a moral status and are worth preserving. They disagree over what exactly is worthy of protection and how much weight should be given to securing their integrity (however it is defined) relative to our duties of international justice.

The division of the world into states is arguably justifiable on functional grounds. to the extent that states appear as "first approximations of optimal units for allocating and producing the world's resources". If we think that states matter simply as local units of efficient production and distribution. then this would be the main consideration when evaluating immigration policies. Public order arguments would still matter. likewise claims pertaining to a society's economic capacity to secure its material reproduction. but not arguments relating to its cultural integrity or way of life. Unless. of course. the capacity of states to act as efficient units of production and distribution is linked to their being distinctive political communities with a particular culture of shared meanings worth preserving.

Over twenty years ago. Michael Walzer defended such a view. based on the idea that "distributive justice presupposes a bounded world within which distribution takes place". Since the goods to be divided. exchanged and shared among individuals have social meanings that are specific to particular communities. it is only within their boundaries that conflict can be resolved and distributive schemes judged either just or unjust. The crucial assumption here is that the "political community is probably the closest we can come to a world of common meanings. Language. history. and culture come together [...] to produce a collective consciousness". Politics itself. moreover. as a set of practices and institutions that shape the form and outcome that distributive conflicts take. "establishes its own bonds of commonality". To reject political communities' right to distribute the good of membership is to undermine their capacity to preserve their integrity. It is to condemn them to become nothing more then neighbourhoods. random associations lacking any legally enforceable admissions policies. The probable result of the free movement of individuals would be "casual aggregates" devoid of any internal cohesion and incapable of being a source of patriotic sentiments and solidarity. In a world of neighbourhoods. membership would become meaningless. The upshot of this is that we should recognize the political community's right to regulate admission with a view to securing its cultural. economic and political integrity.

Walzer's position. notably his choice of analogies. has been extensively discussed. His assumption that sovereign states constitute communities of shared meanings appears particularly shaky. Most often. existing states incorporate various political communities that are themselves internally pluralistic: linguistically. culturally and ideologically. In such cases. one would be hard pressed to identify the community whose integrity is at stake. Indeed. few states correspond to the picture Walzer envisages as the appropriate context for distributive justice.

This is not to say that political communities are merely functional units. As Habermas argues. if the communitarian position appears irrelevant in the face of the complexity and internal diversity of modern societies. it reminds us that modern states are a "political form of life" that cannot be "translated without remainder into the abstract form of institutions designed according to general legal principles". As forms of life. they include "the *politicocultural* context in which universalistic principles must be implemented. for only a population *accustomed* to freedom can keep the institutions of freedom alive". Here. Habermas refers yet again to his distinction between the political culture. which develops around universalistic constitutional principles. and the wider. background culture. It is the integrity of the former. not the latter that must be preserved: immigrants should be expected to integrate into the political culture of their new country. which means more than simply embracing abstract liberal-democratic principles.

They must "willingly engage" with the particular form that these principles take in a given society with its own specific history. Given that they come from different cultures. newcomers will bring distinct perspectives to the interpretation of the political constitution and may well affect its future development. But to the extent that their contribution can be understood as part of the democratic conversation. rather than as a conversation stopper. one cannot justify stricter limits to immigration on such grounds. What presumably can be argued is that the capacity of the polity to integrate newcomers in the political culture should be considered when setting admissions policies.

Liberal nationalists like Will Kymlicka make a similar argument: they claim that liberal egalitarian aims such as equality of opportunity and solidarity stand a much better chance of being realized in the context of a strong national culture. defined as a "societal culture" involving a "common language and social institutions". All things being equal. maintaining and strengthening such cultures serves a vital interest of individuals and liberal egalitarians should not strive for fully open borders. But does this mean that our interest in a strong national culture outweigh our duty to pursue international justice? From a liberal egalitarian perspective. the answer is clearly no.

The right of political communities to protect their integrity stands only under conditions of rough international equality. Under such conditions. limits to immigration would not cause substantial harm. but "would only reserve for the nationals of a country what aliens already have in their own country — namely. the chance to be free and equal citizens within their own national community". Under the present situation of radical inequality. however. restrictive policies of immigration allow richer countries to "hoard an unfair share of resources" and cannot be squared with the principle of the moral equality of persons. which requires that "we care equally about the well-being of all individuals. wherever they are born. and however little we interact with them".

Kymlicka doesn't say how we should interpret his conclusion as pertains to present policies of immigration: must we demand that the borders of Western democracies be opened until they honour their duties of international justice? Should we rather underscore their dual moral obligations to fight global poverty and allow in more immigrants? Or. since global poverty and injustice are the problems. wouldn't it be better to address them directly and see them as our first moral priority ? As Kok-Chor Tan remarks. the argument should be understood as supporting "the primacy of international justice. rather than as a claim about how to prioritize public policies and goals".

This primacy implies "that national projects of well-off nations lose their legitimacy if these nations are not also doing their fair share as determined by their duties of justice". Whether or not liberals should concentrate on reforming the international system as Thomas Pogge has urged or fight for both greater international distributive justice and more open borders as Veit Bader advises is a matter of strategy. The two prescriptions are by no means incompatible; insisting on the illegitimacy of restrictive immigration policies under current conditions may be a way to put rich countries on the spot and prod them to accept their moral responsibilities towards the world's poor.

LIBERAL NATIONALISM

Liberal Nationalism is a kind of nationalism identified by political philosophers who believe in a non-xenophobic form of nationalism compatible with liberal values of freedom. tolerance. equality. and individual rights. Ernest Renan and John Stuart Mill are often thought to be early liberal nationalists. Liberal nationalists often defend the value of national identity by saying that individuals need a national identity in order to lead meaningful. autonomous lives and that democratic polities need national identity in order to function properly.

Liberal nationalism. also known as civic nationalism or civil nationalism. is the form of nationalism in which the state derives political legitimacy from the active participation of its citizenry. from the degree to which it represents the "general will". It is often seen as originating with Jean-Jacques Rousseau and especially the social contract theories which take their name from his 1762 book *The Social Contract*. Civic nationalism lies within the traditions of rationalism and liberalism. but as a form of nationalism it is contrasted with ethnic nationalism. Membership of the civic nation is considered voluntary. Civic-national ideals influenced the development of representative democracy in countries such as the United States and France.

Liberal nationalism lies within the traditions of rationalism and liberalism. but as a form of nationalism it is contrasted with ethnic nationalism. Membership of the civic nation is considered voluntary. as in Ernest Renan's classical definition in "Qu'est-ce qu'une nation?" of the nation as a "daily referendum" characterized by the "will to live together". Civic-national ideals influenced the development of representative democracy in countries such as the United States and France.

States in which civic forms of nationalism predominate are often ex-settler colonies such as the United States. Canada. Mexico. Brazil. and Argentina. in which ethnic nationalism is difficult to construct on account of the diversity of ethnicities within the state. A notable exception is India. an ex-plantation colony. where civic nationalism has predominated due to the country's unparalleled linguistic. religious and ethnic diversity.

Civic-nationalist states are often characterized by adoption of the *jus soli* for granting citizenship in the country. deeming all persons born within the integral territory of the state citizens and members of the nation. regardless of their parents' origin. This serves to link national identity not with a people but rather with the territory and its history. and the history of previous occupants of the territory unconnected to the current occupants are often appropriated for national myths. In the United Kingdom. the Conservative Party and UK Independence Party which advocate British Unionism/British Nationalism and the Scottish National Party and Plaid Cymru. which advocate independence from the United Kingdom. and the Social Democratic and Labour Party. which supports a United Ireland. and Alliance Party of Northern Ireland are civic nationalist. Also. civic nationalism in post-Soviet Ukraine has prevailed since the Orange Revolution. Outside Europe. it has also been used to describe the Civil war era Republican party in the United States.

This is in contrast to ethnic nationalist political parties like the far-right British Nationalist Party and many nationalist parties found elsewhere in Europe. The SNP and Plaid Cymru were the first political parties to field elected candidates of an ethnic minority background in the devolved institutions of their respective nations–Bashir Ahmad in the Scottish Parliament. Mohammad Asghar in the Welsh Assembly; both are Muslims of origin from British India.

NATIONAL COMMUNISM

The term National Communism describes the ethnic minority communist currents that arose in the former Russian Empire after Vladimir Lenin's Bolshevik Party seized power in October 1917.

Left-wing socialists in Ukraine and the Muslim areas of the former tsarist empire also developed distinct variants of communism that continued in the USSR until 1928. Ukrainian and Muslim varaints differed from each other on two points in particular. The Muslims believed the fate of world revolution depended on events in Asia not Europe. They also argued alliances with the national bourgeoisie were necessary for the duration of the liberation struggle.

Class divisions had to be ignored.otherwise the national bourgeoisie would turn away from national liberation. ally with their imperial counterparts and thus ensure the ultimate collapse of any revolutionary struggle and national liberation. In its Muslim variant it was a synthesis of nationalism. communism and anarchism as well as religion. Muslim communists included people from both left and right wing groups which predated the Revolution. joining the between 1917 and 1920—some of whom later were Narkomnats. under the People's Commissar Joseph Stalin.

CIVIC NATIONALISM

Civic nationalism defines the nation as an association of people who identify themselves as belonging to the nation. who have equal and shared political rights. and allegiance to similar political procedures. According to the principles of civic nationalism. the nation is not based on common ethnic ancestry. but is a political entity whose core identity is not ethnicity. This civic concept of nationalism is exemplified by Ernest Renan in his lecture in 1882 "What is a Nation?". where he defined the nation as a "daily referendum" dependent on the will of its people to continue living together".

Civic Nationalism is a kind of non-xenophobic nationalism compatible with liberal values of freedom. tolerance. equality. and individual rights. Ernest Renan and John Stuart Mill are often thought to be early liberal nationalists. Liberal nationalists often defend the value of national identity by saying that individuals need a national identity in order to lead meaningful. autonomous lives and that liberal democratic polities need national identity in order to function properly.

Civic nationalism lies within the traditions of rationalism and liberalism. but as a form of nationalism it is contrasted with ethnic nationalism. Membership of the civic nation is considered voluntary. as in Ernest Renan's "daily referendum" formulation in What is a Nation?. Civic-national ideals influenced the development of representative democracy in countries such as the United States and France.

ETHNOCENTRISM

Whereas nationalism does not necessarily imply a belief in the superiority of one ethnicity over others. some nationalists support ethnocentric protectionism or ethnocentric supremacy. Studies have yielded evidence that such behaviour may be derived from innate preferences in humans from infancy. The term ethnocentrism is a more accurate and meaningful term.

NATIONAL PURITY

Some nationalists exclude certain groups. Some nationalists. defining the national community in ethnic. linguistic. cultural. historic. or religious terms may then seek to deem certain minorities as not truly being a part of the 'national community' as they define it. Sometimes a mythic homeland is more important for the national identity than the actual territory occupied by the nation.

LEFT-WING NATIONALISM

Left-wing nationalism refers to any political movement that combines left-wing politics with nationalism. Many nationalist movements are dedicated to national liberation. in the view that their nations are being persecuted by other nations and thus need to exercise self-determination by liberating themselves from the accused persecutors. Anti-revisionist Marxist-Leninism is closely tied with this ideology. and practical examples include Stalin's early work *Marxism and the National Question* and his Socialism in One Country edict. which declares that nationalism can be used in an internationalist context. fighting for national liberation without racial or religious divisions. Other examples of left-wing nationalism include Fidel Castro's 26th of July Movement that launched the Cuban Revolution ousting the American-backed Fulgencio Batista in 1959. Ireland's Sinn Féin. Wales's Plaid Cymru. Scotland's SNP. the Awami League in Bangladesh and the African National Congress in South Africa.

TERRITORIAL NATIONALISM

Territorial nationalists assume that all inhabitants of a particular nation owe allegiance to their country of birth or adoption. A sacred quality is sought in the nation and in the popular memories it evokes. Citizenship is idealised by territorial nationalist A criterion of a territorial nationalism is the establishment of a mass. public culture based on common values and traditions of the population.

Pan-Nationalism

Pan-nationalism is unique in that it cover a large area span. Pan-nationalism focuses more on "clusters" of ethnic groups.

ULTRANATIONALISM

Ultranationalism is a zealous nationalism that expresses extremist support for one's nationalist ideals. It is often characterized by authoritarianism. efforts towards reduction or stoppage of immigration. expulsion and or oppression of non-native populations within the nation or its territories. demagoguery of leadership. emotionalism. scapegoating outsiders in socioeconomic crises. fomenting talk of presumed. real. or imagined enemies. predicating the existence of threats to the survival of the native. dominant or otherwise idealized national ethnicity or population group. instigation or extremist reaction to crack-down policies in law enforcement. efforts to limit international trade through tariffs. tight control over businesses and production. militarism. populism and propaganda.

Prevalent ultranationalism typically leads to or is the result of conflict within a state. and or between states. and is identified as a condition of pre-war in national politics. In its extremist forms ultranationalism is characterized as a call to war against enemies of the nation/state. secession or. in the case of ethnocentrist ultranationalism. genocide. Fascism is a form of palingenetic ultranationalism that promotes "class collaboration". a totalitarian state. and irredentism or expansionism to unify and allow the growth of a nation. Fascists sometimes promote ethnic or cultural nationalism. Fascism stresses the subservience of the individual to the state. and the need to absolute and unquestioned loyalty to a strong ruler.

ANTI-COLONIAL NATIONALISM

This form of nationalism came about during the decolonialisation of the post war period. It was a reaction mainly in Africa and Asia against being subdued by foreign powers. This form of nationalism took many guises. including the peaceful passive resistance movement led by Gandhi in the Indian subcontinent Benedict Anderson argued that anti-colonial nationalism is grounded in the experience of literate and bilingual indigenous intellectuals fluent in the language of the imperial power. schooled in its "national" history. and staffing the colonial administrative cadres up to but not including its highest levels. Post-colonial national governments have been essentially indigenous forms of the previous imperial administration.

CRITICISMS

Critics of nationalism have argued that it is often unclear what constitutes a "nation". or why a nation should be the only legitimate unit of political rule. A nation is a cultural entity. and not necessarily a political association. nor is it necessarily linked to a particular territorial area - although nationalists argue that the boundaries of a nation and a state should. as far as possible. coincide. Philosopher A.C. Grayling describes nations as artificial constructs. "their boundaries drawn in the blood of past wars". He argues that "there is no country on earth which is not home to more than one different but usually coexisting culture. Cultural heritage is not the same thing as national identity".

Nationalism is inherently divisive because it highlights perceived differences between people. emphasizing an individual's identification with their own nation. The idea is also potentially oppressive because it submerges individual identity within a national whole. and gives elites or political leaders potential opportunities to manipulate or control the masses. Much of the early opposition to nationalism was related to its geopolitical ideal of a separate state for every nation. The classic nationalist movements of the 19th century rejected the very existence of the multi-ethnic empires in Europe. Even in that early stage. however. there was an ideological critique of nationalism. That has developed into several forms of anti-nationalism in the western world. The Islamic revival of the 20th century also produced an Islamic critique of the nation-state.At the end of the 19th century. Marxists and other socialists produced political analysis that were critical of the nationalist movements then active in central and eastern Europe.

In the liberal political tradition there is widespread criticism of 'nationalism' as a dangerous force and a cause of conflict and war between nation-states. Nationalism has often been exploited to encourage citizens to partake in the nations' conflicts. Such examples include The Two World Wars. where nationalism was a key component of propaganda material. Liberals do not generally dispute the existence of the nation-states. The liberal critique also emphasizes individual freedom as opposed to national identity. which is by definition collective.

The pacifist critique of nationalism also concentrates on the violence of nationalist movements. the associated militarism. and on conflicts between nations inspired by jingoism or chauvinism. National symbols and patriotic assertiveness are in some countries discredited by their historical link with past wars. especially in Germany. Famous pacifist Bertrand Russell criticizes nationalism of diminishing individual's capacity to judge his or her fatherland's foreign policy. William Blum has said this in other words: "If love is blind. patriotism has lost all five senses." Albert Einstein stated that "Nationalism is an infantile disease... It is the measles of mankind." The anti-racist critique of nationalism concentrates on the attitudes to other nations. and especially on the doctrine that the nation-state exists for one national group to the exclusion of others. This view emphasizes the chauvinism and xenophobia that have often resulted from nationalist sentiment.

Norman Naimark relates the rise of nationalism to ethnic cleansing and genocide. Political movements of the left have often been suspicious of nationalism. again without necessarily seeking the disappearance of the existing nation-states. Marxism has been ambiguous towards the nation-state. and in the late 19th century some Marxist theorists rejected it completely. For some Marxists the world revolution implied a global state; for others it meant that each nation-state had its own revolution. A significant event in this context was the failure of the social-democratic and socialist movements in Europe to mobilize a cross-border workers' opposition to World War I. At present most. but certainly not all. left-wing groups accept the nation-state. and see it as the political arena for their activities.

Anarchism has developed a critique of nationalism that focuses on its role in justifying and consolidating state power and domination. Through its unifying goal it strives for centralization both in specific territories and in a ruling elite of individuals while it prepares a population for capitalist exploitation. Within anarchism this subject has been treated extensively by Rudolf Rocker in *Nationalism and Culture* and by the works of Fredy Perlman such as *Against His-Story. Against Leviathan* and "The Continuing Appeal of Nationalism".

In the Western world. the most comprehensive current ideological alternative to nationalism is cosmopolitanism. Ethical cosmopolitanism rejects one of the basic ethical principles of nationalism: that humans owe more duties to a fellow member of the nation. than to a non-member. It rejects such important nationalist values as national identity and national loyalty. However. there is also a political cosmopolitanism. which has a geopolitical programme to match that of nationalism: it seeks some form of world state. with a world government. Very few people openly and explicitly support the establishment of a global state. but political cosmopolitanism has influenced the development of international criminal law. and the erosion of the status of national sovereignty. In turn. nationalists are deeply suspicious of cosmopolitan attitudes. which they equate with eradication of diverse national cultures. While internationalism in the cosmopolitan context by definition implies cooperation among nations and states. and therefore the existence of nations. proletarian internationalism is different. in that it calls for the international working class to follow its brethren in other countries irrespective of the activities or pressures of the national government of a particular sector of that class. Meanwhile. most anarchists reject nation-states on the basis of self-determination of the majority social class. and thus reject nationalism. Instead of nations. anarchists usually advocate the creation of cooperative societies based on free association and mutual aid without regard to ethnicity or race.

ANTI-NATIONALISM

Anti-nationalism denotes the sentiments associated with the opposition to nationalism. arguing that it is undesirable or dangerous. Some anti-nationalists are humanitarians or humanists who pursue an idealist form of world community. and self-identify as world citizens. They reject chauvinism. jingoism and militarism. and want humans to live in peace rather than perpetual conflict. They do not necessarily oppose the concepts of countries. nation states. national boundaries. cultural preservation or identity politics.

Some anti-nationalists oppose all types of nationalism. even ethnic nationalism among oppressed minority groups. This strain of anti-nationalism typically advocates the elimination of national boundaries. Variations on this theme are often seen in Marxist theory. Marx and Engels rejected nationalism as a whole. believing *"the working class have no country"*. More recently. certain groups descended from the Maoist tradition of Marxism have moved towards this fiercely anti-nationalist stance in a different way than Trotskyists. saying that although it may be a painful and unpopular position to hear. ultimately opposing all nationalism strengthens proletarian internationalism. Many Trotskyists. however. such as Chris Harman. were critical of nationalism while advocating support for what they saw as progressive national struggles.

In recent times. Islamism has been described as anti-nationalist movement. emphasizing Muslims and discarding the notion of nationality. Anarchism has developed a critique of nationalism that focuses on nationalism's role in justifying and consolidating state power and domination. Through its unifying goal. nationalism strives for centralization. both in specific territories and in a ruling elite of individuals. while it prepares a population for capitalist exploitation. Within anarchism. this subject has been treated extensively by Rudolf Rocker in *Nationalism and Culture* and by the works of Fredy Perlman. such as *Against His-Story. Against Leviathan* and "The Continuing Appeal of Nationalism".

In his "Aphorisms on the Wisdom of Life". Arthur Schopenhauer rejected nationalism. seeing it as an abandonment of personal identity. The philosophy of Friedrich Nietzsche can also be seen as opposing all forms of nationalism. although he opposed virtually every other form of social movement and ideology as well. Søren Kierkegaard's philosophy is a criticism and vehement rejection of Christian nationalism.

BANAL NATIONALISM

Banal nationalism refers to the everyday representations of the nation which build an imagined sense of national solidarity and belonging amongst humans. The term is derived from Michael Billig's 1995 book of the same name. Today the term is used primarily in academic discussion of identity formation and geopolitics.Examples of banal nationalism include the use of flags in everyday contexts. sporting events. national songs. symbols on money. popular expressions and turns of phrase. patriotic clubs. the use of implied togetherness in the national press. for example. the use of terms such as *the* prime minister. *the* weather. *our* team. and divisions into "domestic" and "international" news. etc... Many of these symbols are most effective because of their constant repetition. and almost subliminal nature.

Michael Billig's primary purpose in coining the term was to clearly differentiate every-day. endemic nationalism from extremist variants. He argued that the academic and journalistic focus on extreme nationalists. independence movements. and xenophobes in the 1980s and 90s obscured the modern strength of nationalism. by implying that it was a fringe ideology. He noted the almost unspoken assumption of the utmost importance of the nation in political discourse of the time. for example in the calls to protect Kuwait during the 1991 Gulf War. or the Falkland Islands in 1982.

He argues that the "hidden" nature of modern nationalism makes it a very powerful ideology. partially because it remains largely unexamined and unchallenged. yet remains the basis for powerful political movements. and most political violence in the world today. However. in earlier times calls to the "nation" were not as important. when religion. loyalty. or family might have been invoked more successfully to mobilize action. He also uses the concept to dispute post-modernist claims that the nation-state is in decline. noting particularly the continued hegemonic power of American nationalism.

BUSINESS NATIONALISM

Business nationalism is a right-wing economic nationalist ideology held by a sector of the political right in the United States.

Business nationalists are ultraconservative business and industrial leaders who favour a protectionist trade policy and an isolationist foreign policy. Locked in a power struggle with corporate international interests. business nationalists often use populist rhetoric and anti-elite scapegoating to build a broader base of support in the middle class and working class.

In the past. business nationalism has also been the main sector in the U.S. from which union–busting campaigns have emerged. Sectors of business nationalism also have promoted white supremacist segregationism. the Red Scares. anti–immigrant sentiment. and allegations of Jewish banking conspiracies.

HISTORY

Ultraconservative business and industrial leaders who saw the New Deal implemented in the United States between 1933 and 1936 as proof of an imagined sinister alliance by international finance capital and communist-controlled labour unions to destroy free enterprise became known as "business nationalists".

In the mid-1930s. Gerald L. K. Smith carried the banner for business nationalists. many of whom were isolationists and would later oppose the entry of the United States into World War II. Smith received public and financial support from wealthy businessmen who were concentrated in "nationalist-oriented industries". These included the heads of national oil companies Quaker State. Penzoil. and Kendall Refining; automakers Henry Ford. and John Francis Dodge and Horace Elgin Dodge. Two business nationalists who networked other ultraconservatives were J. Howard Pew. president of Sun Oil. and William B. Bell. president of the chemical company American Cyanamid.

Pew and Bell were on the executive committee of the National Association of Manufacturers. Pew also funded the American Liberty League. Sentinels of the Republic. and other groups that flirted with fascism prior to World War II. After World War II. Pew funded conservative Christian evangelicals such as Reverend Billy Graham.

The John Birch Society. founded in 1959. incorporated many themes from pre-WWII right-wing groups opposed to the New Deal. and had its base in the business nationalist sector. The society heavily disseminated an ultraconservative business nationalist critique of corporate internationalists networked through groups such as the Council on Foreign Relations. Today business nationalism is represented by ultraconservative political figures such as Pat Buchanan.

CRITICISM

According to progressive scholar Mark Rupert. the right-wing anti-globalist worldview of business nationalists "envisions a world in which Americans are uniquely privileged. inheritors of a divinely inspired socio–political order which must at all costs be defended against external intrusions and internal subversion." Rupert argues that this reactionary analysis seeks to challenge corporate power without comprehending the nature of "capital concentration and the transnational socialization of production." The reactionary analysis absent this understanding breeds social alienation and intensifies "scapegoating and hostility towards those seen as outside of. different or dissenting from its vision of national identity." As alienation builds. more overtly fascistic forces will attempt to pull some of these angry people into an ideological framework that further justifies demonization of the chosen "Other."

Investigave reporter Chip Berlet argues:

- When populist consumer groups. such as those led by Ralph Nader. forge uncritical alliances with business nationalists to rally against GATT and NAFTA. an opportunity emerges for the anti–elite rhetoric of right wing populism to piggy-back onto a legitimate progressive critique. Why is this a problem? Business nationalism carries with it its right-wing baggage. Pat Buchanan's rhetoric is an example of this baggage. His racist. antisemitic and zenophobic inclinations reflect business nationalism's right-wing national chauvinism. At the core of right wing populism is the "producerist narrative" where the main scapegoats are people of colour. especially Blacks. This narrative diverts attention from the White supremacist subtext. It uses coded language to mobilize resentment against people of colour through attacks on issues immediately relevant to them. such as welfare. immigration. tax. or education policies. Women. gay men and lesbians. abortion providers. youth. students. and environmentalists are also frequently scapegoated in this manner.

Enabling and (Dis)abling Discourses of Social Citizenship

Theories of citizenship have traditionally been predicated upon notions of the universal subject – a subject which presupposes a white. able. male body. engaged in market participation. Citizenship discourses appear to offer very little to people with disabilities either theoretically or practically as disability has been absent from most all key citizenship debates. Dominant theories of liberal citizenship highlight individualism and rights. Civic republicanism and communitarianism stress obligations. participation and community. These hegemonic ideologies of citizenship have offered a dichotomy of rights versus participation with space only for the able bodied subject engaged in market participation.

In response. feminist theories have presented a variety of alternatives informed through themes of private versus public. inclusion versus exclusion and have expanded the range of participation from the market to care-giving and attempted to offer the subject as embodied. However. even in the most radical of reconstructions. dichotomies remain a central tenet and the continuous reference point is always that of the able body. leaving no space for disabled subjectivity. Helen Meekosha and Leanne Dowse pose the important question. "How do we begin to rewrite the story of what it means to be a disabled citizen?"

Given the inherent problems with current notions of citizenship. an enabling discourse cannot be concerned with participation versus rights. private versus public or inclusion versus exclusion as a person with a disability is a oxymoron within these bifurcated models.

The disabled citizen cannot become a subject unto his/her own if trapped at the intersection of existing binary oppositions. The question therefore can be posed. how do we reconstruct a story of what it means to be a disabled citizen if we are presupposing that the citizen remains an unproblematic subject? To understand how disability and citizenship intersect. a deconstruction of dominant citizenship discourses highlighting the absence of disability is necessary before a reconstruction of citizenship inclusive of a differently abled subject can be achieved.

Contemporary theories of liberal citizenship often begin with an analysis of T. H. Marshall's post-war conception of citizenship which focuses on according people a number of citizenship rights. While it is beyond the scope of this paper to engage in a comprehensive debate on Marshall's theory. his influential theory will be briefly outlined to demonstrate how the subject within contemporary liberal citizenship requires a deconstruction beyond what has been achieved in the literature thus far.

According to Marshall. citizenship is a matter of ensuring that everyone is treated as a full and equal member of society. Marshall offers a tripartite view of citizenship. dividing it along the lines of civil. political and social. and is concerned with notions of liberty and equality. achievable through civil and political rights which grant full and equal membership. Citizenship is defined as:A status bestowed to those who are full members of a community. All who possess the status are equal with respect to the rights and duties with which the status is endowed. There is no universal principle that determines what those rights and duties shall be. but societies in which citizenship is a developing institution create an image of an ideal citizen against which achievement can be measured and towards which aspiration can be directed.

For Marshall. the fullest expression of citizenship requires a liberal-democratic welfare state so civil. political and social rights can be guaranteed to all. The welfare state in Marshall's view ensures that every member of society feels like a full member and is able to participate in and enjoy common life. When any of these rights are withheld or violated. people will be marginalised and unable to participate. This model has often been referred to as 'passive citizenship' due to the absence of any obligation to participate in public life. While Marshall did not specifically engage with disability. he believed that social rights enabled what he termed the 'the disadvantaged' to enter the mainstreams of society and effectively exercise their civil and political rights. Social rights for Marshall range from the right to a modicum of economic welfare and security to the right to share to the full in the social heritage and to live the life of a civilised being according to the standards prevailing in the society.

The liberal view of the citizen is inherently problematic for people with disabilities on a number of complex levels. The key site of rendering the disabled subject invisible is that the universal notion of citizenship as a 'status' and as a set of 'rights' confers the subject as equal outside of societal structures. This is poses a series of problems for people with disabilities as it is often the societal structures which render them oppressed. An individual cannot achieve full participation if the means to achieve such participation are contributing to the very exclusion they wish to overcome. In other words. if we use Marshall's notion that to *withhold* rights renders the individual unequal and unable to participate as a citizen (therefore no longer possessing the necessary full status). this assumes that equality *precedes* the rights universally granted. and only by removing such given rights does a person become marginalised. Furthermore. it is underpinned by assumptions that once such rights are granted. the status itself is free of both socio-cultural and political-economic inequalities.

This is problematic for the individual who is unable to participate in any citizenship realm due to their citizen 'status' being inherently bound in socio-cultural and political-economic injustices. What of the individual who is further marginalised by attempts to grant them full participation? To enable a person to be granted full and equal rights. what ever is being granted must be value free. People with disabilities within a liberal framework cannot achieve such value free justice. nor full equality. nor can they ever achieve the status of 'citizen'. for the reference point remains an unproblematised abled bodied individual with capacities assumed to be equal. Within such a framework. the implication of granting social rights (thereby assuming ability to equally participate in civil and political rights) is in itself problematic and requires further deconstruction. as such rights overlook the fact that it is societal structures themselves which are a site for injustices. In the example of social security – which is a social right according to Marshall and a means for achieving access to the political and civil realms – the ability to access and obtain social security benefits does not remove the multiple and complex barriers which a person with a disability faces. Social rights therefore do not in themselves enable the disabled subject to compete equally in civil and political society.

An alternative view to liberalism is civic republicanism (or communitarianism) and there has been a revival of these ideologies in response to the rights based notions found in liberalism. These discourses view citizenship as an activity or as practise. not just a status. Central to the civic republicanism notion of citizen is a conception of individuals as not being logically prior to society. In civic republican discourse it is believed that a citizen should undertake certain duties and responsibilities and be loyal to the state rather than to individual interests. Communitarians object to the asocial concept of the self in liberalism as the self is seen as both socially constructed and embedded in a cultural context. Civic republicanism has focussed on the need to create a political community and a common bond between citizens which closes the differences of class. religion and culture. This discourse purports that identity is shared within a political community and this identity is seen as stemming partly from self-determination and partly from a common history.

Such a view has been critiqued by Meekosha and Dowse who argue that notions of active citizenship require people to take their responsibilities seriously as well as claiming their rights and this poses problems for people who have different or competing communities. such as people with disabilities. Modern states are not socially and culturally homogonous. and as the idea of civic virtue was founded upon the twin premises of a tightly knit community and politically active citizens it is clearly problematic today.

Civic republicanism is not a rights based manner of thinking and therefore. according to Adrian Oldfield the discourse tends to assume that "citizens possess the knowledge and skills. the level of wellbeing. amount of time. and the freedoms of speech and association that are all necessary for the practice of citizenship". This statement is reflective of how a person with a disability would find it difficult to achieve citizen subjectivity as the tenets within this discourse are founded upon the unproblematised subject. This is further highlighted through the way in which civic republicanism stresses a rough economic equality among citizens. As people with disabilities experience a range of injustices at both the socio-cultural and political-economic levels. this discourse of citizenship will find it difficult to create a space for disability or a person with a disability. as the genesis of the 'citizen' is an undifferentiated individual. Using the example of current labour market structures. it would be questionable whether alleged common employment history or common bonds experienced within the workplace are similar for both a person with a disability and an able-bodied worker.

In response to both liberal and civic republicanism views of citizenship. feminist literature has made valuable contributions to citizenship discourses and created embodied spaces in which to deconstruct the universalist. male notions of citizenship. While the range of feminist work on citizenship is quite varied and complex. this chapter will now examine several key feminist alternatives in order to demonstrate how they remain incomplete for people with disabilities. and in particular. for women with disabilities.

Carol Pateman in her explanation of patriarchal institutions offers a radical critique of the concept of universal citizenship in classical political theory and has been widely influential in enabling spaces within citizenship discourses to be inclusive of women. Pateman (1992) suggests that women are excluded from politics as a result of the private public divide being based upon a male norm. She believes that a sexually differentiated citizenship which distinguishes between men and women as different but equal individuals is ideal. Pateman (1992) maintains that women should be included as citizens based upon their caring work and that women should be incorporated into citizenship discourses as 'women' - rather than having a gender-neutral citizenship. Citizenship needs to be rethought from the viewpoint of the female citizen. Pateman argues that if both sexes are to be full citizens "the meaning of sexual difference has to cease to be the difference between freedom and subordination". Citizenship in this view needs to include women and once it does so. Pateman believes that the concept of citizen would change. This theory. while worthy of far more attention than can be given here. is problematic for people with disabilities - and in particular for women with disabilities as it presumes that women are a homogenous category firstly capable of 'caring' tasks. and secondly willing to do such work.

This point has been taken up by Mary Dietz (1992) who states that as long as feminists only focus on social and economic concerns around children. family. schools. work or wages etc. they will not articulate a truly political vision or address the problem of citizenship. Citizenship cannot be reformulated to 'fit women'. but rather should be deconstructed from the dichotomies upon which it is constructed. A gendered discourse of citizenship is problematic for women who do not fit into the normalised gender. such as women with disabilities. The double oppression which disabled women and subsequently such a gendered theory of citizenship contributes further to the injustices which people with disabilities face. Meekosha and Dowse argue that feminist analysis which separated the private from the public has not incorporated an examination of people with disabilities. Women with disabilities often inhabit a unique space somewhere between the private and the public. while seen as remaining a 'burden' in both. People with disabilities are conceived as having neither familial responsibility or public presence and are not constituted in traditional 'masculine' terms or embraced by feminist critique which equates care-giving with responsibility as a form of citizenship.

An alternative view of citizenship has been offered by Ruth Lister (2003) whose view is premised upon her claim that citizenship is a process. not just an outcome. where the struggle for rights is equally as important as the rights obtained. This perspective Lister argues. enables citizens to be active participants in political and welfare institutions rather than passive holders of rights. Lister maintains that the balance between rights and obligations and the nature of each is at the heart of mainstream debates on citizenship. She argues that whilst citizenship rights are represented as essentially abstract and universal. it is possible to incorporate notions of diversity and difference into the conceptualisation without sacrificing the principle of common and equal rights which in itself is necessary for the accommodation of difference.

Lister proposes that a reconception of citizenship should be formulated through synthesising the rights and participatory traditions via the notion of human agency. Lister feels that by embracing elements of the two main historical citizenship traditions. citizenship can emerge as a dynamic concept in which "process and outcome stand in a dialectical relationship to each other". Lister suggests that the idea of human agency as citizenship is conceived as both a status involving a wider range of rights. and as a practice involving political participation. To be a full citizen means to be able to enjoy the rights of citizenship necessary for agency and social and political participation. and to act as a citizen involves fulfilling the full potential of the status.

This theory is certainly beneficial for people with disabilities as it begins to address how it is not just the outcome of rights that is important (as in the case of liberal and civil republican views) but also the means through which full citizenship is achieved. The disability movement is engaged in a constant struggle to obtain and to reaffirm rights and the means for participation. Lister also avoids a gendering of citizenship through her notion of human agency which can overcome the current exclusionary dichotomies found in many citizenship discourses. However. the notion of human agency for people with disabilities within Lister's framework is problematic as Lister appears to imply human agency is a given. and that it is the *means* for attainment of full citizenship. where as in fact for people with disabilities. the ability to exercise human agency itself is at the core of the struggle for full citizenship and therefore a deconstruction of it is necessary *preceding* its use to attain citizenship. Furthermore. the concepts of 'status' and 'participation' which Lister utilises have not been sufficiently deconstructed from their original flawed meanings within the liberal and civic republicanism traditions. It is questionable whether the socio-cultural and political-economic injustices which underpin such concepts can be overcome through binding them with human agency. It is also debatable as to whether the synthesis of two historically problematic theories will actually create one *un*problematic theory. For people with disabilities who have been excluded from the very definitions of status and participation. and whose human agency is challenged and constrained on a range of complexities. more than a synthesis of existing citizenship discourses is required to enable a space for their own subjectivity.

It is the structural conditions that contribute to rendering people with disabilities as less than full citizens and this is an area which is not been given sufficient attention by many feminist theories. Models of citizenship which privilege 'female tasks' such as private caring. or privilege an unproblematised notion of human agency remain homogenised towards an able body and exclude important group differences. The exclusion from key citizenship debates of the historical and social circumstances of individuals has been taken up by Iris Marion Young who offers a radically alternative view of citizenship.

In Young's (1998) view. citizenship requires the development of a theory based not on the assumption of an undifferentiated humanity but rather on the assumption that there *are* group differences and some groups are actually or potentially disadvantaged. Young believes that the best way to realise the inclusion and participation of everyone in full citizenship is by the concept of differentiated citizenship. This approach to citizenship has been widely acclaimed by other feminists as it offers a rearticulation of citizenship which is inclusive of diversity and difference. Young's theory can be useful as it attempts to be inclusive of not just women. but of other oppressed groups – namely people with disabilities.

Young (1998) importantly raises the point that rights and rules which are universally formulated are blind to differences of race. culture. gender. age or disability and thereby perpetuate rather than undermine oppression. This is the evident problem in both liberal and civil republican discourses of citizenship.

Young believes that the universal notions found in contemporary theories of citizenship are problematic as they place citizenship above particular group and individual differences.

In Young's view. there are two key meanings attached to universal citizenship. Firstly. universality is defined according to what citizens have in common as opposed to how they differ. Secondly. universality presupposes the laws and rules apply to everyone equally and is therefore blind to individual and group differences. As previously noted. for particular groups such as those with a disability. it is the norms and laws which perpetuate rather than eliminate injustices.

The inclusion and participation of everyone in social and political institutions. Young suggests. requires the articulation of special rights which attend to group differences. In seeking a differential theory of citizenship. Young is aware of a contradictory problem which can occur which she refers to 'the dilemma of difference'. Young notes how for oppressed and disadvantaged groups seeking full inclusion and participation. they must continue to deny that there are any essential differences so that there is no justifications where such groups can be denied the equal opportunities to participate in the socio-cultural and political-economy realm. Conversely. Young further notes how such groups have found it necessary to affirm that there *are* often group-based differences which make the application of a strict principle of equal treatment. especially in competition for positions. unfair because such differences put those groups at a disadvantage. Young gives the example of how there has been some success in winning special rights for people with physical and mental disabilities in the past twenty years and suggests this is a clear case of where promoting equality in participation and inclusion requires attending to the particular needs of different groups.

While Young's differentiated citizenship theory has much to offer oppressed groups and individuals - and in particular for people with disabilities. it offers a substantial base for obtaining subjectivity - some key problems persist. Nancy Fraser (1997) has been critical of Young for having an essentialist notion of the groups and for privileging cultural groups. While Young's group differentiated theory may be suitable for Native Americans or Jewish Americans. it is less applicable for other groups such as people with disabilities. gays and lesbians. women or African Americans. Young's definition of a social group also attempts to cover both cultural and political-economic phenomena which is problematic. Fraser (1997) maintains a single conception which encompasses several disparate modes of collectivity (such as gender. race. ethnic groups. sexualities and social classes) may result in the loss of important conceptual distinctions. For a person with a disability. the assumption of homogeneity overlooks differences within disability. Often disability is wrongly viewed as an overarching category. however there are significant variations in the type. degree and experiences of disability and these distinctions are underpinned by difference in gender. class. race and/or sexuality. Fraser (1997) suggests that a group differentiation perspective can lead to one of the modes of collectivity being implicitly dominant where its characteristics will be projected as the characteristics of all social groups. This latter point is crucial for a person with a disability as often it is the disability which is seen first and foremost and other characteristics. such as gender. sexuality or class are subsumed. An inclusive theory of citizenship for people with disabilities cannot reside upon simply 'group differentiation' and so while Young offers us a hopeful theory. it is only the first step and remains incomplete. Nancy Fraser's (1998) work on redistribution and recognition attempts to fill some of the absent spaces that can be found with the above citizenship discourses. Fraser overlooks disability in her work. however her theory of justice can Non-etheless be drawn on and utilised by people with disabilities in developing an embodied theory of citizenship.

Fraser proposes two broadly conceived. analytically distinct. understandings of justice. The first is socioeconomic which stems from the political-economic structures of society. Examples are exploitation. economic marginalisation and deprivation. For people with disabilities a key area of injustice is access to the labour market. Furthermore. for those who choose or are forced to live outside the labour market. a person with a disability is marginalised and deprived in the structure of the social security system. The second type of injustice Fraser notes is cultural or symbolic which stems from social patterns of representation. interpretation and communication.

Examples include cultural domination. non-recognition and disrespect. Although Fraser maintains there are various differences between socioeconomic injustice and cultural injustice. both are pervasive in contemporary societies and both are inherently bound in processes and practices that systematically disadvantage some groups of people. While Fraser does not include people with disabilities in the groups discussed. it can be argued that people with disabilities are clearly and most obviously systematically disadvantaged through the twin processes of socio-cultural and political-economic practices. Importantly. Fraser (1998) notes how her distinction between economic injustice and cultural injustice is an analytical one. as in practice the two are intertwined.

It is Fraser's (1998) view that the remedy for economic injustice is political-economic restructuring which could involve redistributing income. reorganising the division of labour or transforming other basic economic structures. Collectively these are referred to as 'redistribution'. For people with disabilities. the achievement of full and inclusive citizenship cannot be realised without labour market and social security issues being addressed. as these form the twin pillars of disability policy. thereby forming the heart of justice and citizenship for people with disabilities. Fraser (1998) believes that the remedy for cultural injustice is cultural or symbolic change. which could involve revaluing disrespected identities or recognising and valorising cultural diversity. Collectively these are referred to as 'recognition'. For people with disabilities. the stigma. ignorance and fear of disability requires redressing. While the disability movement has made invaluable contributions to promoting differently abled views. it is unfortunate that (as of yet) these have not translated into a full and equal recognition of disability.

Fraser (1998) states that recognition claims often take the form of calling attention to the specificity of some groups and thus tend to promote group differentiation. While in contrast. redistribution claims often call for abolishing economic arrangements which underpin group specificity and thus tend to promote group de-differentiation. This means the politics of recognition and redistribution have mutually contradictory aims as the former promotes group differentiation whereas the latter undermines it. Fraser rightly notes how the two kinds of claims thus stand in tension with each other and can interfere or even work against one another. While the following issue will be more fully explicated in forthcoming work. it is critical to draw attention here to how the contradictory aims of redistribution and recognition mirrors the tensions found in employment Programmes and social security benefits for people with disabilities. The OECD refer to these as "twin but contradictory goals" and state that "how to reconcile these twin goals has yet to be resolved". This inherent problem. while not targeted to disability. is also realised by Fraser who states:

The redistribution-recognition dilemma is real. There is no neat theoretical move by which it can be wholly dissolved or resolved. The best we can do is try to soften the dilemma by finding approaches that minimise conflicts between redistribution and recognition in cases where both must be pursued simultaneously.

Along with redistribution and recognition remedies. Fraser argues that we also need to develop an alternative version of anti-essentialism. one which permits the link between a cultural politics of identity and difference with a social politics of justice and equality. This is what is inherently missing from other citizenship discourses delineated within this paper. For people with disabilities. full and equal citizenship cannot be attained until the very structures of injustices which stem concurrently from socio-cultural and political-economic realms are deconstructed to be inclusive of the disabled body. As Meekosha and Dowse rightly note. major citizenship debates are influenced by race. ethnicity. class or gender identity but all neglect disability and people with disabilities. Therefore. citizenship discourses which focus on dichotomies of rights versus participation. or private versus public. or inclusion versus exclusion are inherently flawed for a person with a disability. The reference point within such bifurcated models rests upon normative judgements of the abled bodied subject. It is the fundamental source of subjectivity which must be interrogated for full and equal citizenship to be realised. and for people with disabilities. it is the normative vision of the able bodied citizen which must be unbound from its inherent socio-cultural and political-economic injustices. To refer back to the original question posed of how do we begin to rewrite the story of what it means to be a disabled citizen? We begin this story through making the *able*-bodied citizen absent. and only then can the disabled subject be realised.

4

Citizenship and Rights

CITIZENSHIP

The conception of gender justice affects the ways in which claims to citizenship and entitlement are pursued.(Shamim and Sever 2004) Citizenship has been traditionally understood in a formal sense. that is. it is based on equal and formal citizenship for all adults born within the territory of a state. With the ending of colonialism in the context of South Asia. all adults were to be included in suffrage. and political inequality thus eliminated. However. feminists have challenged these formal understandings of citizenship. asserting that women still have a secondary status in political and public life. Women are also paid less than men and seem to be less respected than men in public life. They are often characterized as 'second-rate citizens'.

The analysis of gender justice suggests that citizenship is intimately connected to understandings of gender difference and whether women are included on the same terms as men. are treated as naturally weak and inferior. or as sometimes requiring different treatment and sometimes similar treatment in order to enjoy full access to their rights as citizens. If a woman. for example. is merely considered as naturally and inherently different from a man. then as evidenced in South Asia and elsewhere. difference in treatment in terms of the rights and privileges accorded through citizenship and the claims to entitlements will be justified merely on the basis of that difference.

If however. women are considered to be the same. and gender difference largely ignored. then citizenship will be understood in terms of formal equal treatment and similar treatment. This will not enable women to claim special rights. an entitlement to special treatment in order to accommodate the differences between men and women that do exist. For example. pregnancy or childcare is largely ignored in the sameness approach. Women are treated the same as men and any special treatment based on women's role in child bearing and rearing is regarded as a violation of the equality clause or as an exception to the principle of equality rather than integral to it. Finally. if gender justice is viewed from the perspective of patriarchy. any claims to citizenship always will be exposed as deeply flawed. as inherently based on oppressing women through their sexuality and holding some undefined. omnipresent system of patriarchy responsible for women's oppression.

Thus. citizenship is not just about membership and the rights and responsibilities that membership bestows. It is also connected to the way in which women are included or excluded based on the assumptions about gender difference on which citizenship is based.

In the legal arena. the literature reflects very different understandings of citizenship. and influences the ways in which gender justice is pursued. In the context of South Asia. the definition of citizenship was heavily influenced by the legacy of the colonial encounter. Citizenship was something that the 'white man' invented and was focused on the idea of the citizen as someone who was virtuous and rational. who had no kinship ties. In contrast. the colonial subject was viewed as lacking citizenship. as chaotic. different and incapable of taking on the responsibilities demanded of citizenship. This conception of citizenship. as linked to notions of reason. capacity to choose. as well as civilizational development was quite prevalent. It was reminiscent of the attitude towards women. both in the subcontinent as well as in the west. who were regarded as infantile. incapable of decision-making and in need of protection. The law was employed as a means for defining citizenship in terms of an unstated Eurocentric norm. It was. at its core. a definition based on racial distinctions. on exclusions and the techniques of 'othering'. At the same time. the colonial power desired to redefine the colonial subject through a move to universalize and rationalize laws as well as to create a native population through Western education and create elites that mimicked the West. Thus the disciplining of sexuality in the colonial context which was perceived as corrupting and excessive. as well as the representation of the Western citizen to the colonial subject as good. decent. enlightened and civilized through the technologies of law and education. were integral to the definitions of citizenship and of who could be incorporated into such definition and in what ways. A uniform criminal legislation was enacted in 1833. which inaugurated the process of 'disarming' Indian society and moving towards the creation of a universal legal subject. The moral compass of the colonial power was inserted into the legal agenda. and used to justify the banning of a litany of practices—infanticide. sati. child marriages—in the name of rational law and civilizing the native into a recognizable and more familiar subject of liberal rights discourse.

The image of citizenship as pure. virtuous and rational has been challenged in the feminist and postcolonial scholarship. It has also been contested on the ground. in the context of the early struggles for freedom and rights fought by anti-colonial movements. the struggle for rights and equality by women and other disadvantaged groups. and the contemporary conditions of globalization. Anti-colonial struggles opened up new definitions of citizenship. as an identity that enables rights claims. Women have claimed rights to citizenship in Pakistan. India and Nepal; along with freedom from non-discrimination and freedom from violence. Religious minorities have claimed rights to retain special temporary measures as well as the right to be governed by their personal laws. in order to retain their integrity and freedom from majoritarianism. These claims have challenged the West's notions of universality and exposed the notion that the universal subject. or idea of the pure citizen. had built into it an exclusionary potential.

In the contemporary period. citizenship has been subjected to new concerns and challenges (Purvis and Hunt 1999; Isin and Wood 1999; Fraser 1997 Young 1990). The conflicts between different religious and ethnic groups. as in India. Bangladesh and Sri Lanka. have resulted in an increased strain in the boundaries of citizenship. where different groups are pitted against one another in their claims for recognition. Challenges have been made by religious and conservative forces against claims to citizenship by minorities in their own countries. Some examples include the claims of Ahmadiyas in Pakistan. the Nepali refugees in Bhutan. or the Muslims in India.

Citizenship is increasingly being informed by xenophobia. exclusions and other forms of alienation. that treat 'the other' as a threat to national and social cohesion and national identity (and security). It is for this reason that a review and understanding of the colonial constructions of citizenship are critical in order to appreciate the current shifts and contemporary constructions of citizenship. In the contemporary period. citizenship is increasingly essentializing identities. contingent on static definitions of caste. religion. age as well as class. as more groups compete for access to the scarce state resources and benefits. In other words. citizenship is being used as a tool for inclusion as well as exclusion. and cannot be understood in purely universalistic terms or as having equal applicability to all.

In the context of women. claims to citizenship have at times been based on the recognition of their gender difference. Historically. women have been denied rights to citizenship in their individual capacities and their citizenship determined by a male member such as a father or husband. Such exclusions were based on essentialist assumptions about women. They were not deemed capable of exercising rights to self-determination or engaging the public democratic or political process by virtue of their inferiority to men. This. in turn. has tended to essentialize gender identities: women are cast primarily as caretakers. mothers and wives in need of protection. Such an assumption has led to law-reform proposals that actually curtail rather than advance women's rights to gender justice. An example is the previous Indian government's law reform proposal on domestic violence that was more concerned with the protection of the institution of the family and marriage. and women's roles within this institution. It sanctioned the right of men to beat their wives with reasonable cause. which included instances where a wife made a grab for her husband's property.2 A second example includes the recent interest in sexual harassment in Nepal and India. which has come to be informed by moralistic assumptions about women's sexual conduct and the need to sexually sanitize the workplace. At the same time. ignoring these differences does not address how difference has been used to discriminate against and subordinate women. The critical point is that the ways in which differences are understood and defined have a considerable influence on the way in which citizenship comes to be understood and defined.

The contemporary conditions of globalization have further altered understandings of citizenship. Since the 1980s. the processes of globalization have resulted in increased economic privatization and deregulation. Simultaneously. we have witnessed the emergence of new non-state actors. groups and communities who are migrating and no longer identified exclusively within one nation. There is an increased dependence on the market to provide essential services such as health or childcare. The unequal distribution of wealth leaves some citizens with less purchasing power to access these services and contributes to the impoverishment of marginalized groups such as women. Feminist academics. advocates and women's organizations argue that unless development planning and practice take into account unequal power relations on the basis of gender. women's position—as well as that of other marginalized groups—will remain unchanged and might even worsen. Finally. undocumented migrants. of which women constitute at least fifty percent. are crossing borders and gravitating towards the large metropolitan centres. setting up a new strata of informal citizenship that destabilizes further 'pure forms' linked exclusively to one nation.

RIGHTS

Feminist legal studies and practices have begun to explore the question of the role of law in feminist struggles from a multiplicity of perspectives. many of which defy simple classification. A new perspective on the role of law and rights in the context of South Asia is emerging. one based on post-colonialism. I now review some of the recent literature in this area. which exemplifies the emergence of this approach. It is important to pursuing a gender justice project specifically in the context of South Asia. although it has ramifications well outside of this region. Postcolonial approaches to rights and law are varied and defy any simple classification. One common position. however. is that they do critique the basic philosophical tenets of the enlightenment—rationality. objectivity and subjectivity. Postcolonialism rejects the concepts of objectivity and neutrality that are ostensibly the central characteristics of law. insisting the law is always based on biases and a point of view. Quite specifically. that law is based on inclusions and exclusions that are determined invariably from a majoritarian perspective. This view is based partly on the historical experiences with law. where the sovereignty of the Asian subcontinent was denied in the name of the imperial project and justified on the grounds that the colonial subject was so culturally and socially different. that he or she was not entitled to sovereignty or rights. Difference was a ground for denying rights. and was not an argument posited in opposition to the notion of universal rights. but inherent in the universal project. Rights could only be conferred on those who had reached a certain stage of civilizational maturity and the colonial ruler was best situated to determine when that stage had been reached.

Feminist legal studies have begun to develop increasingly complex and nuanced analyses of law's role in women's oppression. and its potential role in challenging that oppression. Interestingly. some of the most insightful work that has initially been written comes from disciplines other than law. Feminist historians have played a leading role in the articulation of a more complex understanding of the role of law in social change. Lata Mani. Radhika Singha and Tanika Sarkar are among the feminist historians who have critically examined the complex relationship between law in colonial India and women's subordination. Singha. for example. considers the ways in which law-making was a cultural enterprise. where the colonial state could draw upon differences such as rank. status and gender. She explains how the state re-ordered these identities in ways that produced an exclusive definition of its sovereign rights. so as to define who was or was not entitled to benefits conferred. In addition to feminist historians. feminist work on law has begun to emerge within the social sciences and humanities more generally. In their ground-breaking discursive analysis of the Shah Bano case. Zakia Pathak and Rajeswari Sunder Rajan have examined law as discourse. and the way in which this discourse constitutes subjects. More recently. Rajeswari Sunder Rajan has examined the relationship between the postcolonial. Indian nation-state. law and Indian women's actual needs and the contradictions produced through this relationship. She argues that law and citizenship define not only the scope of political rights for women. but also their cultural identity and everyday life.

Postcolonial legal scholarship has only recently begun to develop these feminist perspectives. Archana Parashar. in her study of family law reform. examines and evaluates some of the insights of debates within feminist legal studies. She uses the insights of these debates to further her understanding of the role of law in social change. while rejecting those aspects of the debates that do not fit the Indian context. In developing her analysis of the role of legislation and the promotion of gender justice. Parashar argues for the importance of law reform in women's struggles. However. her view of the nature of the role of law reform is informed by a consideration of the limits of law. She argues. for example. that 'instead of dismissing law reform as a means of achieving equality for women. it is more productive to realize the limitations of law and have appropriate expectations that law reform by itself will be insufficient to change society and end women's oppression.' She argues that law can serve an important symbolic value: 'Symbolic legislation can be of liberating value as it can provide a focus around which forces of change can mobilize.' In this respect. Parashar's work marks an important shift in feminist legal analysis. in its integration of rigorous and detailed legal analysis with a feminist perspective attentive to both the limitations and possibilities of law.

Other scholars have similarly begun to complicate feminist understandings of law. Nivedita Menon has explored questions of the conceptualization of rights within the context of women's struggles around abortion. sexual violence and reservations. Menon's work can be seen as a discursive analysis of the women's movement's engagement with law. In the context of abortion. for example. she argues that the women's movement has demanded that women have a right to choose and have control over their bodies. Yet. within the context of sex selection. the same groups have argued for a limitation on the same right. Menon attempts to illustrate the contradictions within the liberal discourse of rights for feminism. She argues that rights are discursively constituted—that rights only acquire meaning within specific contexts and specific discourses. In other words. rights may have a radical potential within feminist frameworks. but once they are put into the context of the broader political economy. their meanings may change and their contradictory character exposed.

Flavia Agnes' work has also been an important contribution to the development of more complex and nuanced analyses of feminist engagement with law. Throughout her work. Agnes interrogates the effect of law reforms on women and questions whether laws intended for women's benefit have lived up to their promise. Her work on violence against women. for example. addressed the failure of law to adequately address the reality of violence. Through a detailed examination of laws addressing rape. dowry. domestic violence. prostitution. indecent representation of women. sati (the practice which relates to the immolation of widow on her husband's funeral pyre) and sex discrimination tests. Agnes explores the broader questions of why law has had so little effect in women's lives. and whether law can bring about social change. In her analysis of rape laws. for example. Agnes reveals the ultimate failure of the campaign for reform in the early 1980s to bring about a transformation in the definition of rape. She illustrates the extent to which 'the same old notions of chastity. virginity. premium on marriage and fear of female sexuality are reflected in the judgements of the post-amendment law.'

Agnes' analysis of the other legislative provisions intended to protect women against violence similarly attempts to reveal the extent to which the reforms did not fundamentally challenge and transform the underlying assumptions about women's identities. She exposes how law is susceptible to being appropriated by a reactionary politics. illustrated in her analysis of the debates on the Uniform Civil Code in India. and how these are located in a highly charged communal context. She reveals how communalism seeps into some recent judicial decisions. exposing the contested nature of law and rights. Agnes is also critical of both the women's movement's failure to develop an explicitly secular agenda. and the resulting—though unstated—Hindu norm that has come to characterize the movement.

The postcolonial literature that is emerging in the context of South Asia reveals that law is no longer viewed in terms of an either/or dichotomy. It is neither a mere instrument of social change nor of patriarchy. What is emerging is a much more complex analysis born from postcolonial location and experience. Law was received in the Asian subcontinent as already exclusive and subordinating. It was introduced into the subcontinent as a mechanism for denying the colonial subject rights and freedoms that could only be acquired through civilizational maturity and the development of the capacity to reason.

During the freedom struggle. it is clear that rights also served a progressive end. because the freedom fighters invoked civil and political rights in order to acquire independence. Yet the struggle itself speaks to the contradictory nature of law and rights. and how it is a contested terrain. In the context of women. there is evidence that law has been used as both a subordinating tool as well as a liberating one. Women have won the right to vote. to education and also have succeeded in law reform in the area of sexual violence. But as the literature indicates. such achievements cannot be read as clear victories. They have at times been achieved by reinforcing gender difference. In the case of rape for instance. a woman may succeed in her claims if she is willing to present herself as chaste. pure. virginal and modest. This representation is deeply entwined with the demands of nationalism and for feminism to position itself at times as anti-Western. so that they do not compromise their nationalist credentials. The new literature is exposing how certain assumptions about women are embedded in legal discourse and how gender and the constitution of women's subjectivities need to be understood against the backdrop of the colonial encounter.

At one level. it would seem that rights discourse is ultimately unable to represent the interests of marginalized and disadvantaged groups. However. this position would be met with considerable resistance from women. *dalits* (lower castes). Muslims and other disadvantaged communities who have used rights in their struggles for social change. Rights remain important to people who have never had them. and a perspective that argues against rights can only come from a privileged position. from those whose rights are already secure.

At the same time. there is a need to move beyond the limitations of what I have described above as 'a rights-based approach.' Remaining confined to a universal understanding of rights. does not attend to its potential to be exclusive (as demonstrated by the history of colonialism) and also to be appropriated by more reactionary agendas (as demonstrated by the use of rights discourse by right wing nationalist entities. such as the Hindu Right in India). The rights based agenda can be used in pursuit of gender justice. only so long as it remains attentive to historical antecedents and fact that rights can be appropriated by the more powerful and can entrench notions of gender difference in ways that are not necessarily liberating for women.

A MAPPING OF HUMAN RIGHTS ISSUES

This chapter sets out the issues which inhabit the human rights landscape in areas of ordinary governance.

CUSTODIAL VIOLENCE

Custody death. torture in custody and custodial rape have been subjects of much concern. Custodial violence has been on the agenda of civil rights groups for over two decades. and reports documenting instances of violence and its systemic occurrence. have been instrumental in the campaigns against custodial violence. Although custody deaths have found an acknowledgment from the state. and the NHRC has issued directions to the states it is difficult to assess if this has resulted in any reduction in the incidence of custody deaths.

- To report of the NHRC any death in custody within 24 hours of the occurrence. and
- To videotape the post-mortem proceedings.

NHRC reports show a marked increase in the reported cases of custody deaths each year. This is attributed. by the NHRC. to increased reporting and not to increased incidence of the crime; this. however. needs to be further investigated. The incidence of custody deaths demonstrates more undeniably the brutalisation of the processes of law enforcement by the police and armed forces. However. custodial torture (not resulting in death) is not at the focus of campaigns to reduce custodial violence. There are few places which have taken up the treatment of the victims of torture as victims of torture. The Indian state. in the meantime. has resisted attempts (including that of the NHRC) to have it ratify the Torture Convention.

In recent reported cases from the Gauhati High Court. it is 15 and 16-year olds who are found to have been victims of state violence. and the defence of the state has been that they were hardened militants. Custodial rape has found an expanded definition-in terms of power rape-in the Penal Code. 1860. However. these provisions have hardly been invoked.

In the meantime. most often. judicial perceptions of the victim of custodial rape have in significant measure. discredited the victim's version. and blamed the victim resulting in reduction of sentence for policemen convicted of rape to less than the minimum prescribed in law. From Mathura to Rameeza Bi to Maya Tyagi to Suman Rani-these women have become symbols of patriarchal prejudices. Campaigns in the matter of custodial rape have invoked their name. and they are now names that are etched into the history and legend of the women's movement. In the meantime. the legal dictum that the identity of a victim of rape be not disclosed to protect her privacy has been set in place.

PROJECT DISPLACEMENT

Project displacement. for the construction of large dams or for power projects. for instance. have led to protest movements directly involving the affected people. The NBA has utilised strategies and tactics of protest-including *jal samarpan*. human chains. working on the funders and the contractors to withdraw. participating in the proceedings before. and surrounding. the World Commission on Dams-which have refused to let the issue be drowned out. This has also seen the manufacturing of conflicting forces. such as the pro-dam lobby which is believed to be largely state-sponsored.

Human rights issues that arise include:

- Displacement. *per se*
- The poverty of rehabilitation. and often. the impossi-bility of rehabilitation
- The impoverishment that results from displacement
- The non-reckoning of cultural and community identity and of rights.

What constitutes development has come into severe question in this arena. The Land Acquisition Act 1894 has been at the centre of protests. Among the strategies adopted to deal with the coercive nature of the law has been the drafting of alternative legislation. The obduracy of the state in not approving a policy for rehabilitation of the displaced has also been cause for protest.

THE INTERNALLY DISPLACED DUE TO CONFLICTS

The large-scale internal migration caused by political violence has created classes of internal refugees. During the years of militancy in the Punjab. after the anti-Sikh riots in 1984. and the movement of Kashmiri Pandits out of the valley have provided visible evidence of such migration. While the violence that preceded the migration has been squarely addressed in human rights terms. the rehabilitation and return of the migrants after displacement appears to have been only on the margins of the human rights movement.

REFUGEES

India has not ratified the 1951 UN Convention on Refugees. nor has it signed the 1967 protocol. The Indian state has generally resisted visits from the UNHCR to camps where refugees are housed. Activists say that the Indian state has been relatively benign towards refugees. In 1999. India hosted more than 2.92.000 refugees; which includes more than 16.000 persons from Afghanistan. 65.000 Chakmas from Bangladesh. 30. 000 Bhutanese of Nepali origin. 50.000 Chin indigenous people from Myanmar and about 39.000 pro-democracy student activists from Rangoon and the Mandalay region. 1.10.000 Sri Lankan Tamils of whom 70.000 are in camps and 40. 000 outside. 1.10.000 Tibetans and around 7000 persons from other countries.

The assassination of Rajiv Gandhi in 1991 has reportedly altered the treatment meted out to the Sri Lankan refugees. According to a fact-finding report of a civil liberties organisa-tion in Tamil Nadu. Sri Lankan refugees fall into three categories: those who are in the 133 refugee camps; refugees who maintain themselves outside the camps; and those who have been identified as belonging to militant groups who were kept in virtual rigorous confinement in the three special camps.

In August 1995. 43 inmates of the Special Camp at Tippu Mahal. Vellore escaped and a one-man commission set up by the state describes the structure and administration of the camps. The refugees were found to be prisoners in these camps and. as even the state appointed commission had remarked. 'admittedly these inmates or most of them are in rigorous confinement in the special camps for five or six years continuously.' The testimony of the two inmates to the fact-finding team also revealed that the camp in Vellore had among its inmates at least 12 disabled persons.

The Government of India does not appear to have any policy on how to deal with refugee-prisoners in their camps. The protection of Chakma refugees in the state of Arunachal Pradesh. and their right to have their claim for citizenship considered. was canvassed by a civil liberties group before the NHRC.

The Supreme Court. approached by the NHRC. directed that the threats held out to the Chakmas by the local citizens be dealt with by the state. It also asserted that their applications for being granted citizenship be considered under the Citizenship Act. The difficulties besetting refugees even after long years of residence in a state. with state acquiescence. were in evidence here.

LAND ALIENATION

The loss to communities of right over land is widespread. and various movements to recover control over land and related resources have been active particularly in the past decade and a half. though some movements go back many decades.

The issue of tribal land alienation was linked with that of displacement. and the judicial system was used to get an order declaring unconstitutional the transfer of land from a tribal to a non-tribal through the medium of the state (in its land acquisition capacity). Recent efforts to delete this constitutional protection given in Schedule V of the Constitution are being resisted as a denial of basic protection given to tribals. paving the way for their displacement and impoverishment.

The issue of land alienation was one of the primary issues in the struggle for separate statehood for Uttaranchal. and till today is identified as one of the main rights violations occurring in the state. In Kerala. the issue is differently positioned. While the loss of land to the tribal is viewed as a violation of their rights and protection of those rights. the settlers are largely people who are themselves on the economic margins.

While groups from within the tribal communities have been demanding restoration of alienated land. and the High Court has supported their stand. other human rights advocates maintain an uneasy silence since the contest appears to be between two vulnerable communities.

RIGHT OVER RESOURCES

The right of the forest dwellers to reside in forests. and for those dependent on forest produce to have access to forests. is contested terrain. Till recently. there were conservation groups which demanded that removing tribals from within forest areas was necessary in the interest of conservation. This stand has softened somewhat. and a more symbiotic relationship between the forest and the dweller recognised as possible. The problems are now spoken of in terms of overpopulation. and over-grazing. in the forest area.

State policy is. however. widely perceived as being inimical to the continuance of the forest dweller within the forest. 'Settling' of rights and interests is therefore met with deep suspicion. as is happening in Madhya Pradesh. Activists have therefore been mobilising the grassroots-in MP. it was through a *padayatra* over a period of six months-to resist the conservation projects which may end up pauperising the dwellers. and. further. may denude the forest too.

There have been attempts in the early '90s to prepare a new Forest Bill that will contain within it the interests of conservation. and of the people. Efforts such as this have stalled the legislation proposed by the state which groups and movements see as being opposed to rights-including the right to livelihood. to culture. to security. to shelter. among others-even while the alternative bills have hardly ever been adopted. An activist identified the problem of land and resources being related to how possession and ownership of land are perceived.

There are three kinds of property he said:

1. Private property
2. Public property
3. Common property

What is held as 'public property' by the state. he said. has been treated as property owned by the state. and not held in trust by the state. It is the notion of common property that has to be resurrected and advanced. The entry of mining interests into Orissa has. for instance. brought into the open the problem that is inherent in globalisation when it comes into conflict with local interest.

The unequal. triangular contest between multinational mining interests. the state which binds itself to protecting the multinational interest on Indian territory. and the local dwellers-in the case of mining. it is often tribals-manifests itself as a human rights issue.

Aquaculture. which brings in corporations to exploit resources through prawn culture. for instance. has been resisted on grounds of loss of livelihood. long-term destruction of marine life and consequent degradation of the environment.Corporatised aquaculture and shrimp farms have been banned. Deep-sea trawlers have also been banned. and the livelihood and lives of fisher communities salvaged. So. too. with prawn culture. Human rights activists see setbacks to these efforts at preservation of community livelihoods and of the environment in the Aquaculture Bill that has been presented to the Parliament in 2000.

The Aruvari Sansad (Water Parliament) in Ajmer district in Rajasthan. which. with the help of the Tarun Bharat Sangh. an NGO. has wrested control over the river. the check dams it has built along it. the revived rivers and the fish that have sprung into being in the river is an uncommon assertion over water and water resources to the exclusion of agencies of the state.

The issue of land reforms and the redistribution of land was encountered in Andhra Pradesh. The Peoples War Group. for instance. avers that land reform is at the root of their attacks against the state. The problem of professional land grabbers. and the response of land invasion to take possession of land which should rightly belong to the invading community. was also seen in Andhra Pradesh. State response has been to treat the attacks. and invasion. as public order. or law and order. problems.

The loss of tribal land through land alienation-something that the law limits-has raised other issues in Kerala. for instance. The land had been bought from the tribals by settlers who are themselves economically and socially marginalised. A prolonged legal battle. where the court had directed the return of the land to the tribals. has not seen a solution to the contending interests of two communities. each in need of protection from expropriation.

URBAN SHELTER AND DEMOLITION

There has been a routinising of the emergency visible in the matter of cleaning up of the cities. In 2000-2001. Delhi has seen a spate of demolitions of 'slums'. The slum dwellers have been divided up into eligibles and ineligibles. with the eligibles being given very small plots of land on which they are required to construct houses within six months on a licence basis.

The size of the plot ensures that it is only a 'slum' that develops. The 'ineligibles' are not thereafter considered by state policy. Housing rights activists too do not appear to have been able to identify what happens to the ineligibles when demolition occurs.

In Bangalore. housing rights groups have been attempting to demonstrate the effort and money that 'encroachers' expend on the land on which they settle; and that they have worked for their entitlement to alternative plots. In Bombay. and to a lesser extent elsewhere. there have been attempts to involve the slum dwellers in reconstructing the area in a manner which will let the slum disappear. while they are given places in high-rise tenements in the same area with the rest of the space to be used commercially. In Patna. an order of the High Court in a PIL. requiring the municipal corporation to demolish encroachments. resulted in a demolition spree that an embarrassed court had to step in to stop.

The illegal status of the urban dweller who cannot afford to purchase legality has been aggravated by B.N. Kirpal.J saying: 'Establishing or creating slums. it seems. appears to be good business and is well organised...Large areas of public land. in this way. are usurped for private use free of cost... The promise of free land. at the taxpayers' cost. in place of a jhuggi. is a proposal which attracts more land grabbers. *Rewarding an encroacher on public land with free alternate site is like giving a reward to a pickpocket.*'

Unlike South Africa. where the state's obligation to provide shelter before destroying even an illegal habitat was recognised. drawing upon international law. there is no such recognition in Indian law or judicial decisions. Activists and campaigners therefore face an unenviable. if unavoidable. task of combating the anti-poor stand of the state.Pavement dwelling. and houselessness. was raised in the '80s and. though it may never really have disappeared. it has resurfaced more rigorously since the demolitions have begun in Delhi. Migrant workers living on pavements have been particularly vulnerable to random attacks in areas of militant violence.

Newspapers have reported such occurrences in the '90s. This issue affecting migrant labour particularly needs to be addressed. The 'clearing' of pavements by removing hawkers has been a phenomenon visible in most cities. Eviction of hawkers. and of dwellers. is a significant issue. and the demands include recognition not only of shelter. land and monetary compensation. but of livelihood too.

LIVELIHOOD

Apart from issues of rights over resources. and in the context of displacement and relocation. the death of cotton farmers has. for instance. raised questions about protection of livelihood. Liberalisation has resulted in loss of jobs to large numbers in the workforce. and we hear of deaths among the working classes. This is an area that seems to demand closer attention.

The withdrawing of protective labour legislation. which is proposed. such as the 'abolition' part of the Contract Labour (Prohibition and Regulation) Act 1970. or the prohibition of night work for women except where specifically attempted. it is feared. is likely to shrink the rights of workers to a great degree. Freedom of association is also being re-cast in a new Trade Unions Bill. which labour leaders and activists believe is meant to stifle the powers of labour to group together and be heard. The casualisation of labour which the changes portend are expected to drastically reduce the bargaining power of labour.

In 1989. a PIL filed by two social/political activists from Orissa. led to the express recognition of starvation as a violation of fundamental rights. In 1994. the NHRC acknowledged that starvation is a violation of human rights and ordered the state to pay compensation to the families of victims of starvation in Kalahandi in Orissa.

In March/April 2001. academics/researchers from the Delhi School of Economics and the Madras Institute of Development Studies have asked for distribution of buffer stocks that the government has stored in its godowns. to stem the tide of hunger among those with low purchasing power. The juggling with the public distribution system. and the defining and re-defining of the poverty line and consequently of 'below poverty line' is causing particular concern. The death of 17 protesters chased by the police into the Tamaraparani river. and over 200 injured in the incident has been compared to the killing of innocent persons by the British at Jallianwallabagh 80 years ago. On July 23. 1999. a solidarity procession organised by several political parties proceeded to the Collectorate in Tirunelveli Town in South Tamil Nadu. demanding an early solution of the wage dispute that had been the cause of discontent and agitation among tea workers in the Manjolai Tea Estate.

The also demanded the immediate and unconditional release of 652 tea estate workers who had been kept in the Tiruchi jail for six weeks following a demonstration before the same Collectorate on June 7 and 8. 1999. Talks on the labour dispute having failed. the political parties decided to present a charter of demands to the Collector.

As the processionists neared the Collectorate. the police attempted to prevent the jeep which had the leaders of the agitation in it from proceeding further. As the crowd milled around. the events that ensued included a lathi charge by the police. the lobbing of tear gas and the police also opened fire. A video footage shows an injured person. bleeding. being carried away by four policemen. This injured person remains unaccounted for.

The police then chased the people down the banks of the river Tamaraparani forcing the people to jump into the water to save themselves from the police force. Photographs graphically reveal the pursuit of the people by the police into the river. even pushing the people back into the water. 17 people drowned. There were injuries on the person of the drowned victims. testifying to ante-mortem police brutality.

This episode constitutes a new threshold to police violence and brutality in labour related agitation and protest. The 'clearing' of pavements by removing hawkers has been a phenomenon visible in most cities. Eviction of hawkers. and of dwellers. is a significant issue. and the demands include recognition not only of shelter. land and monetary compensation. but of livelihood too.

SEXUAL HARASSMENT AT THE WORKPLACE

This issue acquired visibility with the decision of the Supreme Court in *Vishaka*. Earlier efforts at having the problem addressed. as. for instance. in the Delhi University. has drawn strength from the guidelines set out in the Judgement. It was widely reported. however. that it was still proving difficult to get institutions to adopt the guidelines and act upon it. The Madras High Court. for instance. was reportedly averring that the guidelines did not apply to the court; and allegations of sexual harassment by a senior member of the Registry were given short shrift.

The process of setting up a credible grievance redressal mechanism was reportedly being watered down in the recommendation of a committee to the Delhi University. In Kerala. a Commission of Enquiry was set up after Nalini Netto. a senior official of the Indian Administrative Service. pursued her complaint of sexual harassment against a serving minister of the state cabinet-which is seen as a diversion from a representative investigative and redressal forum.P E Usha. in Kerala. faced hostility in her university when she followed up on her complaint of sexual harassment. There have been allegations of sexual harassment of women employees by senior persons within institutions working on human rights. and in progressive publications. which too have shown up the inadequacy of the redressal mechanisms.

- Translating the guidelines into norms in different institutions and workplaces;
- Finding support systems for women who are sexually harassed
- Breaking through thick walls of disbelief are reckoned to be the priorities

This has also been introduced into programmes on gender sensitisation for judicial officers. Sexual harassment accompanied by violence has become a common feature with cases of acid throwing where there is unrequited love. and harassment which has culminated in the murder of a hounded girl.

Rape

In the '80s and into the early '90s. was widely discussed. and alternative drafts and definitions essayed. While following *Tukaram and Ganpat's* case. 'power' rape was partially introduced into the law. The definition of rape. consent and the status of marital rape in law has however not been altered. Again. while the campaign's gains are witnessed in the Supreme Court holding that. as a rule. the victim's version should not require corroboration and that it should be given credence:

- The trauma of the trial continues.

- The law's sanction to delving into character evidence concerning the victim remains in the Evidence Act despite the flood of criticism and protest it has provoked.

In Uttaranchal. an issue not uncommon in investigations into. and trial of. rape surfaced. It was reported that women who were raped at Muzaffarnagar are being pressurised not to testify in the criminal cases not only by the police but also by their own community and political leaders. particularly since monetary compensation has been paid. In 1994. the National Commission for Women (NCW) was asked by the Supreme Court to propose a scheme for establishing Rape Crisis Centres. and for a Criminal Injuries Compensation Board. which could care for victims of crime.

This is yet to materialise. In the meantime. the women's movement in Rajasthan has got the administration to provide monetary relief to victims of rape. unconnected with trial and conviction. Though this has. at least occasionally. resulted in the veracity of the accusation being challenged as having been made so as to obtain the sum in compensation. it is seen as a move to helping the woman recover.Rape as reprisal was symbolised in Bhanwari Devi's experience. Bhanwari Devi. a *saathin* working in Rajasthan in and around her village. was part of a wider network of women who were involved in a state-sponsored programme of empowerment particularly of women and girls.

Her intervention to thwart the practice of child marriage in the community around her is commonly acknowledged as having resulted in the gang rape that was inflicted on her-as punishment. by men of the dominant community who were outraged by her intervention. The acquittal of the alleged rapists. more especially the reasoning of the court. based on caste and hierarchies of belief. accentuates the re-victimising of the woman.

The low rate of conviction for rape. and the protest from women's groups. were held out to justify a proposed amendment to criminal law to provide death penalty for the offence of rape. The conflict between provisions of the death penalty and human rights has surfaced. even if gradually. and the groups we met. as well as the National Commission for Women. have rejected the proposal for death penalty for the offence of rape.

DEATH PENALTY

The civil liberties movement has been consistent in its opposition to the death penalty. For a brief while. there were some sections in the women's movement who supported-either vocally. or by their silence-the imposition of death penalty for rape. This too has been retracted. and death penalty for rape opposed. After the period in the early '80s. when the Supreme Court drew up the `rarest of rare' rule. there has been a downward slide. particularly discernible in the 1990s.

- Multiple death sentences.

- Death penalty to minors. and
- Death sentence while reversing acquittal are not uncommon.

The campaign against execution of two youths in Andhra Pradesh who had been convicted of burning a bus which killed 23 passengers saw concerted action. which resulted in their sentence being commuted by the President.

The confirmation of the sentence of death on women is a relatively recent phenomenon. Ramashri's sentence was reduced to life by the Supreme Court. even as the court rejected the right of the NCW to intervene. The sentence of death imposed upon Nalini. convicted in the Rajiv Gandhi assassination case. has been opposed by human rights groups. along with the sentence of death meted out to three others in the same matter.

Death sentence confirmed despite dissent among judges of benches of the Supreme Court on the sentence that should be imposed is another. disturbing. occurrence. Even doubts about the age of the accused-whether he had been less than 16 years of age and therefore a juvenile-were not sufficient to dispense with death sentence where death was awarded by a majority of judges.

That the young accused was defended by legal aid lawyers and that 'It is reasonable to presume. in such circumstances. that the amicus curiae or advocate appointed on State brief. would not have been able even to see the petitioner. much less collect instructions from him. during the second and third tiers' was noticed only by the minority judge. Dearth of data. and difficulty of access to data is one obstacle to effectively countering the retentionists.

In the meantime. the proliferation of death penalty in recent statutes. viz..:

- The Narcotic Drugs and Psychotropic Substances Act 1985 (and as amended in 1988)
- National Security Guards Act 1986
- TADA 1987 (which lapsed in 1995. but trials under which continue)
- Arms Act 1950
- Indo-Tibetan Border Police Act 1992
- The Scheduled Castes and Scheduled Tribes (Prevention of Atrocities) Act 1989
- Commission of Sati (Prevention) Act 1987
- S. 364 A IPC as introduced in 1993-'kidnapping for ransom. etc.'

There has been a deafening silence from the NHRC on the issue of the death penalty.

FAKE ENCOUNTERS (EXTRA-JUDICIAL KILLINGS)

In India. extra-judicial killings by the police or the security forces are called 'encounter killings'. meaning that the killing occurred during an armed encounter between the police or security forces and the victim. The killing by the state forces is most often declared to be defensive. cases of attempted murder and other related offences are registered against the victims. and the cases closed without further investigation since criminal cases come to an end upon the death of the accused.

Despite being 'unnatural deaths'. and the victim having being killed. no investigation ensues to determine whether the death was in fact in an actual encounter. nor whether the use. and the extent of use. of force was justified. This is an acknowledged strategy of the state for eliminating certain kinds of opposition to the state and the established order.

In Andhra Pradesh. for instance. the naxalites have been the targets; in Punjab. it was the militant; in Mumbai. it is those who are alleged to be part of the underworld. Civil liberties groups. journalists and lawyers have consistently challenged this practice over the past two decades.

The demand as it has been articulated after recent episodes has been:

- For doing away with state violence in the form of killings in fake encounters. and
- That all cases of encounter killings ought to be registered as first information reports (FIRs) and investigated before the case is closed. The practice of registering cases against the deceased and terminating the proceedings even before it begins is being vigorously challenged. The NHRC too has issued directions endorsing this recommended practice. but to little effect. These court. and out-of-court. battles have carried on throughout the '80s and the '90s to the present.

The Committee of Concerned Citizens (CCC). a group of individuals in Andhra Pradesh. has approached encounter killings differently. Addressing both naxalite groups and the state. the CCC has been working at de-escalation of violence. While the naxalite response has taken the CCC to the issue of land reforms as being fundamental in understanding violence of the opposition. the state. it is widely believed. is pursuing the path of unbridled unleashing of the use of encounters.

The numbers killed in encounters have increased in the two years when the process of reconciliation was being negotiated by the CCC. making some of them ask if intervention by the human rights actors was actually prompting the state to escalate the violence.The human rights community has had to contend with the issue of impunity which is immediately seen as arising from thee non-registration and the non-investigation of cases.

INVOLUNTARY DISAPPEARANCES

The Punjab disappearances were brought into the open by two human rights defenders. Khalra and Kumar. Khalra was himself thereafter 'disappeared'. Investigations into these disappearances-which were uncovered when mortuary records in three districts of the Punjab were scrutinised and 'unidentified' and partially identified persons were found to have been cremated without informing the families of the deceased-was handed over by the Supreme Court to the

NHRC.The manner in which the matter was reduced to a point where the State of Punjab agreed to pay compensation of '1 lakh (*without admitting liability*) to the families of 18 persons who had been disappeared and the NHRC's tolerance of this stand of the state. is striking in the *general denial of the phenomenon of disappearances*.

This was after the CBI had found that bodies of several persons had been cremated surreptitiously in the late '80s and early '90s-585 persons who had been subsequently identified had been cremated after being labelled as unidentified. Around 330 of them had been partially identified and over 1200 remained to be identified.

The deficiency of compensation as a measure of reconciliation is also evident.Disappearances appear to be a pattern where there is militant resistance to the state. Case law speaks of this phenomenon in the Northeast. In fact. the first major case of compensation for disappearance after being picked up by the armed forces was from the Northeast.

On February 27. 2001. newspapers reported that it was alleged in the Lok Sabha. without being effectively countered. that the number of persons missing from the custody of the security forces and the police has risen to 2174 in Jammu and Kashmir; 76 cases had been registered and only one person had been challaned so far.

- Acknowledgment of involuntary disappearances
- Investigation. and seeking to establish what happened to the disappeared so that families and the community can finally know
- Prosecution and punishment. for reasons of deterrence too. and
- Compensation as a measure of atonement are being sought to be worked into the system.

It was also reiterated that reconciliation would be impossible to achieve without such acknowledgment. identification of the disappeared and reparation. That Khalra disappeared even while the matter was being taken to the Supreme Court is a statement on impunity.

The theme of impunity was laid out when K.P.S. Gill. the policeman in-charge in Punjab through the waning years of militancy. lashed out in protest when a policeman.

Sandhu. committed suicide while facing multiple charges of excesses committed during the years of militancy. The schizophrenic attitude of the process which rewarded him when he killed 'terrorists'. and later sought to prosecute him for abuse of power even amounting to murder. stood exposed.

According to K.P.S. Gill:

- Blamed the judiciary for having been inactive. or of playing safe. when captured terrorists were brought before it. and
- Held out the threat that if pursued by prosecution. the police would be unavailable to deal with militancy another time.

EXTRAORDINARY LAWS

These have been one of the means of routinising the enactment of laws that are normally promulgated in an emergency or in extraordinary situations.

The Terrorist and Disruptive Activities (Prevention) Act 1987 (TADA) was contested for:

- Its denial of fair trial standards-*e.g.*. it reduced the tiers of appeal
- The provision regarding making confessions to a police officer admissible in evidence
- The broad contours of the law on what constitutes terrorism. and
- Potential and proven abuse-for *e.g.*. the largest number of TADA detenues were in Gujarat. where militant activity was not present.

The public condemnation of TADA. political opposition to it. the NHRC's spirited intervention and the state's assessment that it was no longer necessary. led to the law not being reenacted when it lapsed in 1995. There have. however. been further attempts to revive the law-as in the Prevention of Terrorism Act recommended in 1999 by the Law Commission. for instance.

Further. state laws in Maharashtra. Andhra Pradesh and. more recently. in Madhya Pradesh and Karnataka-as a measure against organised crime-have brought the TADA back into their states under a hardly disguised identity. Tamil Nadu has also proposed a Prevention of Terrorism Bill along similar lines.

The Armed Forces Special Powers Act 1958 (AFSPA) is another law which provides extraordinary powers. It has been in force in the Northeast for these years. The TADA and the AFSPA survived challenge before the Supreme Court in the '90s. This has caused a serious rethink on the courts as a situs for testing the legitimacy of such extraordinary laws that deny fundamental rights. and breach human rights principles. It is evident that it is only vigilance. and resistance. which is keeping the proliferation of these laws in check.

The arrest and detention of civilians under extraordinary laws. like the TADA. also appears to be routine. It has been alleged. for instance. that villagers in the vicinity of Veerappan. the sandalwood smuggler's beat are routinely subjected to harassment. search and detention. In the negotiations for the release of actor Rajkumar who was taken hostage by Veerappan on July 30. 2000. the release of 51 detainees being held under TADA since 1992 on suspicion of having participated in the murder of policemen was in issue.

Human rights activists claim that many of them were local people who had been roped in as being 'associates' of Veerappan. When a civil liberties organisation moved the court for release of those so incarcerated. the petition was not entertained. But during the negotiations. the government of Karnataka showed a readiness to release them in the interests of law and order. and also. significantly. since others released on bail earlier 'have not repeated the offences and they have not involved themselves in any similar offences and terrorist activity have not been noticed recently in the area. '

PREVENTIVE DETENTION

When the Constitution came into being in 1950. preventive detention laws were avowedly intended to be a transient measure. During the emergency. the Maintenance of Internal Security Act 1971 (MISA) was among the more infamous laws which allowed for preventive detention of persons in the avowed interest of maintenance of internal security.

There are now a number of legislations which permit preventive detention. in the states and at the centre. The National Security Act 1980 (NSA) is an instance of the latter. The A.P. Prevention of Dangerous Activities of Bootleggers. Dacoits. Drug Offenders. Goondas. Immoral Traffic Offenders and Land Grabbers Act 1986 is an example of the former.

Public protest against the continuance of these laws is almost inaudible despite:

- The long periods. sometimes up to two years. that a person may be kept in preventive detention
- The tardiness of the procedure prescribed-*e.g.*. the executive may be given up to three months to get the opinion of the Advisory Board which may effectively have a person in custody under executive order up to ninety days
- The range of activities that are allowed to be covered by preventive detention laws that are unconnected with public order or law and order.

Unlike the challenge to the TADA. preventive detention laws have not engaged the human rights community in any sustained manner.

DETENTION

A range of detentions including those that were plainly illegal came to light during the course of our work:

- The incarceration of persons deemed to be 'non-criminal lunatics' (NCLs) or the wandering mentally ill in jails was investigated in a PIL before the Supreme Court. These are persons picked up under the Police Acts of the states. or under police powers in other laws such as the Indian Lunacy Act 1912. or its successor law. the Mental Health Act 1987. They are treated as`nuisances'. or bracketed as being dangerous. this providing the rationale for putting them away. The term NCL is in contradistinction to`criminal lunatics'. that is. those accused of crime but found to be mentally ill or suffering from mental disorder. For years NCLs were received in jails as places of`safe custody' under the Indian Lunacy Act 1912 and later under the Mental Health Act 1987. In the states of West Bengal and Assam. where the Supreme Court sent Commissioners to investigate. it was found that many of those in jails as NCLs were in fact not mentally ill at all. but had been placed there deviously. to serve some completely unrelated purpose. For instance. a 70-year woman was found to have been put away as an NCL apparently because her landlord was using it as a means of evicting her. We heard resonances of this reasoning from a lawyer-activist in Chennai.

- The Supreme Court declared. in August 1993. that using jails as places of safe custody to house non-criminal mentally ill persons (NCMI) is unconstitu-tional. Apart from the state of Assam. which admitted in an affidavit in the Supreme Court to continuing the practice. the NHRC has intermittently reiterated that NCMI should be housed in places other than jails. It is plain that the practice continues.
- This is an area that has not been widely addressed within the human rights community. NHRC's recognition of the issue too has been desultory.
- There is evidence in law reports. and activists have admitted to have knowledge of. the practice of hostage taking by the police where the person to be apprehended is not within reach of the police. Relatives of the person sought are then picked up and kept in custody till he surrenders. This appears to have happened with some regularity in Punjab. but we also heard of it in Delhi and Andhra Pradesh. for instance. This breach of the law needs further investigation and response.
- There have been reports of people spending long years in jail. which could have been averted if prisons were not as inaccessible as they are. *Rudul Sah.* the man who spent fourteen years in jail because he had been considered unfit to stand trial. and continued to remain untried despite having been declared fit. is one wellknown instance. Recent instances from Bihar and West Bengal reveal that the neglect that occasions such illegal incarceration continues. The incapacity of a person to follow up on his trial and sentence. and to procure orders in time has been known to keep him in prison long after he was due to have been released. The inability to furnish bail or sureties was reportedly one such reason for the large undertrial population.
- It is evident that systemic changes are imperative if these questions of personal liberty are to be addressed.
- In custodial institutions other than prisons-in 'protective homes' for women. for instance. the problem of custody versus shelter has been raised. Protective homes are established under the Immoral Traffic (Prevention) Act 1956 (ITPA). Since they are the only statutory institutions that can house women for 'protection' as also for 'correction'. they act as places of custody. operating within the executive-magistracy system. We met women in 'protective custody' in the Agra Protective Home. who were witnesses in a case to be

tried in Jhansi; they desired to leave and they had been in the institution for nearly two years. But the law would not let them. 'Rescued' women were placed in these institutions. but the purpose of 'rehabilitation' was found to be too inadequate to make the difference.

- Prison jurisprudence since the late '60s recognises that prisoners do not lose all their rights because of imprisonment. Yet. there is a loss of rights within custodial institutions which continue to occur. For instance. it was found that the HIV status of all the women in the Agra Protective Home was public knowledge. and there was no confidentiality attaching to this information. There was segregation within the institutions of those found to be HIV positive. and. for a while. the Supreme Court too endorsed this. The rules governing women in these institutions uncannily resemble prison rules-such as those concerning visitors. letters. and even punishment for conduct within the institutions.
- Persons working in this area said that this was an area which called for an injection of human rights experience and perspectives.
- The non-release of persons cured of mental illness from institutions was also reported to be a problem. We repeatedly met the need for halfway homes and support services which could help a person be restored to liberty.
- In Delhi. we heard of persons who had been picked up as being persons of Bangladeshi origin. who were kept in custody in a night shelter till they could be repatriated if they were. in fact. found to belong to Bangladesh and the Foreigners Act 1946 could be invoked to effect this move. There was concern that even the basis of identifying them as possible foreigners was not clear and that dispelling suspicion of nationality could well be more difficult for the poor and the dispossessed.

It is also found that it is common practice to pick up people for questioning. and not record their presence in the police station till the police is ready to present them before a magistrate-a way of thwarting the constitutional requirement that every person taken into custody be produced before a magistrate within 24 hours.

Apart from the illegality of such detention. it also makes difficult proving torture in custody during the period of illegal. unrecorded. detention. Human rights activists suggest that telegrams be dispatched to the Chief Minister. the Director General of Police. the Superintendent of Police. and the Governor for instance. when information about such illegal detention is obtained. to establish the time of detention. The conditions of persons with mental illness in institutions have been cause for human rights concern. In Gwalior Mental hospital. for instance. it was found that persons with mental illness were left in nakedness; the explanation was that they tore their clothes if they were given them. The press raised the issue. Chaining of mentally ill patients was also a practice. and this was outlawed by an order of the court.

One difficulty in ensuring that such violations do not occur. and in getting the law implemented. is access. The human rights community has not engaged with the problems faced within the walls of custodial institutions. Imaginative answers which will make open institutions of what are now bureaucratic. and closed. institutions is an imperative. The hysterectomy controversy in the early 1990s in Pune represents another aspect of the control and decisionmaking within custodial institutions.

The hysterectomy of girls below 18 years of age. who were mentally retarded. raised controversy about the decision made by the professionals. The professionals involved in making the decision neither denied that the hysterectomy was being done. nor did they did see it as a violation. It was justified as being in the best interests of the hygiene of the mentally retarded girl. as making practicable the care of the mentally retarded.

The response did not rule out the possibility of sexual abuse when within the institutions. but said it would protect the girls from pregnancy in the event of such an encounter. The persons responsible for the decision responded angrily to the charges of human rights violations. The Medical Council of India. however. distanced itself from this position. and declared the practice as being against their norms. The intervention of the media and the human rights community precluded further hysterectomies from being done.

MISSING WOMEN

There are various situations which throw up the issue of 'missing' women. The lopsided sex ratio in many states. and the juvenile sex ratio in even a state such as Kerala (which is held out by planners and economists as the model performer on the population front). is one area where women. and girls. go`missing'.

In Orissa. we heard of the phenomenon of 'Jhansi' marriages and 'Gwalior' marriages. Girls from very poor homes were escorted by a 'broker' to be married to men in Jhansi or Gwalior. and he would bring back a bride price of ` 10.000 to `25.000 to be given to the girl's family. While some of these marriages had been found to be genuine. the possibility of some of these women being trafficked was not ruled out. Also. what a girl/woman did if deserted or ill-treated was not clear.There was therefore an attempt by activists to keep track of women who had not been heard from for over a period of three months. so that their whereabouts could be verified and their safety ascertained. In July 1999. activists had begun the process of documenting the 'missing' woman. In Delhi. we were informed that missing persons reports when women go missing from their marital homes were hardly ever related with unidentified bodies of women who were declared to have committed suicide by drowning. for instance. The paucity of information. and the difficulties in follow up. has kept this issue in the margins of human rights concerns.

HOMICIDE IN THE MATRIMONIAL HOME

Often identified as being dowry-related deaths. unnatural deaths of women in their marital home has acquired prominence. Like encounter killings. acknowledgment has not led to a reduction in the incidence of such homicide. In Andhra Pradesh in 1990 a civil liberties organisation raised the issue of violation of women's rights as a human rights issue by comparing the number of dowry deaths and the number of encounter killings during one time period-about 2000 dowry deaths. and 300 deaths in encounters.

In Bangalore. a women's group keeps a watch in the Burns Ward of the leading government hospital. and also scrutinises newspapers for reports of deaths of young women. which they then follow up. They also had a 'Truth Commission' where a tribunal heard the narratives of the families of girls/women who had been the victims of dowry deaths.

The inadequacies of investigation. and the many slips in the judicial process which results in a low rate of prosecution and a lower rate still of conviction. was observed everywhere. The definition of 'dowry death' in the Penal Code. based on preponderance of probability and a shifting of onus represents a significant shift in criminal law and jurisprudence.

In the meantime. the Dowry Prohibition Act has been hardly at all implemented. Most states still have no Dowry Prohibition Officers. The maintenance of list of things given and received is still not mandatory. S. 498 A. which was brought in to deal with cruelty in the matrimonial home. has suffered criticism as being abused. sending the family of the man to prison till bail is procured.

Some women's groups. however. contended that the abuse was only marginal. and that this was the only provision in law which could hold the perpetrator of domestic cruelty accountable. Some also spoke of bringing into law the notions of right to matrimonial home and matrimonial property as other approaches of protecting women on whom cruelty is practised.

DOMESTIC VIOLENCE

In locating domestic violence in the terrain of human rights. one point of view was that it is not the identity of the perpetrator alone which can be allowed to determine whether a victim has been subjected to a human right violation or not: that it is a man or his family who exercises their power to harass. assault and injure a woman. and not the state which is the perpetrator. should then make no difference to the place for this violence in human rights discourse.

Also. it is state practice. and endorsement. of patriarchy that keeps such violence in the home. we were told:

- Crime against women cells in police stations
- Counselling centres
- Help lines
- Short stay homes-which. though. are few in number have been set up in many cities.

There has also been a concerted effort to bring in a law to deal with domestic violence. A Bill prepared. debated and presented to the government by a women's organisation has been adopted by Parliament for discussion. which is a significant step in a non-governmental role in law making. S. 498 A was introduced into the Penal Code in 1983.

It makes cruelty to a woman within the matrimonial home punishable with imprisonment up to three years and fine. It is a cognisable. non-bailable. offence. Widespread violence against women. and increasing evidence of women dying unnatural deaths in the matrimonial homes provoked the women's movement to demand a change in the criminal law.

The offence is non-bailable. that is a complaint under s. 498 A. once registered as an FIR. would result in the arrest of the members of the matrimonial family of the woman. They would have to be granted bail by a court before release. and this could keep them in custody for varying periods of time. In matters of remission of sentence. too. offenders convicted under s. 498 A may be excluded.On the one hand. there have been complaints of the misuse of this provision. and the consequent harassment. often incarceration. of many members of the family complained against. On the other. there is little scope to deny that the incidence of cruelty. including physical cruelty. which leads even to death. is extraordinarily high. This is an issue yet unresolved; the Domestic Violence Bill may have some impact on it.

In the meantime. an activist lawyer asserts that the phenomenon of violence and death in the matrimonial home should not need to be linked invariably with the phenomenon of dowry; violence and cruelty are independent entities within many homes. An activist also told us: when a man beats his wife regularly. and the wife gets him soundly thrashed by the police. civil liberties groups are sometimes confused on what stand to take.

SATI

The burning of Roop Kanwar on the pyre of her husband in Rajasthan in 1986. has reintroduced sati into mainstream discourse. Questions of volition. custom and communal pride have been raised justifying the practice. State inaction has been at issue. In 1987. the Commission of Sati (Prevention) Act was enacted making abetment of sati an offence; and the death penalty was introduced as an alternative sentence.

The attempt to commit sati was made punishable with imprisonment for a term up to six months or with fine. or both; this has been contested ever since its inception as punishing the victim. The 'glorification' of sati. where a temple is constructed and a dead woman worshipped bringing in money to the family. has also been made punishable.

This last is constantly under contest-as denying the right to practise a religion. Women's groups in Rajasthan see this as a particularly important provision in taking away the material incitement in the commission of sati. The communal violence of much of the protest against this law. and of the practice itself. is a telling statement of the capacity of patriarchy to deny a place for human rights.

CHILD MARRIAGE

Though a law prohibiting child marriage has been in the statute books since 1929. it is still performed in many parts of India. For instance. the practice of performing child marriages on *Akas Teej*. it is reported. has not stopped in Rajasthan. It is widely believed that the gang rape of Bhanwari Devi was intended as a lesson. since she was active in preventing child marriages. Another aspect of child marriage was revealed when Ameena. a girl of about 12 years. was married to an old man from Saudi Arabia who was to take her out of the country as his bride.

CHILD LABOUR

Apart from the employment of children in work. including those classified as hazardous. it was reported that:

- Children continue to be sold into labour. The parents of a young girl from Assam were paid a sum of money for the girl to be brought to Delhi as a domestic worker. Her plight came to light when she ran away from the ill-treatment she suffered. and she was given shelter by a social activist.
- Child workers employed in homes and in commercial workplaces. were subjected to ill-treatment. The chaining of bonded child labour in the carpet industry near Varanasi so that they could not escape was reported. Injuries on the person of domestic child workers in Delhi sometimes resulting in death. have been reported intermittently in the press. In Maharashtra. a civil liberties organisation took the state and a contractor to court when the latter ill-treated. resulting in death. one of the young boys he had brought with him from Tamil Nadu.

These manifestations of violence against the child disguised as child labour calls to be addressed. The vulnerability of the child has also been seen in Delhi. for instance. where child domestic workers have been accused of killing their employers. or in being accomplices to outsiders. The 'social clause' on child labour does not result in doing away with child labour. we were told. but causes segregation.

There were dissenting voices on the ILO Convention on the Elimination of the Worst Forms of Child Labour. The provisions which speak of child prostitution and child pornography as labour are unacceptable. they said. 'These are crimes. not labour.' we were told. Further. when Indian law is so strict that it says that non-payment of minimum wages amounts to bonded labour-a provision that is not found in any international convention-what use is one more convention. we were asked.In 1993. the Supreme Court declared that education is a fundamental right till a child reaches the age of 14 years. Education for the child has got tangled with the issue of child labour; sending the child to school is projected as a necessary step to ending the practice of child labour.

In Andhra Pradesh. an organisation working in the area of education for children has done away with the uncertainties of definition by working on the premise that every child out of school is child labour. They have therefore arrived at a non-negotiable: that every child must belong in a school.

In this view. NFE centres. for instance. would be a means of perpetuating child labour. So. too. with the adjusting of school timings to accommodate the working child. In the meantime. this 1999 Convention is being canvassed for signature. and ratification by the Indian State.

The convention defines 'the worst forms of child labour' as comprising:

- All forms of slavery or practices similar to slavery. such as the sale and trafficking of children. forced or compulsory labour. debt bondage and serfdom;
- The use. procuring or offering of a child for prostitu-tion. for the production of pornography or for porno-graphic performances;
- The use. procuring or offering of a child for illicit activities. in particular for the production and trafficking of drugs as defined in the relevant international treaties;
- Work which. by its nature or the circumstances in which it is carried out. is likely to jeopardize the health. safety or morals of children.

This is in consonance with the recent trend among UN organizations to directly involve human rights in standard-setting. and the creating of binding obligations of states in their area of operation.

THE 'NEGLECTED' CHILD

Street children have their peculiar vulnerability. In Bangalore. a study reveals that almost every street child has been sexually violated at some time or another. They are also specially susceptible to drugs. Street children. however. take care of themselves. and often of each other. It does not appear that institutionalising them is an answer to their needs. nor do they seem willing to trade their liberty for a life off the streets.In Bangalore. Bombay and Delhi. we heard of drop-in centres: places where children could drop in for a wash. some lessons. to keep their savings and to discuss their problems with others. if they so chose. They were. however. reported to be vulnerable to being 'rounded up' and sent periodically into state institutions from where they would need help to emerge. or from where they would 'escape'.

Women in prostitution have faced the possibility of their children being forcibly separated from them. following an order of the Supreme Court in *Gaurav Jain v. Union of India.* A 'raid' conducted by Delhi Police in 1990. in which 112 'children' were picked up from the GB Road area was an indication of what such a power being given to the police could mean to the women and their children. The recent changed law on 'children in need of care and protection' even prescribes adoption as an option that may be enforced by the state.

CHILD ABUSE

There has been increasing evidence of child abuse. and more particularly child sexual abuse. being pervasive. The perpetrator is often a near relative or someone close to the family. This adds to the vulnerability of the abused child. and. apart from the confusion and sense of shame which the child experiences. it is also that there is a problem with a refuge which the child can access. The dependence on the family as a support structure in times of abuse breaks down when the offending event occurs in the home.

Following what is widely considered as a useful intervention in the Supreme Court in the *Vishaka* guidelines regarding sexual harassment in the workplace. the matter of child abuse has also been taken to the court. and the Law Commission has been inducted into setting the parameters for care and action in cases of child sexual abuse.

THE 'UNWANTED' GIRL CHILD

The declining sex ratio. particularly the declining juvenile sex ratio. even in Kerala which is celebrated in economic writings and in state policy for having achieved a high rate of literacy and negative population growth. has begun to seriously engage. among others. researchers and women activists. The low status of women continues to be reflected in the practice of infanticide including in some parts of Tamil Nadu. foeticide. sex-selective abortion which the amniocentesis technology has made common. and mal-nourishment among girl children.In Usilampatti Taluk. reportedly. the ratio of female: male is 879:1000. Since 1986. the issue of female infanticide has been in focus in this area. More recently. scanning centres have mushroomed in the area. and female foeticide is rampant among those who are able to afford it. We were told that. in Tamil Nadu. there are around 2000 scan centres. most of which are unregistered. A researcher reported his encounter with the sale of girl children by communities in Andhra Pradesh to persons who then placed them for adoption. He drew attention to the astonishing fact that there is. as of now. no law to control. or punish. the sale of children. The involvement of adoption agencies in A.P. in what is allegedly the sale of children has since come to public attention. in April 2001.

PROSTITUTION

The fear of AIDS. it is perceived. has given the issue of prostitution a visibility. This has. however. led to attributing to women in prostitution the trait of being a 'high risk group'. even as it has been contended that it is high risk behaviour and not high risk groups that should be targeted. It appears that patterns of funding have impacted on this identification of the prostitute woman as belonging to a high-risk group. The demand for prostitution to be recognised as 'sex work' has been raised. with dignity of the woman in prostitution as its basis.

There are differing perceptions about prostitution-one which sees it as exploitative of women. and another that views it as representing the 'agency' of the women in the profession. There are various shades of meaning given to 'exploitation' and 'agency' which lies in the spaces between these two positions. Decriminalisation is also proposed. and disputed. on differing understandings of what decriminalising will mean. and do.

Most of the people we spoke to on the issue of prostitution. however. felt after a discussion emphasising the difference. that the practice of prostitution should be delinked from the issue of trafficking. In this context. trafficking is seen to be the sale and purchase of women and girls. and. more recently. boys. into prostitution.

While 'voluntariness' is a term with graded meanings. especially since economic compulsions and social exclusion are not uncommon causes for entering into the practice of prostitution. it is the distinctly involuntary nature of trading in human beings that is at the hub of trafficking. Trafficking in minors is a scourge that is commonly referred to as a crime to be curbed.

We encountered the issue of organising women in prostitution in two different ways. In Calcutta. a 'samiti' of sex workers are articulating their position. and taking a pro-active lead in matters of preventing the entry of minors into the profession in their area of operation. They also said that. if trafficking be seriously dealt with. they be allowed to. legally. participate in curtailing trafficking-for who else was more likely than the people already in the profession to know when women and girls were bought and sold. they asked.

In Mumbai. a respondent working among prostitute women for over a decade. advocated 'collectivisation' but had a problem with adopting the norm of forming unions of women in prostitution. While she did find that the state was doing very little about trafficking. she was convinced that if sex work were seen as 'real work' under the law. all efforts to curb trafficking would cease. It was also suggested that 'sex work is real work' is a funderdriven agenda. and. that those who do not adopt this line were being deliberately excluded.

In Kerala. however. a different perspective emerged where a distinction was drawn between the demand that persons in sex work should get all labour rights and the rights based approach. As a feminist. our respondent espoused the rights based approach. There was a recognition that most feminist ideologies oppose commercial sex workers coming together; the commercialisation of the body was identified as the problem.

Also. most people do not believe in the agency of commercial sex workers. it was explained. There was an opposition to licensing since that would only lead to further exploitation. The issue has been invisibilised over the years. and with people in high places being involved. it has helped to send it further underground.

The *Surinelli* and *Vidhura* cases have however increased confidence to complain; and people are now listening differently. Another women's activist opposed the use of the term 'commercial sex worker': prostitution is not productive work. she said. But her main problem was that she saw prostitution as reinforcing patriarchy. and that endorsing prostitution as work would fall into the snare patriarchy has set for the women's movement.

In the matter of trafficking. it was pointed out that proposals for checking all women travelling on their own. particularly across borders was a move detrimental to the interests of women and could end up curbing their right to free movement and achieve little else.

PRISONS

The conditions in jails; solitary confinement; the refusal to make condoms available in Tihar jail on the ground that homosexuality is an offence in law. and this would be seen as fostering an illegality; the inhuman treatment of prisoners. including their being kept in leg irons. for instance; overcrowding of prisons; the right of prisoners. including undertrials. to vote are issues that have been raised repeatedly over the years. The courts have been the arena of contest.

The inadequacy of medical services in prisons. often resulting in the death of prisoners has been much in evidence. Apart from the inconclusive enquiry into the death of Rajan Pillai. when he was in jail. High Courts and the NHRC have been confronted repeatedly with this issue. Statistics in the Annual Reports of the NHRC reveal that there are a much larger number of deaths in judicial custody than there is in police custody.

Given the frequency and seriousness of the complaints about medical services in prisons. it would bear investigation to find out how many of the deaths in judicial custody are. in fact. occasioned by medical negligence. The condition of persons on death row does not appear to have been investigated so far. Nor the effect that execution of prisoners has on their families. The inaccessibility to legal services that is endemic in most prisons. has been identified as a human rights issue. but has not been resolved yet.

There are reports of prison riots which were allegedly caused by the poor conditions in prisons including insufficient provision of food. and the maltreatment. including the brutalising. of prisoners. On November 17. 1999. for instance. a riot broke out in Chennai Central Prison. It left at least nine persons dead. and one more succumbed to injuries on November 19. 1999. There were at least seven prisoners with bullet injuries who were referred to the government general hospital.

The figures of those injured and dead in the riots varies. but it appears to be around 100 prisoners. The deputy jailor was killed in the riots. The simmering discontent seems to have had to do with inadequate food. the meagre water supplied to the prisoners. and the torture meted out to them by the prison staff.

The death of a prisoner tortured and killed in the Central Prison in July 1999. which was explained away without an enquiry as being a suicide. seems to have caused resentment and anger among the prisoners. It was the death of Boxer Vadivel. a prisoner believed to have been tortured for over three days between 12th and 15th of November. and the torture of two other prisoners by the Deputy Jailor which sparked off the riots.

Jeyakumar was burned alive. The prisoners claimed to a fact-finding team that the rebellion had already come under control when antiriot police were brought in and prisoners were indiscriminately targeted. For instance. a prisoner who was physically disabled. and could not have posed any threat to the police. was shot at point blank range. The anatomy of a prison riot. and what it means in the context of human rights. and of punishment. calls to be investigated in full. and addressed. Prison riots have been erupting sporadically. leaving little reason to doubt that they are symptomatic of a systemic malaise.The condition of medical care in prisons is woeful. and cases before the High Courts and the NHRC testify to this fact. The inordinately large number of deaths in judicial custody. as reflected in the figures set out in the Annual Reports of the NHRC. is also an indicator. That prisons are death traps becomes apparent.

Overcrowding of prisons. with a large population of undertrial prisoners spending extended periods in jail-a recent press report cites a survey conducted by the State (Jail) Department in Bihar which shows 154 undertrial prisoners in Bhagalpur jail for over 20 years awaiting trial and they are now over 70 years old-only strains the system further. Systemic changes and bold initiatives are imperative.So far. the Supreme Court's directive in 1979 to release undertrial prisoners on personal recognisance bonds. and periodic intervention thereafter by the Supreme Court. has provided ad hoc relief. There is little to indicate that there has been any fundamental re-thinking on this matter. On the other hand. recent legislation is severe in matters of bail. and persons arrested under the NDPS Act 1985. for instance. regardless of the nature of their participation in the offence. are not entitled to bail.

In Mumbai. social workers reported that they have been allowed access to prisoners to help them re-establish. and maintain. contact with their families. and to provide related support services to the prisoners. They admitted to shutting their eyes to human rights violations in prisons since any intervention of that nature would jeopardise even the services they are now able to provide.In Chennai and in Mumbai. the '80s and a part of the '90s saw active provision of legal aid to prisoners; in Chennai. the High Court legal aid board was engaged in this process. In Delhi. legal literacy. literacy. meditation and yoga and legal aid has reached Tihar jail. The setting up of the NHRC appears to have had some impact on the accessibility of prisons. as have the many PILs which challenged the conditions within.

WAGES TO PRISONERS

The work that prisoners do has been devalued in a decision of the Supreme Court in *State of Gujarat v. High Court of Gujarat.*

A judge in the case has held that:

- Prisoners are not entitled to minimum wages. particularly where they have been sentenced to rigorous imprisonment. and it is part of their sentence to do hard labour
- The non-payment of wages in prison will not amount to a violation of the constitutional dictum on the right against exploitation
- Where they do earn a wage. apart from deductions for their maintenance in the prison. monies may be taken from it to pay to the victim as compensation.

There is a complete negation of the rehabilitative potential of work and wages. and a re-introduction of the purely punitive in this Judgement of the court that human rights advocates and activists will have to contest.

SEXUALITY

Discrimination against. and harassment of. those with a sexual orientation different from the heterosexual is being more openly addressed in the past ten years than it was earlier. Yet. coming out openly is still an act of courage. And we were told how homosexual couples were susceptible to arrest and extortion. Just the knowledge that a person is a homosexual would render him vulnerable. they said. The lesbian groups that we met spoke about the difficulty of coming out. and the support services that were needed to help resist. principally. the families. One of the ways of providing that support is in the initiation of 'help lines'.

FREEDOM OF EXPRESSION

The rise of communalism has been accompanied by an assault on free expression. The vandalising of M. F. Hussain's paintings because he had painted a nude Saraswati many years ago; the destruction of the exhibition organised by SAHMAT in Varanasi because it depicted Rama differently from how the vandals believed he should be depicted; the protests. and their vulgarisation when the protesters paraded in their underwear in front of Dilip Kumar's house. against the film 'Fire'; the concerted attacks on the filming of 'Water'-all these are instances of intolerance. which have denied free expression. with the implicit-sometimes explicit-support of the state. The banning of the play on Nathuram Godse following protests and disturbances are part of a pattern.

More recently. there have been reports of a government circular that conferences. seminars. workshops...which include participants from abroad require clearance from the government. including the External Affairs Ministry. Human rights are specifically in the list. And it is particularly applicable to people from Pakistan. China. Bangladesh. Sri Lanka and Afghanistan.

DALITS

The practice of untouchability has persisted. and dalit activists and unions have been making efforts to demonstrate its pervasiveness and variety. even while they contest its practice. In Andhra Pradesh. in a study done by dalit activists. 46 ways of practising untouchability have been documented. In Kerala. there was collaboration underway between caste groups and dalits in combating caste and brahmanism. In Gujarat. a study of the practice of untouchability has been recently done.

Some groups working among dalits. and including some dalit groups. have been lobbying to place caste as an agenda in the World Conference against Racism. The definition evolving in the conference. which includes discrimination based on descent and occupation is seen as an acknowledgment of caste discrimination. This is an avowed effort to internationalise the issue of caste-based discrimination and oppression. This issue permits an exploration into the relationship between a movement-in this case. the dalit movement-and groups working with dalits and/or dalit issues in terms of their respective politics and priorities.

Police firing on a group of dalit villagers in Nadunalumoo-laikkinaru in Tamil Nadu in 1991 is believed to have occurred to put down a young leadership that was emerging in the village. A chain of circumstances from the support given to the villagers by activists. to filing the matter as a case in the Supreme Court. to three committees which investigated the matter. to the awarding and disbursement of compensation to the injured villagers and the court order which prohibited the indicted policemen from being posted in the vicinity appears to have empowered the village. It has also bolstered their confidence that help could well come from beyond the village. In Melavalavur it was a different story. This is a panchayat which is reserved for dalit leadership within the panchayat system.

When elections were first to be held:

- The dalits were chastised. subjected to a community fine of '2000 and warned to withdraw their nominations.
- In the second round. the administration urged the dalits to file nominations. which they did. The ballot boxes were taken away by the non-dalit villagers.
- The third time around. the administration promised protection and conducted the elections amidst threats and tight security. About a month after the elections. the dalit panchayat leader. Murugesan. and five of his comrades were waylaid when they were travelling in a public bus. and brutally hacked to death on the highway.

This was in June 1997. Since then. another election has nominally installed a dalit as panchayat head. But the village lives in a state of permanent terror. A police outpost has been set up. but in that part of the village from where the threat to the dalits emanates. A memorial has been constructed to the memory of the six dead men.

The Scheduled Castes and Scheduled Tribes (Prevention of Atrocities) Act has been on the statute books since 1989. There are however hardly any convictions under this Act. Dalit activists say that there are many loopholes in the law which help offenders slip out of both the Atrocities Act as well as the Penal Code. An activist made particular mention of s. 3 (iv) and (v) of the Act in illustrating the non-user of this law. Studies on the working of this Act have been started in some states.

Manual scavenging. and the disinterest of the state in putting an end to this inhuman practice which involves the carrying of excreta manually. and which additionally aggravates caste-based exclusion has been identified as a priority for action in Andhra Pradesh and Tamil Nadu.

MEDICAL RESEARCH

The connection between abortion. in vitro fertilisation and gene manipulation was drawn to ask how the question of human rights could be considered in this context. The poser was: ought it not to be the primary question whether neo-eugenics through gene manipulation should be resisted. or was it to be asked in terms of the mother's choice to have a 'blue-eyed baby girl'? Depo Provera. a contraceptive drug. was introduced into the Indian market without conducting Phase IV trials. which meant that the Indian state conducted no research specific to Indian users before deciding to introduce the drug in the market. The issue in Phase IV trials of Net-oen was of informed consent. In the pre-liberalisation phase. we were informed. all research was to be undertaken by the ICMR. But post-liberalisation. there has been a dramatic change. and the trend has been for pharmaceutical companies. or the NGOs funded for the purpose. to conduct research; their agenda is not beyond suspicion.

Pharmaceutical companies have been attempting to dilute the guidelines for scientific research on human subjects. The Nuremberg Code was very strict. The later Helsinki declaration. we were told. relaxed these rules. And efforts are underway to further relax the notion of informed consent for the greater common good. These efforts have been stalled at the international level. But ICMR's 'Ethical Guidelines for Biomedical Research on Human Subjects' has been amended in 2000 to allow proxy consent in some cases. such as in epidemiological situations or in the larger public good.

In 1997. the Indian government signed an agreement with the USA that would allow Indian citizens to be used as research subjects in an international research project on human genome for furthering 'international good'. Since this became known. there have been protests-that the bodies of Indian citizens do not belong to the state that it can sign them away.

Court battles around banned drugs being sold in the Indian market have sometimes resulted in prospective banning. But the plea of the pharmaceutical company that the stocks be not destroyed. but that they be allowed to transport it to another jurisdiction outside India has been allowed. Sharing information with other potential markets becomes of importance. and ways of doing this may have to be established.

POPULATION POLICIES

There has been a deliberate re-introduction of 'incentives' and 'disincentives'. and of punitive measures into state policy:

- The birth of a third child beyond a period of gestation from the commencement of state laws on the subject (including Himachal Pradesh. Rajasthan and Haryana) will disqualify a person from standing for elections to the panchayat. or to continue in office.
- Medical termination of pregnancy and tubectomy has been included in the Maternity Benefit Act 1961 for 'benefit' under the law. The threatened denial of 'maternity benefit' for the birth of the third child and thereafter was. however. shelved after concerted protest. The new provision puts an onus on the woman to keep the size of her family low.
- There are private proposals pending in various state legislatures including Delhi and Andhra Pradesh to disentitle the third child to ration under the Public Distribution System. and for the parent to be penalised in their jobs if they hold a government job. The Delhi proposal even included provisions that the family could not be allowed

to procure a house if there was a third child! These have not yet become law. but they have not disappeared from the public debate altogether.

- 'Social marketing' of contraceptive drugs. supported in Uttar Pradesh by large grants from funders. has been the subject of protest from. particularly. women activists. Social marketing. which includes across-the-counter sales. would inevitably lead to ill-informed use of the contraceptives. without an understanding of the sideeffects. or of the meaning of symptoms that may manifest upon use. The prioritising of reducing population at the cost of women's health is being stoutly resisted.

ORGAN TRANSPLANT

A racket in the sale of kidneys was exposed in Karnataka in the late 1980s and early '90s. There were allegations that the 'donor' was duped and his kidneys were removed and 'donated'; or that the donor had sold his kidneys as a commodity may be sold to raise resources-poverty was the characteristic that distinguished the donor. A series of exposés confirmed that there was a pattern to the sale and purchase of kidneys. which implicated. among others. doctors and hospitals.

The dust refused to settle. and in 1994. Parliament enacted the Transplantation of Human Organs Act 1994. which allowed organ donation either only after death. or where the receiver was a near relative of the donor. or it is actuated by 'affection. or attachment towards the recipient.' In the last-mentioned case. an Authorisation Committee has to approve the donation. The Act. in its prefatory text. says it is 'to provide for the regulation of removal. storage and transplantation of human organs for therapeutic purposes and for the prevention of commercial dealings in human organs.'

The issue seems to have acquired a subterranean residence since. This may be an area which must be regularly revisited to prevent exploitation. and worse. In a different context. the issue of surrogacy has entered Indian parlance; but the human rights. and legal. implications have not been pursued with much rigour.

TRAFFICKING

While trafficking in women is rampant in many parts of the country. and also across borders. it is Kerala that the sexual exploitation of women and trafficking has been exposed. and the accused brought to trial and conviction. The *Surinelli* case. the *Ice Cream Parlour* case and the *Vidhura* case are undiluted narratives of sexual exploitation. In the *Surinelli* case. forty persons. including prominent political figures and persons from the establishment among them. were convicted after a prolonged trial in 2000. They are now on bail while their appeal is pending.

Some women's activists have been studying the issue of migration and trafficking-whether for prostitution. labour in sweat shops. domestic work which is often ill-paid and oppressive. or as mail order brides—while recognising that while migration makes women vulnerable to exploitation-and violence. migration is often not wholly involuntary. Women. for instance. migrate to escape violent domestic situations too. Shorn of its moral content. activists say. the law regarding trafficking could actually help women trafficked into situations for which they did not bargain.

CONCEPT OF CITIZENSHIP AND RIGHTS

The concept of citizenship involves the concept of rights. Citizenship is both a status and a set of rights. As American Chief Justice Earl Warren declared. 'Citizenship is man's basic right for it is nothing less than the right to have rights' A citizen is someone who possesses rights which are denied to non-citizens and to resident aliens and foreigners. Similarly. according to Rawls. 'The position of equal citizenship is defined by the rights and liberties required by the principle of equal liberty and the principle of fair equality of opportunity.

When the two principles are satisfied. all are equal citizens'. However. all rights are not citizenship rights. Citizenship is a status bestowed on those who are full members of a national community and citizenship rights are those which derive from and facilitate participation in this 'common possession'. They are rights of a person in the community of a nation-state which are ultimately secured by the state. These rights in a way impose certain limitations upon the state's sovereign authority. and entail certain duties from other persons.According to Marshal. the growth of citizenship has been 'stimulated by both the struggle to win (those) rights and by their enjoyment when won'. Examining the concept of citizenship in the context of social classes. Marshal pointed out that its unique element can be defined in terms of specific set of rights and the social institutions through which these rights are exercised. Tracing the development of the institutions of modern citizenship. Marshal writes that while capitalism created inequalities. citizenship created a status through which members shared equal rights and duties. The three elements of citizenship rights identified by Marshal are: Civil. political. and social.

The civil element of citizenship is composed of rights necessary for individual freedom and institutions most directly associated with it are the rule of law and a system of courts. They include right to properly. contract. freedom of speech. religious practice. assembly and association. Moreover. they can be used to create groups. associations. corporations and movements of every kind. They are a kind of power against the state. The political aspect consists of a set of political rights such as right to take part in the elections and right to serve in bodies endowed with political authority. Such rights are associated with the parliamentary institutions. The social component of rights subsumes the right to share the social heritage.Citizenship in the twentieth century has been associated more with the development of the idea of social rights. After the second world war. the belief that the stale has a duty to ensure social justice and an adequate level of welfare for all its citizens has rapidly gained ground. The guiding principle of the policies commonly implemented has been that the state should raise funds through taxing the rich and these funds should be used for educational and health services and protecting the citizens from illness. unemployment and old age. etc. If by citizenship we mean the recognition of reciprocal rights and responsibilities. then the state has an obligation to provide basic welfare to its citizens.

The rich have an obligation to contribute funds for social welfare and the beneficiaries of the welfare state have an obligation not to abuse these rights and services. In this sense. the provisions for welfare are unrelated to the specific status of citizenship. Heater has called this aspect of citizenship as 'social citizenship'. This is a belief that since all citizens are assumed to be fundamentally equal in status and dignity. none should be so depressed in economic and social conditions as to make a mockery of this assumption. Therefore. in return for the loyalty and virtuous civic conduct displayed by the citizens. the state has an obligation to smooth out any gross inequalities by a guarantee of basic standard of living in terms of income. shelter. health and education.

Essential minimum standard in these areas of life should be enjoyed as a right of citizenship. irrespective of wealth. bargaining power. sex. age or race. Further. no stigma should be attached to the communal source of provisions. Thus the modern idea of citizenship includes not only civil and political dimensions but also a social component. However. it would be imprudent to assume that the different component of rights of modern citizenship are equally guaranteed by the state. Not only are the civil and social rights founded on different principles and basis. there may exist some tension with each other.

The social rights are always under a threat to be eliminated by the civil rights. In recent years. the debate over citizenship rights has broadened to include recognition to a variety of groups such as groups struggling for the rights of women and ethnic minorities. rights of children. the poor of the third world. and even rights of animals and plants. Some writers have interpreted these new social movements as shifting and widening the definition of social and political membership to encompass previously excluded and oppressed social groups. They look to an expanded set of rights to match a broader and cosmopolitan concept of citizenship. In this way rights come to define our identity as citizens of a global community. However. inspite of popularity. the belief is unfounded because the hope that they can be included in a reformed and fuller concept of citizenship rights is practically not feasible.

WHAT ARE RIGHTS WHAT ARE RIGHTS ?

There are two types of right: Negative rights and Positive rights.

Negative Rights Negative Rights

Put simply a negative right is the right to be left alone. Specifically it is the right to think and act free from the coercive force of others. Free from muggers. fraudsters and restrictive laws and taxes. A negative right is an absolute. Even the slightest violation breaks this right. Imagine that a man stops you in the street once a week and forces you to stand still for one minute - hardly a life changing violation - yet your right to be free of the coercion of others is being broken. The degree to which this right is violated changes from place to place but I know of no country where it is not routinely violated by the state.

Remember that a person cannot claim this right while violating the same in others. A mugger cannot claim a right to be left alone whilst mugging people.The kind of society where this right is prevalent is a society whose government exists only to protect the individual from the force of others. The American Constitution and Bill of Rights are the closest examples - which. sadly. modern day America is abandoning daily.

Positive Rights Positive Rights

These are rights to something. A right to food. to Health care. to education - whatever. The reality of a positive right is that whatever the object of the right is. it needs to be created before the 'right' can be fulfilled. This creates an obligation upon others to create it and it is the basis for slave societies and statist dictatorhips.In the UK positive rights exist and each person who is taxed and restricted via legislation into providing the object of the right is working a proportion of his/her life as a slave. This may seem a bit extreme. but it isnt. Unless you agree entirely with your payment of every tax and everything the government then spends your money on. you are being forced to work for ends you have *not* given your consent to - just like a slave. Slavery was outlawed. but it crept back under the guise of the 'public good'.

The reason most people tolerate. or even give apathetic support to it. is because they are not thinking about which principles are being abandoned and which of their own rights they are giving up by doing so. Many people find the costs of obeying restricitive laws and paying 50per cent in tax irritating but. amazingly. no more than that. "Its not all that bad!" They might say - I would suggest turning back the tide of controls and restrictions now before it is terribly bad - it has happened in other countries. however naively you might imagine "it cant happen here". The answer is to ask. whenever some new scheme is proposed by the government. "at whose expense?" and you will find that the expense is your freedom.

WHERE DO RIGHTS COME FROM? WHERE DO RIGHTS COME FROM?

A common question asked of political rights is where do they come from and how are they granted. There are several different justifications for the inclusion of rights in a constitutional system. These vary slightly depending on how the political philosophy views the individual. Since the enlightenment focused social endeavour on individual autonomy as the primary source. the notion of universal political rights have risen. This is present in republicanism. liberalism. libertarianism and progressivism. All these political philosophies focus on the individual as the dominant political entity.

Republicanism views the purpose of government as ensuring the liberty of the individual. Tyranny or despotism has no place in a republican system. The rights or just demands of an individual's agreeance to follow the will of the majority in a government system come with the assurance of freedom from tyranny or arbitrary government.A bill of rights becomes a political technology that ensures the liberty of the individual and describes tyranny. It creates a sphere of exclusion for government that it cannot legislate over.

Dan Deniehy took a natural rights view of republicanism. This describes moral perfection as the end result of human achievement. maturation and growth. Deniehy writes that tyranny and despotism are the dominant affliction against this purpose.Consequently the tyranny becomes a crime against mankind's destiny - a crime against nature. This is a non-religious argument for natural rights. The religious argument for natural rights is quite simply that rights are granted by God. This is less sophisticated than Deniehy's argument and reliant on faith.

Progressives view rights as an intrinsic function of being human. For this reason they are often called Human Rights by the progressive movement. The progressives view rights as being greater than the simply eradication of tyranny and protection of liberty as republicans do and often include more ambiguous rights of a social nature such as the right to dignity or the right to education.These are fine principles to maintain. however. they do not have a place in a constitutional document as they are nearly impossible to quantify. For instance writing brutally explicit language on the right to dignity is impossible.Libertarians view rights in terms of the intrinsic value of the individual. This philosophy often terms them individual rights. Libertarianism does not have the same focus on tyranny as republicanism does and is merely interested in the primacy and dominance of the individual as a political being.

Of these justifications for rights I believe the republican definition to be superior. It is constitutionally achievable through explicit constitutional language and separation of powers. The focus on the eradication of tyranny and political equity are important principles in democratic and representative systems.

Under republicanism rights are a very essential political technology which better serves the protection of liberty from arbitrary government.

LEGAL RIGHTS AND THE STATE LEGAL RIGHTS AND THE STATE

While claims for human rights appeal to our moral self. the degree of success of such appeals depends on a number of factors. most important of which is the support of governments and the law. This is why so much importance is placed on the legal recognition of rights.

A Bill of Rights is enshrined in the constitutions of many countries. Constitutions represent the highest law of the land and so constitutional recognition of certain rights gives them a primary importance. In our country we call them Fundamental Rights. Other laws and policies are supposed to respect the rights granted in the Constitution. The rights mentioned in the Constitution would be those which are considered to be of basic importance. In some cases these may be supplemented by claims which gain importance because of the particular history and customs of a country. In India. for instance. we have a provision to ban untouchability which draws attention to a traditional social practice in the country.So important is the legal and constitutional recognition of our claims that several theorists define rights as claims that are recognised by the state. The legal endorsement certainly gives our rights a special status in society but it is not the basis on which rights are claimed. The rights have steadily been expanded and reinterpreted to include previously excluded groups and to reflect our contemporary understanding of what it means to lead a life of dignity and respect.

However. in most cases the claimed rights are directed towards the state. That is. through these rights people make demands upon the state. When I assert my right to education. I call upon the state to make provisions for my basic education. Society may also accept the importance of education and contribute to it on its own. Different groups may open schools and fund scholarships so that children of all classes can get the benefit of education. But the primarily responsibility rests upon the state. It is the state that must initiate necessary steps to ensure that my right to education is fulfilled.

Thus. rights place an obligation upon the state to act in certain kinds of ways. Each right indicates what the state must do as well as what it must not do. For instance. my right to life obliges the state to make laws that protect me from injury by others. It calls upon the state to punish those who hurt me or harm me. If a society feels that the right to life means a right to a good quality of life. it expects the state to pursue policies that provide for clean environment along with other conditions that may be necessary for a healthy life. In other words. my right here places certain obligations upon the state to act in a certain way.

Rights not only indicate what the state must do. they also suggest what the state must refrain from doing. My right to liberty as a person. for instance. suggests that the state can not simply arrest me at its own will. If it wishes to put me behind bars it must defend that action; it must give reasons for curtailing my liberty before a judicial court. This is why the police are required to produce an arrest warrant before taking me away. My rights thus place certain constraints upon state actions.

To put it another way. our rights ensure that the authority of the state is exercised without violating the sanctity of individual life and liberty. The state may be the sovereign authority; the laws it makes may be enforced with force. but the sovereign state exists not for its own sake but for the sake of the individual. It is people who matter more and it is their well-being that must be pursued by the government in power. The rulers are accountable for their actions and must not forget that law exists to ensure the good of the people.

KINDS OF RIGHTS KINDS OF RIGHTS

Most democracies today begin by drawing up a charter of political rights. Political rights give to the citizens the right to equality before law and the right to participate in the political process. They include such rights as the right to vote and elect representatives. the right to contest elections. the right to form political parties or join them.

Political rights are supplemented by civil liberties. The latter refers to the right to a free and fair trial. the right to express one's views freely. the right to protest and express dissent. Collectively. civil liberties and political rights form the basis of a democratic system of government. But. rights aim to protect the well-being of the individual. Political rights contribute to it by making the government accountable to the people. by giving greater importance to the concerns of the individual over that of the rulers and by ensuring that all persons have an opportunity to influence the decisions of the government.

However. our rights of political participation can only be exercised fully when our basic needs. of food. shelter. clothing. health. are met. For a person living on the pavements and struggling to meet these basic needs. political rights by themselves have little value. They require certain facilities like an adequate wage to meet their basic needs and reasonable conditions of work. Hence democratic societies are beginning to recognise these obligations and providing economic rights.

In some countries. citizens. particularly those with low incomes. receive housing and medical facilities from the state; in others. unemployed persons receive a certain minimum wage so that they can meet their basic needs. In India the government has recently introduced a rural employment guarantee scheme. among other measures to help the poor. Today. in addition to political and economic rights more and more democracies are recognising the cultural claims of their citizens. The right to have primary education in one's mother tongue. the right to establish institutions for teaching one's language and culture. are today recognised as being necessary for leading a good life. The list of rights has thus steadily increased in democracies. While some rights. primarily the right to life. liberty. equal treatment. and the right to political participation are seen as basic rights that must receive priority. other conditions that are necessary for leading a decent life. are being recognised as justified claims or rights.

Rights not only place obligations upon the state to act in a certain way — for instance. to ensure sustainable development — but they also place obligations upon each of us. Firstly. they compel us to think not just of our own personal needs and interests but to defend some things as being good for all of us. Protecting the ozone layer. minimising air and water pollution. maintaining the green cover by planting new trees and preventing cutting down of forests. maintaining the ecological balance. are things that are essential for all of us. They represent the 'common-good' that we must act to protect for ourselves as well as for the future generations who are entitled to inherit a safe and clean world without which they cannot lead a reasonably good life.Secondly. they require that I respect the rights of others. If I say that I must be given the right to express my views I must also grant the same right to others. If I do not want others to interfere in the choices I make — the dress I wear or the music I listen to — I must refrain from interfering in the choices that others make. I must leave them free to choose their music and clothes. I cannot use the right to free speech to incite a crowd to kill my neighbour. In exercising my rights. I cannot deprive others of their rights. My rights are. in other words. limited by the principle of equal and same rights for all.

Thirdly. we must balance our rights when they come into conflict. For instance. my right to freedom of expression allows me to take pictures; however. if I take pictures of a person bathing in his house without his consent and post them on the internet. that would be a violation of his right to privacy.

Fourthly. citizens must be vigilant about limitations which may be placed on their rights. A currently debated topic concerns the increased restrictions which many government are imposing on the civil liberties of citizens on the grounds of national security. Protecting national security may be defended as necessary for safeguarding the rights and well being of citizens.

But at what point could the restrictions imposed as necessary for security themselves become a threat to the rights of people? Should a country facing the threat of terrorist bombings be allowed to curtail the liberty of citizens? Should it be allowed to arrest people on mere suspicion? Should it be allowed to intercept their mail or tap their phones? Should it be allowed to use torture to extract confession?

In such situations the question to ask is whether the person concerned poses an imminent threat to society. Even arrested persons should be allowed legal counsel and the opportunity to present their case before a magistrate or a court of law. We need to be extremely cautious about giving governments powers which could be used to curtail the civil liberties of individuals for such powers can be misused.Governments can become authoritarian and undermine the very reasons for which governments exist — namely. the well being of the members of the state. Hence. even though rights can never be absolute. we need to be vigilant in protecting our rights and those of others for they form the basis of a democratic society.

CRITICAL EVALUATION CRITICAL EVALUATION

According to Heater. citizenship as a useful political concept has been so much overloaded in the twentieth century that there is a danger of its being disintegrated. The nature and utility of citizenship in the Greek city-state was totally different from the ways in which the concept has been realized in the modern nation-state. The concept which evolved to provide a sense of identity and community is on the verge of becoming a source of communal dissension. There are problems of disagreement over the interpretation and actualization of the idea of citizenship. More importantly. the granting of citizenship to virtually all inhabitants of the globe has given rise to a number of contradictory problems. some of which can be identified.

Firstly. if citizenship means political participation. then there has been a tendency towards a low level of participation by the people in the political process. And yet if all citizens are equal. then they must have equal opportunity and motivation for participatory activity. Secondly. citizenship is distorted by the process of gross inequalities in economic and social spheres. In fact the concept of social citizenship is still an area for greater pessimism. Social equality has been achieved only in a fraction of countries. At global level. social citizenship is far from being a reality both in theory and practice.

Thirdly. in underdeveloped countries where vast gaps exist between rich and poor. the benefits of citizenship are yet to reach to the low and marginal groups. These societies still cling to local. communal. religious or tribal loyalties and the sense of national cohesion is conspicuous by its absence. Fourthly. in the multicultural societies. serious tensions are emerging with regard to minority rights. And lastly the women liberation movements have put a serious question mark on the concept of citizenship because citizenship had deliberately excluded women not only from the political process but also from a number of social and economic rights.

LIBERTARIAN CRITIQUE OF CITIZENSHIP

The modern western democratic tradition associates citizenship with the liberal version of individual rights. By 1980s. more citizens were enjoying freedoms of thought. expression. assembly and association. The state. in the name of welfare measures. intervenes positively in the life of the individual.The demands and opportunities for the citizen to participate have never been greater.

But of late. the reaction against this intervention has been equally powerful. There is a tendency to withdraw from civil concerns in order to pursue a private. family life and a revulsion to the need to participate democratically in order to preserve political freedom. The proponents of elite theory argue that a view of politics which gives central role to citizenship in the sense of participation is an illusion. Political power is the handiwork of elites and at the very best. the involvement of citizens is limited in choosing between the competing elites on political agenda drawn up by the elites and on the goals determined by the elites.

On the other hand. libertarian writers like Hayek and Nozic leave little room for rich citizenship because they see government as empire rather than being an institutional structure serving certain common good. The duty of the citizen. they claim. is to observe certain rules of this game such as to pursue one's own interest and observe the rights of others. They define citizenship in terms of forbearance. *i.e.*. as not interfering in the rights of others rather than actually participating in the realization of certain communal values through political activity and political institutions.

The duty of the citizen is not to attempt for certain common good but to maintain the legal framework which secures space for them to realize their private non-civic interests. In short. they have brought the conflict between.political-social citizenship and socio-economic citizenship to the forefront once again.

EQUALITY

The Constitutions of Bangladesh. India. Nepal. Pakistan and Sri Lanka include the right to equality and a provision that does not regard special measures enacted for the benefit of women and children as violative of the equality provision. Before discussing the meaning of equality and its effect on gender justice. I must add a note of caution. Despite the legal interpretations to the meaning of equality. its understanding and effect is also shaped by the very different political. religious and cultural contexts of each South Asian country. All—with the exception of Nepal—were once colonies. and won their independence in the first part of the twentieth century. Yet each has developed in very different ways. While feudal relations continue to influence power at the local levels. India and Sri Lanka are distinctively different from Pakistan and Bangladesh. which have experienced long periods of military rule. Bhutan is a monarchy and a closed society. It is currently using 'authenticity' criteria for conferring citizenship. Nepal was once a monarchy. and is now a relatively new democracy. This democracy is currently (at the time of writing) being threatened by the Maoist insurgency and its political struggle with the monarchy. India and Sri Lanka are democracies. but have experienced considerable political turmoil in the form of self-determination movements.

ethnic and religious strife. Thus. by pointing out the commonalities in the pursuit of gender justice through equality discourse. it is important to keep in mind the diverse political. social. economic and cultural formations of these different countries.

Equality has eluded any simple or uniform definition. In the context of constitutional law and equality theory. two approaches to equality are clearly identifiable in political and legal discourse: a formal and a substantive approach. In the formal approach. equality is seen to require equal treatment—that is. all those who are the same must be treated the same. It is based on treating likes alike. The constitutional expression of this approach to equality has been in terms of the similarly situated test—the requirement that those who are similarly treated should be treated similarly. Within this approach. equality is equated with sameness. Only individuals who are the same are entitled to be treated equally. Any differential treatment of individuals or groups who are the same is seen to constitute discrimination (Singh 1976; Dwivedi 1990). The first step in the similarly situated analysis is to determine who is to be compared to whom. If the individuals or groups in question are seen as different. then no further analysis is required. because the difference justifies the treatment. Accordingly. when groups are not similarly situated. then they do not qualify for equality. even if the differences among them are the product of historic or systemic discrimination.

In contrast. the focus of a substantive equality approach is not simply with the equal treatment of the law. but with the actual effect of law. The explicit objective of a model of substantive equality is the elimination of the substantive inequality of disadvantaged groups in society. As Parmanand Singh observes. it 'takes into account inequalities of social. economic and educational background of the people and seeks the elimination of existing inequalities by positive measures'. Substantive equality is directed at eliminating individual. institutional and systemic discrimination against disadvantaged groups. which effectively undermines their full and equal social. economic. political and cultural participation in society.

The dominant understanding of equality in South Asia is heavily influenced by the liberal tradition. and based on assumptions of sameness. In other words. if you are the same you are entitled to equal treatment. Sameness becomes the pre-requisite to a challenge of discrimination. At the same time. the equality clause in each of the constitutions makes specific exceptions to the dominant understanding of equality as sameness. Reservations for scheduled castes and tribes. and special treatment for religious minorities and women have generally been regarded as exceptions to the dominant understanding of equality. rather than as integral to equality. Yet. these exceptions have rendered the universal understanding of the concept at times ambiguous and highly polarized. For example. the way in which gender difference is understood has a profound effect on the entitlements and rights that women are accorded. If gender difference is irrelevant and all persons should be entitled to formal equal rights. what happens to differences that have actually disadvantaged or historically been used to subordinate women. such as pregnancy or child care? If gender difference is regarded as an exception to equality. it can justify highly protectionist legislation. If gender difference is read as integral to equality. then historical disadvantage. rather than sameness or difference. becomes central to the understanding of equality.

Three approaches to the question of gender difference can thus be identified: protectionist. sameness and compensatory. A protectionist approach assumes that women are different from men—women are understood as weaker. subordinate and in need of protection. In this approach. any rule or practice that treats women differently than men can be justified on the basis that women and men are different. and that women need to be protected. The second approach is an equal treatment or sameness approach. In this approach. women are understood to be the same as men. that is to say. for the purposes of law they are the same. and must be treated the same. Any legislation or practice that treats women differently from men is seen to violate the equality guarantees. This sameness approach has been used to strike down provisions that treat women and men differently. It has. however. also been used to preclude any analysis of the potentially disparate effect of gender neutral legislation. In the third approach. women are understood as a historically disadvantaged group. and as such. in need of compensatory or corrective treatment.

Within this approach. gender difference is often seen as relevant and as requiring recognition in law. It is argued that a failure to take difference into account will only serve to reinforce and perpetuate the difference and the underlying inequalities. There are competing understandings of equality as well as to gender difference that exist in different countries in South Asia. The judicial approaches have been overwhelmingly influenced by a formal approach to equality. and a protectionist approach to gender difference. This formal approach to equality. in which equality is equated with sameness. and the protectionist approach to gender difference. in which women are understood as weak and in need of protection. has operated to limit the efficacy of these constitutional challenges. Some examples of a protectionist approach to gender difference include the provisions of the Nepali Constitution. which preclude Nepalese women from passing their nationality on to their children or to a spouse of foreign nationality). presumably on the grounds that women are incapable of assuming a nationality independent from that of their husbands. coupled with the simultaneous concern over national and cultural purity.

Similar to it is Section 488 of the Indian Code of Criminal Procedure. 1872. It requires men to pay maintenance to their wives. but imposes no corresponding duty on women to maintain their husbands. The provision is based on the assumption that women are economically dependent on their husbands. The amount of maintenance is usually minimal. reflecting how women's contribution to the household is regarded as supplemental or nominal. Section 488 was challenged as violating the equality clause in the Indian Constitution (Article 14) The Court upheld the section. stating that it applied to all women in similar circumstances. that is to all women deserted by their husbands and that such legislation favouring this class of people was not arbitrary. (Thamsi Goundani v. Kanni Ammal. All India Reports 1952 Madras 529.) Although the decision was beneficial from the perspective of the individual woman seeking maintenance from her husband. the reasoning was based on a formal approach to equality. It suggests that those who were similarly situated could be treated the same. The court also emphasized the issues of gender difference. treating the difference between men and women as natural. stating explicitly that woman were weaker than men and thus. in need of special treatment. The language suggests a protectionist approach to gender. In Pakistan. in 2003. the Supreme Court of Pakistan overturned a 1997 verdict of a High Court that voided the marriages of adult Muslim women without the permission of the woman's father or guardian. The decision challenges the protective assumption that informed the High Court's decision. and adopts the sameness standard when it comes to consensual marriages by either adult men or women. The case illustrates that formal equality remains an important goal for securing gender justice. while at the same time. emphasizing that formal equal treatment does not necessarily redress the underlying structural and systemic conditions as well as assumptions about gender difference which reinforce gender discrimination and women's subordinate status.

The role of equality rights litigation in challenging laws that allegedly discriminate on the basis of sex is contradictory. Judicial approaches have operated to limit the extent to which differential treatment of women is seen to be discrimination. And even where such differential treatment is perceived as tantamount to discrimination. the results are not always unequivocally positive. For example. while some cases have either struck down laws that have created legal obstacles to women's equality. the reasoning on which the results are based often reinforce assumptions about women as the weaker sex and vulnerable. Conversely. cases in which courts uphold laws that are designed to address women's substantive inequality may be done on the basis of similarly problematic reasoning. The analysis belies the assumption that legal engagements can 'solve' the problem and produce gender justice in result. even though on the face of it. the law appears gender-neutral.

The language of equality has played a central role in the struggle of the women's movement to bring about gender justice. And yet the language of equality is also used by those who oppose efforts to improve women's social and economic position. In its guise as formal equality. it has been used as a shield against efforts to develop programmes that are specifically directed at improving the conditions of women. It is also a concept that can and is being used by the Hindu Right or Muslim fundamentalists. in their attack on minority rights. One example of this in India is the case of Shah Bano. where a 73-year-old Muslim woman. who was divorced by her husband to whom she had been married for 40 years. brought a petition demanding maintenance from her husband under Section 125 of the Indian Criminal Procedure Code. According to Muslim personal law. she would only have been entitled to maintenance for the period of the *iddat*. that is. three months after the divorce. In April 1985. the Supreme Court held that she was entitled to maintenance under Section 125. and that allowing this maintenance would not violate the Koran. Conservative and orthodox forces within the Muslim community were outraged: they regarded the decision as an encroachment on the authority of Muslim theologians. An independent member of parliament introduced a Bill to save Muslim personal law. The women's movement. along with progressive Muslim organizations. campaigned against the Bill. The Hindu Right also campaigned vigorously against the Bill. which in its view was simply another example of the Congress government 'pandering to the minorities'.

5

Corporate Citizenship

In some respects. we might like to think that things have come a long way since the early days of the Social Issues in Management Division of the Academy of Management when corporations were in the words of Prakash Sethi 'up against the corporate wall.' Similarly. it can seem that much has changed since the early days of 'lobbying the corporation' began to draw attention to potential and actual corporate abuses against society—and its stakeholders—and the natural environment. Or since the ethics scandals of the 1970s and 1980s in the Defence contracting industry that resulted in the creation of the Foreign Corrupt Practices Act and spawned the implementation of codes of conduct in associated industries. and. ultimately. the Ethics Officers Association. Or since the wave mergers and acquisitions in the 1980s and early 1990s that resulted in a whole new rationale for getting rid of people: downsizing. rightsizing. restructuring. with all of the related 'social issues.'

Then again. maybe not so much has changed when we look at the almost incredible array of corporate scandals. accounting frauds. executive greed. short-sightedness. and ethical problems that greeted the opening of the new millennium. What have we actually learned from management theory generally. never mind the business in society field. which is so much more peripheral? Good corporate citizenship/good management practice is hardly rocket science. What needs to be done and generally how things 'ought' to be is actually pretty obvious. The problem appears to be translating what we know into practice.... thus much in the world of practice is the same as...or worse than it was in the field's early days. in part because of the forces of globalization and attendant growth of corporate power has creating shifting centers of power and influence in the world. By its nature that power is explicitly focused on what Frederick (1975) calls economizing and power aggrandizing. rather than the more civilizing. relationally-oriented pressures that come from civil society.

Indeed. investor capitalism. which puts shareholders front and center as the stakeholder of interest. has dominated economic and corporate thinking for at least 25 years. Perhaps not so much has changed. after all. Globalization and outsourced manufacturing have created significant Labour and human rights issues in developing countries. where Labour. human rights. and environmental standards are weak or Non-existent. simultaneously weakening the economies of local (home) communities and taking advantage of the disadvantaged systematically. Companies in the US now broadly participate in politics through contributions to political action committees that at least have the appearance of significant influence. ...Well. maybe corporate practice hasn't changed all that much. after all. The question is whether the evolution in theories have brought us relevant understanding.

Academic thinking about corporate citizenship. variously termed corporate social responsibility. corporate responsibility. corporate social performance. business citizenship. and corporate citizenship. as well as business ethics. stakeholder management. relationships. and engagement. arguably *has* made significant progress over the past 35 years or so this paper will attempt to demonstrate. So has corporate responsibility from a company perspective. at least in some respects. scandals and malfeasance aside. But the practice and academic streams are in many respects parallel universes. Further. if we were to truly look at the whole range of management theories or management practices. what we call corporate citizenship would be far from central. Parallel universes thus exist within management disciplines. within the business in society field itself in the stakeholder and corporate responsibility streams. and between theory and the realm of corporate practice. The gap between business in society or corporate citizenship theory and mainstream management disciplines is obvious and needs little attention. The recent call to action issued by Swanson and Frederick (2002) on the IABS and SIM listservers has drawn sufficient attention to this reality that it need not be considered in detail here.

Fundamentally. this paper asks business in society scholars some foundational questions. What is our role in fostering the profusion of language? Should some rationalization take place or some consolidation of terminology? What is our role in *bridging* parallel universes that already exist. *i.e.*. within the field. by creating some sort of consistency of conceptualization and agreement about terminology. rather than generating still more terms that appear to describe basically the same phenomena so as to set 'our' work apart from that of others? Or bridging between scholarship and business practice. *i.e.*. to what extent does and should our scholarly work reflect actual business practice? Or in other disciplines. bridging among the various academic disciplines that have evolved within the past 25 years that focus on fundamentally the same constructs on which business in society scholars are interested?

DEFINING CORPORATE CITIZENSHIP

This chapter focuses on parallel streams that exist within the field of business in society and between the field and corporate practice. While the paper will not provide an exhaustive literature review from a scholarly perspective. it will touch on the eras since the early days when the business in society field began to take shape using Bill Frederick's very helpful (and seminal) CSR framework. and illustrating how the CSR's have evolved into corporate citizenship. responsibility. reputation. and relationships in the present era. One thing that is truly important if the field is to progress is to begin to agree on terminology and its appropriate usage.

The metaphor of a branching (evolutionary?) tree neatly describes how the field has evolved to its current understanding of corporate citizenship. an understanding that begins to link the relatively parallel universes of theory and practices. and also illustrates how various conceptual branches are related to each other. Towards that it. it will be helpful to layout the general definitional framework that guides this discussion. because it is increasingly clear that common definitions are needed to provide credibility and legitimacy to the field. Although not all of these terms were in use at the start of the field. arguably a few of them can now be considered core or root concepts. related to each other. building both the theoretical and practical bases of the field. The root concepts. to my mind. are:

CORPORATE CITIZENSHIP (CC)

Corporate citizenship is manifested in the strategies and operating practices a company develops in operationalizing its relationships with and impacts on stakeholders and the natural environment. Some degree of corporate citizenship (on a scale from poor to excellent) is present in all of these relationships and in the ways that companies treat stakeholder/nature. Note that this definition attempts to integrate two separate streams of thinking: corporate (social) responsibility/performance and stakeholder theory. Corporate citizenship is an increasingly popular term in business practices. albeit there is considerable controversy about whether a corporation can (or should) act as a citizen.

Business Citizenship

Business citizenship is similar to corporate citizenship. involving the 'broader perspective on business rights and duties. stakeholder relationships. opportunities. and challenges that accompany the ...global economy.

CORPORATE RESPONSIBILITY (CR)

Corporate responsibility is the degree of (ir)responsibility manifested in a company's strategies and operating practices as they impact stakeholders and the natural environment day-to-day.. Some level of responsibility is integral to any corporate action or decision that has impacts. Corporate responsibility cannot be avoided because it is integral to action. and thus forms the root or foundation of corporate citizenship. Notably. this terminology is increasingly being used in business practice as a substitute or alternative for corporate citizenship. hence the definitions are used interchangeably.

Corporate *Social* Responsibility (CSR or CSR1)

Corporate social responsibility is the subset of corporate responsibilities that deals with a company's voluntary/discretionary relationships with its societal and community stakeholders. CSR is typically undertaken with some intent to improve an important aspect of society or relationships with communities or non-governmental organizations (NGOs) (Non-profits). CSR is frequently operationalized as community relations. philanthropic. multi-sector collaboration. or volunteer activities. CSR as generally used falls into what Carroll termed the discretionary and ethical responsibilities of business.

CORPORATE SOCIAL PERFORMANCE (ASSESSMENT)

Corporate social performance focuses on the principles of (social) responsibility at the institutional (legitimacy). organizational (responsibility). and individual (managerial discretion) levels. the processes of responsiveness (said to be environmental assessment. stakeholder management. and issues management). and outcomes (social impacts. Programmes. and policies). Basically. CSP provides a framework by which a company's relationship to and activities in society and with respect to stakeholders and the natural environment can be assessed. illustrating that principles. processes. and outcomes all need to be taken into account. The CSP framework was 'reoriented' by Swanson (1995) in an effort to integrate normative and descriptive approaches to business in society through concepts of value neglect and attunement. thereby avoiding what Freeman (1994) terms the separation thesis. which suggests that values can be separated from practice.

STAKEHOLDER THEORY

Popularized by Ed Freeman (1984). stakeholder theory essentially argues that a company's relationships with stakeholders (and treatment of the natural environment) is core understanding how it operates and adds value as a business; indeed. Freeman (2003) argues that stakeholder relationships are the very basis of value added and strategic initiative. Stakeholder language has been widely adopted in practice and is being integrated into concepts of corporate responsibility/citizenship by scholars who recognize that it is through a company's decisions. actions. and impacts on stakeholders and the natural environment that a company's corporate responsibility/citizenship is manifested.

Other definitions that will be useful for differentiating among the constructs used in the field follow:

- Corporate Community Relations (CCR) or Involvement (CCI). Corporate community relations is a (boundary-spanning) corporate function that typically encompasses corporate practices that enable the company to form (hopefully positive) relationships with members of communities in which it operates or with which it has relationships. and with 'society' at various levels (local. state/provincial. regional. national and global). CCR typically includes specific functions such as a foundation or philanthropic Programme (corporate philanthropy). volunteer activities. in-kind giving. and multi- or inter-sector partnerships/collaboration. Corporate community involvement (CCI) can be thought of as the processes associated with company interaction with community-based stakeholders. at whatever level of community is appropriate.
- Corporate Reputation. Corporate reputation encompasses the perceptions that companies' external and internal stakeholders have about their strategies. practices. and products/services. corporate responsibility/citizenship. and performance across a broad range of stakeholder and environmental measures. not just financial measures.

In our journey through the progress of corporate citizenship. we will see that many other terms also frame this discourse. One of the important objectives of this review is an effort to get the field to agree on terminology so that as it translates into practice there can be consensus about the underlying meanings. In my opinion. too many terms with different implications are now used interchangeably or in limited ways.

CSR1-4 AND CSP

Without going through a complete history of the field of business in society...and I would note that what we study is business *in* society. not business *and* society. we can see that there has been considerable development of (and. one hopes. advances in) scholarship. research. and practice. Research and scholarship have been paralleled at least partially by developments in corporate practice. What isn't fully clear is whether there is yet any synthesis into a theory of business in society—or corporate citizenship—that is broadly accepted. In fact. there may well be a yet not integrated and emerging theory of corporate citizenship. but it is a theory about and in practice. rather than a synthesis of the numerous streams of scholarly literature. Corporate citizenship as it stands today is more a theory of practice that comes largely from a few progressive companies. consulting firms. and the European Union. rather than a broad consensus of business practitioners or scholars.

Let us start this journey through the thicket of corporate citizenship terminology with the CSRs. In what became an important framework that continues to shape the conceptualization of the field. Bill Frederick argued for a progression of CSRs over a period of about 30 years. Frederick's typology begins with corporate social responsibility (CSR1) (the 1960s and 70s). moves to corporate social responsiveness (CSR2) (the late 1970s and 1980s). and ultimately to what (somewhat unfortunately. as he later recognized) he termed corporate social...rectitude (CSR3) (mid-1980 onward). More recently. Frederick argued that a significantly broader understanding of the role of companies in the world through a study of natural science and meaning (spirituality) needed to be undertaken through CSR4. Cosmos. Science. and Religion (spirituality).

The development of corporate responsibility or the ways that company practices impact stakeholders and the natural environment. Other terms that have been used to describe these responsibilities are corporate citizenship (which I use interchangeable with corporate responsibility to reflect the wide array of integral responsibilities) and business citizenship. The broad and integral responsibilities of the firm are underpinned by the concepts developed through stakeholder theory (which. according to some scholars. has multiple forms). As the definitions above suggest. the term corporate 'social' responsibility is used here to reflect the in-practice definition of the manifestation of a company's efforts to improve the society(ies) within which it operates. including the natural environment. but the emphasis is on the specifically social ('do-good.' volunteer. philanthropic. multi-sector collaborative) efforts.

Complimenting Frederick's CSRs are multiple additional branches prominent since the 1980s: corporate responsibility. corporate reputation. and corporate relationships give us three CRs related to the ways companies manifest their stakeholder/environmental relationships. Rather than viewing them as linearly developing later stages replacing the earlier. as Frederick implicitly did. it may be helpful to view them as branches from the trunk of corporate social responsibility. which rests on corporate responsibility(ies). corporate citizenship. stakeholder relationships. and assessment of that performance (corporate social performance). key root concepts in the field as it exists today.

These concepts exist. that is. side by side. simultaneously. rather than having evolved one from the other. more like an evolutionary tree with multiple branches that co-exist than a single successful evolutionary set of advances with a lot of dead ends. In this evolutionary sense. responsibility is the trunk (with integrity. perhaps at the root. though we won't go there at this point) and multiple branches emerging over time sometimes sequentially. sometimes emerging simultaneously. not all of which fit under the CSR rubric. Corporate citizenship as it stands today is the whole tree with all branches relevant.

CSR1: CORPORATE SOCIAL RESPONSIBILITY

The first stage of business in society literature focused on corporate social responsibility. CSR1.. CSR1 rested on two foundational principles. charity and stewardship. and six fundamental precepts. Despite the evolution of terminology that Frederick articulates. the term corporate social responsibility has largely stuck. both in the academic world and in the world of corporate practice. at least until the more recent emergence of the term corporate citizenship and its related term corporate responsibility (dropping the word social). CSR1 basically argued that with the rights that companies demanded in society came with a series of responsibilities and that as actors in societies companies had an obligation to behave responsibly. meeting its obligations voluntarily to avoid problems that would otherwise emerge. In practical usage. the term tends. as the definition above suggests. to mean the 'social' or 'do good' things that companies do. e.g.. multi-sector collaboration and partnerships aimed at bettering society in some way. community relations activities. philanthropic Programmes and strategies. and volunteer activities. In this view. companies could and should be held responsible for their actions and decisions as they affected society and ought to live up to a higher set of standards then simple adherence to the law for the good of all. Notably. the language of social responsibility is the language that has survived and. in many respects. shaped the field. for many practitioners today still believe that CSR(1) is all there is to the corporate citizenship paradigm.

CSR2: CORPORATE SOCIAL RESPONSIVENESS

The CSR1 era lasted from the 1960s until about the late 1970s. when it was not replaced but complimented by the advent of CSR2. corporate social responsiveness. The emergence of CSR2 reflected a more proactive stance on the part of companies that was recognized in the parallel universe of scholarship. most notably in the work of Preston and Post (1975). Responsiveness means that companies took explicit and forward-looking action to deal with external constituencies (whom we would now call stakeholders) and social/public policy issues. typically by evolving what Preston and Post termed boundary-spanning functions. Preston and Post also argued that corporate-society interaction needed to be viewed not as separate and non-interacting streams but through the lens of an 'interpenetrating systems model.' Companies. using boundary-spanning functions. attempted to cope more proactively than always reactively with problems and issues their activities raise in spheres other than the economic sphere. inherently recognizing their interdependence (interpenetration) with society.

Issues management became another branch of the evolutionary tree of corporate citizenship during the 1980s and. in some respects. continuing today. Wartick (1988) made a link between corporate financial performance and the capacity to manage issues well. a perspective taken global by Nigh and Cochran (1994) and strategic by Mahon and Waddock (1992) using the lifecycle perspective popularized by Preston and Post (1975). Taken a more systemic. network-oriented perspective based on some of the literature on multi-sector collaboration. Austrom and Lad (1989) proposed that alliances might create a new context for organizations. new values. and new ways of thinking. some of which can today be seen to be emerging in practice. *e.g.*. through the initiatives of the UN Global Compact or the evolution of the Global Reporting Initiative as a multi-stakeholder effort.

According to Frederick (1987). CSR 2 was more pragmatic or practice oriented than CSR1 had been. Indeed. CSR2 seems to have been drawn from the experience of companies rather than from calls for more responsibility coming from scholars or activists such as Ralph Nader. Two substreams emerged from this thinking. One stream was a micro-organizational stream emphasizing structural changes within the company to enable it to be more responsive to external issues. a stream whose progenitors were Ackerman and Bower (1975).

The second stream within CSR2. according to Frederick. was the macro dimension. which focused on public policy and was epitomized by the seminal work of Preston and Post (1975). Although Preston and Post (1975) famously spoke about the public responsibilities of managers. in practice. those public responsibilities became subsumed soon enough to the at least theoretical responsibilities that managers bore to the shareholder as the shareholder revolution began in the early 1980s under the rhetoric of shareholder first promoted by the increasingly dominant Chicago-school economists. led most notoriously by Milton Friedman and in the political context of the socially conservative Reagan era.

CSR3: CORPORATE SOCIAL...RECTITUDE

The third iteration of CSR was. according to Frederick (1987). in somewhat unfortunate terminology that was never widely adopted. corporate social rectitude or CSR3. CSR3 reflected the dramatic growth of interest in business ethics within the general business in society field in the mid and later 1980s. CSR3. according to Frederick. emphasized both social values derived from the socio-political environment and the emergence of a great deal of conceptual writing about business ethics.. Led largely by converted philosophers. the business ethics component of the business in society field emphasized ethical decision making processes. codes of conduct. and efforts to infuse companies with a broader set of values than narrow economic self-interest. As Frederick defined it. rectitude or ethics involved ‘a pervasive sense of rightness. respect. and humanity’ that would put values and ethics ‘at the center of a company’s concerns. its policies. and its major decisions’. Unfortunately. in practice. little of the sort happened. and as Liedtka pointed out. the field of business ethics has had little demonstrable effect on business practice. despite the common values across many management systems and approaches that she identified in that seminal—but under-cited or acknowledged—paper. The broader focus on values. however. has had some impact on practice. as is made clear in the work not only of Liedtka. Wicks (2001). and also the seminal management research of Collins and Porras (1996. 1997) and Senge (1990). as both theorists and progressive practitioners began to recognize the power in articulating and deploying inspirational vision and values within companies.

CSP: CORPORATE SOCIAL PERFORMANCE

Another stream emerged around 1991 when Donna Wood. building on the work of Wartick and Cochran (1985). drew up an integrated framework corporate social performance that linked the major streams to date using principles. processes. and outcomes as the guiding framework. Basically. the CSP framework provided an outline of what needs to be considered in assessing corporate (social) responsibility or performance. as well as an overview of the dominant (at the time) processes associated with that performance. the CSP framework was primarily intended to advance theory and research in the field rather than to influence practice. Somewhat more restrictive (narrowly focused) than the current understanding of corporate responsibility and corporate (business) citizenship. the CSP framework focused dominantly on the social (vs. broader stakeholder and environmental) impacts of corporate performance and rightly belongs in the CSR1 and CSR2 streams as identified by Frederick (1987).

As an assessment tool. the CSP model is helpful in pointing scholars and practitioners alike at the policies. processes. and performance arenas that must be evaluated to assess social responsibility. It. however. largely ignores (except for a bow to stakeholder management) the integral responsibilities of companies associated with impacts on stakeholders that began to surface with the evolution of stakeholder theory and emergence of the language of corporate citizenship in the late 1990s. As Swanson (1995) pointed out. the CSP approach fails to integrate ethical/value processes and the moral foundation for managerial and corporate action with the economic rationale that is notable in the economic paradigm. In 'reorienting' the CSP model. Swanson (1995) argued for an interactive orientation focused at four levels of analysis: CSR macroprinciples. CSR microprinciple. corporate culture. and social impacts.

Using Frederick's (1995) insightful and provocative nature-based approach to foundational corporate values. Swanson argues that corporate decisions should be made on the basis of what Frederick (1995) says are basic values that shape companies. economizing (efficiency) and ecologizing (not wasting resources). as well as power seeking (aggrandizement). which provide both negative and positive duties (benefits) to society. Swanson further argues for integration of both the normative and descriptive approaches to business in society through the concepts of value neglect (which highlights the problems of lack of integration) and value attunement to bring the responsibility and responsiveness streams together. thereby attempting to overcome what Freeman (1994) has called the separation thesis (the separation of ethics and business practice).

CSR4: COSMOS. SCIENCE. RELIGION (SPIRITUALITY)

In a late-1990s keynote address to the Social Issues in Management (SIM) division of the Academy of Management. claiming that scholars had 'exhausted' the primary analytic framework of CSR. Frederick (1998) added a fourth wave to his CSR framework. CSR4. invites the field away from a corporate centric focus Towards a Cosmos (C) or naturalistic and science-based orientation as a proxy for all of the natural sciences. Frederick pushed (and continues to push) for an understanding of the naturalistic basis on which human social institutions arise. through the "S" in this wave. *i.e.*. Science (S). and Towards a type of understanding of man's search for meaning embodied in Religion (R) or spirituality.

Interestingly and as a side-bar. the latter orientation of spirituality in business shaped itself largely outside the business in society field at least within practice and in the Academy of Management. emerging as the Management Spirituality and Religion (MSR) group. separate from the more business-centric Social Issues in Management (SIM) division. This path is much the same as had been followed by the Organization and Natural Environment (ONE). Gender and Diversity in Organizations (GDO) (formerly Women in Management). and. more recently. Critical Management Studies (CMS). The spirituality in business movement. derived in some respects from interpretive methodologies that focus on meaning making and its role in fostering successful businesses. attempts to build values into business through emphasizing spirituality (or religion) and meaning. personal and organizational awareness. and development along a number of important dimensions. Furthering this side-bar. it is important to note that while the business in society field in some respects spawns such outgrowths. few business in society scholars actually participate in them. In particular the emergence of CMS poses a problem for business in society scholarship if it assumes the role of what Freeman (1989) in his SIM division chair's address called 'crits.' That critical role has now been largely subsumed within the CMS. not the SIM. division of the Academy of Management.

Frederick's (1998) effort move the business in society field Towards a less corporate-centric perspective builds on his important book. *Values. Nature. Culture. and the American Corporation* (1995). which used a natural science perspective to analyze the values that underpin business. As noted above. the fundamental values that underscore the role of business in society were. according to Frederick (1995). economizing. or prudent and efficient use of resources. commonly known as efficiency. and power aggrandizing. or augmenting and preserving the power of managers and organizations. These values stand in some tension with a third important value cluster identified by Frederick (1995). ecologizing processes. which like nature create cyclical and sustainable processes and patterns of use and reuse of raw materials. In my own book. *Leading Corporate Citizens* (2002). I attempt to move these values to the sectors or spheres that constitute human society (economic—economizing values. political—power aggrandizing values. and civil society—relationship or civilizing values). along with the natural environment as underpinning with its ecologizing values. Although SIMians (IABSians. and SBEians...to use Frederick's terminology welcomed Frederick's intellectual efforts. the field remains largely focused within a corporate-centric paradigm while other fields (as the previous paragraph dramatically illustrates) adopt the wider and more critical perspective once the hallmark of the business in society field. As Frederick (2003. personal communication) points out. 'if [business in society scholarship is] to remain centered on the corporation and miss the lessons to be found in the parallel universe of science and the cosmos—then we can expect others to do it.'

CORPORATE SOCIAL RESPONSIBILITY

Corporate social responsibility (CSR. also called corporate conscience. corporate citizenship or sustainable responsible business/ Responsible Business) is a form of corporate self-regulation integrated into a business model. CSR policy functions as a self-regulatory mechanism whereby a business monitors and ensures its active compliance with the spirit of the law. ethical standards and international norms. In some models. a firm's implementation of CSR goes beyond compliance and engages in "actions that appear to further some social good. beyond the interests of the firm and that which is required by law." CSR aims to embrace responsibility for corporate actions and to encourage a positive impact on the environment and stakeholders including consumers. employees. investors. communities. and others.The term "corporate social responsibility" became popular in the 1960s and has remained a term used indiscriminately by many to cover legal and moral responsibility more narrowly construed.

Proponents argue that corporations increase long term profits by operating with a CSR perspective. while critics argue that CSR distracts from business' economic role. A 2000 study compared existing econometric studies of the relationship between social and financial performance. concluding that the contradictory results of previous studies reporting positive. negative. and neutral financial impact. were due to flawed empirical analysis and claimed when the study is properly specified. CSR has a neutral impact on financial outcomes. Critics questioned the "lofty" and sometimes "unrealistic expectations" in CSR. or that CSR is merely window-dressing. or an attempt to pre-empt the role of governments as a watchdog over powerful multinational corporations.Political sociologists became interested in CSR in the context of theories of globalization. neoliberalism and late capitalism. Some sociologists viewed CSR as a form of capitalist legitimacy and in particular point out that what began as a social movement against uninhibited corporate power was transformed by corporations into a 'business model' and a 'risk management' device. often with questionable results

CSR is titled to aid an organization's mission as well as a guide to what the company stands for to its consumers. Business ethics is the part of applied ethics that examines ethical principles and moral or ethical problems that can arise in a business environment. ISO 26000 is the recognized international standard for CSR. Public sector organizations (the United Nations for example) adhere to the triple bottom line (TBL). It is widely accepted that CSR adheres to similar principles. but with no formal act of legislation.The notion is now extended beyond purely commercial corporations. *e.g.* to universities.

DEFINITION

Business dictionary defines CSR as "A company's sense of responsibility towards the community and environment (both ecological and social) in which it operates. Companies express this citizenship (1) through their waste and pollution reduction processes. (2) by contributing educational and social Programmes and (3) by earning adequate returns on the employed resources."

A broader definition expands from a focus on stakeholders to include philanthropy and volunteering.

CONSUMER PERSPECTIVES

Most consumers agree that while achieving business targets. companies should do CSR at the same time. However not all CSR activities are popular. Most consumers believe companies doing charity will receive a positive response. Somerville also found that consumers are loyal and willing to spend more on retailers that support charity. Consumers also believe that retailers selling local products will gain loyalty. Smith (2013) shares the belief that marketing local products will gain consumer trust. However. environmental efforts are receiving negative views given the belief that this would affect customer service. Oppewal et al. (2006) found that not all CSR activities are attractive to consumers. They recommended that retailers focus on one activity. Becker-Olsen (2006) found that if the social initiative done by the company is not aligned with other company goals it will have a negative impact. Mohr et al.(2001) and Groza et al. (2011) also emphasise the importance of reaching the consumer.

APPROACHES

Some commentators have identified a difference between the Canadian (Montreal school of CSR). theContinental European and the Anglo-Saxon approaches to CSR. It is said that for Chinese consumers. a socially responsible company makes safe. high-quality products; for Germans it provides secure employment; in South Africa it makes a positive contribution to social needs such as health care and education. And even within Europe the discussion about CSR is very heterogeneous.

A more common approach to CSR is corporate philanthropy. This includes monetary donations and aid given to Non-profit organizations and communities. Donations are made in areas such as the arts. education. housing. health. social welfare and the environment. among others. but excluding political contributions and commercial event sponsorship.

Another approach to CSR is to incorporate the CSR strategy directly into operations. For instance. procurement of Fair Trade tea and coffee.

Creating Shared Value. or CSV is based on the idea that corporate success and social welfare are interdependent. A business needs a healthy. educated workforce. sustainable resources and adept government to compete effectively. For society to thrive. profitable and competitive businesses must be developed and supported to create income. wealth. tax revenues and philanthropy.

The Harvard Business Review article *Strategy and Society: The Link between Competitive Advantage and Corporate Social Responsibility* provided examples of companies that have developed deep linkages between their business strategies and CSR. CSV acknowledges trade-offs between short-term profitability and social or environmental goals. but emphasizes the opportunities for competitive advantage from building a social value proposition into corporate strategy. CSV gives the impression that only two stakeholders are important - shareholders and consumers. Many companies employ benchmarking to assess their CSR policy. implementation and effectiveness. Benchmarking involves reviewing competitor initiatives. as well as measuring and evaluating the impact that those policies have on society and the environment. and how others perceive competitor CSR strategy.

Cost-benefit analysis

In competitive markets a cost-benefit analysis of CSR initiatives. can be examined using a resource-based view (RBV). According to Barney (1990) "formulation of the RBV. sustainable competitive advantage requires that resources be valuable (V). rare (R). inimitable (I) and non-substitutable (S)." A firm introducing a CSR-based strategy might only sustain high returns on their investment if their CSR-based strategy could not be copied (I). However. should competitors imitate such a strategy. that might increase overall social benefits. Firms that choose CSR for strategic financial gain are also acting responsibly.

RBV presumes that firms are bundles of heterogeneous resources and capabilities that are imperfectly mobile across firms. This imperfect mobility can produce competitive advantages for firms that acquire immobile resources. McWilliams and Siegel (2001) examined CSR activities and attributes as a differentiation strategy. They concluded that managers can determine the appropriate level of investment in CSR by conducting cost benefit analysis in the same way that they analyze other investments.

Reinhardt (1998) found that a firm engaging in a CSR-based strategy could only sustain an abnormal return if it could prevent competitors from imitating its strategy.

SCOPE

Initially. CSR emphasized the official Behaviour of individual firms. Later. it expanded to include supplier Behaviour and the uses to which products were put and how they were disposed of after they lost value.

Supply chain

Incidents like the 2013 Savar building collapse pushed companies to consider how the Behaviour of their suppliers impacted their overall impact on society. Irresponsible Behaviour reflected on both the misbehaving firm. but also on its corporate customers. Supply chain management expanded to consider the CSR context. Wieland and Handfield (2013) suggested that companies need to include social responsibility in their reviews of component quality. They highlighted the use of technology in improving visibility across thesupply chain.

IMPLEMENTATION

CSR may be based within the human resources. business development or public relations departments of an organisation. or may be a separate unit reporting to the CEO or the board of directors. Some companies approach CSR without a clearly defined team or programme.

Engagement plan

An engagement plan can assist in reaching a desired audience. A corporate social responsibility individual or team plans the goals and objectives of the organization. As with any corporate activity. a defined budget demonstrates commitment and scales the program's relative importance.

Accounting. auditing and reporting

Social accounting is the communication of social and environmental effects of a company's economic actions to particular interest groups within society and to society at large.Social accounting emphasizes the notion of corporate accountability. Crowther defines social accounting as "an approach to reporting a firm's activities which stresses the need for the identification of socially relevant Behaviour. the determination of those to whom the company is accountable for its social performance and the development of appropriate measures and reporting techniques." Reporting guidelines and standards serve as frameworks for social accounting. auditing and reporting:

- AccountAbility's AA1000 standard. based on John Elkington's triple bottom line (3BL) reporting
- The Prince's Accounting for Sustainability Project's Connected Reporting Framework
- The Fair Labour Association conducts audits based on its Workplace Code of Conduct and posts audit results on the FLA Web site.
- The Fair Wear Foundation verifies labour conditions in companies' supply chains. using interdisciplinary auditing teams.
- Global Reporting Initiative's Sustainability Reporting Guidelines
- Economy for the Common Good's Common Good Balance Sheet
- GoodCorporation's standard developed in association with the Institute of Business Ethics
- Synergy Codethic 26000 Social Responsibility and Sustainability Commitment Management System (SRSCMS) Requirements — Ethical Business Best Practices of Organizations - the necessary management system elements to obtain a certifiable ethical commitment management system. The standard scheme has been build around ISO 26000 and UNCTAD Guidance on Good Practices in Corporate Governance.The standard is applicable by any type of organization.;
- Earthcheck Certification/ Standard
- Social Accountability International's SA8000 standard
- Standard Ethics Aei guidelines
- The ISO 14000 environmental management standard
- The United Nations Global Compact requires companies to communicate on their progress (or to produce a Communication on Progress. COP). and to describe the company's implementation of the Compact's ten universal principles.
- The United Nations Intergovernmental Working Group of Experts on International Standards of Accounting and Reporting (ISAR) provides voluntary technical guidance on eco-efficiency indicators. corporate responsibility reporting. and corporate governance disclosure.
- The FTSE Group publishes the FTSE4Good Index. an evaluation of CSR performance of companies.

In nations such as France. legal requirements for social accounting. auditing and reporting exist. though international or national agreement on meaningful measurements of social and environmental performance has not been achieved. Many companies produce externally audited annual reports that cover Sustainable Development and CSR issues ("Triple Bottom Line Reports"). but the reports vary widely in format. style. and evaluation methodology (even within the same industry). Critics dismiss these reports as lip service. citing examples such as Enron's yearly "Corporate Responsibility Annual Report" and tobacco companies' social reports.

In South Africa. as of June 2010. all companies listed on the Johannesburg Stock Exchange (JSE) were required to produce an integrated report in place of an annual financial report and sustainability report. An integrated report reviews environmental. social and economic performance alongside financial performance. This requirement was implemented in the absence of formal or legal standards. An Integrated Reporting Committee (IRC) was established to issue guidelines for good practice.

Ethics training

The rise of ethics training inside corporations. some of it required by government regulation. has helped CSR to spread. The aim of such training is to help employees make ethical decisions when the answers are unclear. The most direct benefit is reducing the likelihood of "dirty hands". fines and damaged reputations for breaching laws or moral norms.

Common actions

Common CSR actions include:

- Environmental sustainability: recycling. waste management. water management. renewable energy. reusable materials. 'greener' supply chains. reducing paper use and adopting Leadership in Energy and Environmental Design (LEED) buildind standards.
- Community involvement: This can include raising money for local charities. providing volunteers. sponsoring local events. employing local workers. supporting local economic growth. engaging in fair trade practices. etc.
- Ethical marketing: Companies that ethically market to consumers are placing a higher value on their customers and respecting them as people who are ends in themselves. They do not try to manipulate or falsely advertise to potential consumers. This is important for companies that want to be viewed as ethical.

Social license

"Social license" refers to a local community's acceptance or approval of a company. Social license exists outside formal regulatory processes. Social license can nevertheless be acquired through timely and effective communication. meaningful dialogue and ethical and responsible Behaviour. Displaying commitment to CSR is one way to achieve social license. by enhancing a company's reputation.

POTENTIAL BUSINESS BENEFITS

A large body of literature exhorts business to adopt measures non-financial measures of success (*e.g.*. Deming's Fourteen Points. balanced scorecards). While CSR benefits are hard to quantify. Orlitzky. Schmidt and Rynes found a correlation between social/environmental performance and financial performance.The business case for CSR within a company employs one or more of these arguments:

Triple bottom line

"People. planet and profit". also known as the triple bottom line form one way to evaluate CSR. "People" refers to fair labour practices. the community and region where the business operates. "Planet" refers to sustainable environmental practices. Profit is the economic value created by the organization after deducting the cost of all inputs. including the cost of the capital (unlike accounting definitions of profit).

This measure was claimed to help some companies be more conscious of their social and moral responsibilities. However. critics claim that it is selective and substitutes a company's perspective for that of the community. Another criticism is about the absence of a standard auditing procedure.

Human resources

A CSR Programme can be an aid to recruitment and retention. particularly within the competitive graduate student market. Potential recruits often consider a firm's CSR policy. CSR can also help improve the perception of a company among its staff. particularly when staff can become involved through payroll giving. fundraising activities or community volunteering. CSR has been credited with encouraging customer orientation among customer-facing employees.

Risk management

Managing risk is an important executive responsibility. Reputations that take decades to build up can be ruined in hours through corruption scandals or environmental accidents. These draw unwanted attention from regulators. courts. governments and media. CSR can limit these risks.

Brand differentiation

CSR can help build customer loyalty based on distinctive ethical values. Some companies use their commitment to CSR as their primary positioning tool. *e.g.*. The Co-operative Group. The Body Shop and American Apparel Some companies use CSR methodologies as a strategic tactic to gain public support for their presence in global markets. helping them sustain a competitive advantage by using their social contributions as another form of advertising.

Reduced scrutiny

Corporations are keen to avoid interference in their business through taxation and/or regulations. A CSR Programme can persuade governments and the public that a company takes health and safety. diversity and the environment seriously. reducing the likelihood that company practices will be closely monitored.

Supplier relations

Appropriate CSR Programmes can increase the attractiveness of supplier firms to potential customer corporations. *E.g.*. a fashion merchandiser may find value in an overseas manufacturer that uses CSR to establish a positive image—and to reduce the risks of bad publicity from uncovered misBehaviour.

CRITICISMS AND CONCERNS

CSR concerns include its relationship to the purpose of business and the motives for engaging in it.

Nature of business

Milton Friedman and others argued that a corporation's purpose is to maximize returns to its shareholders and that obeying the laws of the jurisdictions within which it operates constitutes socially responsible Behaviour.While some CSR supporters claim that companies practicing CSR. especially in developing countries. are less likely to exploit workers and communities. critics claim that CSR itself imposes outside values on local communities with unpredictable outcomes.

Better governmental regulation and enforcement. rather than voluntary measures. are an alternative to CSR that moves decision-making and resource allocation from public to private bodies. However. critics claim that effective CSR must be voluntary as mandatory social responsibility Programmes regulated by the government interferes with people's own plans and preferences. distorts the allocation of resources. and increases the likelihood of irresponsible decisions.

Motives

Some critics believe that CSR Programmes are undertaken by companies to distract the public from ethical questions posed by their core operations. They argue that the reputational benefits that CSR companies receive demonstrate the hypocrisy of the approach.

Misdirection

Another concern is that sometimes companies use CSR to direct public attention away from other. harmful business practices. For example. McDonald's Corporation positioned its association with Ronald McDonald House as CSR while its meals have been accused of promoting poor eating habits.

Controversial industries

Industries such as tobacco. alcohol or munitions firms make products that damage their consumers and/or the environment. Such firms may engage in the same philanthropic activities as those in other industries. This duality complicates assessments of such firms with respect to CSR.

STAKEHOLDER INFLUENCE

One motivation for corporations to adopt CSR is to satisfy stakeholders.

Branco and Rodrigues (2007) describe the stakeholder perspective of CSR as the set of views of corporate responsibility held by all groups or constituents with a relationship to the firm. In their normative model the company accepts these views as long as they do not hinder the organization. The stakeholder perspective fails to acknowledge the complexity of network interactions that can occur in cross-sector partnerships. It relegates communication to a maintenance function. similar to the exchange perspective.

Ethical consumerism

The rise in popularity of ethical consumerism over the last two decades can be linked to the rise of CSR. Consumers are becoming more aware of the environmental and social implications of their day-to-day consumption decisions and in some cases make purchasing decisions related to their environmental and ethical concerns.

Socially responsible investing

Shareholders and investors. through socially responsible investing are using their capital to encourage Behaviour they consider responsible. However. definitions of what constitutes ethical Behaviour vary. For example. some religious investors in the US have withdrawn investment from companies that violate their religious views. while secular investors divest from companies that they see as imposing religious views on workers or customers.

Creating shared value

Non-governmental organizations are also taking an increasing role. leveraging the media and the Internet to increase the visibility of corporate Behaviour. Through education and dialogue. the development of community awareness in pushing businesses to change their Behaviour is growing.

Creating Shared Value (CSV) claims to be more community aware than CSR. Several companies are refining their collaboration with stakeholders accordingly.

Public policies

Some national governments promote socially and environmentally responsible corporate practices. The heightened role of government in CSR has facilitated the development of numerous CSR Programmes and policies. Various European governments have pushed companies to develop sustainable corporate practices. CSR critics such as Robert Reich argued that governments should set the agenda for social responsibility with laws and regulation that describe how to conduct business responsibly.

Regulation

Fifteen European Union countries actively engaged in CSR regulation and public policy development. CSR efforts and policies are different among countries. responding to the complexity and diversity of governmental. corporate and societal roles. Studies claimed that the role and effectiveness of these actors were case-specific.

The variety among companies complicates regulatory processes. Self-regulation allows each corporate actor to balance profits and social responsibility without cumbersome governmental involvement. Studies suggest that mandated CSR distorts the allocation of resources and increases the likelihood of irresponsible decisions.

Bulkeley cited the Australian government's actions to avoid compliance with the Kyoto Protocol in 1997. over concerns of economic loss and national interest. The Australian government claimed that the pact would damage Australia more than any other OECD nation. In November 2007. the new Prime Minister Kevin Rudd ratified the protocol.

Canada adopted CSR in 2007. Prime Minister Harper encouraged Canadian mining companies to meet Canada's newly developed CSR standards.

Laws

In the 1800s.the US government could take away a firm's license if it acted irresponsibly. Corporations were viewed as "creatures of the state" under the law. In 1819. the United States Supreme Court in Dartmouth College vs. Woodward established a corporation as a legal person in specific contexts. This ruling allowed corporations to be protected under the Constitution and prevented states from regulating firms. Recently countries included CSR policies in governtment agendas.

On 16 December 2008. the Danish parliament adopted a bill making it mandatory for the 1100 largest Danish companies. investors and state-owned companies to include CSR information in their financial reports. The reporting requirements became effective on 1 January 2009. The required information included:

- CSR/SRI policies
- How such policies are implemented in practice
- Results and management expectations

CSR/SRI is voluntary in Denmark. but if a company has no policy on this it must state its positioning on CSR in financial reports.

In 2014. India became the world's first country to enact a mandatory minimum CSR spending law. Under Companies Act. 2013. any company having a net worth of 500 crore or more or a turnover of 1.000 crore or a net profit of 5 crore must spend 2per cent of their net profits on CSR activities. The rules came into effect from 1 April 2014.

Crises and their consequences

Crises have encouraged the adoption of CSR. The CERES principles were adopted following the 1989 Exxon Valdez incident. Other examples include the lead paint used by toy maker Mattel. which required the recall of millions of toys and caused the company to initiate new risk management and quality control processes. Magellan Metals was found responsible for lead contamination killing thousands of birds in Australia. The company ceased business immediately and had to work with independent regulatory bodies to execute a cleanup. Odwalla experienced a crisis with sales dropping 90per cent and its stock price dropping 34per cent due to cases of E. coli. The company recalled all apple or carrotjuice products and introduced a new process called "flash pasteurization" as well as maintaining lines of communication constantly open with customers.

GEOGRAPHY

Corporations that employ CSR behaviors do not always behave consistently in all parts of the world. Conversely. a single Behaviour may not be considered ethical in all jurisdictions. *E.g.*. some jurisdictions forbid women from driving. while others require women to be treated equally in employment decisions.

UK retail sector

A 2006 study found that the UK retail sector showed the greatest rate of CSR involvement. Many of the big retail companies in the UK joined the Ethical Trading Initiative.an association established to improving working conditions and worker health.

Tesco (2013) reported that their 'essentials' are 'Trading responsibility'. 'Reducing our Impact on the Environment'. 'Being a Great Employer' and 'Supporting Local Communities'. J Sainsbury employs the headings 'Best for food and health'. 'Sourcing with integrity'. 'Respect for our environment'. 'Making a difference to our community'. and 'A great place to work'. etc. The four main issues to which UK retail these companies committed are environment. social welfare. ethical trading and becoming an attractive workplace.

Top ten UK retail brands in 2013 based on Retail Week reports:

Retailer	Annual Sales £bn
Tesco	42.8
Sainsbury's	22.29
Asda	21.66
Morrisons	17.66
Mark and Spencer	8.87
Co-operative Group	8.18
John Lewis Partnership	7.76
Boots	6.71
Home Retail Group	5.49
King Fisher	4.34

Anselmsson and Johansson (2007) assessed three areas of CSR performance: human responsibility. product responsibility and environmental responsibility. Martinuzzi et al. described the terms. writing that human responsibility is "the company deals with suppliers who adhere to principles of natural and good breeding and farming of animals. and also maintains fair and positive working conditions and work-place environments for their own employees. Product responsibility means that all products come with a full and complete list of content. that country of origin is stated. that the company will uphold its declarations of intent and assume liability for its products. Environmental responsibility means that a company is perceived to produce environmental-friendly. ecological. and non-harmful products." Jones et al. (2005) found that environmental issues are the most commonly reported CSR Programmes among top retailers.

STAKEHOLDERS. CORPORATE RESPONSIBILITY1.2.3. AND CORPORATE CITIZENSHIP

Two major streams of the business in society field since 1984 have been the CSR/CSP emerging into corporate citizenship streams and the largely separate stakeholder stream. both underpinned in many ways by the growing emphasis on business ethics. Only recently. has theory begun to merge stakeholder thinking into thinking about corporate responsibility or citizenship. Other important streams that emerged during the last two decades of the 20th century and into the present time include a focus on corporate reputation and another separate emphasis on corporate (stakeholder) relationships and engagement. Together. these streams constitute the current progress of corporate citizenship.

STAKEHOLDER THINKING

Thinking about stakeholder (stakeholder theory) evolved rapidly over the time period since Freeman's (1984) seminal book first popularized the concept. As with corporate responsibility theory. the language surrounding stakeholder theory has also shifted over time. Freeman's (1984) general idea was that managing stakeholder relationships are essential to managing any enterprise. indeed represent the very basis on which companies are founded and managed. and are critical to strategic management in particular. Companies cannot. in this view. exist without stakeholder relationships and relationships by their nature are inherently normative because of the mutuality of interests they imply. This proposition avoids what Freeman has called the separation hypothesis which says that business and ethics can be discussed independent of each other (or. implicitly. that corporate 'social' responsibility can be divorced from stakeholder or corporate responsibility). Companies. in the stakeholder view. will be more successful when they have better stakeholder relationships.

Stakeholder language was later adapted to become stakeholder *management*. with the attendant (and largely mistaken) implication that all stakeholders could (should). in fact. be 'managed' by companies. Over time. Freeman (1994) has argued that narratives or stories about company performance are central to building coherence in understanding stakeholder relationships and company practices and performance. Others have argued for three types of stakeholder theory: descriptive. instrumental. and normative (falling into. Freeman would likely say. the separation thesis). Some theorists suggest that stakeholder theory should be considered core to the theory of the firm. although this suggestion has not made the leap into practice to date. Drawing on the work of Preston and Post (1975). Clarkson (1995) argued that stakeholders could be both primary and secondary. depending on the impacts of the company on them (or vice versa). The core idea is that companies cannot exist without relationships to stakeholders and these relationships carry with them moral implications.

Stakeholder thinking basically argues that because corporate activities affect and are affected by the actions of internal and external constituencies (stakeholders). the *relationships* and practices that a company develops with respect its stakeholders are central to the company's long-term effectiveness and have implicit moral weight. As I have elsewhere argued. responsibility is integral to any corporate relationship or practice at some level (from very poor to excellent). but cannot because of its integral nature be avoided. This argument is fundamentally the same one that Freeman (1994) makes in arguing against the separation thesis.

The dominant framing of stakeholder relationships. stakeholder management. has important and generally unrecognized implications that stakeholders can and should be *managed* much as internal corporate processes and employees (who are. of course. important stakeholders) can be managed. The implicit power dynamic of this language. however. makes it problematic for external stakeholders who are attempting to influence corporate practice. not to be under the dominance of the company and fails to recognize the inherent mutuality of *relationships*. The most widely cited framework of 'stakeholder management' is that of Mitchell. Agle and Wood (1997). which makes explicit the one-way operationalization of stakeholder dynamics. as well as the power implications. The alternative language. stakeholder relationships (or relationship management) represents another emerging stream of thinking.

CORPORATE RESPONSIBILITY (CR1)/CORPORATE (BUSINESS) CITIZENSHIP

By the mid-to-late 1990s. new terminology and thinking about what we shall from here on call corporate responsibility (CR) began to emerge. Donaldson (1992) published an important book that linked international business. the forces of globalization. and business ethics. The term corporate responsibility drops the word social so popular in previous language development to reflect the emerging sense that responsibilities are integral to corporate actions. decisions. behaviors. and impacts. Generically. these decisions. behaviors. and impacts can be called corporate practices—and those practices inherently affect stakeholders and the natural environment. In turn actions of stakeholders (and the status of the natural environment) affect a company's ability to carry out its work. thus corporate responsibility (nee corporate citizenship) integrally links corporate practices. stakeholders. and the integral responsibilities associated with relationship.

The term corporate responsibility is generally comparable in usage to the term corporate citizenship (CC). which largely emerged from British thinkers rather than from the business in society field in the US as previous developments had largely done. CR/CC is similar to business citizenship. as articulated by Wood and Logsdon (2001) and Logsdon and Wood (2002). Business citizenship incorporates the rights and duties of companies. stakeholder relationships. and opportunities and challenges of the global business environment. It is premised partly on political theory. which in the early days of the business in society field. was more central than it currently is.

The terms corporate responsibility and corporate (business) citizenship integrate stakeholder relationships into their operationalization for the first time. uniting the two dominant streams in the business in society field. because in addition to focusing on the social implications of business activities. they also incorporate issues related to companies' performance with respect to specific stakeholders and the natural environment. This integration makes stakeholder- and environment-related performance central to CR. Mutual. holistic relationship-based interactions are part of the core foundation of corporate citizenship and in an emerging form of CR. that of corporate relationships.

Important work in the business ethics arena also typifies this period. particularly Donaldson and Dunfee's integrative social contracts theory. Donaldson and Dunfee argue for the existence of foundational values that they call hypernorms that are global in scope and that can be applied in any context. Picking up on this term in our study of responsibility management systems in corporate practice. Charles Bodwell and I have argued for values we term foundational values as the basis for developing comparable codes of conduct and stakeholder/ecological practices across companies in different contexts.

During the 1990s and early 2000s. two other CRs became popular: corporate reputation and corporate relationships (including notions of stakeholder engagement). As 'corporate social responsibility' partially morphed into 'corporate responsibility' (CR1) in the world of practice. companies also began paying attention to their corporate reputation (CR2). in part as a result of renewed anti-corporate activism during the 1990s. Simultaneously. corporate (stakeholder) relationships (CR3 or CSR4a) emerged as an important set of operating principles and processes within the boundary-spanning functions that companies had begun developing in the 1970s and 1980s.

CORPORATE REPUTATION (CR2)

The work of Charles Fombrun and colleagues brought considerable academic attention to the issue of corporate reputation during the 1990s. Emerging partially from the perspective of protecting a company's brand image. and hence from the marketing field. the study of corporate reputation drew attention to the reality that underlying a company's public image (or public relations activities) was a reputation that could either attract or turn away key stakeholders. Fombrun started the Reputation Management Institute at New York University. which both influenced and made a bridge to practice. and also began to do stakeholder-based surveys of companies' reputation. Additionally. the journal *Corporate Reputation Review* provided an outlet for academic papers (focused somewhat on practice) that highlight issues of corporate reputation.

In the business in society field. early work by Wartick (1992) explored corporate reputation by looking at media exposure. Integration of corporate reputation into business in society field. uniting much of the empirical work on corporate (social) responsibility/performance. and a key element of the progress of corporate citizenship.

CORPORATE (STAKEHOLDER) RELATIONSHIPS (CR3. CSR4A)/ STAKEHOLDER ENGAGEMENT

As the language of stakeholder theory diffused into corporate and popular parlance. the term stakeholder management gained a degree of dominance.

taking a central place in important works like the Post. Preston and Sachs (2002) book. *Redefining the Corporation* and their related paper. Managing the Extended Enterprise: The New Stakeholder View." in *California Management Review*. Others. however. focused on the relational aspects of stakeholder. emphasizing stakeholder engagement as a long-term process of mutual interaction (*e.g.*. Svendsen. 1998. Harrison and St. John. 1996; Freeman and Gilbert. 1988) and recognizing that stakeholder relationships are the foundation of the perceptions that make up corporate reputation.

Stakeholder engagement processes partially grew out of attention to public-private partnerships. which have evolved into multi-stakeholder collaboration and dialogue to bring multiple interests together around important social. political. and economic development issues. Engagement on a relatively equal footing means power sharing. interaction. and partnership and is highlighted in emerging multi-stakeholder dialogues being sponsored. for example. by the United Nations' Global Compact's Learning Forum among numerous others.

Engagement with corporate executives on sensitive issues is also an important strategy of the social investment movement. particularly social investors who submit shareholder resolutions. Some organizations like the Interfaith Center on Corporate Responsibility sponsor about 100 shareholder resolutions annually. some of which are withdrawn after engagement with company executives on the relevant issue.

A TIPPING POINT FOR CORPORATE CITIZENSHIP?

Many factors push in the direction of corporate responsibility/citizenship and against the forces of shareholder dominance of Chicago School economic model. which puts shareholder interests above those of other stakeholders. But it obvious from looking at the very brief overview of what is happening in scholarship and practice that these factors have yet to cohere into a system with the power or strength of the economic model and what Mike Jensen calls the single objective function of profitability. Stakeholder theory and corporate citizenship's triple bottom line demand complexity of objective functions. a capacity to 'take' multiple perspectives. which is also a given for productive stakeholder engagement of any sort.

The triple bottom line approach demands multiple objective functions and new. more holistic measurement systems (*e.g.*. balanced scorecard. holistic performance assessment. social audit.

The Global Reporting Initiative. with its association with AA 1000 (stakeholder and sustainability). SA 8000 (Labour). ISO 14000 (environmental) standards and processes. pushes both corporate citizenship practice and scholarship in new directions that demand greater integration rather than less. As I have argued elsewhere. however. creating a tipping point for corporate citizenship demands a far more systemic and holistic approach to corporate responsibility (and performance in general) and its assessment than has existed to date. Below. we will briefly outline what we believe to be the essential components for making corporate citizenship real:

- *Responsibility Management Systems*: coherent. systemic. and holistic internal responsibility management systems that acknowledge the mutuality of interests of companies and their stakeholders and the natural environment (with appropriate external support from consultants and industry or related organizations/associations). and
- *Responsibility Assurance Systems and Processes*: externally credible responsibility assurance comprised of generally (globally) accepted foundational principles and standards promulgated by credible institutions. globally accepted and credible reporting standards and guidelines for at least the triple bottom line. and credible external verification. monitoring. and certification systems.

Let me explain. One key factor to make corporate citizenship real is the evolution of recognized and accepted responsibility management systems analogous to accepted quality and environmental management systems. The second key factor is a holistic and integrated responsibility assurance system. which from what I can see now. involves three additional elements. The first key element is globally accepted standards and principles. *e.g.*. those of the Global Compact. Sullivan Principles. Caux Principles. OECD Guidelines for Multinational Corporations. ILO conventions. or. more likely. some synthesized and rationalized combination of the core elements of these and related principles. Second. there will need to be generally accepted social end environmental (and financial) reporting standards for which Global Reporting Initiative (GRI) seems to be the leading contender at the moment. The third element of the responsibility assurance system is credible and generally accepted. verifiable assessment. certification. and monitoring systems (along the lines of AA 1000 stakeholder engagement/triple bottom line and SA 8000's Labour assessment practices).

How do we know such a system is needed? Well. one of the characteristics of the scandals of 2002 (and surrounding years) is that much trust in the system has been destroyed. Some 600 companies have joined the UN Global Compact. agreeing to live up to the nine principles. but they represent but a drop in the bucket compared to the 70.000 multinational firms in existence. not to mention the millions of small and medium-sized enterprises that hardly receive any attention at all in the literature on corporate citizenship. Of the GC signatories. as of early 2003. only 44 were US companies. yet US companies clearly dominate the global business environment. Progress has been made on corporate citizenship. but from these very cursory overview. it is clear that much more needs to happen both to link the parallel universes of practice and scholarship that now exist and to integrate the CR and stakeholder streams within the business in society field. Yet. as Frederick (1998) might well out. all of this is still corporate centric. while as the world's problems today dramatically illustrate. there is life in society beyond companies.

WHAT REMAINS FOR CORPORATE CITIZENSHIP SCHOLARS?

We have come far. Corporate citizenship has made progress. But there is obviously a distance yet to be traveled to complete the journey Towards making corporate citizenship real. in integrating the parallel universes within scholarship and with practice. and Towards expanding the purview and impact of the business in society field. There is plenty of work left to do to continue the progress of corporate citizenship. in both the scholarly and practitioner realms. The corporate scandals of 2002. the many protests against globalization. the long-term economic implications of war and a politically-inward United States within a globalized world highlight some of the many important issues related to corporate citizenship that still demand attention. Such issues provide an outline for the future development of corporate citizenship research that may be helpful to consider. Scandals drew attention to the conflicts on corporate political involvement/strategies. unhealthy political ties. corruption. lack of transparency. and lack of accountability for impacts of many large companies today. They draw attention to the reality that many people do. in practice. separate their morality and their humanity from economic and business decisions.

The activist pressures that emerged around issues related to outsourcing in the 1990s (*e.g.*. human rights abuses. labor rights. sweatshop working conditions. pay scales. living standards. population control. corruption. and environmental degradation) highlight further areas of concern. Issues of ecological sustainability. while receiving significant attention from environmental scholars. need to be re-introduced into the corporate citizenship/ responsibility agenda. in part to integrate the extensive attention the ecology that has emerged in the European Union (in particular). Other issues. such as AIDS in the workplace. water resources/scarcity. war (*e.g.*. Iraq) and its impacts on business. making work more meaningful and balancing human life and the spheres in which human civilization operates. all demand attention. And these issues simply scratch the surface. Important questions need to be asked and answered and business in society scholars have critical roles to play in that process.

6

Conceptions of Citizenship

INTRODUCTION

Citizenship has been redefined in the United States. and its privileges and rights have been extended since the ratification of the Constitution. While the initial conception of a citizen was a white male. it has been redefined to include women and people of Colour. Although citizenship is no longer explicitly defined along gender or racial lines. the legacy of its original conception is salient in welfare state policies. lawmaking. and the exercise of constitutional rights. A particular instance in which this is evident is in the arena of abortion politics. Since the legalization of abortion. state and federal governments have imposed restrictions that serve as barriers to access. Furthermore. the United States has a stratified welfare state that lacks uniform policies and fails to provide adequate social support for parenthood. Due to the nature of pregnancy and childrearing. these policies and restrictions are gender specific and hinder the ability of women. particularly those of Colour. from exercising their constitutional and social rights. Consequently. this initial conception of citizenship is problematic because each law and right is modeled after a white male and disregards the different experiences and positions of women and those of Colour. Reproductive choice is constrained and shaped by race and gender.

In this paper. I will examine the utilization of abortion according to the theories of citizenship and the welfare state. I will look at how access is shaped by race. gender. and social policy. This paper is organized into four parts. Part I reviews theories of citizenship and the welfare state and part II outlines the research methods used to analyze the predictors of abortion rates. The third part analyzes these findings. and the final part discusses the implications of these findings.

CONCEPTIONS OF CITIZENSHIP

Citizenship can be defined in many ways. but historically it has been grounded in the conception of a man (Schwarzenbach. 2003; Isenberg. 1998). In the United States. the initial conception of a citizen was equated with being a white male. Race was socially constructed to privilege whiteness. and this was a prerequisite for citizenship. Birthright was not equated with rights. citizenship. and an American identity. As a result. one was entitled to citizenship based solely upon skin Colour. To be white meant to be a citizen and a moral. self assured. independent. and politically sophisticated being; to be non white was to be unfit for citizenship. immoral and dependent. It was impossible for one to claim to be a citizen if one was not white. regardless of gender.

Besides being white. a citizen was an abstract legal person assumed to be autonomous. self determining. and self interested. These qualities were typified as masculine characteristics. and women were inherently excluded. Collectively. women did not possess the qualities associated with citizenship. and their status as native-born citizens did not garner them the same rights afforded to similarly situated men. Even though women were born in the United States. they could make no claim to citizenship because they were not men.

Through long and difficult struggles that for black women continued into the 1960s. formal citizenship was extended to women and Non- whites. However. women have not truly benefited from the extension of this male version of citizenship. This "universal" definition has been thrust upon them and women and Non- whites have not been fully incorporated as full members within society. In the realm of civil. political. or social rights. the incorporated actors were imagined to be men. Laws assume a generic (white male) citizen. Women are disadvantaged because these laws fail to consider their specific circumstances and experiences such as pregnancy. childbirth. and caregiving. Not only are these impacted by gender. but these experiences of motherhood are also shaped by race.

Women have been extended citizenship rights on the same terms as men instead of citizenship rights that accommodate women's specific interests. Although all persons can make claims to formal equality. informal discrimination continues to abridge citizenship. Women and men gained the constitutional right to abortion in the 1973 *Roe v. Wade* decision. Although this was grounded in the right to privacy derived from the Fourteenth Amendment. the Court decided that as a pregnancy progressed. the states have a compelling interest in protecting the potential life of a fetus. Since the *Roe* decision. states have passed legislation eroding access to abortion.

Because a citizen is assumed to be a white male. these laws assume a male actor and as a result. these restrictive abortion laws discount or ignore women's rights and interests. The right to privacy and abortion is a constitutional right. yet legislation infringes upon the exercise of these rights. Men are inherently able to exercise their constitutional right to an abortion. and they benefit from the assumptions of citizenship and laws. Due to the biological nature of pregnancy. it is the rights of women that are being encroached.

Despite this recognition. laws and practices create barriers to abortion access that inhibit a woman's constitutional right to an abortion. The "gender neutral" and "race neutral" laws and constitutional rights that are granted to women and people of Colour are meaningless if they are unable to exercise those rights. Although women have the constitutional right to abortion. various "gender neutral" and "race neutral" laws and practices serve as barriers to its access. However. since only women are afflicted with pregnancy. only they have been unable to exercise this right. Even though citizenship and laws are believed to be neutral. they have unfavorable consequences for those who are not white men. The experiences and interests of women have been forced to fit into the patriarchal paradigm of citizenship that has privileged white men's behaviors and norms. Attempts to be gender neutral do not acknowledge the inherent biological differences between women and men.

Though women have been bestowed with citizenship rights. this does not mean that they are full members in the community or equal to men. To be a full member of the community means having the ability to exercise the constitutional right to an abortion. The extension of a white male version of citizenship does not mean that citizens are equal before the law and the Constitution. It does not consider the biological. economic. and social conditions that inhibit the practice of formal equality. If reproductive choice is constrained. then women have not been fully incorporated in society and can hardly claim to be full citizens. To be equal means to be equal with respect to the rights and duties which come with being a citizen. Due to the biological nature of pregnancy. barriers to abortion access limit women's ability to exercise this same right and be truly equal to men.

Laws that govern abortion are shaped by traditional attitudes towards women and assume that their most important role is as a wife and mother. A gendered version of citizenship is bestowed upon women when the state assumes responsibility over women's reproductive lives and primacy is given to their role as a mother instead of an individual. When this occurs. it is assumed that women are incapable of making their own decisions. Yet. a citizen has been defined as an autonomous and independent thinking individual. Citizenship rights are abridged when the state questions women's competency and ability to make decisions regarding their reproduction.

Reproductive restrictions inhibit the exercise of full citizenship because it views women as mothers first and as individuals second. This is evident because funding is available for non-elective abortions; thus it makes assumptions about women's roles as mothers and gender their rights and liberties as citizens. Citizenship encompasses more than political rights; it also includes social rights. Fundamental to citizenship is the reproductive freedom to not only have access to abortion. but also favorable conditions and resources to raise children. Although women are granted a gendered version of citizenship that encourages motherhood. welfare state policies promote a specific type of motherhood. If states view women primarily as mothers. then it would make sense for them to have policies to assist and promote parenthood. Instead. our welfare state has policies that seem to simultaneously discourage parenthood and abortion.

LIT REVIEW

Conceptions of motherhood and citizenship are shaped by social policy. race. and gender. These can impact abortion rates in the United States. Past research has been devoted to determining the factors that impact abortion rates in the United States. However. these focus on the effect that demographics. region. and abortion access have on abortion rates. Instead of considering how abortion and motherhood are shaped by state policy. past studies have taken a more limited economics of abortion approach by considering the impact of supply and demand on rates.

Studies conducted after the passage of Roe in the 1970s show that abortion rates are lower in areas with rural populations. This is because there is a scarcity of abortion providers in these areas. Abortion access may also be inhibited in areas with a large Catholic population. Borders and Cutright (1979) and Wetstein (1996) find that rates are lower in these areas. but Hansen (1980) finds that a higher proportions of Catholics actually increases the abortion rate. Conversely. rates tend to be higher among areas with high Jewish populations. Studies show inconsistent evidence that increased black populations lead to higher abortion rates. States with higher socioeconomic status have higher rates.

Abortion rates are strongly predicted by provider availability and abortion funding; these may be the most powerful predictor of abortion rates. Rates are higher in areas with increasing numbers of abortion providers and available physicians. Rates are also higher in areas in which Medicaid funds the procedure. Restrictive abortion policies serve as barriers to access and lower rates. Abortion policy has an indirect effect on rates because it governs provider availability and funding. Access to publically funded abortions leads to higher rates. Lower abortion costs increase the abortion rate and not funding abortion increases the rate.

Abortion rates are also lower in states with a high proportion of poor families. but Borders and Cutright (1979) find that rates are higher in states with high rates of poor women and women on public assistance.

Further research shows that public opinion can impact abortion rates. Wetstein (1996) argues that mass preferences. policy. and mass Behaviour are related. Attitudes Towards abortion will impact state policies that will in turn impact abortion rates. For example. in states with more support for abortion. there are less access restrictions so rates are higher. In contrast. in states that are more hostile to abortion. rates are lower Gober. 1994). Differences in state policies reflect the mass attitudes towards abortion and sexual Behaviour. Employment and educational opportunities for women have an impact on abortion rates. As increasing numbers of women enter the workforce and higher education. abortion rates increase. Welfare state benefits can also impact rates. Higher wages for men and women and generous AFDC benefits have lower abortion rates. In contrast. states with low welfare benefits operate to encourage young pregnant women to marry while state with increased welfare benefits operate to encourage single motherhood among whites. Not surprisingly. higher marriage rates lead to lower abortion rates.

Finally. the composition of the state legislatures impact abortion rates. Republican governors are shown to have an increase in abortion rates. The presence of pro-choice governors and greater percentages of women in the state legislatures leads to few abortion restrictions and thus. abortion rates. Blank. George. and London (1996) find that party control and voting patterns in the state legislatures have no effect on abortion rates.

For a more comprehensive understanding of the abortion rates in the United States. we must also consider how reproductive choice and abortion rates are shaped by social policy and race. Because the United States does not have a comprehensive welfare state. this lack of public assistance may constrain a woman's choice to have children and inadvertently encourage abortion. There are several theories as to why the United States has not developed a comprehensive welfare state.

CAPITALISM AND DEMOCRATIC CITIZENSHIP

Capitalism. by shifting the locus of power from *lordship* to*property*. made civic status less salient. as the benefits of political privilege gave way to purely 'economic' advantage. This eventually made possible a new form of democracy. Where classical republicanism had solved the problem of propertied elite and labouring multitude by restricting the extent of the citizen body (as Athenian oligarchs would have liked to do). capitalist or liberal democracy would permit the extension of citizenship by restricting its powers (as the Romans did). Where one proposed an active but exclusive citizen body. in which the propertied classes ruled the labouring multitude. the other could—eventually—envisage an inclusive but largely passive citizen body. embracing both elite and multitude. but whose citizenship would be limited in scope.

Capitalism transformed the political sphere in other ways too. The relation between capital and labour presupposes formally free and equal individuals. without prescriptive rights or obligations. juridical privileges or disabilities. The detachment of the individual from corporate institutions and identities began very early in England (it is. for example. reflected in Sir Thomas Smith's definition of a commonwealth as 'a societie or common doing of a multitude of free men collected together and united by common accords and covenauntes among themselves'. and in the individualistic psychologism that runs through the tradition of British social thought from Hobbes and Locke to Hume and beyond); and the rise of capitalism was marked by the increasing detachment of the individual (not to mention individual property) from customary. corporate. prescriptive and communal identities and obligations.

The emergence of this isolated individual did. needless to say. have its positive side. the emancipatory implications of which are emphasized by liberal doctrine. with its constitutive concept (myth?) of the sovereign individual. But there was also another side. In a sense. the creation of the sovereign individual was the price paid by the 'labouring multitude' for entry into the political community; or. to be more precise. the historical process which gave rise to capitalism. and to the modern 'free and equal' wage labourer who would eventually join the body of citizens. was the same process in which the peasant was dispossessed and deracinated. detached from both his property and his community. together with its common and customary rights.

Let us consider briefly what this means. The peasant in precapitalist societies. unlike the modern wage labourer. remained in possession of property. in this case land. the means of labour and subsistence. This meant that the capacity of landlord or state to appropriate labour from him depended on a superior coercive power. in the form of juridical. political and military status. The principal modes of surplus extraction to which peasants were subject—rent and tax—typically took the form of various kinds of juridical and political dependence: debt-bondage. serfdom. tributary relations. obligations to perform corvée labour. and so on. By the same token. the capacity of peasants to resist or limit their exploitation by landlords and states depended in great measure on the strength of their own political organization. notably the village community. To the extent that peasants were able to achieve a degree of political independence by extending the jurisdiction of the village community—for example. imposing their own local charters or replacing landlord representatives with their own local magistrates—they also extended their economic powers of appropriation and resistance to exploitation. But however strong the village community became from time to time. there generally remained one insurmountable barrier to peasant autonomy: the state. The peasant village almost universally remained as it were outside the state. and subject to its alien power. as the peasant was excluded from the community of citizens.

It is here that Athenian democracy represents a radically unique exception. Only here was the barrier between state and village breached. as the village effectively became the constitutive unit of the state. and peasants became citizens. The Athenian citizen acquired his civic status by virtue of his membership in a deme. a geographical unit generally based on existing villages. The establishment by Cleisthenes of the deme as the constituent unit of the polis was in a critical sense the foundation of the democracy. It created a civic identity abstracted from differences of birth. an identity common to aristocracy and *demos. symbolized by the adoption by Athenian citizens of a demotikon. a deme-name. as distinct from (though in practice never replacing. especially in the case of the aristocracy) the patronymic. But even more fundamentally. Cleisthenes' reforms 'politicised the Attic countryside and rooted political identity there'. They represented. in other words. the incorporation of the village into the state. and the peasant into the civic community. The economic corollary of this political status was an exceptional degree of freedom for the peasant from 'extra-economic' exactions in the form of rent or tax.*

The medieval peasant. in contrast. remained firmly excluded from the state and correspondingly more subject to extra-economic surplus extraction. The institutions and solidarities of the village community could afford him some protection against landlords and states (though it could also serve as a medium of lordly control—as. for example. in manorial courts). but the state itself was alien. the exclusive preserve of feudal lords. And as the feudal 'parcellization of sovereignty' gave way to more centralized states. the exclusivity of this political sphere survived in the privileged political nation. Finally. as feudal relations gave way to capitalism. specifically in England. even the mediation of the village community. which had stood between peasant and landlord. was lost. The individual and his property were detached from the community. as production increasingly fell outside communal regulation. whether by manorial courts or village community (the most obvious example of this process is the replacement of the English open-field system by enclosure); customary tenures became economic leaseholds subject to the impersonal competitive pressures of the market; smallholders lost their customary use-rights to common land; increasingly. they were dispossessed. whether by coercive eviction or the economic pressures of competition. Eventually. as landholding became increasingly concentrated. the peasantry gave way to large land-holders. on the one hand. and propertyless wage labourers. on the other. In the end. the 'liberation' of the individual was complete. as capitalism. with its indifference to the 'extra-economic' identities of the labouring multitude. dissipated prescriptive attributes and 'extra-economic' differences in the solvent of the labour market. where individuals become interchangeable units of labour abstracted from any specific personal or social identity.

It is as an aggregate of such isolated individuals. without property and abstracted from communal solidarities. that the 'labouring multitude' finally entered the community of citizens. Of course. the dissolution of traditional prescriptive identities and juridical inequalities represented an advance for these now 'free and equal' individuals; and the acquisition of citizenship conferred upon them new powers. rights. and entitlements. But we cannot take the measure of their gains and losses without remembering that the historical presupposition of their citizenship was thedevaluation of the political sphere.

the new relation between the 'economic' and the '.political' which had reduced the salience of citizenship and transferred some of its formerly exclusive powers to the purely economic domain of private property and the market. where purely economic advantage takes the place of juridical privilege and political monopoly. The devaluation of citizenship entailed by capitalist social relations is an essential attribute of modern democracy. For that reason. the tendency of liberal doctrine to represent the historical developments which produced formal citizenship as nothing other than an enhancement of individual liberty the freeing of the individual from an arbitrary state. as well as from the constraints of tradition and prescriptive hierarchies. from communal repressions or the demands of civic virtue—is inexcusably one-sided.

Nor can we assess the ideological effects of the modern relation between individual citizen and civic community or nation. without considering the degree to which that 'imagined community' is a fiction. a mythical abstraction. in conflict with the experience of the citizen's daily life. The nation can certainly be real enough to inspire individuals to die for their country; but we must consider the extent to which this abstraction is also capable of serving as an ideological device to deny or disguise the more immediate experience of individuals. to disaggregate and delegitimate. or at least to depoliticize. the solidarities that stand between the levels of individual and nation. such as those forged in the workplace. the local community. or in a common class experience. When the political nation was privileged and exclusive. the 'commonwealth' in large part corresponded to a real community of interest among the landed aristocracy. In modern democracies. where the civic community unites extremes of social inequality and conflicting interests. the 'common good' shared by citizens must be a much more tenuously abstract notion.

Here. again. the contrast with ancient democracy is striking. Constructed upon the foundation of the deme. the democratic polis was built upon what Aristotle in the Nicomachean Ethicscalled a natural community. That this 'real community' had real political implications is suggested by the tangible consequences of peasant citizenship. Nor was the contradiction between civic community and the realities of social life as great in Athenian democracy as in the modern democratic state. Modern liberal democracy has in common with ancient Greek democracy a dissociation of civic identity from socio-economic status which permits the coexistence of formal political equality with class inequality. But this similarity disguises a deeper difference between the two forms of democracy. reflecting radically different relations between 'political' and 'social' or 'economic' planes in the two cases.

The right to citizenship was not determined by socio-economic status; but the power of appropriation. and relations between classes. were directly affected by democratic citizenship. In Athens democratic citizenship meant that small producers. and peasants in particular. were to a great extent free of 'extra-economic' exploitation. Their political participation—in the assembly. in the courts. and in the street—limited their economic exploitation. At the same time. unlike workers in capitalism. they were still not subject to the purely 'economic' compulsions of propertylessness. Political and economic freedom were inseparable—the dual freedom of the demos in its simultaneous meaning as a political status and a social class. the common people or the poor; while political equality did not simply coexist with. but substantially modified. socio-economic inequality. In this sense. democracy in Athens was not 'formal' but substantive.

In capitalist democracy. the separation between civic status and class position operates in both directions: socio-economic position does not determine the right to citizenship—and that is what is democratic in capitalist democracy—but. since the power of the capitalist to appropriate the surplus labour of workers is not dependent on a privileged juridical or civic status. civic equality does not directly affect or significantly modify class inequality—and that is what limits democracy in capitalism. Class relations between capital and labour can survive even with juridical equality and universal suffrage. In that sense. political equality in capitalist democracy not only coexists with socio-economic inequality but leaves it fundamentally intact.

THE AMERICAN REDEFINITION OF DEMOCRACY

Capitalism. then. made it possible to conceive of 'formal democracy'. a form of civic equality which could coexist with social inequality and leave economic relations between 'elite' and 'labouring multitude' in place. Needless to say. however. the conceptual possibility of 'formal democracy' did not make it a historical actuality. There were to be many long and arduous struggles before the 'people' grew to encompass the labouring multitude. let alone women. It is a curious fact that in the dominant ideologies of Anglo-American political culture these struggles have not achieved the status of principal milestones in the history of democracy. In the canons of English-speaking liberalism. the main road to modern democracy runs through Rome. Magna Carta. the Petition of Right and the Glorious Revolution. not Athens. the Levellers. Diggers and Chartism. Nor is it simply that the historical record belongs to the victors; for if 1688. not Levellers and Diggers. represents the winners. should not history record that democracy was on the losing side?

It is here that the American experience was decisive. English Whiggery could have long remained content to celebrate the forward march of Parliament without proclaiming it a victory fordemocracy. The Americans had no such option. Despite the fact that in the struggle to determine the shape of the new republic it was the anti-democrats who won. even at the moment of foundation the impulse Towards mass democracy was already too strong for that victory to be complete. Here. too. the dominant ideology divided governing elite from governed multitude; and the Federalists might have wished. had it been possible.

to create an exclusive political nation. an aristocracy of propertied citizens. in which property—and specifically landed property—remained a privileged juridical! political/military status. But economic and political realities in the colonies had already foreclosed that option. Property had irrevocably discarded its extra-economic 'embellishments'. in an economy based on commodity exchange and purely 'economic' modes of appropriation. which undermined the neat division between politically privileged property and disenfranchised labouring multitude. And the colonial experience culminating in revolution had created a politically active populace.

The Federalists thus faced the unprecedented task of preserving what they could of the division between mass and elite in the context of an increasingly democratic franchise and an increasingly active citizenry. It is now more generally acknowledged than it was not very long ago that US democracy was deeply flawed in its very foundations by the exclusion of women. the oppression of slaves and a genocidal colonialism in relation to indigenous peoples.

What may not be quite so self-evident are the anti-democratic principles contained in the idea of democratic citizenship itself as it was defined by the 'Founding Fathers'. The framers of the Constitution embarked on the first experiment in designing a set of political institutions that would both embody and at the same time curtail popular power. in a context where it was no longer possible to maintain an exclusive citizen body. Where the option of an active but exclusive citizenry was unavailable. it would be necessary to create an inclusive but passive citizen body with limited scope for its political powers.

The Federalist ideal may have been to create an aristocracy combining wealth with republican virtue (an ideal that would inevitably give way to the dominance of wealth alone); but their practical task was to sustain a propertied oligarchy with the electoral support of a popular multitude. This also required the Federalists to produce an ideology. and specifically a redefinition of democracy. which would disguise the ambiguities in their oligarchic project. It was the anti-democratic victors in the USA who gave the modern world its definition of democracy. a definition in which the dilution of popular power is an essential ingredient. If American political institutions have not been imitated everywhere. the American experiment has Non-etheless left this universal legacy.

Plato's Protagoras referring to the Athenian practice of letting shoemakers and blacksmiths. rich and poor alike. make political judgments. This passage. which gives _expression to the democratic principle of isegoria. not just freedom but equality of speech. neatly identifies the essence of Athenian democracy. Here. by contrast. is a quotation from Federalist no. 35. by Alexander Hamilton:

The idea of actual representation of all classes of the people. by people of each class. is altogether visionary.... Mechanics and manufacturers will always be inclined. with few exceptions. to give their votes to merchants in preference to persons of their own professions or trades... they are aware. that however great the confidence they may justly feel in their own good sense. their interests can be more effectually promoted by merchants than by themselves. They are sensible that their habits in life have not been such as to give them those acquired endowments without which. in a deliberative assembly. the greatest natural abilities are for the most part useless.... We must therefore consider merchants as the natural representatives of all these classes of the community.

Some of the most essential differences between ancient and modern democracy arc nicely summed up in these two quotations. Alexander Hamilton is spelling out the principles of what he elsewhere calls 'representative democracy'. an idea with no historical precedent in the ancient world. an American innovation. And here. shoemakers and blacksmiths are represented by their social superiors. What is at stake in this contrast is not simply the conventional distinction between direct and representative democracy. There are other more fundamental differences of principle between the two conceptions of democracy contained in these two quotations.

The concept of isegoria is arguably the most distinctive concept associated with Athenian democracy. the one most distant from any analog in modern liberal democracy—including its closest approximation. the modern concept of free speech. Alexander Hamilton was no doubt an advocate of free speech in the modern liberal democratic sense. having to do with protecting the right of citizens to express themselves without interference. especially by the state. But there is in Hamilton's conception no incompatibility between advocating civil liberties. among which the freedom of _expression is paramount. and the view that in the political domain the wealthy merchant is the natural representative of the humble craftsman. The man of property will speak politically for the shoemaker or blacksmith. Hamilton does not. of course. propose to silence these demotic voices. Nor does he intend to deprive them of the right to choose their representatives. He is. evidently with some reluctance. obliged to accept a fairly wide and socially inclusive or 'democratic' franchise. But like many anti-democrats before him. he makes certain assumptions about representation according to which the labouring multitude. like Sir Thomas Smith's 'lowest person'. must find its political voice in its social superiors.

These assumptions also have to be placed in the context of the Federalist view that representation is not a way of implementing but of avoiding or at least partially circumventing democracy. Their argument was not that representation is necessary in a large republic. but. on the contrary. that a large republic is desirable so that representation is unavoidable—and the smaller the proportion of representatives to represented. the greater the distance between them. the better. As Madison put it in Federalist io. the effect of representation is 'to refine and enlarge the public views. by passing them through the medium of a chosen body of citizens...'. And an extensive republic is clearly preferable to a small one. 'more favorable to the election of proper guardians of the public weal'. on the grounds of 'two obvious considerations': that there would be a smaller proportion of representatives to represented. and that each representative would be chosen by a larger electorate. Representation. in other words. is intended to act as a filter. In these respects. the Federalist conception of representation—and especially Hamilton's—is the very antithesis of isegoria.

We have become so accustomed to the formula. 'representative democracy'. that we tend to forget the novelty of the American idea. In its Federalist form. at any rate. it meant that something hitherto perceived as the antithesis of democratic self-government was now not only compatible with but constitutive of democracy: not the exercise of political power but its relinquishment. its transfer to others. its alienation.

The alienation of political power was so foreign to the Greek conception of democracy that even election could be regarded as an oligarchic practice. which democracies might adopt for certain specific purposes but which did not belong to the essence of the democratic constitution. Thus Aristotle. outlining how a 'mixed' constitution might be constructed out of elements from the main constitutional types. such as oligarchy and democracy. suggests the inclusion of election as an oligarchic feature. It was oligarchic because it tended to favour the gnorimoi. the notables. the rich and well born who were less likely to be sympathetic to democracy. Athenians might resort to election in the case of offices requiring a narrowly technical expertise. notably the top financial and military posts (such as the military office ofstrategos to which Pericles was elected); but such offices were hedged about with stringent measures for ensuring accountability. and they were clearly understood as exceptions to the rule that all citizens could be assumed to possess the kind of civic wisdom required for general political functions. The quintessentially democratic method was selection by lot. a practice which. while acknowledging the practical constraints imposed by the size of a state and the number of its citizens. embodies a criterion of selection in principle opposed to the alienation of citizenship and to the assumption that the demos is politically incompetent.

The American republic firmly established a definition of democracy in which the transfer of power to 'representatives of the people' constituted not just a necessary concession to size and complexity but rather the very essence of democracy itself. The Americans. then. though they did not invent representation. can be credited with establishing an essential constitutive idea of modern democracy: its identification with the alienation of power. But. again. the critical point here is not simply the substitution of representative for direct democracy. There are undoubtedly many reasons for favouring representation even in the most democratic polity. The issue here is rather the assumptions on which the Federalist conception of representation was based. Not only did the 'Founding Fathers' conceive representation as a means ofdistancing the people from politics. but they advocated it for the same reason that Athenian democrats were suspicious of election: that it favoured the propertied classes. 'Representative democracy'. like one of Aristotle's mixtures. is civilized democracy with a touch of oligarchy.

WELFARE STATE THEORIES

AMERICAN EXCEPTIONALISM

Social policy in the United States is shaped by its political history and is consistent with a liberal regime type (Amenta. Bonastia. and Caren. 2001). The country was founded upon general attitudes of distrust of a central government. Thus. nobody trusted the government to adequately and efficiently manage a comprehensive welfare state. More importantly. attitudes of individualism and meritocracy meant that it was not appropriate for the government to redistribute benefits to mitigate inequalities. It is widely believed that equality of opportunity is equated with minimal government intrusion. Each person is assumed to be on a level playing field. and upward mobility is possible with a strong work ethic.

The guiding values of the welfare state disadvantage women. particularly those of Colour. Capitalist values of meritocracy. achievement. and individualism are values constructed by white males. The American welfare state assumed a white male actor. and its extension has forced women and Non- whites to adopt and conform to these values. Welfare state benefits such as Social Security initially assumed a white male breadwinner with a dependent wife at home to assume the caregiving role. As a result. the welfare state is a two-tiered track that reproduces gender and racial hierarchies. Instead of expanding the welfare state to accommodate women's unique needs and experiences. they are instead expected to conform to the male model of the welfare state and its values.

INSTITUTIONAL RACISM AND SEXISM

The institutional structure of the welfare state shaped its policies and its impacts. Federalism prevented the formation of a strong. unified central government. and this was an obstacle to the formation of centralized redistributive policies. As a result. states were responsible for the administration of welfare benefits. This allowed inconsistent administrations of varying degrees of welfare benefits. Race inhibited the development of a strong. centralized welfare state. and its institutional structure shaped the differential treatment of citizens of different races. A decentralized welfare state allowed local and state politicians and bureaucrats to decide the terms of exclusion and inclusion. It allowed states to discriminate against blacks and prevent them from claiming benefits. They could discriminate against recipients and dictate the development of policies and Programmes. Race is a divisive issue in welfare state politics. and policies reflect the racial structures and hierarchy in the United States. Policymakers did not Favour universal policies and social assistance because it was antithetical to American values and because these would benefit blacks. Race institutionalized a hierarchical structure of social policy by assigning social insurance to white working and middle classes and assigning poor women and Non- whites to public assistance. Social insurance was considered a socially acceptable form of welfare with deserving recipients. while public assistance was a socially unacceptable form that stigmatized its recipients. White workers were worthy recipients of Old Age Insurance. Blacks were initially excluded from this form of social insurance. and the classification of beneficiaries by class and Labour market attachment promoted racial divisions. This two tiered welfare state distinguished socially acceptable welfare benefits from stigmatizing benefits. The path dependent nature of the liberal welfare state institutionalized and reinforced race and gender hierarchies. These practices failed to grant women and Non- whites complete social rights.

The structure of the welfare state is a reflection of our political institution and race and gender relations. It is embedded in a society that grants unequal status to different racial groups. resulting in an order that reflects power structures and reinforces racial differences. The institutionalization and path dependence of these policies will inhibit more inclusive and comprehensive policies. Social support is scarce. and women and Non- whites are stigmatized when they accept public assistance. This is because our value system discourages a reliance on the government to overcome disadvantages. Instead. many think that women and the poor should rely upon their own resources and are responsible for their own position in society.

Race shapes attitudes Towards welfare state spending and Programmes. Opposition to welfare spending is largely a result of the perception that those who benefit are lazy and overwhelmingly black. and many Americans are reluctant to fiscally support social spending that may benefit this particular group. Because of this. I expect that in states with higher populations of blacks will have lower levels of social support that may lead to higher abortion rates. Programmes that are oriented towards poor and disadvantaged children do not receive overwhelming support because its beneficiaries are likely to be black.

CONCEPTIONS OF MOTHERHOOD

Access to abortion and public assistance are shaped by conceptions of motherhood. Historically. women have been incorporated into the welfare state as dependents since workers were assumed to be men. The welfare state effectively separates the wage earners from the caregivers by promoting individualism. independence and self-reliance for men while promoting dependence. reliance. and paternalism for women. This creates a two-tiered system in which the former deserves welfare benefits while the latter is stigmatized. Because citizenship is linked with employment. state supported dependence undermines women's claim to citizenship. According to the male model of citizenship. employment is a prerequisite for autonomy and independence.

Table. Abortion Rate Predictors. 2004.

State Social Spending on Children. 2004	-3428.556* (1501.564)
Percent of Women in State Legislatures. 2003	490** (.130)
Percent Black Population. 2000	.258** (.091)
Abortion Providers. 2000	.065** (.013)
Women's Labour Force Participation. 2004	1.640* (.738)
(constant)	-70.802 (33.442)
R-squared	.614

* p<.05 ** p<.01

Table. Abortion Rate Predictors. 2005.

State Social Spending on Children	-2702.54 (1397.142)
Percent of Women in State Legislatures. 2004	.512** (.131)
Percent Black Population. 2000	.294** (.093)
Abortion Providers. 2000	.062** (.013)
Women's Labour Force Participation. 2005	.518 (.784)
(constant)	-20.657 (35.882)
R- squared	.582

* p<.05 ** p<.01

Universal conceptions of work and citizenship are gendered. and women cannot depend on liberal welfare policies to mitigate inequalities and grant them full personhood. Welfare state policies were modeled after a male worker. and it has inadequately accommodated women since they have entered the Labour force. Women are faced with the dilemma of pressing for equality with men while also pressing for support for women in their roles as housewives and mothers.

Support for motherhood is bound in racial and ethnic terms. as well as marital status. Welfare state policies promote motherhood and implicitly discourage women's employment and independence. Social policy aimed at women was initially designed to benefit them as wives and mothers and discourage their employment. Support for public day care and aid to single mothers is divisive because opposition fears that it will break up the traditional family and promote women's independence. Welfare benefits do not allow mothers to be completely independent. Instead. they are faced with the double burden of balancing work and caregiving. or they must be dependent upon a man for financial support. Women's citizenship is further compromised and shaped by race. Motherhood serves as a gatekeeping function.

and the racially stratified welfare state is mediated by gender. Historically. white women became guardians of civilization. and the fitness of the nation depended on women=s reproduction and their role as mothers. Race is used to organize society. and since this is transmitted through blood lines it became necessary to control white women=s fertility. White women fulfilled their destiny and womanly duties by producing white babies to populate the free world. Reproduction was white women=s gift and duty to the family. community. and nation.

The structure of the welfare state continues to privilege white motherhood. The right to motherhood is a class privilege. and social policy inadvertently discourages poor women. particularly those of Colour. from being mothers. Welfare state benefits differ according to race and gender; white middle class women are encouraged to stay home with their children. while poor mothers are required to work outside the home. Implicit in these policies is the belief that poor women and women of Colour are not suitable for motherhood. These women are not considered to be deserving of welfare benefits because poverty is a personal shortcoming that can be reproduced in subsequent generations.

7

The Political Philosophical Foundations of Citizenship

LIBERAL THEORY OF POLITICAL THOUGHT

Throughout the modern period. the most predominant perspective in Western political thought has been the liberal theory. The advancement of political theory has been achieved through ongoing debates between this and other opposing standpoints. Consequently. most modern political theoretical debates can be situated within a broad liberal tradition. Other traditions. which have emerged. constitute critiques of liberal theory. None of these traditions however is a closed. internally consistent cluster of thoughts. Instead. political traditions are pliable conceptual realms that occasionally overlap.

Amongst the range of political philosophical perspectives there are four roughly distinguishable strands. These are liberal theory. the consensual order. participatory republicanism and moderate post-modern pluralism. This chapter will briefly outline the general ideas contained in each of these strands. highlighting key representative thinkers. The main tenets of these perspectives will be further elaborated upon within the following sociology section. which highlights the political orientations of each strand.

Out of the four perspectives named above. liberalism is considered to be the most dominant in the areas of philosophy and political theory. This perspective strongly emphasises the individual and rights are mostly based on liberties that apply to everyone. In this view. legal and political rights are prioritised and are balanced by only a few obligations. particularly the obligation to obey laws. The relationship between these rights and obligations is a contractual and reciprocal one. Political parties grounded within this view tend to aggregate the various issues raised by interest groups and most political activity takes place within representative legislatures.

One philosopher. well renowned for his Liberal theory of citizenship is Rawls. Rawls is widely considered to be one of the most important political philosophers of the late twentieth century. In his theory of justice as fairness.

Rawls presents a framework that explains the significance of political and personal liberties. equal opportunity and cooperative arrangements that are beneficial to the less advantaged of the society.

Quite apart from many of his liberal counterparts. Rawls aims to explore the rights of free and equal individuals as part of a social cooperation theory. Rawls seeks to achieve this by associating justice with the idea of fairness. Rawls postulates that when co-operation between individuals is fair. justice can then be insured. And justice in essence. becomes fairness. In this sense Rawls approach represents a shift in the liberal focus from private to public but without forsaking the traditional concern for the rights of the individual.

In his quest for a basic structure for social order. Rawls seeks a social contract type agreement. Rawls suggests that as a prerequisite to the establishment of fairness. those who are in the original position of contracting must operate from behind a 'veil of ignorance'. pertaining to their social positioning. Rawls argues that such conditions will enable individuals to develop a framework of political justice and consequently construct a society of free and equal individuals.

In recent years a new strand of liberalism has emerged. The neo-liberalist strand is. like traditional liberalism. committed to individualism. The aim of neo-liberalists is to address the dangerous imbalance inherent in individual – state relationships. In this view the state has become too involved in the economic and social life of the citizen and therefore stands accused of robbing individuals of self-respect and liberty. The neo-liberalist ideal of citizenship is one that centralises the nineteenth century liberalist notion of 'self help' and individual responsibility.

The consensual order perspective incorporates communitarianism and civic republicanism. In contrast to liberalism. communitarianism emphasises community goals achieved through mutual support and group action. participation and integration. Whilst communitarianism places more emphasis on obligations it also seeks to preserve individual rights. However here. the relationship between obligations and rights in this sense is less immediate than in the liberal tradition. Civic republicanism bears many similarities to communitarianism in its emphasis on the obligations of citizens. However this emphasis is articulated from the standpoint of civic virtue rather state requirement. Within this perspective. the state is seen to be responsible for the enforcement of obligations on the members of society. however civil society also enforces obligations to a certain extent. The work of Rousseau with its emphasis on community. clearly reflects these general sentiments.

Rousseau begins from the standpoint that men are naturally unequal and that as societies evolve from a state of primitiveness into civilisations these inequalities are replaced by politically imposed inequalities. which are totally separate from the former. These inequalities progress in their extremity and if the process remains uninterrupted the final phase is that of the establishment of the master-slave society. Rousseau visualises savagery and Civilization at two opposing ends of the development spectrum. yet postulates that they are not much better than each other. Whilst the state of savagery is unable to accommodate rationality in the absence of language. the onset of Civilization leads to depravity and corruption. Rousseau therefore suggests that between these two states there is "the simple human community where humanity has been achieved and corruption still lies ahead" and that this political constitution must be found in order to foster the conditions necessary to establish a simple human community in the modern age.

In Social Contract (1762). Rousseau outlines what he deems to be the political conditions necessary for the political reformation of society. These involve the defence and protection of each person and their goods and the sustaining of both societal unity and the freedom of each individual. Rousseau suggests that this process begins with each person yielding his or her natural rights to the community. These are then exchanged for civil rights. which enable individuals to become citizens of the state. This transaction impacts upon the citizen's will. who. whilst still willing as an individual also becomes a constituent of the general will.

The third group of theories is that of participatory democracy. This perspective is composed of expansive democratic and neo-republic theories. The expansive democratic element emphasises the rights and participation of the lower classes and other marginalized groups to a greater extent than the previous perspectives. The focus here is on the balancing of group rights with individual rights and obligations with a view to establishing a self-identity that unites individual interests through community activities whilst also preserving the individual's civil rights. Central to expansive democracy are the principles of empowerment. participation and deliberation in and through democratic processes. Similar to this view. neo-republicanism advocates that citizens should partake in shared public action with other citizens. adopt an office which incorporates formal rights and duties and establish a plurality (as opposed to a majority) to guide the community. The ideal here is for the state and civil society to create deliberative institutions such as deliberative poling.

Philosophical representation of the ideologies held within this perspective. are embodied in the work of Habermas. Habermas's aim is to piece together a social theory that propels the cause of human emancipation whilst still preserving an inclusive. universalist moral framework. He views the rationalisation. humanisation and democratisation of society as resulting from the institutionalisation of the potential for the rationality ingrained within the communicative modes common to humans. In this sense Habermas advocates a discursive democracy. which suggests a direct correlation between the prevalence of democracy and its ability to generate communication. This democratic form is grounded in a type of argumentative communication. which places greater focus on deliberation than consent.Moderate postmodernist theories are the most recent addition to the political philosophical debates arena. Theories contained within this group can be arbitrarily divided into two categories. those who propose that citizenship is dead. and those who whilst accepting the notions of citizenship and politics. advocate significant modifications geared towards the establishment of group or particularistic rights. One of the theories contained within the latter category is that of radical pluralism. Within this view it is envisaged that there will be an ongoing contention referred to by Mouffe as agonistic pluralism. A process through which antagonism is transformed into shared consensus on basic democratic issues. According to Mouffe. the antagonistic form of democracy involves confrontations between individuals who agree on basic foundational rules but have differing interpretations of these rules and disagree on key political and moral issues. Central to this model is the notion of the active protesting citizen.

LIBERAL THEORIES OF INTERNATIONAL RELATIONS

Liberals argue that the universal condition of world politics is *globalization*. States are. and always have been. embedded in a domestic and transnational society. which creates incentives for economic. social and cultural interaction across borders. State policy may facilitate or block such interactions. Some domestic groups may benefit from or be harmed by such policies. and they pressure government accordingly for policies that facilitate realization of their goals. These social pressures. transmitted through domestic political institutions. define "state preferences" –that is. the set of substantive social purposes that motivate foreign policy. State preferences give governments an underlying stake in the international issues they face. Since the domestic and transnational social context in which states are embedded varies greatly across space and time. so do state preferences. Without such social concerns that transcend state borders. states would have no rational incentive to engage in world politics at all. but would simply devote their resources to an autarkic and isolated existence. To motivate conflict. cooperation. or any other costly foreign policy action. states must possess sufficiently intense state preferences. The resulting globalization-induced variation in social demands. and thus state preferences. is a fundamental cause of state Behaviour in world politics. This is the central insight of liberal international relations theory. It can be expressed colloquially in various ways: *"What matters most is what states want. not how they get it."* –or- *"Ends are more important than means."*

Liberal theory is distinctive in the nature of the variables it privileges. The liberal focus on variation in socially-determined state preferences distinguishes liberal theory from other theoretical traditions: realism (focusing on variation in coercive power resources). institutionalism (focusing on information). and most non-rational approaches (focusing on patterns of beliefs about appropriate means-ends relationships). In explaining patterns of war. for example. liberals do not look to inter-state imbalances of power. bargaining failure due to private information or uncertainty. or particular non-rational beliefs or propensities of individual leaders. societies. or organizations. Liberals look instead to conflicting state preferences derived from hostile nationalist or political ideologies. disputes over appropriable economic resources. or exploitation of unrepresented political constituencies. For liberals. a necessary condition for war is that social pressures lead one or more "aggressor" states to possess "revisionist" preferences so extreme or risk-acceptant that other states are unwilling to submit.

Three specific variants of liberal theory are defined by particular types of preferences. their variation. and their impact on state Behaviour. *Ideational liberal* theories link state Behaviour to varied conceptions of desirable forms of cultural. political. socioeconomic order. *Commercial liberal* theories stress economic interdependence. including many variants of "endogenous policy theory." *Republican* liberal theories stress the role of domestic representative institutions. elites and leadership dynamics. and executive-legislative relations. Such theories were first conceived by prescient liberals such as Immanuel Kant. Adam Smith. John Stuart Mill. John Hobson. Woodrow Wilson. and John Maynard Keynes-writing well before the deep causes (independent variables) they stress (*e.g.* democratization. industrialization. nationalism. and welfare provision) were widespread.

This essay introduces the liberal approach in three steps. It presents two distinctive assumptions underlying and distinguishing liberal theories. Then it further explicates the three variants of liberal theory that follow from these assumptions. Finally. it reviews some distinctive strengths that liberal theories tend to share vis-à-vis other types of international relations theory.

TWO UNIQUE ASSUMPTIONS UNDERLYING LIBERAL THEORY

What basic assumptions underlie the liberal approach? Two assumptions liberal theory make are the assumptions of *anarchy* and *rationality*. Specifically. *states (or other political actors) exist in an anarchic environment* and *they generally act in a broadly rational way in making decisions*. The anarchy assumption means that political actors exist in the distinctive environment of international politics. without a world government or any other authority with a monopoly on the legitimate use of force. They must engage in self-help. The rationality assumption means that state leaders and their domestic supporters engage in foreign policy for the instrumental purpose of securing benefits provided by (or avoiding costs imposed by) actors outside of their borders. and in making such calculations. states seek to deploy the most cost-effective means to achieve whatever their ends (preferences) may be. Liberal theory shares the first (anarchy) assumption with almost all international relations theories. and it shares the second (rationality) assumption with realism and institutionalism. but not non-rationalist process theories.

Liberal theories are distinguished from other rationalist theories. such as realism and institutionalism. by two unique assumptions about world politics: (1) States represent social groups. whose views constitute state preferences; and (2) Interdependence among state preferences influences state policy. Let us consider each in turn.

ASSUMPTION ONE: STATES REPRESENT SOCIETAL PREFERENCES

The first assumption shared by liberal theories is that *states represent some subset of domestic society. whose views constitute state preferences*. For liberals. the state is a representative institution constantly subject to capture and recapture. construction and reconstruction. by domestic social coalitions. These social coalitions define state "preferences" in world politics at any point in time: the "tastes." "ends." "basic interests." or "fundamental social purposes" that underlie foreign policy. Political institutions constitute a critical "transmission belt" by which these interests of individuals and groups in civil society enter the political realm. All individuals and groups do not wield equal influence over state policy. To the contrary. their power varies widely. depending on the context. Variation in the precise nature of representative institutions and practices helps define which groups influence the "national interest." Some states may represent. ideal-typically. the preferences of a single tyrannical individual. a Pol Pot or Josef Stalin; others afford opportunities for broad democratic participation. Most lie in between. The precise preferences of social groups. weighted by their domestic power. shape the underlying goals ("state preferences") that states pursue in world politics. Sometimes. non-governmental organizations (NGOs) and other actors may form transnational alliances to assist social forces. "State-society relations"—the relationship between a state and its domestic (and transnational) society in which it is embedded—lies at the center of liberal theory.

Liberals believe that state preferences cannot be reduced to some simple metric or preference ordering. such as seeking "security" or "wealth". Most modern states are not Spartan: They compromise security or sovereignty in order to achieve other ends. or. indeed. just to save money. Nor do modern states uniformly seek "wealth." Instead they strike rather strike complex and varied trade-offs among economic. social and political goals. Nor. finally do they seek "power" in the sense of "domination": Many countries would clearly rather spend money on "butter" rather than "guns." To see how consequential the variation in goals can be. one need look no further than the implications for international relations of Germany's evolution from Adolf Hitler's preference for militant nationalism. fascist rule. autarky. and ruthless exploitation of

German *Lebensraum* under *Das Dritte Reich* to the social compromise underlying the postwar *Bundesrepublik Deutschland*. which favored capitalist democracy. expanding German exports. and peaceful reunification. Similarly one can look at the striking change in policy between Maoist and post-Maoist China. Soviet and post-Soviet Russia. Imperial and post-Imperial Japan. and so on.

ASSUMPTION TWO: INTERDEPENDENCE AMONG STATE PREFERENCES INFLUENCES STATE BEHAVIOUR

The second core assumption shared by liberal theories is that *the interdependence among of state preferences influences state Behaviour.* Rather than treating preferences as a fixed constant. as do realists or institutionalists. liberals seek to explain variation in preferences and its significance for world politics. The precise distribution and nature of the "stakes" explains differences in state policy and Behaviour. States. liberals argue. orient their Behaviour to the precise nature of these underlying preferences: compatible or conflictual. intense or weak. and their precise scope. States require a "social purpose" — a perceived underlying stake in the matter at hand — in order to pay any attention to international affairs. let alone to provoke conflict. inaugurate cooperation. or take any other significant foreign policy action. If there is no such interdependence among state objectives. a rational state will conduct no international relations. satisfying itself with an isolated and autarkic existence. Conflictual goals increase the incentive for of political disputes. Convergence of underlying preferences creates the preconditions for peaceful coexistence or cooperation.

The critical theoretical link between state preferences. on the one hand. and state Behaviour. on the other. is the concept of policy interdependence. Policy interdependence refers to the distribution and interaction of preferences—that is. the extent to which the pursuit of state preferences necessarily imposes costs and benefits (known as *policy externalities*) upon other states. independent of the "transaction costs" imposed by the specific strategic means chosen to obtain them. Depending on the underlying pattern of interdependence. each of the qualitative categories above. the form. substance. and depth of conflict and cooperation vary according to the precise nature and intensity of preferences.

The existence of some measure of divergent fundamental beliefs. scarcity of material goods. and inequalities in domestic political power among states and social actors renders inevitable some measure of pluralism and competition among and within states. Unlike realists such as Waltz and Morgenthau. liberals do not assume these divergent interests are uniformly zero-sum. At the same time. liberals reject the utopian notion (often attributed to them by realists) of an automatic harmony of interest among individuals and groups in international society. Nor do liberals argue. as realists like Morgenthau charge. believe that each state pursues an ideal goal. oblivious of what other states do. Liberals argue instead that each state seeks to realize distinct preferences or interests under constraints imposed by the different interests of other states. This distribution of preferences varies considerably. For liberals. this variation—not realism's distribution of capabilities or institutionalism's distribution of information—is of decisive causal importance in explaining state Behaviour.

A few examples illustrate how liberal theories differ from realist. institutionalist or non-rational ones. We have already encountered the example of war in the introduction. in which liberals stress states with aggressive preferences. rather than imbalances of power. incomplete information. or non-rational beliefs and processes. Another illustration is trade policy. Economists widely agree that free trade is superior welfare-improving policy choice for states. yet trade protection is often practiced. To explain protectionism. liberals look to domestic social preferences. An important factor in almost all countries is the competitive position of affected economic sectors in global markets. which generates domestic and transnational distributional effects: Protectionism is generally backed by producers who are globally uncompetitive; free trade by producers who are globally competitive. Moreover. even if the state is a net beneficiary from free trade. domestic adjustment costs may be too high to tolerate politically. or may endanger other countervailing domestic social objectives. such as domestic social equality or environmental quality. Certain domestic political institutions. such as non-parliamentary legislative systems. which governed US trade policy before 1934. grant disproportionate power to protectionist interests.

This differs from realist explanations of trade protectionism. which tend to stress the role of "hegemonic power" in structuring trade liberalization. or the need to defend self-sufficient national security within the prevailing zero-sum geopolitical competition. perhaps by maintaining self-sufficiency or by aiding allies at the expense of purely economic objectives. Institutionalists might cite the absence of appropriate international institutions. or other means to manage the complex informational tasks and collective action problems—negotiation. dispute resolution. enforcement—required to manage free trade. Those who focus on non-rational theories (psychological. cultural. organizational. epistemic. perceptual or bureaucratic) might stress an ideological disposition to accept "mercantilist" theory. shared historical analogies. and the psychological predisposition to avoid losses.

To further illustrate the importance of patterns of policy interdependence. consider the following three circumstances: zero-sum. harmonious and mixed preferences. In the case of *zero-sum* preferences. attempts by dominant social groups in one state to realize their preferences through international action may necessarily impose costs on dominant social groups in other countries. This is a case of "zero-sum" preferences. similar to the "realist" world.

Governments face a bargaining game with few mutual gains and a high potential for interstate tension and conflict. Many ancient cities and states. including those of Ancient Athens. often imposed imperial tribute on defeated neighbors or. in extremis. killed the male population. cast women and children into slavery. and repopulated the town with their own citizens—a situation approximating zero-sum conflict. Today. it might still be argued that there are certain cases—trade in agricultural goods by industrial democracies. for example—where entrenched national interests are so strong that no government seriously considers embracing free trade. In the case of *harmonious* preferences. where the externalities of unilateral policies are optimal (or insignificant) for others. there are strong incentives for quiet coexistence with low conflict and (at most) simple forms of interstate coordination. For example. advanced industrial democracies today no longer contemplate waging war on one another. and in some areas governments have agreed to mutual recognition of certain legal standards without controversy.

One case of *mixed* preferences is bargaining. where states can achieve common gains (or avoid common losses. as with a war) if they agree to coordinate their Behaviour. but may disagree strongly on the distribution of benefits or adjustment costs. Under such circumstances. one of the most important determinants of bargaining power is the intensity of the preferences of each party; the more intense their preference for a beneficial settlement. the more likely they are to make concessions (or employ coercive means) in order to achieve it. Another situation of mixed motives is a situation where interstate coordination can avoid significant risks and costs. as in agreement to avoid naval incidents at sea. or to share information on infectious diseases. In such situations. institutional pre-commitments and the provision of greater information can often improve the welfare of all parties.

Liberals derive several distinctive conceptions of power. very different from that of realism. One form of international influence. for liberals. stems from the interdependence among preferences that Keohane and Nye (*Power and Interdependence)* call "asymmetrical interdependence." All other things equal. the more interdependent a state is. the more intense its preference for a given outcome. the more power others potentially have over it; while the less a state wants something. the less a state cares about outcomes. the less intense its preferences. the less power others have over it. Situations of asymmetrical interdependence. where one state has more intense preference for an agreement than another. create bargaining power. In trade negotiations. for example. smaller and poorer countries are often more dependent on trade and thus benefit more from free trade. and thus tend to have a weaker position and make more concessions in the course of negotiations.

Enlargement of the European Union is a recent instance. Relative preference intensity can also influence the outcome of war. but in a different way. Nations are in fact rarely prepared to mortgage their entire economy or military in conflict. so their power depends not on their coercive power resources. but on their resolve or will. This is why smaller states often prevail over larger ones. Vietnam. for example. did not prevail over the US in the Vietnam War because it possessed more coercive power resources. but because it had a more intense preference at stake.

FROM ASSUMPTIONS TO THEORIES

Taken by themselves. these liberal assumptions—the international system is anarchic. states are rational. social pressures define state preferences. interdependence among preferences dictates state Behaviour—are thin. They exclude most existing realist. institutionalist. and non-rational theories. but they do not. taken by themselves. define very precisely the positive content of liberal theory. Some might rightly complain that simply pointing to state preferences opens up an unmanageably wide range of hypothetical social influences on policy.

Yet. in practice. research has shown that. in practice. the range of viable liberal theories that test out empirically are relatively few. focused. and powerful. Three broad variants or categories of liberal theory exist: *ideational. commercial. and republican liberalism.* At the core of each lies a distinct conception of the social pressures and representative institutions that define state preferences. and the consequences for state Behaviour. Some of these have proven. empirically. to be among the most powerful theories in international relations. Let us consider each in turn.

STATE PREFERENCES BASED ON DOMESTIC SOCIAL VALUES AND IDENTITIES

Ideational liberalism views *domestic social identities and values* as basic determinants of state preferences. Drawing on a liberal tradition of political philosophy dating back to John Stuart Mill. Giuseppe Mazzini. Woodrow Wilson. and John Maynard Keyes. liberals defines social values as the set of preferences held by various individuals and groups in society concerning the proper scope and nature of legitimate state objectives. In particular. nations and groups within nations differ in their conceptions of what a legitimate domestic order is—that is. their conception of which social actors belong to the polity and what is owed them.

Thus for liberals. ends that may appear universal—such as the Defence of political sovereignty and national security—are not necessarily ends in themselves. but are justified only insofar as they are means to realize the specific underlying preferences of social actors concerning "legitimate social order." Some states. such as aggressive states like Hitler's Germany. willing place security and sovereignty at risk in order to achieve conquest. Other states may place security at risk to maintain peace or prosperity. None of these choices are necessarily "irrational"; they simply involve varying sets of social preferences.

Foreign policy. in the ideational liberal view. is an effort to realize these views domestically. Social actors provide support to the government in exchange for institutions that accord with their identity-based preferences and are therefore deemed "legitimate". Similarly. actors will sometimes advocate foreign policies that subvert the existing domestic social order. On the liberal view. the effect of conceptions of social legitimacy on state Behaviour depends on patterns of interdependence among these ideals—in other words. on the transnational externalities created for others by attempts to realize those preferences in one place. Liberal theories predict that where national conceptions of legitimate borders. political institutions. and socioeconomic equality are compatible. generating positive or negligible externalities. peaceful coexistence is likely.

Where social identities are incompatible and create significant negative externalities—as when one state views the promotion of its legitimate borders. political institutions. and socioeconomic standards as requiring aggression or demands *vis-à-vis* another state—tension and zero-sum conflict is more likely. Where national claims can be made more compatible through reciprocal policy adjustment. efforts to cooperate explicitly through international institutions are more likely.

Some social preferences about a legitimate social order are particularly important. such as those pertaining to the proper location of national borders. the nature of political institutions. and the scope of socioeconomic regulation.

National Identity: One basic type of social identity concerns the scope of the "nation": specifically. the legitimate location of national borders and the allocation of citizenship rights. Where borders coincide with underlying patterns of identity. coexistence and even mutual recognition are more likely. but where there are inconsistencies between borders and underling patterns of identity—as there have been in the Balkans for over 100 years. in central Europe in the mid-19th century. and in many places in the world today—greater potential for interstate conflict exists. Over the last century and a half. from mid-nineteenth century nationalist uprisings to late twentieth-century national liberation struggles. the desire for national autonomy constitutes the most common issue over which wars have been fought and great power intervention has taken place. The Balkan conflicts preceding World War I and in the former Yugoslavia after the end of the Cold War are notorious examples. Not by chance is scenario planning for China/United States conflict focused almost exclusively on Taiwan—the one jurisdiction where borders and national identity (as well as political ideology) are subject to competing claims.

Political Ideology: The second basic type of social identity stems from individuals and group commitments to particular forms of political institutions.

Where the realization of legitimate domestic political institutions in one jurisdiction threatens its realization in others (negative externalities). conflict is more likely. From Ancient Greece. where oligarchic and democratic factions in city-states used foreign policy to defend and advance their preferred form of government. to the French Revolution and nineteenth-century Concert of Europe. where monarchies used international cooperation to quash democratic and nationalist revolution. to the Second World War. where democracies and communists fought fascists. to the Cold War. when the United States and the Soviet Union were motivated by divergent political ideologies. disputes over political ideology have fueled international conflict.

Socioeconomic Regulation: The third basic type of social identity relevant for world politics stems from beliefs about legitimate socioeconomic regulation and redistribution. Modern liberal theories (in contrast to the *laissez faire* libertarianism sometimes labeled as quintessentially "liberal") have long recognized that societal preferences concerning the appropriate nature and level of regulation impose legitimate limits on transnational markets. Domestic and international markets are embedded in local social compromises concerning the provision of regulatory public goods. The extent to which countries can cooperate to liberalize markets. for example. depends on the level of conflict or convergence of views about immigration. social welfare. taxation. religious freedom. families. health and safety. environmental and consumer protection. cultural promotion. and many other domestic public goods. These issues have increasingly been the subjects of international economic negotiations. We often see odd domestic coalitions made up of idealists and materialists—so-called "Baptist-bootlegger" coalitions where those who Favour regulation for public spirited reasons ("Baptists") ally with those who benefit in a material sense — around international economic issues. For example. we sometimes observe unions. uncompetitive business and environmentalists all supporting trade protection—for quite different reasons.

STATE PREFERENCES BASED ON ECONOMIC INTERESTS

Commercial liberal theories seek to explain the international Behaviour of states based on the domestic and global market position of domestic firms. workers. and owners of assets. Commercial liberal theory posits that changes in the structure of the domestic and global economy alter the costs and benefits of transnational economic exchange. thus creating pressure on domestic governments to facilitate or block such exchanges through appropriate foreign economic and security policies.

Commercial liberal theory does not predict that economic incentives automatically generate universal free trade and peace. but focuses instead on the interplay between aggregate incentives and distributional consequences. The greater the economic benefits for powerful private actors. the greater their incentive. all other things equal. to press governments to facilitate such transactions; the more costly the adjustment imposed by the proposed economic exchanges. the more opposition is likely to arise. As Dani Rodrik has argued. contemporary trade liberalization generates domestic distributional shifts totaling many times aggregate welfare benefits. Losers generally tend to be better identified and organized than beneficiaries. A major source of protection. liberals predict. lies in uncompetitive. un diversified. and monopolistic sectors or factors of production. Their pressure induces a systematic divergence from laissez-faire policies-a tendency recognized by Adam Smith. who famously complained of mercantilism that "the contrivers of this whole mercantile system [are] the producers. whose interest has been so carefully attended to." This commercial liberal approach to analyzing conflict over foreign economic policy is distinct from those of realism (emphasizing security concerns and relative power). institutionalism (informational and institutional constraints on optimal interstate collective action). and constructivism (beliefs about "free trade"). Extensive research supports the view that free trade is most likely where strong competitiveness. extensive intra-industry trade or trade in intermediate goods. large foreign investments. and low asset specificity internalize the net benefits of free trade to powerful actors. reducing the influence of net losers from liberalization. Similar arguments can be used to analyze issues such as sovereign debt. exchange rate policy. agricultural trade policy. European integration. foreign direct investment. tax policy. and migration policy.

The effect of economic interdependence on security affairs varies with market incentives. A simple starting point is that the collateral damage of war disrupts economic activity: the more vulnerable and extensive such activity. the greater the cost.

A more sophisticated cost-benefit calculation would take into account the potential economic costs and benefits of war. Where monopolies. sanctions. slavery. plunder of natural resources. and other forms of coercive extraction backed by state power are cost-effective means of elite wealth accumulation-as was true for most of human history-we should expect to see a positive relationship. between transnational economic activity and war. Where. conversely. private trade and investment within complex and well-established transnational markets provide a less costly means of accumulating wealth and one that cannot be cost-effectively appropriated-as is most strikingly the case within modern multinational investment and production networks-the expansion of economic opportunities will have a pacific effect. Along with the spread of democracy and relative absence of nationalist conflict. this distinguishes the current era from the period before the

First World War. when high levels of interdependence famously failed to deter war. We see in current Western relations with China a very deliberate strategy to encourage the slow evolution of social preferences in a pacific direction by encouraging trade. Eric Gartzke has recently argued that the "democratic peace" phenomenon can largely be explained in terms of a lack of economic and other motives for war. Even among developed economies. however. circumstances may arise where governments employ coercive means to protect international markets. This may take varied forms. as occurred under nineteenth-century empires or with pressure from business for the United States to enter the First World War to defend trade with the allies.

REPUBLICAN LIBERALISM: STATE PREFERENCES BASED ON SYSTEMS OF DOMESTIC REPRESENTATION

A final source of state preferences is the structure of domestic political representation. While ideational and commercial theories stress. respectively. particular patterns of underlying societal identities and interests related to globalization. republican liberal theory emphasizes the ways in which domestic institutions and practices aggregate and transmit such pressures. transforming them into state policy. The key variable in republican liberalism. which dates back to the theories of Kant. Wilson. and others. is the nature of domestic political representation. which helps determine *whose* social preferences dominate state policy—thereby defining the "national interest".

A simple consequence is that policy tends to be biased in Favour of the governing coalitions or powerful domestic groups favored by representative institutions—whether those groups are administrators (rulers. armies. or bureaucracies) or societal groups that "capture" the state. Costs and risks are passed on to others.

When particular groups with outlier preferences are able to formulate policy without providing gains for society as a whole. the result is likely to be inefficient and suboptimal policy for the policy as a whole. To the extent that most individuals and groups in society tend generally to be risk averse. the broader the range of represented groups. the less likely it is that they will support indiscriminate use of policy instruments. like war or autarky. that impose large net costs or risks on society as a whole. Democracies tend to be choosy about the wars they enter: Selecting lower cost war. not provoking great-power war. and fighting to win. Republican liberal theory thereby helps to explain phenomena as diverse as the "democratic peace." modern imperialism. and international trade and monetary cooperation. Given the plausibility of the assumption that major war imposes net costs on society as a whole. it is hardly surprising that the most prominent republican liberal argument concerns the "democratic peace:' which one scholar has termed "as close as anything we have to an empirical law in international relations" –one that applies to tribal societies as well as modern states. From a liberal perspective. the theoretical interest in the "democratic peace" lies not in the greater transparency of democracies (a claim about information). the greater military power of democracies (a realist claim). or norms appropriate Behaviour (a constructivist claim). but the distinctive preferences of democracies.

This is not. of course. to imply that broad domestic representation *necessarily* generates international cooperation. In specific cases. elite preferences in multiple states may be more convergent than popular ones. Moreover. the extent of bias in representation. not democracy per se. is the theoretically critical point. There exist conditions under which specific governing elites may have an incentive to represent long-term social preferences in a way that is less biased-for example. when they dampen nationalist sentiment. as may be the case in some democratizing regimes. or exclude powerful outlier special interests. as is commonly the case in trade policy.

The theoretical obverse of "democratic peace" theory is a republican liberal theory of war. which stresses risk -acceptant leaders and rent -seeking coalitions. There is substantial historical evidence that the aggressors who have provoked modern great-power wars tend either to be extremely risk-acceptant individuals. or individuals well able to insulate themselves from the costs of war. or both. Jack Snyder. for example. has refurbished Hobson's classic left-liberal analysis of imperialism-in which the military. uncompetitive foreign investors and traders. jingoistic political elites. and others who benefit from imperialism are particularly well placed to influence policy-by linking unrepresentative and extreme outcomes to log-rolling coalitions. Consistent with this analysis. the highly unrepresentative consequences of partial democratization. combined with the disruption of rapid industrialization and incomplete political socialization. suggest that democratizing states. if subject to these influences. may be particularly war-prone. This offers one answer to the paradox posed by James Fearon-namely. why rational states would ever enter into war rather than negotiate their way out.

Parallels to the "democratic peace" exist in political economy. We have seen that illiberal commercial policies-trade protection. monetary instability. and sectoral subsidization that may manifestly undermine the general welfare of the population-reflect pressure from powerful domestic groups. In part this power results from biases within representative institutions. such as the power of money in electoral systems. the absence or presence of insulated institutions. Consider the example of international trade. As we saw in the preceding section. perhaps the most widespread explanation for the persistence of illiberal commercial policies. such as protection. monetary instability. and sectoral subsidization that may manifestly undermine the general welfare of the population. is pressure from powerful domestic groups. The power of such groups is often exacerbated by biases within representative institutions. Where the latter sort of biases exist—and it is seen in most contemporary representative institutions—special interest groups are likely to gain protection through tariffs. subsidies. favorable regulation. or competitive devaluation. Where policy makers are insulated from such pressures. which may involve less democratic—such as "fast track" provisions. executive agreements. and the United States Trade Representative—open policies are more viable. Ironically. in such cases. less "democratic" institutions. in the sense of less "populist" and "participatory" institutions. may in fact be more representative of society as a whole.

THE SCOPE OF THE LIBERAL PERSPECTIVE

We have seen that liberal theory is a coherent family of ideational. commercial and republican theories that share common assumptions about international relations. Such theories explain not only cooperation among liberal states. but pertain to liberal and non-liberal polities. conflictual and cooperative situations. security and political economy issues. and both individual foreign policy and aggregate Behaviour. Such theories challenge the conventional presumption that realism is the simplest. most encompassing and most powerful of major IR theories. Although not all liberal theories are easy to specify. hypotheses about endogenous tariff setting. the democratic peace. and nationalist conflict suggest that liberalism generates many empirical arguments as powerful and parsimonious as those of realism. At first glance. some may object that the claim that state preferences or interests matter—that is. what states want shapes what they do—is trivial. Yet in fact the liberal approach is distinctively different than other widely advocated families of theories. which stress instead the distribution of coercive power. information. cultural beliefs and other characteristics of states. Others may feel that stressing preferences may lead to an impossibly broad and vague approach. because thousands of factors might affect the social demands placed on a modern state. In practice. however. specific liberal theories turn out to be not just powerful but precise and focused as well. Fifty years ago Morgenthau launched the modern post-war field of international relations by proclaiming that international relations theory should avoid "two popular fallacies...the concern with motives...and the concern with ideological preferences." Liberalism seeks to theorize motives. ideologies and preferences—and the empirical data shows that it has done so successfully.

Theories based on the liberal approach can explain. moreover. a number of phenomena for which realist. institutionalist. and non-rational theories of international relations approaches lack a persuasive account.

First. the *liberal approach provides a plausible theoretical explanation for variation in the substantive content of foreign policy*. Neither realism nor institutionalism explains the changing substantive goals and purposes over which states conflict and cooperate. Both focus instead on formal causes. such as relative power. issue density. or the distribution of information—and on formal consequences. such as conflict and cooperation per se. By contrast. liberal theories provide a plausible explanation not just for conflict and cooperation. but for the substantive content of foreign policy. Liberal IR theory offers plausible. parsimonious hypotheses to explain things like the difference between Anglo-American. Nazi. and Soviet plans for the post–World War II world; U.S. concern about a few North Korean. Iraqi. or Chinese nuclear weapons. rather than the greater arsenals held by Great Britain. Israel. and France; the substantial differences between within the Bretton Woods compromise of "embedded liberalism" and the period of "free trade imperialism" that preceded it. divergences between economic cooperation under the EC and NAFTA. and many other cases. Similarly. liberalism makes more sense of the sudden reversal of East–West relations. a shift made possible by the widespread view among Russian officials (so interview data reveal) that Germany was at once ethnically satisfied. politically democratic. and commercially inclined.

Second. *the liberal approach offers a plausible explanation for historical change in the international system.* The static quality of both realist and institutionalist theories. and their lack of persuasive explanations for fundamental long-term change in the nature of international politics. are recognized weaknesses. Global economic development over the past five hundred years has been closely related to greater per capita wealth. democratization. education systems that reinforce new collective identities. and greater incentives for trans-border economic transactions. Realist theory accords such shifts no theoretical importance. but analyzes enduring patterns of state Behaviour reflecting cyclical shifts in power. as in the rise and decline of great powers. Liberal theories. by contrast. forge a direct causal link between economic. political. and social modernization and state Behaviour in world politics. Hence. for example. it is significant to liberals that over the modern period the principles of international order have been decreasingly linked to dynastic legitimacy and increasingly to factors directly drawn from the three variants of liberalism: national self-determination and social citizenship. the increasing complexity of economic integration. and liberal democratic governance.

Third. following on from the second point. *the liberal approach offers a plausible explanation for the distinctiveness of modern international politics.* Among advanced industrial democracies. a stable form of interstate politics has emerged. grounded in reliable expectations of peaceful change. domestic rule of law. stable international institutions. and intensive societal interaction. Whereas realists offer no general explanation for the emergence of this distinctive mode of international politics. liberal theories argue that the emergence of a large and expanding bloc of pacific. interdependent. normatively satisfied states has been a precondition for such politics. Consider. for example.

the current state of Europe. Unlike realist theories. for example. liberal theories explain the near total absence of competitive alliance formation among the leading democratic powers today.

FROM UNICAUSAL TO MULTI-CAUSAL THEORY

We have seen that liberal assumptions about world politics offer a distinct foundation on which a number of powerful theories may be grounded. Yet any good historian. policy-maker or social scientist is instinctively—and rightly—suspicious of mono-causal explanations based on only a single theory. Surely world politics is more complex. What if we want to combine a liberal theory with other theories. liberal or non-liberal? Two final points are worth noting. both of which elaborate the various in which any given liberal theory can be combined with other theories.

First. *various liberal theories work well in tandem with one another.* Not only does liberal theory apply across a wide domain of circumstances. but its three variants—ideational. commercial. and republican liberalism—are mutually reinforcing. They are stronger taken together than separately. Not only do they share assumptions and causal mechanisms. but their empirical implications aggregate in interesting ways. It is widely accepted. for example. that economic development has a strong influence on the viability of democratic governance. with its pacific implications; liberal democratic governments tend in turn to support commerce. which promotes economic development. Such claims can be analytically reinforcing even where they do not make parallel predictions. Anomalies within one variant of liberal theory may be resolved by considering other variants. Positive movement along one liberal dimension—patterns of national identity. democratic participation. or transnational economic transactions—may condone or exacerbate the negative distortions along another liberal dimension.

Norman Angell. whose commercial liberal claims on the eve of World War I included a prediction -that war among major powers was obsolete. is often parodied by secondhand critics. Yet he does not deserve this. Angell staunchly maintained that his well-known "unprofitability of war" thesis in no way implies "the impossibility of war"—a doctrine he dismissed for republican liberal reasons (*i.e.* the fact that not all governments are representative) as a "ridiculous myth." Where representative bias permits special interests to control policy. aggregate incentives for welfare-improving trade are likely to have less effect. Recent studies reveal that the correlation between economic interdependence and peace holds far more strongly among liberal states. Conversely. where democratization heightens socioeconomic inequality. nationalist cleavages. uneven patterns of gains. and losses due to interdependence or extreme heterogeneity of interests—as may have occurred in the former Yugoslavia and other democratizing nations—it may exacerbate international economic and political conflict. Such interaction effects among liberal factors offer a promising area for more detailed analysis. Liberal theories are greater than the sum of their parts.

Second. *liberal theories are easily combined with other international relations theories. generating multi-causal explanations.* Surely there are cases in which a *combination* of liberal and other theories offers a better explanation of state Behaviour than any single sort of theory alone. liberal or otherwise. In such cases. a *multicausal synthesis* is required. But an "anything goes" attitude will quickly lead to complexity. How can we discipline such a synthesis? What model should we use?

Most theorists believe we should synthesize theories by employing realism first (with preferences assumed to be invariant) and then introduce liberal theories to explain whatever is left over. The justification often given is that realist theories deal with the most "important" phenomena in international affairs. coercive threats to national security. and no state will pay attention to liberal factors until they resolve such classic *Realpolitik* issues. Yet such claims arbitrarily privilege realist explanations of any phenomena that might be explained by other theories—and liberal theories. as we have seen. do deal with essential matters of peace and war. Moreover. it is clear—as we have seen above—that conflict often comes about precisely because states have varied interests. and some aggressor states have privileged something above security. this violating the key assumptions of realism.

The truth is in fact the opposite: to the extent that both preferences and coercive other factors matter. *liberal theories enjoy analytical priority in any synthesis.* The assumption of rationality or purposive Behaviour central to realism (like the "bounded rationality" claims of institutionalism) implies action on the basis of a prior. specific. and consistent set of preferences. Unless we know what these preferences are (that is. unless we know the extent to which states value the underlying stakes). we cannot assess realist or institutionalist claims linking variation in the particular means available to states (whether coercive capabilities or institutions) on interstate conflict or cooperation. Nor can we use non-rational decision-making theory to assess whether the means-ends calculations used to realize those interests are rational or not. Preferences determine the nature and intensity of the game that states are playing and thus are a primary determinant of which systemic theory is appropriate and how it should be specified. Variation in state preferences often influences the way in which states make calculations about their strategic environment. whereas the converse—that the strategic situation leads to variation in state preferences—is inconsistent with the rationality assumption shared by all three theories. *In short. liberal theories explain when and why the assumptions about state preferences underlying realism or institutionalism hold.* The reverse is not the case. at least in the short term. In situations where these assumptions do not hold. realism and institutionalism (as well as some variants of constructivism) are not just of limited importance. they are theoretically irrelevant.

The priority of liberalism in multicausal models of state Behaviour implies. furthermore. that collective state Behaviour should be analyzed as a *two-stage process*. States first define preferences—a stage uniquely explained by liberal theories—and *only then* do they debate. bargain. or fight to particular agreements—a second stage explained by realist and/or institutionalist theories of strategic interaction. The two-stage model offers a general structure for research design and theoretical explanation. In those cases where liberal factors only influence strategic outcomes directly. through preferences and preference intensities. liberalism can be tested as a monocausal hypothesis against alternative realist or institutionalist factors. Liberal factors may also influence outcomes indirectly. because the nature of preferences helps determine the relative power and influence of states.. Recall that preferences do not simply shape outcomes. they tell us which realist or institutionalist factors are important and how they relate to state Behaviour. In such cases. explaining (or at least controlling for) variation in state preferences is analytically prior to an analysis of strategic interaction. Without a prior analysis of preferences. only monocausal formulations of realist or institutionalist theory can be tested.

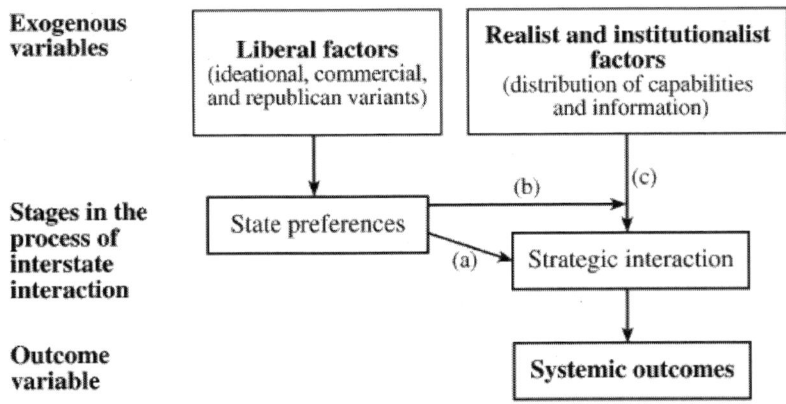

Fig. A tow - stage model of state Behaviour

The primacy of liberal theories in such multicausal explanations may appear to be an abstract admonition. yet it is of real practical importance in interpreting historical experience and current policy.

How are we to understand. for example. Woodrow Wilson's proposal for the League of Nations. often cited as the epitome of liberal "legalism" and "utopianism." At first glance. Wilson's proposal seems to reflect a naive confidence in international institutions. Yet in fact it was a two-stage liberal proposal—and a realistic one at that. From the start. Wilson was skeptical about the *autonomous* influence of international institutions. He cared little about their precise form. because he viewed them as no more than "a symbolic affirmation of the 'rightness' of democracies in their mutual relations." Thus. for example. his initial draft of the League Covenant included no provisions for international law or a supranational court; both were eventually added only at the insistence of more conservative (and more cynical) foreign and domestic politicians. He was skeptical that the League could ever actually override national decisions.

Instead what Wilson termed the "first point" to remember about the League was not institutionalist but liberal: Its membership was to be restricted to those countries enjoying republican government and national self-determination. Insofar as the League was to rely on public opinion. it was to be solely *democratic* public opinion. Based on a multicausal liberal analysis. Wilson explicitly identified a set of narrow preconditions under which collective security institutions could succeed. The League. he argued. would function only if nationally self-determining democracy was a nearly universal form of government among great powers. which in turn controlled an overwhelming proportion of global military power. In 1917. Wilson believed this situation to be imminent: "There are not going to be many other kinds of nations for long.... The Hapsburgs and the Hohenzollerns are permanently out of business." Given Wilson's underlying theory. is it surprising that the League had become moribund by 1936. after twelve European countries had moved from democracy to dictatorship? Or that this shift isolated democratic France and Britain. exacerbating their oft-noted geopolitical dilemmas in Manchuria and Abyssinia? When a similar situation arose in the former Yugoslavia after 1989. in a world where almost all the great powers in the region were liberal democracies—as we have seen above—Western governments intervened to oppose aggression. while avoiding any hint of armed conflict among themselves. Indeed. the absence of serious conflict among Western powers over Yugoslavia—the "World War I scenario"—reflects in large part a shared perception that the geopolitical gains from conflict among democratic governments are low. In this sense. the interwar failure of the League. often cited as a realist refutation of utopian liberal *ideology*. in fact confirms liberal IR *theory*.

Multicausal liberalism helps to explain not only ambitious schemes for cooperation like collective security. but "realist" policy outcomes like power balancing and bipolar conflict. A form of multicausal liberalism underlay the post–World War II U.S. policy of containment—a policy traditionally treated as the embodiment of realism. Containment of the Soviet Union was never simply about power balancing. It was a liberal grand strategy. as made explicit after World War I by Wilson and John Dewey. then after World War II by George Kennan. Kennan. in this regard a liberal. linked the European threat to the nature of the Soviet regime; it is often forgotten that nine-tenths of the seminal "X" article was given over to an analysis of Soviet domestic beliefs. A Western military deterrent would be required. he argued. only until the Bolshevik revolution had run its course. whereupon the Soviet system would collapse of its own accord. The decisive Western actions in the Cold War. according to Kennan. were the reconstruction of Germany and Japan as capitalist democracies through policies like the Marshall Plan. The goal of the policy was the transformation of social purposes and state preferences in Western countries. neither of which would assume much importance in a purely realist analysis.

In the end. the conduct and conclusion of the Cold War proceeded precisely as Kennan's two-stage liberal model had predicted. Realist power balancing served throughout as a static. interim instrument to maintain the status quo. but shifting state preferences explain the outbreak and eventual passing of the conflict. By 1959. standing in a Moscow exhibit of kitchenware. Richard Nixon and Nikita Khrushchev declared that the Cold War would be won and lost not through relative military capabilities. but through the relative economic prowess and ideological attractiveness of the two superpowers. Economic stagnation and a measure of ideological change in the East predated foreign policy change.

If the West. as Khrushchev rashly promised. had been buried under the superior economic performance of the East. the outcome might well have been different. These examples demonstrate the ability of multicausal liberal theories to explain critical twentieth-century foreign policy decisions. such as those taken in 1918. 1947. and 1989. even when national security interests are fully engaged.

In interpreting such cases. the major difference between realist and liberal theories lies not. as is often claimed. in the observation that realist states are concerned about security threats. or even with balancing security threats. Both theories predict this under specific circumstances. Where the two families of theory genuinely differ is on the sources of security threats themselves. with realists attributing them to particular configurations of power (against which states balance). whereas liberals attribute them to extreme conflict among ideological. institutional. and material preferences. (For their part. Institutionalists attribute them to uncertainty and the failure of commitment strategies. and epistemic theorists to particular beliefs about the efficacy or appropriateness of specific policy responses.)

If liberal theories contribute to explaining core realist cases such as bipolar conflict. there is good reason to believe that the most powerful influences in world politics today are not the deployment of military force or the construction of international institutions. but the quiet transformation of the domestic and transnational social values. interests. and institutions that underlie the widely varying preferences states bring to world politics.

THE SOCIOLOGY OF CITIZENSHIP

This chapter will first begin by outlining the classical sociological conceptions of citizenship. which are born within three dominant traditions; liberal theory. communitarian theory and that of radical democracy. The chapter will then proceed to document some of the recent contemporary sociological theories. which will also assist in highlighting a number of issues that are seen to determine the nature of citizenship in our late modern age. Here the key features of the nature of late modern society will be considered and its effects on the nature and positioning of citizenship explored.

LIBERAL THEORY

In its most general sense. citizenship as membership of a political community and is constructed around a set of interrelations between four key elements. these are rights. duties. participation and identity. The conception of citizenship within the liberal tradition has generally focused on the rights of the citizen. This formalistic conception of citizenship is a market centred one. which is based on the principle of equality. This conception effectively presents citizenship and civil society as pre-political forms by placing the citizen within the confines of the private domain.

One of the main theories encompassed within modern liberal thought and one in which there has been a recent revival of interest. is that of Marshall. Although Marshall's theory is widely applicable it is important to note that his analysis was constructed with particular reference to English history. The theoretical standpoint of this theory is often termed as left wing liberalism or the social democratic version of citizenship. Where as liberalism highlights the rights of the citizen and conservatism focuses on the duties of the citizen. Marshall stresses both rights and duties. Marshall saw citizenship as an official legal status associated with full membership of a community. Within this conception. citizens have the right to have rights and all citizens are equal with respect to their rights and duties. Marshall's work bears some resemblance to Marxism in the sense that it redirects the focus placed on civil society and places it on the class system. In fact possibly the most important aspect of Marshall's theory is its explicit proclamation of the relationship between citizenship and social class. Marshall's theory presents a State-based model as opposed to a market based one.

According to Marshall it is following the encompassing of both political and social rights that citizenship develops a more overtly contentious relationship with the class system. Marshall does not see this contention in a purely negative light however. On the contrary. Marshall's theory postulates that through this conflict citizenship or more specifically social citizenship. is able to impact upon the capitalist class system. reducing social inequalities. Marshall did not claim that this interactive relationship marked the end of the class system. but that it enabled citizenship to impose certain modifications upon it. It is for this reason that Marshall states: "citizenship has itself become in certain respects the architect of legitimate social inequality" (Marshall and Bottomore cited in Heater 2004:114) Marshall sees this interactive relationship between social class and citizenship as an ongoing one in which both structures act upon each other. each initiating and shaping changes in the other.

Marshall perceives citizenship as an integrated whole comprised of three interrelated elements; the civil. the political and the social. According to Marshall these three elements have independent histories and institutional bases which could be traced back to the eighteenth Century when civic rights were acquired. through to the nineteenth Century in which Political rights were acquired. through to the twentieth Century which marked the acquisition of social rights. Marshall did however acknowledge a certain amount of elasticity within these stages. Marshall postulates that is was through this accumulative chronological pathway of rights acquisition that citizenship as a concept has evolved. Marshall's account of citizenship is therefore in effect. a theory of social change. which documents the growth of citizenship throughout time.

Two of the main criticisms of liberal theory are; it's perceived inadequate response to the challenge of community and to the challenge of democracy. The first of these criticisms is levelled from the theoretical camp of the communitarians. In contrast to liberalism. communitarianism situates civil society in the community. In this viewpoint participation and identity are emphasised as opposed to rights and duties. Communitarianism is unique in its rejection of contractualism and individualism. which separates it both from liberalism and social democracy. Although communitarian theory can be seen to have drawn the citizenship debate into the political domain. the concept of politics utilised by communitarians. does not encompass democracy. Consequently this viewpoint is often associated with liberal theory. which also stands accused of this shortcoming.

COMMUNITARIANISM

The communitarianism perspective is one which centralises the social sphere and more specifically the community. In fact the formulation of values and order within the community are favoured above the formulation of such aspects on an individual level. Consequently. communitarians have a vested interest in the social units through which values are transmitted and enforced. These include the family. schools and other community based organisations. Whilst all communitarians uphold the general importance of community. they differ in the extent to which they emphasise individual liberties and rights (Christensen and Levinson. eds. 2003).

Within the communitarian viewpoint there are three main categories. these are liberal communitarianism. conservative communitarianism and civic republicanism. Although uniquely individual in their stance. these three forms are held together by a number of permeating strands. Due to the specific philosophical issues it embodies. the liberal communitarian debate is one that is notably separate from other debates within communitarianism. This particular viewpoint is commended for its highlighting of the identity problem within the citizenship debate. Liberal communitarians seek to affix the political community within the context of the cultural community and believe that these circumstances facilitate the discovery of identity. The focus here is a kind of moral. cultural collectivism in which material values are marginalized. This focal area is reflective of Liberal communitarians quest to highlight the importance of cultural identity as opposed to individual rights. The above sentiments are clearly expressed in the work of one of the best-known communitarian theorists. Charles Taylor who offers the most concrete analysis of citizenship issues within the liberal communitarian debate.

Unlike liberal communitarianism. conservative communitarianism has more of a sociological as opposed to philosophical content base. This particular form of communitarianism tends to emphasise the family. religion. tradition. nation and the culture of consensus. Conservative communitarianism is distinguished by its strong consensus on identity issues. its perception of participation as a civic responsibility and its emphasis of social reconstruction.

Emphasis within the civic republicanism perspective is placed on civic bonds this is quite apart from the market or state emphasis found in liberal theory or the moral community emphasis found within mainstream communitarianism. Central to this tradition are participation in public life and commitment. In fact civic republicanism postulates that it is within this context that individualism is able to attain its highest level of expression. The model of citizenship constructed within this perspective is one which is anchored in participation and public action. one in which identity occupies a minor position.

The political ideal here is that of the 'self governing political community' which constitutes the very heart of citizenship notions within the civic republicanism perspective. Democracy is regarded within this tradition with considerable ambivalence. Although civic republicanism did in certain respects accommodate the democratic revolution that followed after it. republicanism has maintained a deep-rooted scepticism of the concept of modern democracy.

Though individual in their approach. Liberal communitarianism. conservative communitarianism and civic republicanism are nevertheless united in their efforts to furnish citizenship with the political dimension that is absent from other state-centred conceptions. All three strands also present community as the central constituent of civil society. It is additionally evident that the above traditions seek to give citizenship a public voice centred around identity and participation. Despite their contrasting perspectives of citizenship. viewpoints within the Liberalist and communitarian traditions still share in their disregard of democratic issues. It is for this reason that both traditions are heavily criticised by theorists who perceive democracy to be central to any valid notion of citizenship.

RADICAL DEMOCRACY

The aim of radical democracy is to deepen the political significance of citizenship to a level that is impossible to attain within liberal and communitarian traditions. It is important to note however. that radical democracy is not so much a theory of citizenship as it is a theory of democracy which has been highly instrumental in transporting the citizenship debate out of the liberal and communitarian realms and giving it a deeper political grounding. Within the liberal tradition. citizenship is reduced to the various rights of the individual. Communitarianism counteracts this view by effectively substituting democracy with the concept of a participative. community based citizenship. Within radical democracy. citizenship is repoliticised through democracy. Not surprisingly the desirable model advocated here is one of democratic citizenship. Within radical democracy there are a number of different perspectives that construct images of citizenship from differing standpoints. These are direct democracy. discursive democracy and feminist perspectives.

Direct democracy emerged during the 1970s and 1980s during a time when much debate was centred around the new social movements. Within this viewpoint the aim is to induce social change through the transformation of democracy. Citizenship here is seen to have the potential to eradicate the separation between state and society if its potential for democratic political participation is realised. A citizenship of participation would effectively transport politics out of the hands of the state and into the domain of society thus bridging the gap between the two. It is this line of thought that characterised the new social movements of the 1970s and 80s. which led to the reintroduction of the idea of 'civil society'. Also underpinning the direct democracy movement was the concept of collective identity. grounded by a common goal. In this sense the direct democracy movement extended the citizenship agenda to the self-creation of society. empowering citizens in a way that could be distinguished from all other previous perspectives.

Following its dominant emergence during the 1960s. 70s and 80s. Direct democracy experienced a steady decline during the 1990s. It was at this time that a number of separate movements arose. One of these successive movements was discursive democracy. Discursive democracy focuses on the deliberative process of democracy and challenges notions of privatism by extending this process into certain 'depoliticised areas'. This model both acknowledges and respects the distinction between state and society but also distinguishes civil society as a third domain which cuts across both state and society. creating a "social basis for autonomous public spheres" (Habermas. cited in Delanty. 2000:41). Discursive democracy is therefore located both in the public sphere and within civil society. which is characterised by a “partly institutional political culture”. Within this model. the public sphere is seen as a space where information. opinions and problems can be articulated and deliberated over. Its capacity to actually solve problems is however limited. It is therefore thought that the process of decision-making lies firmly in the hands of the institutionalised political system.

Within the discursive democracy perspective. contemporary society characterised by its decentred and self-critical nature. This is due to the significant rise in the emergence of competing interest groups and frontline issues of cultural pluralism. which dominate debates surrounding the nature of contemporary society. According to discursive democracy theorists. the only viable response to this social climate is for civil society to become discursive as opposed to self-organising. thus making citizenship the basis of politics instead of segregating the two completely.

Though mindful of the democratic political potential of the autonomous public. discursive theory is nevertheless criticised by feminists who claim that inadequate consideration is given to the pre-discursive domain and that consequently deeper power structures related to identity construction are neglected. Such feminist perspectives and will constitute somewhat of a critique of the theoretical viewpoints that have been presented thus far.

The central complaint of feminist theorists is that little or no attempt is made to politicise the private sphere. which exists outside of the politicised public domain. Feminists therefore promote a politicised view of the private domain together with a pluralist conception of the public domain. Rejecting both the universality of liberal perspectives and the communitarian notion of the unitary community. feminism constructs its argument form the point of group difference also rejecting notions of the homogeneous society constrained by common concepts or goals. Young. suggests that the liberal ideal only serves in privileging dominant groups and excluding women and other subordinated groups. despite the fact that they have equal citizenship status. Such viewpoints are also thought to assume that every individual has equal access to avenues of participation in society. whereas for many groups this is far from reality.

The exclusion of women in particular is emphasised by Foster who along with other feminist theorists states that citizenship is a masculine construct which excludes women through its separation of the private and public domains. The claim here is that “the burden of women’s responsibility for work associated with the private sphere has implications for their legal status as citizens” simply because it places women outside the public domain and therefore outside of the realm of citizenship.

According to young (1989). what is needed are group rights which will enable marginalized and minority groups to uphold their autonomy in the face of dominant groups. The citizenship ideal here is one which accommodates and respects the diverse private identities of individuals enabling the formation of "a group differentiated citizenship and a heterogeneous public" (Young cited in Delanty. 2000:44).

Underlying each of the viewpoints housed within the radical democracy model is the premise that citizenship is located in collective action. the nature of which changes from viewpoint to viewpoint. Under radical democracy. the realms of citizenship are also extended to the domain of the self. One of the main contributions of radical democracy to the citizenship debate is its questioning of the notion of assumed consensus. a notion that is integral to both liberal and communitarian perspectives.

There is no doubt that all of the above perspectives have made valuable contributions to the citizenship debates over the years. They have at the very least maintained thought provoking animation within the citizenship dialogue and have been instrumental to succeeding theorists who in criticising the early perspectives in particular. have in effect anchored and amassed their own arguments. In this sense. these theories can be viewed as the foundation blocks of the modern citizenship debate as we know it. The reality is however. that earlier citizenship debates are often deemed to be inadequately equipped to accommodate issues inherent to the nature of late-modern society. It is on this premise that many of the more contemporary theories have arisen.

CONTEMPORARY SOCIOLOGICAL PERSPECTIVES

Contemporary perspectives of citizenship have been built upon varied perceptions of late-modern society. Ingrained within them are deep considerations of the changed and changing nature of this society and the consequent effects on the nature and positioning of citizenship. The innately complex and multilayered nature of these theories has caused considerable disagreement about their categorisation. For the purposes of this exploration however. the theories covered will be very loosely separated into nationalist and post-nationalist theories. Some theories however can be perceived as belonging to both categories.

Multinational Citizenship is one of the few nationalist theories within the contemporary citizenship debate. Here it is believed that an operational and effective post-modern citizenship can maintain harmonious existence within the confines of nation and state structures. This viewpoint is presented within Harty and Murphy's 'defence of multinational citizenship' (Harty and Murphy. 2005). Whilst Harty and Murphy agree that regional and global integration are indicative of significant challenges to state sovereignty. they disagree with predictions of the complete dissolution of the state and its replacement with regional and/or global authoritative forms (Harty and Murphy. 2005). Instead it is envisaged that state sovereignty will be redistributed both internally. for the purpose of internal autonomy within nations (within nationally plural states) and externally to cater for the realities of global interdependence. Supporters of this viewpoint believe that the adequate provision of access to autonomy for national groups within multinational states is possible. and also that this can be achieved without the transcendence of nation and state boundaries (Harty and Murphy. 2005). Here the aim is to highlight the ways in which institution based solutions can satisfy nationalist demands. The claim is that a multinational citizenship will enable the establishment of a sub-state citizen community with the freedom to select political representatives and with the autonomy to make decisions without interference from external authorities. It is thought that this process can be enabled through appropriate institutional designs. which as a basic principle. must incorporate the equal consideration of the range of national identities for which they cater. This would accord greater autonomy to national groups whilst safeguarding the political and territorial elements of citizenship and fulfilling the traditional demands of the state (Harty and Murphy. 2005).

Postnationalists argue that the process of globalisation has depleted state sovereignty and that this has resulted in the erosion of the political salience of regionally situated national identities and citizenship forms. Theorists within this area envisage the replacement of national identities with identities and citizenship forms that transcend national boundaries (Harty and Murphy. 2005).

One of the more contemporary postnationalist approaches to citizenship is that of cultural citizenship. This theory is based on the premise that we live in an information society in which networks and information are paramount. where time and space are separate and disembedded. where risk and uncertainty have replaced progress and confidence and where consumerism prevails throughout. According to Stevenson (2003). it is in this societal climate that symbolic. mobile cultures have arisen.

Cultural citizenship promotes the development of a communications-based society. in which democratic communication is an institutionalised norm. In this viewpoint. it is under these conditions that social transformation can take place and not through the collective insurgence of workers. The implementation of this communication mode requires individuals to seek beyond their own culturally relative viewpoints to gage and deliberate the perspectives of others and consequently learn from others. "A genuinely cosmopolitan dialogue would need to be underpinned by both the acceptance of universal principles and the recognition of difference. This is the very essence of cultural citizenship" (Stevenson. 2003:25). Further to this point. the development of a cultural citizenship also involves the eradication of assumed identity labelling of particular groups. This in turn involves the questioning of dominant codes and cultures. which enable and encourage such labelling processes.

Whilst cultural citizenship strongly encourages the acceptance and embracing of difference it does not undermine the importance of overarching. inclusive. democratic communities. Indeed the view here is that both ideals can be adequately accommodated in communication-based societies and without the need for the homogenisation of difference. In sum "cultural citizenship includes rights. obligations. civic spaces of participation. respect. identity and difference and individualisation" (Stevenson. 2003:33) and explores the possibility of maintaining solidarity whilst at the same time promoting the creativity of the self.

Another contemporary portrayal of citizenship is forwarded by cosmopolitan citizenship. This theoretical standpoint transcends the boundaries of nation and state yet fails to dispense with either. Like the cultural citizenship viewpoint. the cosmopolitan citizenship perspective places general emphasis on inclusion and the accommodation of difference and acknowledges the 'advanced interconnectivity of cultures' that characterises late-modern society.

Within the cosmopolitan citizenship viewpoint there are several sub-strands. which whilst reflecting similar central concerns. construct cosmopolitanism from differing points of emphasis. The first of these notions of cosmopolitanism emphasises both international and legal aspects. This particular strand was initiated and led by Kant. During the late 1700s Kant proceeded to explore the notion of an international civil society. The central theme running through his work was the principle of reason. which led him to believe that it was necessary to restrict the exercise of power to law. Kant campaigned for a system of international law. which he termed cosmopolitan law. This notion encompassed the possibility of citizenship existing beyond the state.

While Kant's theory of cosmopolitanism is said to have opened the debates arena on the subject of internationalism. many post Kantian theories of cosmopolitanism tended to a certain extent. to be shaped by the concept of nationalism. shifting from the wider focus evident in Kant's work. However in the relationship between civil society and nation. the concept of nation was later replaced with that of the state. Within this paradigm there emerged two viewpoints. that of realism. which promoted the notion of autonomous states and that of functionalism. in which supporting states were at the centre. Both of these views were counteracted by the emergence of arguments for a post-national order. which would induce the dissolving of the state as a sovereign entity. Bull (1977) for instance. whilst remaining heavily sceptical of the notion of global civil society. argues for an order in which sovereignty is shared on multiple levels. Within this diversified discourse of internationalism and citizenship. cosmopolitan citizenship is generally confined to a state centred world. Despite Kant's early efforts. the idea of citizenship beyond the state still remains a subordinated concept within this citizenship model.

The second theory of cosmopolitanism emphasises globalism and holds the concept of a global civil society at its centre. Here. strong emphasis is placed on the cultural and social nature of cosmopolitan citizenship. The emergence of globalisation theory carried with it strong implications of a dissolving significance of nationality and the severing of the link between nationality and identity alongside the rapid growth of cultural pluralism. It was on the general premise of such implications that the theory of global cosmopolitanism arose. The globalisation debate has given voice to a number of different perspectives. all of which conceive the possible existence of a global civil society under pinned by democracy. In contrast to Kant's notion of internationalism these standpoints are overtly anti-statist. From the points put forward within the globalisation debate it is clear that there are various possible ways that globalisation can accommodate cosmopolitanism yet the eventuality itself is not a certainty

Another notion of cosmopolitanism is built on the concept of transnational communities. Within this conception. cosmopolitanism is situated within deterritorialized transnational communities formed of highly mobile cosmopolitan citizens. In fact mobility is a key component to this form of cosmopolitanism. Within this view the identity of the cosmopolitan citizen embodies greater flexibility and these citizens are more likely to be multilinguistic. Since such citizens are typically those who have left their homeland to settle in another country. they are characterised by the multiple loyalties. which transcend physical location. For instance. a British resident who was born and raised in Estonia may have dual loyalty. to Estonia as their homeland and to Britain as their place of abode. This is seen to result in what is often termed. the 'creolisation' of global culture. This is the adaptation of global culture by its recipients. In one sense there is an acknowledgement and assimilation towards the strong currents of the global culture and on the other these currents are rode against and its central force weakened. The flexibility of cosmopolitan citizens which extends to cultural identity also pertains to the citizenship of the individual. which is subject to alteration.

The notion of transnational communities outlined within the cosmopolitan citizenship perspective reflects less of a concern with world governance and more of a concern with the identities of these communities. Within this viewpoint cosmopolitan citizenship is tied to residence and not birth. This theory highlights the impact of cultural issues on citizenship. consequently exposing the inappropriateness of the segregation of public and private spheres in the conceptualisation of citizenship.

A fourth strand of cosmopolitan citizenship is that which places the notion of post nationalism at the centre. Although accorded with a number of different meanings. within the discourse of cosmopolitan citizenship. the term postnationalism refers to the "reflexive transformation of existing national conceptions of group membership". Again. the key factor here is residence. One of the key supporters of the post-national citizenship ideal is Habarmas. At the foundation of Habarmas's proposals is the notion of the dual existence of a constitutional order and a civil society characterised by a discursive democracy and grounded in public spheres. His theory also reflects a strong commitment for both the constitutional state and cosmopolitanism. Habermas visualises the development of cosmopolitanism taking place within the confines of the constitutional state as opposed to it being imposed through global processes. For Habermas postnationalism is more to do with the embedding of cosmopolitism in the realm of constitutional state. than it has to with global civil society. It is these premises that separate Habermas's theory from most other normative cosmopolitan theories. which envision the establishment of global civil society following the dissolving of the nation-state.

It is from the departure point of Habermas's novel theory that Delanty constructs what he terms. the idea of civic cosmopolitanism. Delanty proceeds a step further than Habermas in that he dares to propose a new concept of cosmopolitanism based on the premise that cosmopolitanism poses a real challenge to the forces of globalisation. However Delanty's proposals are not without condition. Delanty postulates that in order for this threat to be a significant one. cosmopolitanism must replace the already unstable institution of nationalism. In order for this to be achieved. the relationship between cosmopolitanism and the community. which still remains monopolised by nationalism. must be re-established.

Delanty's notion of civic cosmopolitanism reconciles nationalism with post-nationalism. thus forming what he terms a self-limiting kind of cosmopolitanism. which avoids both the extremes of particularism and of universalism.. In contrast to other normative cosmopolitan theories. Delanty presents a form of cosmopolitanism that looks not to transcend the political community through "an international organisation of states" but rather through "a pluralist world of political communities".

One post-nationalist theorist. who questions the appropriateness and stability of the notion of citizenship altogether. is Soysal. Soysal argues that due to the effects of globalisation in late modernity. human rights have adopted an enhanced role and position. In fact. Soysal's proceeds further in proposing that human rights are presently replacing citizenship as the primary facilitator of individual autonomy. Soysal argues that the post-war era has cultivated a revolutionised notion of citizenship. which is underpinned by principles of universal personhood as opposed to national belonging.

This shift in principles is said to have occurred against a backdrop of globalisation. which has encompassed international law. the United Nations network. the emergence of global civil society. and the establishment of regional governance. As a result. Soysal argues that human rights are increasingly taking centre stage in the global political arena. as the notion of state sovereignty begins to fade. Put another way. "once relegated to the status of pre-political privatism. human rights are now overriding the rights of citizenship and reshaping democratic politics". Using the example of 'guest workers' in Europe.

Soysal concludes that the fact that these workers had been accorded social and civil rights without being granted official citizenship status. demonstrates the decline in the importance of citizenship benefits caused by the increasing prevalence of human rights. Through this demonstration Soysal also highlighted the frailty of national laws. which can now be overridden by transnational communities via transnational legal institutions such as the European Union (EU). These communities are also able to take advantage of the incorporation of international human rights laws into national law. From Soysal's viewpoint this evidence shows that social membership is seen to be a post-national phenomenon built on personhood as opposed to citizenship itself.

Taylor further supports the above view point. Taylor postulates that in the late modern age. risk has become a global common denominator and thus has created common interests and concerns. According to Taylor. the current social climate has given way to a more overarching and unified agreement on the importance of human rights in the late-modern age.

Another theory which emphasises the nature and form of rights in its portrayal of citizenship is multicultural citizenship. Multicultural citizenship is one which combines concerns for the universal rights and membership in liberal nation states. with those for the challenge posed by ethnic plurality. While many liberal theorists believe that the universal rights accorded through citizenship safeguard the cultural membership of individuals. theorists within this school of thought envisage the need for additional rights for vulnerable minority groups. in order for such groups to sustain themselves amidst the dominant culture(s).

Within this perspective there are two general versions both of which reflect differing conceptualisations of the relationship between multicultural citizenship and universal citizenship. On the one hand. feminists and (post) marxists perceive a critical and antagonistic relationship where both concepts are seen as opposites. In this view. universal citizenship facilitates the prevalence of oppression whilst multicultural citizenship allows for marginalized voices to be heard. At the centre of the feminist contribution to the multicultural citizenship debate is the theme of 'oppression'. According to young (1989. 1990). society is formed of different groups which are either dominant or oppressed. This strand of differentiated citizenship therefore concerns the denouncing of universal rights and the provision of special rights for oppressed groups. This suggests a politics for difference and not one geared towards the possibility of integration (Janoski and Gran. 2002).

On the other hand. this notion of 'oppression' is hardly featured in Kymlicka's liberal version of multicultural citizenship. Within this viewpoint the notion of universal rights is an acceptable one. However it is the inadequate number of them for certain groups that remains problematic. Kymlicka (1995) campaigns for the establishment of group differentiated rights for particular minority cultures in addition to the universal rights bestowed upon all. The central concept here is 'societal culture' which is effectively synonymous with the majority culture. Within a culturally plural society this evokes issues of equality and justice. which can only be confronted through the according of special rights to aid in the recognition and protection of minority cultures.

Unlike many other post-war liberals Kymlicka argues that General human rights cannot replace or subsume minority group rights. as these are unable to adequately confront important questions relating to cultural minority groups. This ultimately results in cultural minorities being left vulnerable to injustice at the hands of the dominant group. thus aggravating ethnocultural conflicts. It is for this reason that Kymlicka advocates a supplementing of traditional human rights with special minority rights in order to minimise or avoid altogether such disputes. which too often result in bloodshed and loss of lives.

In his presentation of multicultural citizenship Kymlicka aims to show that the emergence of 'politics of difference' brought about through the increased mobilizing of national groups need not pose a threat to liberal democracy. In fact kymlicka demonstrates that many of the demands of such groups correspond with liberal principles of social justice and freedom. Whilst the allocation of minority group rights to particular groups may seem discriminatory. Kymlicka argues that it does in fact correspond with the liberal principle of equality. Instead of giving these groups an unfair advantage. these rights are seen to compensate for the inevitable disadvantage they experience. existing within multinational societies.

From the information within this section it is clear that citizenship is indeed a complex and multifaceted notion and one which has been constructed and reconstructed on a number of different levels. As times have changed so to has the nature and positioning of citizenship. Within the contemporary advanced industrial society citizenship is a negotiated and constructed form and is in this sense reflective of the continually shifting. diverse and ultimately uncertain social climate. Within this climate. individuals are able to shape their own histories and piece together multilayered identities. It is important that citizenship education accommodates for this pliability and adopts a concept of citizenship that embodies a broad outlook. thus allowing greater scope for inclusion and genuinely engaged involvement.

POLITICAL PARTICIPATION

Apart from the embodiment of particular norms and values. citizenship may also be seen as a matter of civic behaviour. a willingness to support the perpetuation of democratic society through active participation in politics and public affairs (Pattie. Seyd and Whiteley. 2004). This Political participation is widely viewed as a positive aspect of democratic society. which cultivates integration. encourages individual identification with the wider community and generally enhances social solidarity. According to White (1993). it is a key requirement for a meaningful democratic society. There is much disagreement among political scientists concerning the definitional boundaries of political participation. One commentator states that Birch (1993). defined political participation as an activity which "is essentially a case for substantial numbers of private citizens [...] to play a part in the process by which political leaders are chosen/or government policies are shaped and implemented." According to Huntington (1991). political participation involves two dimensions. These are participation and contestation. Huntington's definition also implies the existence of civil and political liberty to speak. assemble and publish in the name of political debate. and also the freedom to conduct electoral campaigns.

Political engagement incorporates both conventional and unconventional acts. Conventional or institutional participation refers to involvement in electoral party politics. This form of participation refers to the political venues of participation that are established. monitored and encouraged by the state and includes acts such as voting. standing for office or participating in political party campaigns Unconventional or non-institutional participation on the other hand refers to acts such as demonstrating. leafleting or petitioning such acts may be legitimate or illegal.

Whilst many traditional accounts of political engagement have tended to focus on the conventional political activities. there have been recent calls for the widening of the definition of political participation in light of new forms of activism that have arisen in recent decades. There are also claims that narrow traditional conceptions of political participation create a deceptive portrayal of political activity levels within contemporary society. As stated by Pattie. Seyd and Whiteley. " the citizen audit survey reveals that citizens have not contracted out of politics. but rather are engaged in a multiplicity of political activities beyond the traditional ones". It has also observed that unorthodox forms of participation are increasing in popularity and importance and therefore need to be adequately considered within participation debates.

Both conventional and unconventional forms of participation can be divided into three main categories. The first of these is that of individualistic participation. Individualistic forms can be undertaken by the individual. without assistance from others. Such forms may involve the donation of money to organisations and voting. One of the more invisible individualistic forms of participation is 'consumer citizenship'. Many politicians conceive active citizenship to consist of the influencing of public services to respond to customer preferences. However. consumer citizenship implies that citizens are able to influence the political process by using their purchasing power and that in doing so. such citizens are participating politically. Contact participation is from the respondent's viewpoint. also individualistic. however also requires the participation of representatives or officials. This form involves such activities as writing to the media or speaking to a Member of Parliament. Lastly. collective participation involves the joining together of citizens for political purposes. Collective participation activities may involve attending political meetings or participating in demonstrations.

PARTICIPATION TRENDS

Concerning contemporary liberal democracies. several trends of political participation have been identified. These are:

- An increasingly informed and critical citizenry
- A decline of trust in effectiveness of political elites and institutions
- A decline in loyalty to traditional political parties
- A drop in turnout rates in elections
- An increase in unconventional political participation.

Such trends are generally reflected in accounts forwarded by Pattie. Seyd and Whiteley (2004) concerning the current British political climate. Here it has been observed that with the exception of protest forms. collective forms of participation have experienced significant decline. this has been coupled with the weakening of norms central to the perpetuation of collective participation. In tern. writers have also observed a marked increase in individualistic forms of participation. which are thought to have overshadowed collective forms. In light of this evidence. Pattie. Seyd and Whiteley conclude that Britain is largely composed of 'atomised citizens'. These shifts have resulted in the weakening of institutions that facilitate collective participation such as political parties. This movement is further reinforced by the increase in 'cheque-book' participation. With this emergence of atomised citizenship there comes the increased risk of policy fragmentation and failure. If civil institutions become weak then such processes are harder to counteract. A major consequence of this trend is that the state abdication of its responsibility to provide collective goods and services placing it in the hands of the market. The problem with this arrangement is that citizens feel less obligated to a market state. Also. markets are unable to enforce the rule of law needed to sustain an inclusive. fair and cohesive society. State withdrawal will ultimately result in a breakdown in basic security. Another consequence of weakening institutions is the breakdown of communication between ruler and ruled.

Despite these risks however. there are certain advantages of atomised citizenship and market intervention. One such advantage is the provision of increased choice in public services; another is increased efficiency due to the market focus on innovation and cost reduction. A third advantage is the direct correlation between the cost of services and the benefits gained by the user.

DETERMINANTS OF PARTICIPATION

Gaining a full understanding of the relationship between the personal characteristics of citizens and their involvement in political activities has been one of the ongoing goals of political behavioural empirical research. At the most basic level. theories of participation can be divided into two categories: those which focus on individual or personal attributes and those which highlight the effects of wider social networks. Traditional theories of participation determinants tend to focus on personal or individual characteristics. These studies have generally found the main determinant factors of participation to be individual resources such as education. income or socio-economic status and age or experience. It has been found that those with greater resources in these fields tend to have greater political involvement. In the case of age for instance. it has been found that there is what appears to be a universal increase in participation as people grow older. suggesting that experience is in itself. a political resource. In times past. women have been found to participate less than men. These differences have narrowed considerably and have almost disappeared in industrial democratic societies.

Income has also been identified as a key determinant factor with those at the lower end of the income scale displaying lower levels of political engagement.

Unemployed individuals are even less likely to be politically active because they do not have access to social networks existent within the workplace through which political participation is facilitated. In addition such individuals have very low levels of residential stability. This hinders participation because they are less likely to be integrated in their communities and therefore less likely to have a stable network of neighbours and friends.

Whilst the individuals most likely to be apathetic and non-participatory are those who lack power and resources. these individuals are those most likely to desire state intervention on their behalf. This creates a vicious cycle of frustration. as the lack of political involvement among such individuals constitutes a significant barrier to the implementation of state intervention. Another aspect of non-participation is the emergence of 'cheque-book' participation. This essentially involves one individual subcontracting out his or her participatory duties someone else. Maloney suggests that this type of participation is responsible for much of the recent growth of interest groups such as green peace and shelter. Skocpol (2002). further suggests that the establishment of such organisations often rests in the hands of political entrepreneurs who generate funds through direct mail which are then used to hire pollsters and media consultants to frame policies and lobbying strategies.

More recently. apparent limitations in personal characteristics perspectives. have led to greater emphasis being placed on the environmental determinants of political engagement. A key focal point within this area of research has been the relationship between political participation and individuals' involvement in formal and informal groups. Such groups may include sports clubs. student societies or Book clubs. Although such groups may have few direct links with the political process. they are Non-etheless arenas in which individuals can learn skills that can be utilised within political activities of a higher intensity. They can therefore be considered as training grounds for political participation for many of those involved. It is suggested that involvement in such groups stimulates collective political interest. makes individuals available for mobilisation by the elites and equips people with skills that make participation easier.

Considerably less research has focused on the role of informal groups in political mobilisation. These groups are nevertheless said to underpin civil society and provide vital services. Activities within this area may include involvement in a pub quiz team or the provision of support for neighbours or friends. These activities are valuable because they help to build civic engagement networks and also provide valuable services. One explanation of the relationship between such groups and political participation is that when individuals have friends who participate. they themselves are more likely to do the same. Other research emphasises the size and political orientation of the group as influential factors of political involvement. Another suggestion is that even very basic interactive activities such as playing cards or having lunch with friends may influence participation by enhancing interpersonal trust and compliance to social norms. In addition. there is also evidence to suggest that family interactions can also affect political engagement.

Whilst the above research is highly valuable and enables a clearer understanding of political behaviour. it is nevertheless seen by some to lack detail in certain areas. McClurg (2003) for instance argues that whilst social interaction influences participation the actual affect it has is very much dependant upon the amount of political discussion that occurs within these networks. According to McClurg (2003). social networks can only influence participation through the political substance they encompass thus to fully understand the relationship between social interaction and participation it is necessary to adequately examine this substance as opposed to solely focusing on the social network form.

A more comprehensive and detailed categorisation of political participation theories is given by Pattie. Seyd and Whiteley (2004). The categories used here are choice-based theories and structural-based theories. In the perspective of the choice based theories. actors are seen to be operating within a world where individuals seek to obtain the highest return at the minimum cost. This perspective views citizenship as something which results from the choices that people make which reflect the costs and benefits of the situation in question. The point here is that individuals choose their levels of participation. Within the structural perspective emphasis is placed on the socialisation of individuals into norms. values and behaviours of social groups and those of the wider society. Here. citizens are viewed as products of social forces and structures.

which affect behaviours and attitudes.The first choice theory of participation is the cognitive engagement model. The core idea of this theory is that political engagement is determined by the individual's access to information and their willingness and ability to use it. Education is a central component of this theory because it enables people to acquire and process large amounts of information. Education also enables the acquisition of key skills such as IT and information analysis skills. Increases in education levels coupled with the declining cost of information acquisition. creates a process of cognitive mobilisation which in tern produces politically conscious individuals who have a clear understanding of democratic norms and principles. The cognitively engaged citizen is also a critical citizen who is likely to take action if dissatisfied by state delivery of services. If such citizens feel that they are not receiving adequate benefits. they may be less inclined to acknowledge their obligations as citizens. This is why cognitive engagement is essentially a choice based theory. because it postulates that the political involvement of citizens depends on their perception of the performance of the state system.

One of the main criticisms of this theory is that whilst it explains the importance of information gathering. it is not clear why the individual would want to act on this information or what encourages them to do so. Thus. the process of information acquisition and processing is seen by some as an incomplete explanation for participation.

The second choice based theory is the general incentives theory. This theory specifically explains involvement in high intensity participation. involving political activists. The core idea that underpins this theory is that in order to participate. actors need incentives. These incentives are divided into five types; collective. selective. group. social and expressive.

Collective incentives refer to the benefits of citizenship that are available to all individuals regardless to whether or not they participate. Economists refer to these incentives as public goods. These goods are provided by the state and include. freedom from crime and freedom from invasion. Other goods such as Health care. education and infrastructure are also public goods. In this view it is thought that if individuals perceive policy delivery to be effective then they will be motivated to participate but if they perceive failing delivery then this will function as a deterrent to participation. Here the individual's own belief that they can affect outcomes plays a central role. This is because. even if an individual perceives the system to be an effective one. if they don't think that they can have any influence within it they still will have no motivation to participate.

Selective incentives are the benefits gained as a direct result of participation. Such incentives are exclusive to participants and are not accessible to non-participants. There are two types of selective incentives. process and outcome. Process incentives refer to the perceived benefits of involvement in the participation process itself. The joy of meeting new and interesting people for instance. may be enough of an incentive for someone to get involved in a political activity. Outcome incentives refer to the achievement of certain personal (as opposed to collective) goals whilst participating in the political process. Such incentives help to secure individuals' political commitment for private reasons. For instance a citizen may harbour a private desire to become a local magistrate and this may be their personal incentive for sustained political engagement.

Group incentives refer to the willingness of individuals to be involved in political activities because of the group benefits that will be gained. Individuals propelled by these incentives will often think of the welfare of the group instead of their own welfare. This theory implies that a person may engage in political activity because of the available benefits for a group that is important to them.

The fourth motive for involvement in the general incentives model is drawn from social norms or from the perception of the individual that those around them are supportive of participation and civic values. This viewpoint postulates that a person's level of political involvement will either be inhibited or enhanced by the views of those around them. depending on what they perceive these views to be.

The final set of motives for political engagement outlined within the general incentives model involves the individual's emotional or affective attachments to society. Here it is implied that for some people the motive for political engagement is an emotional attachment to their country. a sense of 'British pride' for instance.

The general incentives model has been criticised for overemphasising the centrality of choice behaviour whilst neglecting the role of socialisation processes in explaining participation trends. Evidence gathered by Barnes and Kaase (1979) for instance. suggests that people become involved in voluntary activities due to their parent's involvement. A person's involvement may also be dictated by the extent to which they are embedded within their community.

Structural theories of participation highlight the influence of macro level forces as opposed to the individual choices made by citizens. The civic volunteerism model is the most prevalent of the structural models. At the centre of this model is the availability of resources. namely; time. money. civic skills. political efficacy and access to political recruitment networks. The central suggestion of this model is that individuals with these resources will participate if the resources have resulted from social structures. education and inherited characteristics from parents. Within this viewpoint. psychological engagement. which is subject to individual choice. is less important than these resources.

Though useful. this type of theory does present a number of problems. The first of these is connected to the proposed correlation of socioeconomic status. participation and civic values. The model fails to adequately explain why significant numbers of high status individuals are not politically engaged. There is also the anomaly that despite the fact that advanced industrial societies are becoming better educated and more affluent. political participation levels continue to decrease. Verba et al (1995). also suggest that this model would benefit from a broader examination of resources including spare time and financial resources in order to provide a more comprehensive explanation of the connection between socioeconomic variables and participation. Another perceived problem with this model is its tendency to focus on supply of participation whilst failing to adequately consider the incentives that underpin political involvement.

The equity-fairness theory. offers an alternative perspective of political participation. Here it is believed that society is composed of various groups who compete for resources. The central notion is that individuals compare themselves with their peers and if these comparisons reveal an unfavourable reflection on the individual. then this can result in frustration or aggression. This aggression may be manifested in the political actions of the individual. In other words. individuals compare their actual life situations with their perceived expectations of that situation. which are constructed through peer comparisons. If there is a significant gap between expectations and actual reality. then relative depravation results. which has consequences for political action. This type of scenario is more commonly manifested amongst objectively deprived groups such as ethnic minorities and individuals with low income. The larger the gap between expectations and reality. the more substantial the political consequences. This model has been used to explore the occurrence of unconventional political activity.

Despite its usefulness in explaining unorthodox political participation. the relevance of the equity-fairness model in the general exploration of political participation is somewhat questionable. It is also possible that relative depravation hinders more conventional forms of participation. These differing effects of relative depravation cause theoretical postulations of the theory to be unclear. The relationship between equity-fairness perceptions and attitudes towards rights and obligations are also said to be inadequately defined.

The last structural model of participation is the social capital model. In the literature. there is much debate about the definition of social capital. Putman (1993) defines it as "features of social organisation such as trust. norms and networks. that can improve the efficiency of society by facilitating co-ordinated actions". Central to this theory is the notion that if individuals trust each other and work cooperatively to solve societal problems then society will be much better off. Generally trust is the key constituent of social capital theory. This trust is strongly embedded in social structures. which transcend time and are concentrated in particular geographical zones. According to social capital theorists it is trust that enables individuals to transcend beyond their immediate networks and connect with others in corporate activities. According to Tocqueville (1990). communities with high levels of social capital feature extensive civic engagement networks and appear to have less crime and higher levels of political participation.

Despite being one of the more predominant models of participation. social capital theory is seen to have some inadequacies. One problem is that that of circularity. When utilised in the explanation of wide forms of participation there is a danger that it could be seen to imply that voluntary activity perpetuates itself in some sort of continuous cycle. This in tern poses the potential problem of broad measures of participation becoming both independent and dependent variables in explanatory models. It has also been suggested that current social capital theory does not adequately account for the causal effects of the socialisation processes.

BME GROUPS AND POLITICAL PARTICIPATION

Over the last two decades. various studies have shed light on the political participation of immigrant groups and the factors which influence participation levels. Drawing from their study of political participation in California. Uhlaner et al for instance. conclude that voting behaviours were influenced by ability to speak English. Cho (1999). also came to similar conclusions and also postulates that immigrants educated outside the United States are less likely to vote than those educated in the United States. In 1999. Junn concluded that immigrants may be less likely to participate in institutional political activities. however are just as likely as natives to be involved in direct unconventional political activities such as protesting.

Since 1974 several studies have demonstrated that non-registration among ethnic minority groups in Britain is notably higher than it is among the white community. This was highlighted in the 1974 sample survey. Another survey reflected the same results in 1979. Over 10 years later in 1991 another survey showed that although participation levels had improved among BME groups they were still notably lower to those of the white population. Consequently. there has been mounting concern about the non-participation of ethnic minority groups. A more recent study undertaken in 1998 discovered that non-registration among black respondents was still very high.

Non-registration has been connected to doubts surrounding the residential status of respondents. others experienced language barriers. There was also a fear of attack from extreme right wing groups who were able to use electoral registers to target individuals from ethnic minority groups. High levels of non-participation. particularly among ethnic minority young people. were also found to have resulted from a general alienation from political processes. High levels of non-participation may also be accounted to the policies and practices of registration offices. which at times fail to meet the needs of ethnic minority electorates.According to Fennema and Tillie (1999. 2001). differences in political participation amongst ethnic minorities are connected to disparities in civic communities. which primarily constitute the amount of ethnic social capital of the group. indicated by involvement in ethnic associational life (Jacobs. Phalet and Swyngedouw. 2004). Here it is predicted that the denser the political ethnic association networks. the more political trust will be generated among the group and the more political activity will be embarked upon.

This model was however found not to be applicable to Brussels where it was found that although there were notably higher levels of ethnic membership among the Turkish community compared to the Moroccan community. there were no notable differences in political participation between the two groups. From this. Jacobs. Phalet and Swyngedouw (2004). conclude that the proposals put forward by Fennema and Tillie need to adequately consider the differences between ethnic social capital and cross ethnic social capital and the relationship that exists between the two. Jacobs Phalet and Swyngedouw. also stress the importance of examining the possible differing effects of ethnic social capital on different ethnic groups.

A similar theoretical viewpoint suggests that political involvement is affected by ethnic residential concentration. The claim here is that those who live in areas which are highly populated with co-ethnics. have greater access to ethnic media and community organisations. This is said to lower the cost of political mobilisation encouraging participation.

Another factor said to affect political involvement amongst immigrants is their prior political experiences. Those who have escaped from oppressive political regimes may be distrustful of the political system and therefore less likely to participate. On the other hand however. they may cherish the opportunity to choose freely the candidate of their preference. which may increase their tendency to vote. The prior political experiences of first generation immigrants may also influence the political participation levels of their children. Studies of political socialisation demonstrate that the voting behaviour of adults is significantly influenced by political activities and discussions of parents during childhood.

Anti-immigrant legislation may also influence immigrant political mobilisation. Where the public benefits of immigrants are placed under threat. the first and second generations are more likely to mobilise against the laws in question for their own benefit and that their relatives. This was shown in the case of the 1996 American elections where it was indicated that immigrant legislation was more prominent for immigrants than it was for other members of the population.

Many of the traditional theories of immigrant adaptation perceive assimilation to be a unilinear process through which social and economic conditions of immigrants improve over time. Over the past decade however.

this view has been strongly challenged in light of the "new" second generation. Many of the revised theories perceive more of a segmented assimilation trend where disparities in group characteristics and incorporation trends lead to unpredictable outcomes.

One such viewpoint is forwarded by Ramakrishnan and Espenshade (2001). who in their examination of immigrant generational status and voting participation found that immigrant political involvement trends were varied according to the racial or ethnic group. The research also found that linguistic barriers may not necessarily be primary obstacles to voting and that previous political experience does not have an effect on voting participation as suggested within more traditional accounts. The study did reveal however. that the presence of anti-immigrant legislation did increase voting participation among immigrants. Overall the findings highlight a need for further systematic research to be conducted concerning immigrant political participation.

YOUNG PEOPLE AND POLITICAL PARTICIPATION

Current representations of young people tend to be quite negative. Youth today tend to be portrayed as self-centred. inconsiderate and apathetic or as a source of trouble. A central constituent of this negative portrayal is the view that young people remain indifferent to social and political issues and alienate themselves from the political world. As concerns for the perceived political apathy of young people have mounted. various approaches and responses to the issue have been forwarded.

In the 1996 MORI Omnibus survey on conventional political participation in Britain it was again confirmed that age is a key determinant of political engagement. In tern. these findings confirmed those of earlier studies. which imply the existence of extensive non-participation and political indifference amongst youth. The study revealed that young people were less likely to vote. join a main stream political party or to engage in political activities that involve any significant costs; either in time. information or finances. The data gathered also revealed clear and systematic variations in levels of political engagement according to employment status. income and class. Unemployed and low-income respondents were much less likely to be politically engaged than those on average or above average incomes. However even when income and social class were accounted for. age was still found to be strongly associated with levels of political engagement.

In light of these findings. Fahmy stresses the importance of examining and confronting the wider social and economic issues when discussing and encouraging the political engagement of young people. According to Fahmy. such an approach has implications for citizenship education. which. apart from its central emphasis on knowledge skills and values. must consider the wider social and economic circumstances of the young people it attempts to reach.

This involves a commitment to tackling the processes of economic exclusion that continue to afflict youth transitions. Fahmy additionally comments that young people are unlikely to benefit from the social and professional networks or civil associations that facilitate involvement in conventional politics. This is partly due to their dependant and subordinate positioning within the life cycle and often within society. This is particularly true of disadvantaged young people.

In its conclusion the report recommends that in order to encourage more wide spread participation. the political views of young people be seriously considered and that serious consideration be given to the accessibility of political structures to groups marginalised by the political process. It is also seen to be necessary to widen avenues for the involvement of young people in formal politics and to develop ways of articulating formal politics using the unconventional forms that young people prefer. This viewpoint accepts that young people have a very limited involvement in formal politics. it also proceeds further in exploring the aetiology of this disengagement with reference to the social and economic disadvantages and the perceived shortcomings of political systems and processes.

Another approach which challenges notions of youth apathy perhaps in a more overt sense. is that forwarded by Rocker. Player and Coleman (1999). Here. young people's involvement in more informal voluntary and campaigning activities is highlighted as an area of political involvement that is often overlooked. Quite apart from the above negative claims. it was found in this study that whilst young people in Britain seem to be somewhat alienated from the world of party politics. they are at the same time very much involved in single-issue campaigning and volunteering activities. This evidence applied to young people from a variety of different backgrounds. It was also found that such activities could help to develop political knowledge awareness. understanding and skills. These results are endorsed by John. Morris and Halpern (2003) who state that whilst young people do not appear to have an interest in conventional politics. they do tend to engage with broader political issues and with a range of group activities.

More recent research funded by the Economic and Social Research Council (ESRC) argues that young people are not politically apathetic but simply have a different understanding of what politics entails. The report also states that most young people desire to be socially engaged but not necessarily in the ways that are traditionally advocated by politicians. In addition the project concludes that young people have a strong interest in political issues and are in fact highly articulate about political issues that affect their lives.

In light of such findings. it is suggested that claims of rampant youth apathy are founded on an overly narrow definition of 'the political'. which excludes what may be seen as the more unconventional political activities. Political participation is widely recognised as a central component of citizenship. This is reflected in the sentiments of the Crick Report and other related texts. Yet political activities seem to be more accessible to some than others. In addition. the political activities of some are more likely to be classified as political than those of others because of the extent to which these activities do or do not correspond with traditional definitions of the political. The groups that typically experience political marginalization are the economically deprived. black and minority ethnic groups and young people. Indeed there are large segments of the British population that fit all three of these categories. Clearly there is a pressing need to ensure that such groups have adequate access to political involvement especially in the light of emergent inclusive notions of citizenship. This may be enabled through the revision of political participation boundaries and a movement beyond the confines of voting behaviour. allowing the consideration of more unconventional forms. It may also be necessary for a paradigm shift to occur in relation to the language used to explain and promote political involvement. In general it is vital that a greater effort is made to ensure that all have equal access to political expression. These debates also have obvious implications for citizenship education. which aims to cultivate active and engaged citizens for the future.

8

Citizenship in Education

The existence of citizenship within the curriculum spans over a number of decades and has adopted a number of forms such as: political studies. Civics. world studies and general studies. During this time there have been various calls for some form of citizenship training. however citizenship education remained a somewhat subordinated area within the UK national curriculum. The emergence of citizenship within the present school curriculum. came about as a result of the *Final Report of the Advisory Group on Citizenship*. published in September 1998. It was due to this report and the ensuing consultation process. that the government in 2002. granted citizenship the prevalent position it now occupies within the school curriculum. This section will outline the concept of citizenship held within education through exploring the main tenets of citizenship education and how citizenship is currently taught. Particular focus will be placed on the secondary school context where the teaching of citizenship has now become a compulsory subject area.

The primary aim of citizenship education as outlined within the current national curriculum. is to equip pupils with knowledge. values and skills that will enable them to become informed and effective citizens within local. national and global society. The particular nature of this aim is heavily related to the social climate in which citizenship education has emerged. Citizenship education has arisen against a social backdrop of considerable social and political upheaval caused by the rise of nationalism and increased disregard for 'civic virtues'. Within this climate global capitalism rivals national democratic institutions and the nation state can no longer be viewed as the given natural order.

These societal characteristics were reflected in research carried out by Professor Crewe and others during the 1990s in which 80 per cent of British students stated that outside of school. they had very little participation in discussions of public issues. For many of these students religion and politics were considered to be prohibited areas of discussion. When questioned about their perceptions of good citizenship only 10 per cent of students mentioned voting or exercising of political rights. The British election study also reported that 25 per cent of 18 to 24 year olds had planned not to vote in the 1992 elections. a figure which rose to 32 per cent in the 1997 general election. Such studies reflect the disengagement and apathy that is seen to be increasingly typical of young people living within contemporary society.

On a broader scale. the cause of citizenship education is further propelled by the "increasingly complex nature of our society. the greater cultural diversity and the apparent loss of value consensus. combined with the collapse of traditional support mechanisms such as extended families". The combined effects of such characteristics threaten the stability of traditional citizenship and national identity. Current citizenship education seeks to confront these societal trends by reasserting the traditional liberal democratic conception of citizenship. It is hoped that this conception will enable the establishment of a common citizenship base in which the multiplicity of identities present in British society can find a place. The education system seeks to achieve this through the exploration of three key areas outlines by the Department for Education and Skills (DfES):

Social and moral responsibility – Pupils learning from the very beginning – self-confidence and socially and morally responsible behaviour both in and beyond the classroom.Community involvement – Pupils learning about becoming helpfully involved in the life and concerns of their neighbourhood and communities. including learning through community involvement and service to the community.Political literacy – Pupils learning about the institutions problems and practices of our democracy and how to make themselves effective in the life of the nation. locally. regionally and nationally through skills and values as well as knowledge - a concept wider than political knowledge alone.

Metaphorically depicted as "three heads on one body". these three areas whilst being independent. are interrelated segments with mutual dependence on each other.These three key areas are reflected within the programmes of study which outline what pupils should be taught and set out the basis for the planning of schemes of work. Programmes of study are based on the work of the Advisory Group on Education for Citizenship. the sentiments of which are encapsulated in the Crick Report. These programmes were completed following a consultation on proposals put forward by the Secretary of State for the revised national curriculum. The programmes of study are complemented by the non-statutory guidelines for personal social and health education for Key stages 3 and 4.

Also interwoven into the programmes of study for citizenship education are three key constituents which function alongside the three key areas of learning to form the complete citizenship learning experience at Key stages 3 and 4. These are divided into three interrelated parts:

- Knowledge and understanding about becoming an informed citizen – this involves: the teaching of legal and human rights and responsibilities; the diversity of identities in the UK; the legal system.

the government and democracy; the role of the media; conflict resolution; and the challenges posed by global interdependence and responsibility.

- Developing skills of enquiry and communication – here pupils should be taught to consider issues. events and problems and to express and justify opinions and contribute to discussions and debates.
- Developing skills of participation and responsible action – pupils should learn how to take account of others experiences and to responsibly participate in activities and reflect on this participation.

ASSESSMENT

From August 2003. teachers are required to assess pupils attainment in citizenship at the end of key stage 3. However. there is no statutory assessment requirement for the end of key stage 4. Instead. schools are advised to decide on the most appropriate methods for monitoring progress and recognising achievement. The QCA Initial Guidance for Citizenship at Key Stage 3 and 4 (2000). advises that assessment in citizenship should be based on the attainment target for citizenship at the end key stage descriptions. These include:

- Pupils' knowledge and understanding of elements of the programme of study
- Pupils' skills development. enquiry. communication. development and action.

According to the end of key stage description. at the end of key stage 3 pupils should be judged on:

- Their ability to demonstrate a broad knowledge and understanding of the topical events they study
- Their understanding of how the public gets information
- Their ability to participate in school and community activities.

Although there is no statutory requirement for assessment at key stage 4. schools are advised that teachers and pupils should collaborate to identify pupils' strengths and development needs in line with the end of key stage description in which it is stated that pupils should be able to:

- Demonstrate knowledge and understanding of the events studied; the rights. responsibilities and duties of citizens. The role of the voluntary sector; forms of government and the criminal justice. legal and economic systems.
- Access and utilise different kinds of information to form and express an opinion; evaluate the effectiveness of different ways of bringing about change in society.

It is advised by the QCA that pupils' progress is recorded in pupil profiles. record sheets or portfolios and that pupils review and record their own progress. Annual reports on citizenship are also required from August 2002.

INCLUSION

"The teaching of citizenship should be relevant to the individual needs and concerns of pupils. connect with their interests and experiences and relate to their abilities and backgrounds"

"Pupils need to be provided with structured opportunities to explore issues actively. problems and events through school and community involvement. and to take part in critical discussions that are challenging and relevant to their lives".

In the teaching of citizenship. teachers are required to adequately consider the following three principles for inclusion.

- Setting suitable learning challenges - Every pupil should have the opportunity to experience success and achieve as highly as possible. This requires teachers to teach the knowledge. skills and understanding to pupils in a way that corresponds with their individual abilities.
- Responding to pupils diverse learning needs – this requires teachers to set high expectations and provide adequate opportunities for all students to achieve including pupils with special educational needs. pupils with disabilities and pupils from a range of diverse cultural and linguistic backgrounds. All students should be able to fully participate. In order for this to be achieved teachers are required to fully implement the requirements laid out in equal opportunities legislation relating to schools.
- Overcoming potential barriers to learning and assessment for individuals and groups of pupils – this requires teachers to adequately consider the particular leaning and assessment needs of pupils in order to enable all pupils to participate effectively. This includes taking account of the type and extent of any difficulty experienced by the pupil.

It is intended that through adherence to these guiding principles. the specific needs of individual and groups of pupils will be met.

POST-16 CITIZENSHIP EDUCATION

In addition to its implementation in schools. citizenship education is also being developed in some 6th forms. colleges and in other informal settings. This citizenship education is being delivered through a Post-16 Citizenship Development Programme which began in September 2001 and is managed by the Learning and Skills Development Agency (LSDA). The programme was originally set up as a pilot initiative to explore different ways of offering citizenship to young people aged 16 and above. During the pilot phase 79 citizenship projects were being run. In September 2004 however. the programme was expanded to include 120 organisations from all over England.

Post-16 citizenship was established in response to recommendations from the Citizenship Advisory Group. who advised that:

- The entitlement to the development of citizenship should be established which applied to all students in the first phase of post-16 compulsory education and training.
- All such young adults should be granted the opportunity to participate in activities that correspond with the development of their citizenship skills and receive recognition for their achievements.

Post-16 citizenship education aims to substantiate and reinforce the citizenship skills developed throughout secondary education. The emphasis at this level is placed on exploring new areas of citizenship and providing opportunities for young people to lead out in activities (www.citizenshippost-16.lsda.org.uk. date accessed: 03/04/2006).

The key concepts of post-16 citizenship education include:

- Rights and responsibilities
- Governments and democracies
- Identities and communities

The guidance issued by the QCA on post-16 citizenship education recommends that learners should have the opportunity to:

- Identify. investigate and think critically about citizenship issues problems or events
- Decide on and participate in follow-up action
- Reflect on recognise and review their citizenship learning

It is intended that through these opportunities. young people will work towards broad learning objectives. Students can then proceed to develop and practice acquired skills through a range of actions and activities.

This section has documented some of the key challenges with which the health and stability of British democracy is currently faced. Citizenship education has been accorded with the rather ambitious task of addressing these challenges through the promotion of a particular conception of citizenship which underpins and directs its processes and content. This conception is one of the 'active citizen' in which an individual is required not only to merely function within a society but to play an active role within it - to possess adequate knowledge and act upon it. Active citizens are empowered citizens who are able to "question. critique and debate the workings and processes of society" and in doing so. contribute to the communitarian ethos that underpins the democratic society.

IMPLEMENTING INCLUSIVE PRACTICE

From a theoretical viewpoint. the constructivist approach to learning is thought to effectively facilitate inclusive teaching practice because of its emphasis on students playing an active role in the construction and development of their own learning. This perspective stands in stark contrast to traditionalist views of students as passive empty vessels in need of the infilling of knowledge by teachers. In the constructivist viewpoint. the student endeavours to make sense of the curriculum presented whilst the teacher facilitates this sense making process. Constructivists also believe that the curriculum is socially negotiated. This suggests that knowledge is both subjective and evolving as opposed to being fixed. Within constructivism. teachers are required to assist students in the critical analysis of the views contained with textbooks instead of presenting them as absolute truth. This perspective allows for the integration of student experiences from beyond the confines of the school.

During research on learning experiences within the multicultural setting. Moll (1988) discovered that the most effective classes for Latino students were those in which they were encouraged to use their personal experience to make sense of school experiences. Moll's research highlighted the fact that in most classrooms. home and community experiences are avoided. However when this area of knowledge is valued. positive effects often result. The integration of personal and cultural knowledge within the classroom can increase the cultural relevance of learning. thus engaging Black and minority ethnic students more effectively. These suggestions are further substantiated by Gay (2004) who stresses the importance of intercultural. multicultural education. which encompasses the exploration of information concerning a range of diverse ethnic groups. According to Codjoe. this will allow schools to become more effective and relevant learning environments for minority students.

The constructivist approach to learning is particularly relevant within inclusive education because it allows the effects of diversity on learning to feature predominantly in dialogues concerning professional development and teacher training. It also requires schools to focus on the improvement of the sensitivity to. and recognition of. diversity within the school organisation.

One of the keys of effective inclusive education. Identified by Gardner (2002). is collaborative learning. An important aspect of collaborative learning is group work. Whilst some educationalists argue that group work results in low-level thinking. a growing number of teachers appreciate the value of group work as an effective teaching and learning method. This is particularly the case among teachers funded through the Ethnic Minority and Traveller Achievement Grant (EMAG) who tend to place great emphasis on bilingual pupils talking with their monolingual peers within small groups. Corden (2000). has identified a number of benefits associated with this mode of learning which include:

- Greater scaffolding of comprehension skills
- Improvements in pupils ability to make connections between the reading and writing process
- Increased corporative behaviour amongst pupils
- Improved interpersonal and social skills
- Improved educational achievement levels

This type of learning is seen as important within inclusive education because it increases pupils' opportunities to share their knowledge. including cultural knowledge. Through collaborative learning. students are also able to develop vital communication and social skills. If the material used reflects aspects of diversity appropriately. then important messages can be conveyed concerning the school's valuing of cultural and social diversity. In addition. an environment where pupils are encouraged to share their thoughts and opinions and where these thoughts and opinions are genuinely valued is likely to lead to psychological security in learning.

Collaboration between colleagues is also seen to be effective within inclusive education. Gardner (2002) emphasises the importance of the effective use of additional staff members in the enhancement of learning and achievement of black and minority ethnic pupils. Here Gardener refers to the corporation of class and support teachers in the planning. delivery and assessment of lessons with the central aim of meeting the diverse needs of pupils. This requires teachers to have mutual respect for each other and to be granted equal status within the classroom. and advocates the sharing of good practice amongst colleagues.

This collaborative ethos can also be adopted as a whole-school approach to inclusive learning. This firstly begins with the ethnic monitoring of pupils to assess the extent to which equal opportunities are being achieved. Without this data. schools can very easily ignore underachievement and the uneven distribution of scarce resources. It is for these reasons that the Parekh Report recommends that educational institutions should be able to demonstrate with the use of statistical data. that disparities in the achievement levels of different ethnic communities are closing. The second phase involves the identification of underachieving groups and the reasons for this underachievement. Thirdly. important decisions will have to be made concerning the allocation of resources for identified pupil groups. The next stage consists of a comprehensive review of pupil needs. in light of curriculum demands. including the cultural implications encompassed within it. It is suggested that working with cultural frames of reference familiar to the target pupils. results in increased access to learning. Collaborative planning. teaching and assessment amongst teaching staff is also likely to engender a more comprehensive approach to teaching and learning. The reporting and dissemination of achievements resulting form collaborative partnerships will also allow for the collation of wider reflections and learning among staff.

In the case of students who speak English as an additional language. it is important that thy too feel valued and included within the classroom. According to Gardner (2002). such students can be made to feel valued and included through the use of different languages within the classroom. If the teacher incorporates even just a few phrases of the pupil's first language this conveys a message of acceptance to the pupil which is likely to lead to the psychological security of the pupil within the school. Some studies have further demonstrated that that teaching the pupil using their first language. has enabled easier access to the curriculum and can actually enable an improved acquisition of the English language compared to students who are taught in English.

Gurnah (1989). proposes that multilingual studies be adopted as a necessary measure of support for black pupils for whom English is an additional language. Gurnah envisages that this area of learning will constitute a holistic and dynamic approach that would present the issues. concerns and aspirations expressed in particular languages. as well as the linguistic rules and conventions. Gurnah postulates that this type of provision will promote the multifaceted nature of British culture and ultimately eradicate the marginalisation of working class ethnic minority children.

According to Gardner. factors that create an inclusive learning environment for EAL students are:

- A stress free learning environment
- Tasks that focus on curriculum access
- Scaffolding learning strategies
- Comprehensible language input
- Collaborative group work
- Supportive pupil networks
- Rich and varied contexts for talking and listening to English
- An inclusive classroom ethos which incorporates Linguistic and cultural diversity
- Opportunities to encounter new concepts through the medium of a first language
- Visual aids
- Explicit modelling of the structures of English

At present there exist multiple challenges in the education of Black and ethnic minority pupils. which have remained consistent for decades. Although there is evidence of progress in some areas. there still remains a significant amount of work to be done. According to Haque (2000). what's needed is a more thorough understanding of what life is like for ethnic minorities living in Britain and what kind of relationship they have with the school. In this view the effectiveness (or ineffectiveness) of the school in bridging the cultural gap between the home and the school warrants further scrutiny. Haque also states that further clarification is needed on the issue of whether differences in the attainments of ethnic groups are related to national origin as opposed to socio-economic. historical or cultural factors which are integral to the ethnic backgrounds of these groups.

Recent literature has additionally highlighted the importance of identity and education. and the need for more careful examination of this interrelation in the light of contemporary multiethnic society. Within the last two decades. the concept of cultural identity within the pluralist nation-state. has become increasingly complex. According to Bbhabha (1994). within this context there is a need for a reconceptualised framework which transcends the concept of 'linear ethnic identities' and contemplates the complex and multilayered nature of identities which are emerging within contemporary society. It is necessary for these issues of cultural hybridisation. adaptation and identity to impact upon the education process. in tern. helping to maximise the potential of black and minority ethnic pupils.

IMPORTANCE OF CITIZENSHIP EDUCATION

Most pupils suggested that citizenship education is important and gave a range of reasons of why this is the case. The reasons given were largely reflective of students' comments concerning the purpose of citizenship education. Young people from the community groups also agreed that citizenship education was important because it gave pupils access to useful information that was applicable to their lives.

A similar viewpoint is also expressed in the following extract:

...[Y]ou've got to learn it in life. Some bits of citizenship teach you about life. like how to get a job and stuff. and that's quite good.

Again the capacity within citizenship to facilitate the learning of life skills that will enable an individual to operate effectively within society. is emphasised here. These comments were further substantiated by comments made by one of the students who stated that in his view the learning was 'too slow' due to the implementation of topics that he deemed to be irrelevant. In this particular case this pupil had pinpointed the topic of 'rubbish' as a 'rubbish' topic. which he personally had no interest in because he didn't feel that he. as an individual. could make a difference by changing his behaviour. Responses from a third group also emphasised the importance of subject matter in the evaluation of the importance of citizenship education. This group did not consider citizenship education to be important because of what they were learning at the time.

Pupils from another group spoke about the value of citizenship from more of an individual empowerment point of view. The pupil has pinpointed the facilitation of knowledge about young people's rights and self respect as key factors of the importance of citizenship education:

[E]nough people probably don't know your rights as a young person you just think 'oh my rights' and go and mess about you don't know ...

It is kind of important because of teaching things about stuff around them and respecting yourself and stuff like that. and what rights you have...

At the same time. pupils were also able to identify certain aspects of citizenship education that hinder/mask its importance within the secondary school context.

As was highlighted in comments pertaining to the purpose of citizenship education. for some pupils. the importance of citizenship was dependant on certain key factors related to the nature of the lesson. In three of the groups. it was indicated that the importance of citizenship education was dependant on the topics being taught and whether or not these topics were deemed to be relevant:

- It depends what the topic is because if it's something like smoking then you already know everything about it. you don't really concentrate as hard as you do on more important stuff like euthanasia or abortion.

The approach of the teacher to the lesson and the actual teaching methods used. were also seen as significant factors of importance. Within the following extract. pupils talk about what they refer to as 'proper lessons' which encompasses a more practical approach to the teaching of citizenship.

On the other hand. the following student commented on the practical and interesting activities that they used to take part in. in citizenship classes that they thought reflected the importance of the subject.

Despite the general agreement among pupils concerning the importance of citizenship education. a minority of pupils also mentioned some additional obstacles. which thwarted the importance of citizenship as a subject. In one of the groups the pupils suggested that whilst citizenship was important. the reality remained that young people of their age failed to understand the true importance of citizenship education. It was also suggested within this group that the reason for this is that many pupils already have knowledge of the values imparted within citizenship from within their own homes.

On the other hand it was again suggested that pupils themselves failed to realise the true importance of citizenship education.

Pupils from another group also commented that in some ways citizenship education is not important because some of the social systems that pupils are thought about are not practically accessible to them.

THE EFFECTS OF CITIZENSHIP

Pupils envisaged that a number of factors impacted on the effectiveness of citizenship education. Pupils in one of the discussion groups explained that the effects of citizenship education in the lives of pupils was dependant on the motivation of pupils which in tern was dependant on the way in which the lesson was taught and the topics that were covered in the lesson.

Similar to the previous sub-sections. one of the groups also commented that if pupils were more engaged in the lesson and the lessons were more active then pupils would 'take it in more'. Pupils also comment that the topics covered within citizenship education have often already been covered within other subjects. The importance of the subject matter was also highlighted with regards to the extent to which BME pupils related to citizenship education. Here there was a significant indication across groups that the extent to which BME pupils related to citizenship education was again dependant on the topics being explored. Two groups suggested that BME pupils relate to citizenship education when the topics of race. racism and equality are covered. This collaborated with comments made within a second group where pupils suggested that BME pupils could relate to citizenship education delivered in former years because these lessons explored real life situations that were close to pupils' own experiences. Another group also highlighted teachers' lack of passion. which was detected in the manner in which lessons were conducted. One pupil mentioned for instance. the non-interactive method where pupils are required to copy from the board. In particular one of the pupils mentioned that when a teacher has clearly put no effort into the lesson this then determines a negative response from pupils who 'cant be bothered'. This again emphasises the effects of lesson delivery on pupil responses towards and perceptions of citizenship education.

Another factor that was seen to hinder the effectiveness of citizenship education was the teachers' lack of knowledge. This was highlighted with two of the group discussions. In one of these groups one of the pupils commented that the teachers don't seem to know right from wrong when discussing issues of race and discrimination.

This extract raises the very tenuous issue of how such sensitive discussions should be dealt with. The question of whether or not the teacher should express his/her personal opinions or remain 'on the fence' in such matters. is brought to the forefront here. In one of the groups the issues of timetabling was also raised. Pupils in this group thought that the lack of time given to citizenship education within the school curriculum limited its effects on pupil's lives. These comments correspond with pupils' identification of the disparity between the importance of citizenship education and its low status.

Here the claim is that citizenship is not taught frequently enough for it to have a significant effect on pupils lives. It is also suggested here that in the latter years of school. citizenship is considered to be of less importance than other GCSE subjects. In addition to the above suggestions. there was also some realisation that the effects of citizenship did to some extent depend on the pupils themselves and whether or not they were prepared to adopt and implement the knowledge disseminated in citizenship education. Pupils from one of the groups also postulated that young people of their age were unable to be significantly affected by citizenship education simply because they had inadequate knowledge of their rights. These pupils seemed to consider knowledge of rights as a prerequisite to the effectiveness of citizenship education in the life of the individual.

PERCEPTIONS OF CITIZENSHIP EDUCATION: COMMUNITY GROUP MEMBERS

Like the school pupils. the young people from community groups viewed citizenship to be an important subject. There was however a retrospective realisation that this was not always the case. Two young people explained that whilst they did not value citizenship education whilst studying it at school. they later realised the importance of the information contained within the subject.

The second young person later proceeded to explain that without studying citizenship at school she would not have known about the Education Maintenance Allowance (EMA) scheme. This young person strongly believed that citizenship education prepared pupils for life after school. These comments relate to comments from school pupils which imply that some pupils fail to see the importance of citizenship education. This lack of perception could also be linked to the hindering factors that mask the importance of citizenship education such as poor delivery and lesson infrequency.

There were various further reasons why citizenship was thought to be important. Firstly. it was thought by one of the young people that citizenship helps with general awareness. Another young person with in the same group suggested that the knowledge and skills gained through citizenship was central to the transition to adulthood and enabled young people to keep up with issues and events on a world-wide scale.

One young person also highlighted the usefulness of citizenship in its incorporation of political issues. an area of teaching which he thought would be useful for young people when engaging with the voting process.

This comment collaborates with the comments of another young person who saw the incorporation of legal and political issues within citizenship education. as a key factor of its effectiveness. This young person appreciated the opportunity provided through citizenship to 'understand the laws' and 'how the government works'.

With regards to the effectiveness of citizenship education. most comments were again positive. pertaining to the knowledge gained and the subject matter covered and the general awareness of social issues and processes. Within one of the group discussions however. one young person suggested that not all pupils would be willing to admit to the usefulness of citizenship education. This comment was made with particular reference to BME pupils. Within this group it was thought that black boys in particular would not be willing to admit to the usefulness of citizenship. This is perhaps indicative of the stigma attached to citizenship and the effects of the unofficial labelling of the lesson as a 'doss lesson'.Like in the pupil discussions. despite these comments however. there was some discrepancy raised concerning the teaching of the subject. Whilst realising the usefulness of the subject in her own life. one of the young people suggested that the effectiveness of the subject depends on who is teaching the lesson.

PERCEPTIONS OF CITIZENSHIP EDUCATION

As with the school pupils and young people from community groups. the views of community group representatives of citizenship education were somewhat ambivalent. In general. community group leaders were very sceptical about the aims of citizenship education. Three of the representatives made strong suggestions that citizenship education was in their view a political tool that is being used to somehow standardise Britishness and ensure that everyone fits with an idealistic traditional model of Britishness. In this view citizenship education was seen to be particularly targeted at BME groups. particularly immigrants entering into British society.

The implementation of citizenship into the school curriculum was also seen to be problematic in that it was felt by some representatives that the structure and foundation of citizenship education had not been given due consideration. Representatives also perceived that citizenship was not given adequate importance within schools.

On the other hand however. community group representatives also realised the usefulness of citizenship education in providing a forum for the exploration of current social issues. In this sense citizenship was seen to be both necessary and important.

NEEDS OF BMES IN THE CONTEXT OF CITIZENSHIP EDUCATION

The two predominant needs that were highlighted within the responses of community group representatives were the need to address identity issues within groups and integration between groups. In terms of self-Identity. one of the representatives also stated that there is a lack of identity amongst BME young people who are unsure about who they are and their position within society. This representative also suggests that these young people 'don't have a sense of belonging' and therefore need to be integrated. This correlates with a response from another representative who stated that there is a need for BME young people to feel a sense of belonging within England.

Here the suggestion is that without a sense of belonging or connection the young person will not have respect for their country of residence. This representative also suggested that the very title of 'citizenship' education causes young people from BME communities to feel distanced and isolated from Britishness and British society. because the integration of the subject in the national curriculum suggests that BME young people are not British enough and need to receive training in that respect. If this is the case then citizenship would be undermining one of its key principles of equality and acceptance. Other representatives also objected to the titling of citizenship education. stating that it again bore connotations of a forceful indoctrination of pupils to ensure that everyone fits into a narrow conception of Britishness.

On the other hand it was widely agreed among representatives that there was a need for young people to gain knowledge and understanding of other community groups and to have respect for other communities. These comments correspond with the strong suggestions from educators that BME youth needed to integrate more with other groups beyond their own. One of the representatives indicated that BME youth do not have a sense of belonging and therefore need to be educated about the benefits of integrating and being part of the wider society. The following statement further suggests that there are stark divisions not only between BME communities and host communities. but even between different BME communities themselves.

Another representative supports this point by explaining that divisions between BME groups is at times caused by mistrust which is born from the experiences of individuals whilst living in their native countries.

Also identified was the need for positive role-modelling within groups. particularly male role models and a need for the reassertion of traditional morals that are upheld within the BME communities. The lack of positive role models was also recognised within the discussions held with community group members. Also highlighted was the need for young people to have active involvement in community activities was also highlighted. In addition one representative also pinpointed the need for understanding of political processes. This particular respondent suggested that young people don't vote simply because they do not understand the voting process.

Bibiography

A.R. Pandey: *Law of Nationality Citizenship and Immigration*, Cyber Tech Publications, Delhi, 2012.

Anupama Roy: *Gendered Citizenship : Historical and Conceptual Explorations*, Orient Longman, New York, 2005.

Anupama Roy: *Mapping Citizenship in India*, Oxford University Press, Delhi, 2010.

Arvind Sivaramakrishnan: *Public Policy And Citizenship : Battling Managerialism in India*, Sage Publication, Delhi, 2011.

Ayelet Harel Shalev: *The Challenge of Democracy: Citizenship Rights and Ethnic Conflicts in India and Israel*, Foundation Books is an imprint of Cambridge University Press India Pvt. Ltd, 2013.

B N Ray: *Citizenship in a Globalising World*, Kaveri Books, Delhi, 2007.

Gurbax Singh: *Law of Foreigners Citizenship and Passports in India*, Universal Law, Delhi, 2011.

Gurpreet Mahajan: *The Public and the Private : Issues of Democratic Citizenship*, Sage Publication, Delhi, 2003.

J.C. Aggarwal: *Principles and Practices Of Teaching Civics and Citizenship Education*, Shipra Publication, Delhi, 2010.

Maitrayee Mukhopadhyay and Navsharan Singh, Zubaan: *Gender Justice, Citizenship and Development*, An Imprint of Kali for Women, 2007.

Meenakshi Thapan: *Contested Spaces: Citizenship and Belonging in Contemporary Times*, Orient BlackSwan, New York, 2010.

Naila Kabeer: *Inclusive Citizenship: Meanings and Expressions*, Cambridge University Press, New York, 2003.

Nira Yuval-Davis and Pnina Werbner: *Women, Citizenship and Difference*, Cambridge University Press, New York, 1999.

Rajeev Bhargava and Helmut Reifeld: *Civil Society, Public Sphere and Citizenship : Dialogues and Perceptions*, Sage Publication, Delhi, 2005.

Rajeshwari Sundar Rajan: *Scandal of the State : Women, Law and Citizenship in Postcolonial India*, Permanent Black, Delhi, 2008.

Rajeshwari Sunder Rajan: *The Scandal of the State : Women, Law, and Citizenship in Postcolonial India*, Permanent Black, Delhi, 2003.

Ranjita Mohanty and Rajesh Tandon: *Participatory Citizenship : Identity, Exclusion, Inclusion*, Sage Publication, Delhi, 2006.

Renu Desai And Romola Sanyal: *Urbanizing Citizenship : Contested Spaces in Indian Cities*, Sage Publication, Delhi, 2011.

Ritty A. Lukose: *Liberalization's Children : Gender, Youth and Consumer Citizenship in Globalizing India*, Orient Blackswan, New York, 2010.

Sumi Krishna: *Women's Livelihood Rights : Recasting Citizenship for Development*, Sage Publication, Delhi, 2007.

Surya Narain Yadav and Indu Baghel: *Citizenship in the Age of Globalisation*, Jnanada Prakashan, Delhi, 2008.

T. K. Oommen: *Classes, Citizenship and Inequality : Emerging Perspectives*, Pearson Education, Delhi, 2003.

T.K. Oommen: *Citizenship and National Identity : From Colonialism to Globalism*, Sage Publication, Delhi, 1997.

T.K. Oommen: *Citizenship, Nationality and Ethnicity : Reconciling Competing Identities*, Polity Press, Delhi, 2001.

Torpey: *Invention Of The Passport, The : Surveillance, Citizenship and the State*, Cambridge University Press, New York, 1999.

V. Geetha and Nalini Rajan: *Religious Faith, Ideology, Citizenship : The View from Below*, Routledge India, 2011.

Zeenat Ara and Shubhra Pant Kothari: *Citizenship and Globalisation*, Abhijeet Publication, Delhi, 2010.

Index